More Profile than Courage

SUNY Series in American Labor History
Robert Asher, Editor

More Profile than Courage

The New York City
Transit Strike of 1966

Michael Marmo

State University of New York Press

Published by
State University of New York Press, Albany

© 1990   State University of New York

For information, address State University of New York
Press, State University Plaza, Albany, N.Y., 12246

Library of Congress Cataloging-in-Publication Data

Marmo, Michael.
    More profile than courage : the New York City transit strike of
1966 / Michael Marmo.
        p.   cm. — (SUNY series in American labor history)
    Bibliography: p.
    Includes index.
    ISBN 0-7914-0261-4. — ISBN 0-7914-0262-2 (pbk.)
    1. Transport Workers' Strike, New York, N.Y., 1966. 2. Strikes
and lockouts—Transport workers—New York (N.Y.)—History—20th
century. 3. Collective bargaining—New York (N.Y.)—Effect of mass
media on. I. Title. II. Series.
HD5325.T72 1966.N48   1990
331.89'2813884'09747109046—dc20   89-36179
                                                                          CIP

10 9 8 7 6 5 4 3 2 1

To the memory of my father

Contents

Preface

As the son of a New York City sanitation employee, my interest in public sector collective bargaining in New York began by osmosis at a very early age. My interest in this project began more than twenty years ago while a graduate student at the University of Illinois's Institute of Labor and Industrial Relations. I am indebted to Milton Derber and Martin Wagner for their encouragement at that time.

I was greatly aided by my access to the Municipal Reference Library of New York City, the files of the Transport Workers Union, and the collection of TWU papers now at the Tammiment Library of New York University. Unfortunately, as of August 1988, the Tammiment collection was still being catalogued and was only partially available.

This study would not have been possible without the willing cooperation of many of the most significant participants. For his help in gaining interviews with many of these individuals I am thankful to my uncle, Pat Marmo.

Robert Asher, the series editor at SUNY Press, provided incisive suggestions and valuable support.

Finally, for her encouragement, smarts, editorial assistance, and ever-present good humor, thanks Morita.

Prologue — Public Sector Bargaining and "Image" Politics

Multilateral Bargaining[1]

Almost twenty years ago, Kenneth McLennan and Michael Moskow coined the term *multilateral collective bargaining* to distinguish public sector negotiations from the essentially bilateral process that prevails in the private sector.[2] They reasoned that because of the public policy issues being considered, various interest groups have a vested concern in the outcome of public sector negotiations, thereby seeking to exert an influence on the bargaining process. Since McLennan and Moskow's seminal work, their approach has become the standard for scholars of public sector bargaining.

The central assumption of virtually all treatments that explicitly or implicitly utilize a multilateral approach to public sector negotiations is that government decisionmakers weigh the political "clout" of each of the interest groups seeking to influence the bargaining process and then make a decision to maximize their political well being. This approach is well-supported in the political science literature and is perhaps epitomized by Anthony Downs who observed that politicians "formulate policies in order to win elections, rather than win elections in order to formulate policies."[3] Following in this tradition, Walter Fogel and David Lewin explain the behavior of politicians in the collective bargaining process by indicating that "they view the electorate as a number of interest groups, and then seek to determine and respond to the relative importance of such groups."[4]

These multilateral models of bargaining, then, owe their intellectual debt to interest group explanations of political behavior. This approach views politicians as approaching their jobs in *tabula rasa* fashion, simply adding the votes of the various interest groups and then implementing into policy the predominant direction of their pressures. Diagramatically, the

1

government official is a centrally located blank box upon which various interest groups, including the union with which they are negotiating, exert pressure:

Figure 1

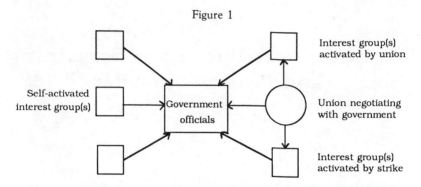

The various interest groups presumed to be putting pressure on government officials in the bargaining process are entities such as Parent Teacher Associations (PTA), welfare rights organizations, and other groups that, without prodding, realize they have a vested interest in the collective bargaining process and attempt to exert pressure. In addition, more sophisticated multilateral models recognize that a union engaged in bargaining can activate other interest groups to put pressure on government officials. For example, a union negotiating with city officials might prevail on other unions or the local Central Labor Council to pressure city government on their behalf. Finally, much has been written of the ability of unions to activate interest groups by virtue of their power to call a strike. When interest groups are activated by the deprivation of critical services, their sole concern is typically that the strike be ended.

Activating Interest Groups—Theory

Perhaps the major shortcoming of these models of multilateral bargaining is that they do not recognize the ability of government officials to "create" support for their policies. Regardless of how it is achieved, a government official will enjoy political support as long as agreement exists between the views of the electorate and the response of the official with regard to those issues that are considered important by voters. Of course, as existing models indicate, government officials can maintain their support by responding to the felt needs of various interest groups. However, a considerable body of recent political science literature indicates that a public official also can achieve congruity between constituent views and government actions by influencing which issues reach the public's awareness and by helping determine the position assumed by the various pressure groups regarding these issues. As perhaps the leading exponent of this view, Murray Edelman, observes, "Political actions chiefly arouse or satisfy people not by granting or withholding their stable substantive demands, but rather by changing the demands and the expectations."[5]

In a complex society, with hundreds of issues clamoring for public attention, individuals and groups must depend, not surprisingly, on external cues regarding which issues are worthy of their consideration. Priorities for discussion of public issues seldom relate directly to the amount of money or manpower to be expended; nor are individuals or groups automatically activated because their own interests will be affected. Instead, matters that experts consider to have a very high priority might arouse only apathy unless they can somehow be elevated to a position of social importance. "The mass public does not study and analyze detailed data [about complex issues]," asserts Edelman; instead, it "ignores these things until political actions and speeches make them symbolically threatening or reassuring . . ."[6]

Although the ability of government officials to determine which issues become salient and their ability to influence "what" individuals and groups think about those issues are conceptually distinct, frequently both of these functions can be achieved by a single act. For example, a news conference by a mayor in which he or she denounces a welfare union's demands as benefiting welfare "cheaters" at the expense of middle-class taxpayers would both make this issue salient for particular interest groups and set the parameters for "how" the issue will subsequently be discussed.

Because government officials are typically unable to directly activate either the mass public or specific interest groups to become part of the collective bargaining process, it is critical that the media be used to achieve such activation. To return to the schematic representation, we now have an "interactive" system in which government officials are both acted on and initiate action. When government officials do activate interest groups, it is by using, or to employ the pejorative connotation, manipulating the media.

Role of the Media

An understanding and appreciation of how the media work is crucial for any individual or group that operates in the public arena. Contrary to their frequent self-characterization as "mirrors of society," the news media, in fact, exercise an enormous degree of discretion in reporting the news.

The media "are not a passive conduit of political activity," one media
analyst has written, but rather "a 'filter' or 'gatekeeper,' whose institutional
interests, definitions and prejudices influence what is reported and what is
not...."[7] Such institutional requisites of the news media determine both
"what" is reported, and "how" it is reported.

Figure 2

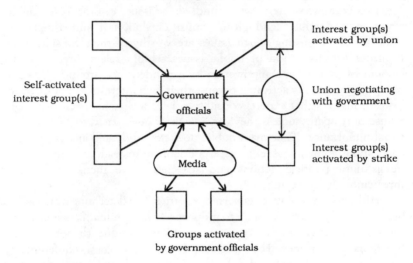

Self-activated
interest group(s)

Interest group(s)
activated by union

Union negotiating
with government

Interest group(s)
activated by strike

Groups activated
by government officials

Although the media now include both print and electronic journalism,
the old newspaper standard of "good copy" still applies as the primary
determinant of whether a story will be covered. More specifically, the
media generally use the following criteria to decide if a story has sufficient
news interest to be reported. Most important, stories are considered
newsworthy if they involve conflict, such as war or strikes. Second, events
should be close to home and should be perceived as having a high impact on
readers or viewers. Next, stories should be "familiar" in the sense that they
should involve familiar situations or well-known individuals. And a final
criterion for television news, the event should have "film value"; that is, it
should be visually suitable for presentation on television.

In addition to these criteria that relate to audience appeal, many stories
are covered simply because they are guaranteed to materialize. Assignment
editors will send reporters to cover news conferences or follow up on news
releases because they are able to predict that a newsworthy story is present.
Thus, a news conference by a mayor to discuss an impending strike is
eminently newsworthy; it is local, involves a well-known politician,

presents conflict, and is guaranteed to take place in time to be reported on the news that evening.

The requirements of a "good story" also dictate "how" the article or report will be presented, the "angle" of the story. Walter Lippmann's observation some sixty-five years ago that newspaper reporting is, in large part, a process of filling an established "repertory of stereotypes" with current news is still valid.[8] In fact, the advent of television news has exacerbated the problem of the news media dealing with problems stereotypically. Because a television news report only lasts a few minutes, it cannot deal accurately with complex issues or long-term trends. As television news executive Reuven Frank has observed, news programs should contain the same elements as fiction or drama; they should have structure and conflict; a problem and its resolution; rising and falling action; and a beginning, a middle, and an end.[9]

Because conflict is presumed to be of greatest interest to the news audience, it is always stressed. If the conflict involves confusing elements, it typically will be reconstructed in the form of a two-sided conflict because confrontations between clearly defined sides are considered most dramatic.[10] Ideally, for maximum dramatic impact, the conflict should pit the forces of good against the forces of evil.

Activating Interest Groups—Practice

Although attempts by government officials to "sell" their policies involves both great effort and a tremendous expenditure of money, it is not typically regarded as being manipulative because it almost always has the trappings of "objective" fact. The historian Daniel Boorstin has dubbed the staging of events by government officials so that they simulate reality, "pseudo-events."[11] Because such pseudo-events are created specifically for the purpose of achieving media coverage, they are potent forces in defining issues as being worthy of societal attention. Pseudo-events typically used by government officials to stimulate one or more groups' interest in what is happening in collective bargaining include media conferences, briefings, interviews, news releases, and news leaks. The success of pseudo-events in garnering media attention is illustrated by one study which indicated that 75 percent of the news stories on local television stations originate from press releases.[12] Thus, a mayor bargaining with a firefighter's union over how a reduction in force should be accomplished might activate black and women's organizations by stating in a news release that the union's proposal to use strict seniority would disproportionately create layoffs among black and women firefighters.

In the attempt by public officials to activate interest groups, their efforts are typically directed at opinion leaders rather than the general public. As one analyst has written, "mass media impact on a handful of political decision makers usually is vastly more significant than similar impact on thousands of ordinary individuals."[13] A newspaper story indicating that a police union is pushing very hard in negotiations to end the city's residency requirement for police officers may be of little interest to the general public. However, the story probably would be of considerable interest to leaders of black organizations who would readily see the implications of such a change on the racial composition of the police department.

Government Influence on What the Public Thinks

Government officials enjoy a uniquely privileged status in being able to influence the way in which public issues are perceived for three reasons: they control the flow of information; they act in an official capacity; and they have access to the media.

Government officials have access to certain information not generally available, and they also can control the dissemination of such relevant facts. By controlling much of the information that is available concerning public sector negotiations, government officials have the power to influence the public's perception of what is taking place. As a study of government agencies concluded, "bureaucratic propoganda uses truth for organizational goals" by "presenting managed and often contrived reports as though they were done 'scientifically' and therefore depict 'objective' truth."[14] For example, a local school board negotiating with a teachers' union might issue a news release indicating that because of the state reimbursement formula and the presence of categorical federal grant monies, the school board's proposal has a *net* cost to the school district that is lower than the union's proposal, even though the total cost of the board's proposal is considerably greater. Lacking such information themselves, interest groups such as the PTA would be hard pressed to disagree with the school board's assessment.

Public officials can also mold opinion regarding public sector negotiations by simply exercising their official powers. A mayor might prevail upon the city's health commissioner to declare a health emergency during a strike by municipal sanitation workers, thereby putting the onus on the union for endangering public health. Or, in those situations where public sector strikes are enjoinable, government officials might initiate legal actions in order to brand the striking union as having no respect for the law.

Finally, government officials can disproportionately influence perceptions of public sector negotiations because their position accords them ready access to the media. If a mayor has a statement concerning negotiations with a municipal union, it will be covered by the media simply because the opinions of well-known officials concerning conflict situations are considered news.

Astute politicians are well aware that the issues involved in public sector negotiations are far too complex to be accurately reflected by the media. They therefore seek to focus attention on a particular aspect of the bargaining process that satisfies media requirements for a "good story," and presents the government officials involved in a favorable light. "Power," writes political sociologist Peter Hall, "is achieved by controlling, influencing, and sustaining your definition of the situation since, if you can get others to share your reality, you can get them to act in the manner you prescribe."[15]

Perhaps the most effective way that government officials define problems to ensure their own success is by the use of condensation symbols. Condensation symbols are names, phrases, maxims, and so on, that evoke highly valued societal or group goals, but which are not subject to empirical verification. The basic function of condensation symbols is to provide instant categorization and evaluation; things that are essential for media presentation.

By using a condensation symbol, a complex set of issues that precipitated a teachers' strike can be reduced to the issue of "whether teachers who were hired to be role models for our children should be allowed to break the law." Or, a set of firefighter negotiations, which might involve such issues as pay parity with police officers, scheduling practices, and a voluntary affirmative action program, will symbolically become a question of "whether employees who have control over life and death situations ought to be allowed to hold a city hostage." In addition to being directed at the general public, condensation symbols can also be directed at specific interest groups as, for example, the characterization of a police union's proposal to carry shotguns in the front of their police cruisers as constituting racial genocide. Each of these examples of the use of condensation symbols contain the same basic elements; they are made for the media; they are stereotypic confrontations of good versus evil; and the government official is depicted as acting from the best of motives.

Resolving Conflicting Expectations

Regardless of how various interest groups are activated or how they come to hold particular expectations of the appropriate course of government action to deal with labor relations situations, a final question remains: how are these conflicting expectations resolved? Harry Wellington and Ralph Winter argue that these differences are resolved by performing a political calculus involving the distribution of fixed economic resources. "What he gives to the union," they observe, "must be taken from some other interest group or from taxpayers."[16] While correct in observing that differing expectations will be resolved on the basis of political considerations, Wellington and Winter exhibit considerable political naiveté in viewing government decisionmaking as involving only the distribution of "material" rewards. In fact, competing claims on government can be met through the allocation of both material and "symbolic" rewards. As political scientist Dan Nimmo reminds us, "...politicians win popular acceptance and support as much because of emotional leadership as their ability to allocate material rewards. The tangible gains that citizens actually accrue are less critical in affirming popular loyalties to regimes than what people think they get."[17]

A wide range of symbolic gestures are available to politicians as a means of gaining acceptability for their actions. Again, one must recognize that granting symbolic rewards is accomplished through the media, so politicians must frame such gestures with the media in mind.

Members of particular interest groups may be reassured through the device of well-publicized consultations with individuals who are perceived as "representing" their interests.[18] Even more reassuring is the establishment of a blue-ribbon committee to dramatize government concern and to delay decisionmaking until such time that the issue will no longer be salient for the interest group in question.[19] Thus, an *ad hoc* parents' group and various black organizations having different opinions on the assignment of teachers to particular schools may all be pacified by establishing a high-level commission to study the question.

In addition to symbolic acts, symbolic rhetorical devices are also available to government officials. Perhaps the most effective rhetorical device, because it meets all media requirements for a "good story," is personifying an enemy so that a dramatic encounter can take place between the forces of good and evil. The enemy might be a labor "boss" who is more interested in maintaining his own job than the fact that citizens simply cannot afford higher taxes, or a state legislature that requires school boards to provide certain programs without providing commensurate financial support. By acting confident and self-assured, in attacking a personified enemy, politicians will probably succeed because most individuals "want to believe that their leaders know what they are doing and so will accept a dramaturgical presentation of such ability on its own terms."[20] However, even if a government official does not completely succeed in a dramatic confrontation, he or she probably will be perceived as having acted heroically, thus remaining worthy of support. Thus, a public official who confronts an unpopular union official on television, and characterizes the union's demands as "unconscionable," might achieve the support of "taxpayer" groups, despite eventually agreeing to healthy wage increases.

Diagramatically, the way in which government officials resolve the demands of competing interest groups is as follows:

Figure 3

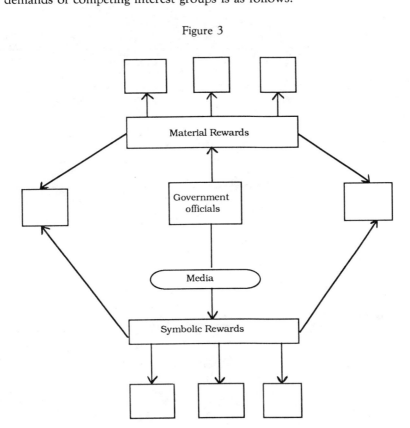

Chapter 1

The Political Milieu

Introduction

The central point in the foregoing model of public sector negotiations is the use of the media by politicians to activate interest groups and distribute symbolic rewards in order to maximize their political goals. The major point of the model and its nuances were dramatically portrayed in the New York City transit negotiations of 1965-1966, in which the two chief protagonists, Mayor John V. Lindsay and Michael J. Quill of the Transport Workers Union (TWU), used the media to further their goals.

Because the model is predicated on the use of the media to achieve political objectives, the political aspirations of Lindsay and the way he used the media to achieve his priorities first must be examined. Later chapters apply the model more directly to the 1965-1966 transit negotiations. Although the analysis centers on the media-conscious performance of Lindsay, the concerns with image politics evidenced by other participants in transit negotiations also are examined.

Lindsay's Election

Thursday, May 13, 1965—John Lindsay began running today for president by way of New York's City Hall. Naturally he did not disclose his ultimate goal. His immediate prospects are dim enough without an unnecessary handicap. In this Democratic town, no Republican, even one as young (forty-three) and lucent as Lindsay, is given any chance of being elected mayor. He has no machine, no troops.[1]

Why would Representative Lindsay, harboring the highest political aspirations at the national level, want to become mayor of New York City? Long considered a political graveyard, no New York mayor had ever been elected to higher office since the city was consolidated at the turn of the century. Furthermore, Lindsay's chances of being elected mayor, on the surface, appeared highly unlikely. Democrats outnumbered Republicans by 3-1/2-to-1 in the city, and the long-moribund Republican party generally was considered an insignificant force in the city's political life.

Lindsay said he was entering the race, "because I believe that with proper leadership our city can once again be restored as the Empire City of the world," and added that, he could not "stand by while the decline and fall of New York continues headlong."[2] Finally, Lindsay blamed the city's problems on the fact that the Republican party had long failed to provide the city's voters with a viable alternative to Democratic rule. During "these long years of one party rule," he charged, New York had "become a place that is no longer for people or for living. There is no leadership and in such a vacuum of leadership there is no standard, no tone, no quality of excellence." Striking a chord that seemed almost ministerial in nature, Lindsay implied that he had been "called" to announce his candidacy because of his "duty, conscience and concern about our city...."[3]

Although Lindsay might well have believed his candidacy was necessary for the survival of New York City, his decision to run for mayor was primarily calculated to serve his own political aspirations. Widely considered to be "presidential timber," the New York Congressman nevertheless found himself hemmed in politically. By the summer of 1965, neither of the two traditional avenues for political advancement, the Senate or the governor's mansion, appeared to be options.

One of the Senate seats was held by fellow Republican Jacob K. Javits, whose term lasted until 1968 and who was expected to run for reelection. The other Senate seat had just been won the previous fall by Robert F. Kennedy and would not come up for reelection until 1970. Thus, when Republican Governor Nelson A. Rockefeller announced that he intended to run for reelection in 1966, the description of Lindsay as a political figure "with great potential but nowhere to go" seemed particularly apt.[4] Faced with such roadblocks, the mayoral election in 1965 was the only option available to Lindsay that would allow him to maintain his political momentum. Lindsay could not simply remain in Congress. The book, *The Future of the Republican Party*, saw Lindsay as "the least tarnished of the Republican presidential possibilities" after the debacle of Barry Goldwater's 1964 presidential campaign but cautioned, "Lindsay's immediate problem is how to break out of the obscurity of the House. It would take years for him to become a national leader from his present post."[5]

In fact, a Lindsay mayoral campaign in 1965 was not nearly as bleak a prospect as most political observers had concluded. As early as 1963, Lindsay had startled a group of political intimates by suggesting that with the paths to the Senate and governorship effectively closed, running for mayor of New York City might be wise. The big cities, Lindsay indicated, were becoming more important in national politics, and this might serve as an excellent power base. Gradually, as the idea was bandied about, the group agreed that "a mayor of New York who qualified legitimately as 'Mr. City' and who did not alienate the fast-growing suburbs around the center cities might go all the way to the White House...."[6] Indeed, 1965 truly could be identified as the year of the city. This was the time when the dual problems of poverty and race came cruelly together in urban areas to produce a recognized "crisis." With this kind of spotlight being directed at municipal problems, the mayor of the nation's largest city would share in that illumination. This scrutiny, however, simply might allow the public to observe the failures that were inevitable in a city whose problems were considered to be virtually insoluble. To the contrary, Lindsay's closest advisors were convinced that because the urban "crisis" was generally conceded to defy solution at this time, regardless of his eventual success, "a dynamic young Mayor, cutting decisively through the municipal morass, can become the focus of national attention, a figure rising even to eclipse some of the Republican governors and senators in whose hands the party's future now seems to rest."[7]

And despite the preponderance of registered Democrats in New York City, Lindsay's advisors were convinced that he could win the election. By the time the New York Congressman decided to run for mayor, several political polls suggested that incumbent mayor Robert F. Wagner, Jr. was vulnerable and that Lindsay might unseat him. In addition, Lindsay was convinced that because he would be viewed as a considerable underdog, a strong showing in the mayoral election would be beneficial, even if he lost.

Having decided that becoming the mayor of New York would aid his career, Lindsay needed to overcome the opposition of the state's leading Republican, Governor Rockefeller. To begin with, Rockefeller viewed Lindsay as a threat to his domination of the state's Republican party. If Lindsay became mayor, he would automatically rival the governor for their party's statewide leadership. Next, if Lindsay defeated incumbent Mayor Wagner, the unofficial leader of the state's Democratic party, Rockefeller feared that Kennedy would fill the void. And quite simply, Rockefeller felt the Republicans would fare better statewide against a Democratic party headed by Wagner instead of Kennedy. Finally, Rockefeller wanted to retain complete control over the state's Republican party in order to mount a presidential campaign in 1968. In this quest, the governor viewed Lindsay as a direct rival. Because both were attractive, liberal Republicans from New York State, they essentially shared the same constituency.

The immediate problem facing the Lindsay campaign was how to energize the stagnant Republican party in the city without the active support of Governor Rockefeller. The Democrats had a captain and often an assistant captain in each of the city's 4,851 election districts, while Republicans did not even have captains in one-half of these districts. In addition, the Democrats, in office for decades, had the patronage that attracts campaign workers. The Republicans, conversely, not only had no leaders, they also had few workers to do the nitty-gritty work of campaigning.

Faced with this virtual "nonparty," Lindsay's top political advisor, Robert Price decided to structure the campaign around young volunteers and to essentially bypass the feeble regular Republican organization. Based on the Price strategy, the volunteers would operate out of nonpartisan storefront headquarters in each of the city's seventy-six assembly districts. This was hardly a new approach for Price who had been successfully using volunteers in each of Lindsay's congressional campaigns.[8]

Lindsay was totally in accord with the Price approach. Asked about the importance of the Republican organization in his mayoral campaign, the candidate responded:

> I can't depend on it for any kind of basic support. I speak at their clubs and show up at their affairs but the core of my political strength has to remain with the volunteers. I have to continue to rely on the new generation. Nobody can argue with young people. Even an old guard election district captain can't argue with boys and girls pushing doorbells. My own test of how well I'm doing in politics is the enthusiasm I can maintain among the youth....[9]

When Lindsay announced his candidacy for mayor of New York, he expected to run against the incumbent Wagner. However, a long-smoldering rift between the "regular" Democrats and the "reform" Democrats caused Wagner considerable disenchantment. Wagner, a "reformer," realized he probably would face a stiff challenge in the primary when New York Senator Kennedy threw his support behind the "regular" Democrats. Faced with such intraparty strife, Wagner succombed to personal concerns when his wife died and decided not to seek a fourth term as mayor. In the ensuing Democratic primary, the slate of candidates put forth by the regular Democrats, Abraham Beame for mayor, Frank O'Connor for city council president, and Mario Procaccino for controller, defeated the Wagner endorsed reform candidates.

The son of a Polish immigrant originally named Birnbaum, the sixty-year-old Beame was a career civil servant. After graduating from City College in 1928, he worked as a high school accounting teacher in the city's school system. After school hours, he engaged in public accounting work, and in 1930 he became a certified public accountant. Beame continued to be employed by the school system until 1946 when he became assistant budget director for the city, a post he held until 1952 when he was promoted to budget director. In 1961, Beame was elected controller. Paralleling most of Beame's career advancement was his active involvement with the Democratic machine. He had long served as a district captain in the Eighteenth Assembly District in Brooklyn. He resigned this party post, however, shortly before Wagner selected him to run on his reform slate in 1961. Being a career civil servant, Beame was "thoroughly familiar with city affairs, . . . knowing all the city offices and most of the people in them . . . . [He] had that valuable bread-and-butter knowledge about who was really responsible for what, where."[10]

John Lindsay: A New-Style Politician

A late 1960s political cartoon depicted a political candidate standing on the rear observation platform of an old-fashioned whistlestop train. On one side, an eager mother lifts up a baby for him to kiss; on the other, a television camera is held up to him. Representative of the "new-style" politicians that emerged at this time, the candidate apparently felt little conflict; he leaned over and kissed the video camera.

T.R. Dye and L.H. Zeigler describe the trend that began in the 1960s:

> The media have become the focus of political campaigning . . . . Campaigns are organized as media events . . . . The voters have come to depend more heavily on television than on any other source of information.
>
> The media have replaced the party as the principal link between the candidates and the voters. Party organizations can no longer "deliver the vote." Even in those few places where party organizations still exist, they can be bypassed by candidates who appeal directly to the voters through television . . . . Party loyalty has declined; there are more "independents" in the electorate than ever before; and among party affiliates there are many who will switch votes for a popular candidate.[11]

Lindsay was one of the first of such new-style, media-oriented politicians. Beame, in contrast, had built his political success by working through the Tammany Hall Democratic political machine.

Ideologically, the two men were virtually indistinguishable on the issues that surfaced during the campaign. Both candidates favored the legalization of off-track betting. Both sought the repeal of the recently passed, and highly unpopular, statewide sales tax. Both men looked increasingly to Washington for financial assistance to aid the city.[12] Although numerous position papers emanated from both camps in the weeks preceding the election, little attention was paid to these documents.[13] While some observers attributed the lack of concern with issues to the similarity of the candidates' views, the fact was that issue oriented campaigns were beginning to disappear from the American political scene. As political analyst Gene Wyckoff observed, "The very pervasiveness of television may serve to inhibit meaningful debate on campaign issues . . . . The differences between alternative ways of getting something done . . . can involve such subtlety and special knowledge as to be largely unexplainable to laymen, especially in the desirable short-sentence, pithy style campaign oratory."[14]

If the electronic media were ill-suited for a discussion of issues, they were particularly amenable to conveying "images." As a result, elections were becoming contests between competing images rather than struggles between differing ideas. As Nimmo has observed, "Politicians employ numerous techniques to adjust to the demands of video campaigning. These techniques are usually based on an appeal to the tastes rather than the convictions of Americans, for television advisors are convinced that personalities and not issue stands or political parties win votes."[15] Almost a generation apart in age, Beame was the old-style politician who would kiss the baby; Lindsay the new-style politico who would kiss the camera. With respect to the image he wanted to project, Lindsay unashamedly attempted to rekindle the sense of urgency and purpose that characterized John F. Kennedy in 1960. "I want to be mayor of our city," he told an overflowing sidewalk crowd, "so I can give it a new start. I want to see the restoration of the greatness of our city. I could stay in the security of the House, I suppose, but the action today is in the streets of the cities." Throughout the campaign, Lindsay made an effort to trade on the Kennedy mystique that was almost "embarrassingly transparent."[16]

In a city in which Democrats overwhelmingly outnumbered Republicans, Democratic party leaders relied on the old-style approach. All Tammany Hall leaders needed to do was to turn-out the Democratic vote and Beame would win in a landslide. The Beame strategy, therefore, was straightforward and low-key: to stress continuously that "Abe Beame was one with the great national leaders of the Democratic party, past and present." "Only the Democratic party is interested in the masses," he said. "It is the party of Roosevelt, of Truman, of Kennedy, Stevenson, Humphrey and Johnson. Remember Medicare, remember Social Security. Let's not take a chance to give that up."[17]

Lindsay, in contrast, tried to disguise his Republican background and to attract voters to his image. The Republican Congressman virtually discarded his Republicanism altogether by running, in his words, "as Lindsay." He ran on a "fusion" ticket with a Democrat and a Liberal as running mates. The word *Republican* appeared on almost none of his buttons, posters, or literature. At one point, Lindsay's refusal to attach the Republican appellation to his campaign material reached the point of self-parody, when his aides produced a button that said generically, "Lindsay Button."

Lindsay and Beame also differed considerably with respect to their personal styles. Beame's personality reflected the consensus-oriented, machine-inspired, career civil servant that he was. Lindsay, as befit the new wave of media-oriented politicians, had a style that was ideally suited to the electronic media. In the age of television, there was no doubt which image would be more compelling to voters:

> Little Abe Beame was a short, undramatic graduate of City College who had slowly climbed the ladder of municipal government . . . . Like it or not, little men with Brooklyn accents are simply not found in the television viewer's mental picture gallery of heroes. And this particular little man had no class, no style, no inspiration, no special inner fire (that is, "demeanor" in image candidates terms) that might compensate for his shortcomings in appearance.[18]

Congressman Lindsay, in contrast, "had everything the American hero on television is presumed to have: blond hair, a face handsome in the tightest close-ups, a well-modulated voice controlled with an actor's discipline, tallness of stature, vigor of youth, the self-confidence of a winner, the sweet smell of success."[19] In a sense, voters were asked to cast their lot with Lindsay because he fit their image of a successful mayor; Beame did not. "Could you imagine," one voter asked rhetorically during the campaign, "Mrs. Beame greeting the Queen of England at Kennedy Airport?"[20]

Rather than attempting cogent analysis, the media furthered this reliance on clichés and stereotypes. The "point was constantly driven home," as William F. Buckley pointed out, "that Abe Beame was ordinary . . . . In due course it became as routine for newspapermen and columnists to describe Beame as 'lackluster' as it was for them to describe Lindsay as 'tall' or 'handsome', or 'glamorous.' . . ."[21]

Virtually alone in his concern with substance rather than style was *Journal American* columnist William S. White, who pointed out that Beame's "very virtues—adult conduct and wise fiscal management—have become vices. He has no 'style!' He is 'dull!' He is short and lacking glamour. He is—though this point is not carefully used—not 'aristocratic' to a curious group of Democratic snobs which is forever screeching against 'discrimination' when practiced by others."[22]

The evidence that the media tended to deal with the confrontation between Lindsay and Beame in stereotypic terms was not merely anecdotal. In a scholarly treatment of the role of the media in this election, Daniel R. Shanor wrote:

> New Yorkers with their six newspapers inundating them with columns backed up by editorials, and their seven television stations swamping them with panel shows and broadcast editorials, found that much of this opinion was of little value to them in making their choice for New York mayor. In the columns, at least, they were being urged not to elect a city official but to participate in an ideological contest, deciding whether the GOP would emerge with a modern John V. Lindsay image or an unreconstructed Goldwaterite image....[23]

Although some columnists made outright endorsements, others Shanor concluded, "made their preferences equally plain in other ways, frequently by describing Lindsay as boyish, handsome and glamorous, or hard-working, new-breed and capable. Abraham Beame...when mentioned at all, was usually dismissed as cautious, colorless and dull, 'the sad, gray little man,' in the words of" one columnist.[24] The media thus contributed, although certainly not in conspiratorial terms, to the Lindsay campaign strategy of attempting to win voters' hearts, rather than their minds.

The reliance that new-style politicians attach to their images is important not only in attracting voters, but also in drawing campaign workers to their causes. Without a strong political party on which to rely, the Lindsay campaign would have to depend on an *ad hoc* collection of volunteers, attracted to the Lindsay image or cause. Such an approach was used even more extensively several years later, of course, in the presidential bids of Eugene McCarthy and George McGovern. In his New York mayoral campaign, Lindsay attracted more than 10,000 active volunteers, most of them young. In addition, another 20,000 were tangentially involved. Together, these 30,000 volunteer workers were able to staff 120 store-fronts throughout the city and personally canvass 70 percent of the voters. "I do not believe," said a Lindsay staffer in analyzing the impact of these efforts, "that any party or combination of parties ever canvassed that high a proportion of the voters in any previous corresponding election."[25]

A final reason for the ascendence of new-style mayors during the 1960s was the divergence that began at that time between their audience and their constituency.[26] The audience comprised those individuals or groups mayors are most interested in impressing, because they can provide them with needed resources and future career opportunities. The constituency, in contrast, refers only to those who can vote in a mayoral election. At one time, as Wilson describes, the audience and the constituency were nearly identical. The mayor was reelected if he pleased his party and a majority of the city's voters. The only resources required (money to finance the next campaign and taxes with which to run the city) were available from within the city. Party workers not only staffed campaign posts, they also filled positions in the administration. However, with the decline of the urban political party and the increasing movement of financial resources out of the central city, mayors had to seek out new sources of organizational and financial support. This is where the audience enters the picture. It

> consists principally of various federal agencies, especially those that give grants directly to cities; the large foundations . . . that can favor the mayor with grants, advice, and future prospects; the mass media, or at least that part of the media—national news magazines and network television—that can give the mayor access to the suburbs, the state, and the nation as a whole. . . .
>
> The audience sets the tone and provides much of the rhetoric for the discussion of urban issues. "Talking the language" of the audience is an important way for a mayor to win esteem and to become a state or even a national figure.[27]

Currying the favor and winning the support of the audience is not inherently detrimental to the interests of constituents. As Roger Starr observes, "The mayor's mythic quality helps determine the level at which the national government will aid New York City. A mayor who is treated by the national press as a glamorous figure is harder for the national government to rebuff than a merely competent gentleman who does not attract the newsmen. . . ."[28] Foundations and private organizations also provided free resources; and, although not as plentiful as federal monies, they often made the difference between running an ordinary administration and one that was newsworthy, exciting, or different. Such support marked a mayor as being on the cutting edge of solving urban problems. As Wilson cynically points out, "The ideal 'pilot project' from the mayor's point of view is one that puts some money into the city treasury, gets some good headlines, provides a few more staff assistants, and then promptly vanishes, without a trace before anyone can start quarreling about what purpose it is to serve or who should control it."[29]

By the mid-1960s the audience was increasingly able to reward, and therefore to shape, the career aspirations of big-city mayors. As more attention was being focused on the cities, mayors could be headed for higher office if they were "adroit enough to get out of city hall and into a safer office before criticisms [began] to mount up."[30]

The mayor of New York enjoyed the easiest access to the national audience of any mayor in the country because New York was the home of the national mass media: of *Time, Newsweek, Life,* and *Look*; of NBC, CBS, ABC; of the *New York Times* (perhaps the only "national" newspaper then); and of the major book publishing houses. Although such media representatives were instrumental in fashioning a national image for John Lindsay, they were in a sense, as much the victim of this image as its creator. While the New York-based national media expressed profound concern with the "urban crisis," they had "little time or energy to spare for the complex, intractable actualities of New York itself." As Irving Kristol and Paul Weaver perceptively observed, "Most of the editors of these magazines, most of the executives of these networks have visited Paris far more often than they have visited Brooklyn.... They are our cosmopolitan parochials."[31]

In developing Lindsay's new-style campaign strategy in the fall of 1965, many tactics were employed that were typical of the image-oriented approach. Although the specifics might vary based on the particular image a candidate sought to convey, a repetoire of tactics for an image based campaign was already fairly well-formulated by this time.

First, as discussed by Edelman, "the public official who dramatizes his competence is eagerly accepted on his own terms." "Willingness to cope is evidently central."[32] In the 1965 mayoral election, Beame implied that the status quo was fine. While conceding that New York City did have problems, he nevertheless constantly reiterated his conclusion—that "there are a lot more things right about New York than there are wrong with it. I want to build on our successful programs."[33] Regardless of the specifics that emanated from the Beame camp, the image that was conveyed was one of resignation and the inability to cope with New York's massive problems. Lindsay, conversely, recognized that giving the impression of competence and implying that he had solutions to the city's problems, most likely would be accepted uncritically. He knew what needed to be done to save the city: the 15¢ subway fare needed to be preserved; the city needed to provide 200,000 new jobs; to create a "slumless city" and a "fearless city." To those age sixty-five and older, he promised to reduce the subway fare during nonrush hours and to have the city pay the $3 monthly insurance copayment under Medicare. How would such programs be financed? Without getting into specifics, Lindsay indicated that such initiatives could easily be financed through the use of federal grants and by saving "$300 to

$400 million annually by eliminating waste in city government."[34] By his public statements, Lindsay obviously relished the challenge of such problems; Beame shrank from them. According to his campaign manager, Robert Price, Lindsay had "to eliminate the inertia among the citizens at large—the feeling that all politicians are the same, that nothing is going to change anyway."[35] And, Price added, "He's already shown at least some movement to the people.... There's action. They're not sure if it's good or bad, but something's happening."[36]

Next, Lindsay "followed the familiar image tactic of associating the opposition candidate with some alleged evil force that could be personified; he attacked three 'villainous' Democratic overlords [Charles Buckley, Bronx; Stanley Steingut, Brooklyn; and Adam Clayton Powell, Harlem] to whom little Abe Beame was allegedly in thrall."[37] He referred to his opponent as "the product of a discredited political machine."[38] This tactic was a natural for television because it was expressed in terms of compassion rather than a direct verbal attack on his opponent; that is, "Lindsay could effectively deprecate Beame by expressing his regret that Beame was a creature of the bosses. Compassion is a familiar attribute of the television hero."[39] Lindsay's attack on the Tammany Hall bosses was ideally suited to the requisites of television. As Lindsay's media advisors well knew, "stories work better on television when there are clear antagonists, especially when they are physically different.... There should be good guys and bad guys."[40]

In the made for television confrontation between Lindsay and the bosses, it was obvious who the "good guy" was. Although frequently portrayed as being somewhat politically naive, there was no question about Lindsay's motivation; he was alternatively referred to as Mr. Clean and the Boy Scout. The term *bosses* has such negative connotations that it makes a discussion of the images of Buckley and Steingut virtually unnecessary. Nevertheless, it helped that both men visually fit the image of the stereotypic boss. Finally, by attacking the bosses, Lindsay could show compassion for "the amiable little bookkeeper," as Jacob Javits had characterized Beame. There was nothing sinister about Beame, this image suggested, he was simply not up to the job.

Related to his attack on the bosses and "in the typical manner of a candidate relying on his attractive television image, John Lindsay became as nonpartisan as possible."[41] He cut himself off from the national Republican party; he secured the nomination of the Liberal party; and he became the candidate of a paper party, "Independent Citizens for Lindsay," to diffuse further his Republican identity. "There is no party behind us," he said. "No organization. No machine. Nothing between us and the people."[42]

As columnist, Maryianne Means, described the Lindsay strategy,

> If Lindsay had his way, nobody would utter the word "Republican" in his hearing. He bills himself as an "independent-nonpartisan" and he displays pictures of himself with Lyndon Johnson. . . . Lindsay is for everything the Democrats are for, only he says he will do it better. He has begged national GOP figures to stay away. When a campaign strategest was asked whether Richard Nixon had been in touch lately, the fellow responded with a grin: "Who?"[43]

Lindsay accepted the cash and campaign aides that were proffered by the national and state Republican parties, but he resisted any public identification as a Republican.

Lindsay's wooing of the Liberal party was masterfully conceived. The Liberal endorsement enabled Lindsay to be perceived as nonpartisan in New York City, yet boosted his stock as a Republican nationwide. The irony of a non-Republican becoming a leading Republican presidential contender did not unduly trouble most observers. As William S. White aptly observed, "Though Lindsay is the spokesman for an un-Republican and basically no-party coalition, his apostles see him, at one and the same time, as the highest hope nationally of the Republican party and also as the matchless symbol of pure, nonpartisan, 'fusion' politics."[44]

The support for Lindsay by the Liberal party was advantageous for many reasons. First, the party had some 60,000 registered members in New York City. Next, it enabled registered Democrats to vote for Lindsay without having to do something that was anathema to many, pulling a Republican lever on a voting machine. Finally, and most significantly, it symbolically demonstrated that a vote for Lindsay was a vote for Lindsay and not for some political party. By being named the standard bearer of two of the three major parties, Lindsay was perceived as being beholden to neither. The imagery was clear. "One of the most important things I've learned in politics," Rockefeller had observed, "is that voters react to you intuitively. . . . And that's the important thing John [Lindsay] has going for him—they can feel his independence."[45]

In this case, however, fact and symbolism diverged. Although Lindsay did essentially dictate terms to his Republican supporters, the endorsement of the Liberal party did not come unencumbered. The Liberal party ostensibly supported Lindsay for only the purest of motives. "No, we will not help to bring political power back to the club houses," said the Liberal's vice-chairman, Alex Rose, in endorsing Lindsay. "Nor will we risk the fate of our city once again by subjecting it to boss rule. . . . We must join all good government forces in all parties for a nonpartisan Fusion administration."[46]

The rhetoric could not be taken at face value, however. As Oliver Pilat describes the Liberal chief's style, "Rose has a flair for making practical decisions on high-sounding grounds...."[47] The Liberal's support of Lindsay apparently involved several quid pro quo's. The Liberal party would have the right to select Lindsay's running mate for president of the city council,[48] and they were also promised a considerable amount of patronage in return for their endorsement.[49] As a former aide to Mayor Wagner described the Rose-Lindsay relationship, "Good Lord, the grip Alex Rose, the power in the Liberal Party, has on John Lindsay is a lot stronger than the influence any individual had on Wagner."[50]

There were a host of internal reasons for the Liberal's endorsement of Lindsay. The party was organized in 1944 after a rift developed in the American Labor Party (ALP), which had been infiltrated by Communists. The two leading figures in the new party were David Dubinsky, president of the International Ladies Garment Workers Union, and Alex Rose, president of the United Hatters, Cap and Millinery Workers Union. As originally formulated, the objectives of the Liberals were to "fight reaction and corruption in both major parties, promote the liberal wing of each, steer clear of Stalinism, help win the war, and work steadily toward a basic political realignment." Traditionally, the Liberals were "an amalgam of trade unionists, middle-class Jewish professionals, and an overlay of upper-echelon intellectuals." By the 1960s, the party was comprised mainly of aging members who had joined at its inception because most younger liberals chose to affiliate with the "reform" Democratic movement. As long as Jews dominated the needle trades industry, the alliance between unionists in this industry, Jewish professionals, and intellectuals of all persuasions was rather stable. But as a majority of the workers in the garment trades became black and Puerto Rican, they did not join the Liberal party in any great numbers. At this point, the coalition that established the party became strained. As a thirty-year-old Liberal lawyer explained, "The union guys aren't liberal, most of them. They're in it for what they can get. The future [of the party] lies in the young intellectuals, and I'm hoping. After all, the unions aren't what they used to be in the party."[51]

Rose and Dubinsky recognized the demographics of their party's support. They would have to endorse Lindsay or risk alienating their younger members. More significant, however, was the fact that a Liberal party endorsement meant a lot more to a Republican candidate than to a Democrat. With Democrats overwhelmingly outnumbering Republicans in the city, comparatively few Republican dissidents would desert their party to vote for a Democrat on the Liberal line. However, when the Liberals backed a Republican, as they did in 1965, there were many more potential Democratic dissidents to vote for the Republican on the Liberal line.[52] In a sense, the Liberals could drive a better bargain with the Republicans than they could with the Democrats. Ironically, when Lindsay reached an "accommodation" or "deal" with the Liberals in return for their support, that support was considered symbolic of his independence.

The new politics is also characterized by the use of public opinion polls to guide campaign strategy. Politicians now design their campaigns with detailed information on what the public thinks so that they may take advantage of support and avoid possible disfavor. As Nimmo observes, "Just as advertisers learn what consumers want and are willing to buy before marketing a product, image makers ask pollsters to determine what electorates look for...."[53] "The results of these early polls [are] used to determine a general strategy—developing a favorable image for the candidate and focusing on a popular campaign theme.... During the campaign, polls can chart the progress of a candidate and even assess the effectiveness of specific themes."[54]

The Lindsay mayoral race "was the nation's first computerized campaign," with campaign workers "provided with a gold mine of information ... checked, tabulated and neatly assembled on punch cards." This detailed data bank enabled campaign workers to determine "which blocks to push hardest in, and which doorbells they needn't waste time ringing. In addition, the punch cards provided up-to-date demographic information on religion and race for each area. Thus campaign literature could be selective and sent precisely to its target .... Nothing like it had ever been seen in the city before."[55]

Voters found the Lindsay image sufficiently compelling during the campaign that he was able to narrowly defeat Beame and become mayor of New York. The Beame loss could be attributed to one glaring miscalculation—he should never have been nominated in the first place. "It was a fatal error for the [Democratic party] bigwigs stemming from the conventional conceit that any condidate of a party that outnumbers its opposition by 3-to-1 cannot lose. It was a fatal error in an age of television."[56] Beame was a perfectly acceptable candidate for an old-style political campaign, but he was certainly no match for Lindsay in a media-oriented, new-style confrontation.

Lindsay's adherence to image politics did not diminish after his election as mayor. In an insightful analysis written on the eve of Lindsay's inauguration, Alan Otten discussed the incoming mayor's approach, "Mr. Lindsay is obviously pleased at these ... frequent press references to himself as 'the Republican Kennedy.' And like the eager New Frontiersmen, he and his top lieutenants count heavily on good looks and pleasant television personality, style, enthusiasm, energy, public and press good will, to help produce a creditable four year record. They believe there'll be many real accomplishments but that astute merchandising and huckstering can create the impression of even greater ones."[57] Concluding that "the Mayor-elect shows an almost unerring instinct for correct political decisions and [is] obviously ambitious and intelligent," Otten was nevertheless sanguine about his ability to govern. So far, Otten observed, "he has not shown much interest in digging deeply into a subject and mastering it; aides say his attention span is something [less than] half a minute, and he displays a distressing tendency to reason in stereotypes and talk in clichés. Top adviser Robert Price... and other Lindsay lieutenants are moving into an area where they've little real experience, and they may find that techniques successful in a political campaign fall short in running a city." Regardless of their real accomplishments, however, they "will probably be made to appear even greater than they are by carefully contrived suggestions of action and motion in other areas. Master-strategest Price believes much good will can be achieved just by having 'that beautiful man' moving around among the populace—riding the subways, dropping in on schools and hospitals, indicating in other ways he truly cares."[58]

As was true of "candidate" Lindsay, incoming-mayor Lindsay intended to rely heavily on the media. "To sell himself and his program... Mr. Lindsay will constantly use radio and television, outlets where he 'projects' particularly well. There'll be television reports to the people, filmed and live press conferences, telethons where the citizens can call in and ask him questions." In fact, the incoming mayor had already been "adroitly using the mass-media to cushion the voters to a realization that change may come a little more slowly than his campaign might have led them to believe. Where the campaign stressed that the city's problems were manageable by the right man, his more recent utterances emphasize the city's dire situation."[59]

The mayor-elect's concern with appearances was perhaps best reflected in the selection of an appropriate condensation symbol or theme, to portray his administration. When a leader of the Ethical Culture Society, Algernon Black, suggested "Proud City," Lindsay was captivated; "It's a good image. I like it." Asked where the sense of pride would come from, Lindsay responded, "It will come from trying, and I think that will lead to accomplishment." Again, it was the pursuit of the goal, rather than its attainment that was Lindsay's primary focus. "It's important to shoot for a Proud City—to aim for it. It gives people a sense of accomplishment, a feeling that they are going somewhere."[60] This theme of a *proud city* was, of course, to be popularized through the media. As soon as the catchword was agreed upon, Lindsay's press secretary leaked a story to the *Journal American* saying that the mayor planned much greater use of WNYC, the municipal radio station, as "part of the Mayor's plan to project the image of

New York as a 'proud city' and to change the people's attitude from dispair, hostility and pessimism to one of participation."[61]

In terms of the way this *proud city* could be achieved, Lindsay was certainly not attracted to the consensus building approach of old-style outgoing Mayor Wagner. Quite to the contrary, the new-style Lindsay observed, "We won't have the cooperation of organized power groups, just Joe Doaks, the consumer."[62] Could you govern successfully without reaching an accommodation with the major power blocs? A close Lindsay aide certainly believed so; ". . . a lot of people in New York who have been claiming for so long that they can deliver blocs of votes may turn out to be wearing the emperor's clothes. Take the labor leaders. I'm not impressed by Mr. Harry Van Arsdale [the head of the New York Central Labor Council] and the voting power he supposedly controls. Oh sure, he can get 200 people to walk around City Hall, but you've got to remember that union members are many other things besides cardholders—they're tenants or homeowners and members of social and religious organizations. They can't be manipulated as if they were one homogeneous mass."[63] In fact, the Lindsay advisor concluded, it might be advantageous politically not to be tied into the so-called ruling elite. "It seems to me . . . that what you have to be especially careful about in politics is choosing your enemies. It's important to have good enemies." Such an approach, of fighting against an identifiable evil force was certainly consistent with an image conscious approach to politics. It was particularly effective, too, where "the demographic shifts that are taking place in New York—the growing numbers of [blacks] and Puerto Ricans—make it all the more important for [Lindsay] to maintain certain enemies."[64]

Perhaps most telling with regard to how successful the mayor-elect was in having the media and the public accept the image he was projecting was a comment by Debs Myers, the former press secretary to Mayor Wagner, several days before the change in administration; "John Lindsay is the only man I've ever heard of who is already the greatest Mayor in history before he takes office."[65]

Chapter 2

An Early Strike

On November 2, 1965, Representative John V. Lindsay was elected the 103rd Mayor of New York City by narrowly defeating his Democratic opponent Abraham Beame. Lindsay, who had received the endorsement of both the Republican and the Liberal parties, thus became the first Republican to win the mayoralty since Fiorello La Guardia was victorious in 1933, 1937, and 1941.

Among the numerous congratulatory messages received by Lindsay the day after his election, was one from Michael J. Quill, president of the Transport Workers Union, offering "sincere congratulations on achieving this high post." The union, which represented employees on the city's subways and buses, also extended an invitation to the mayor-elect to send a representative to sit in on the collective bargaining negotiations between the TWU and the New York City Transit Authority (TA) which were due to get underway the following day, November 4. Quill's telegram continued:

> This invitation is extended to you at this time so that you will be thoroughly acquainted—from the very beginning of our negotiations—with all developments of these critical collective bargaining sessions on contracts that terminate at midnight, December 31, 1965.
>
> We should also inform you that our union has a long-standing commitment with the membership that at 5:00 A.M., January 1, 1966, our traditional slogan of "No Contract—No Work" goes into effect—with no extensions whatsoever.
>
> Again, our congratulations and best regards.[1]

Along with the telegram, Quill sent a copy of the seventy-six proposals his union planned to submit to the TA. If the mayor-elect was on cloud nine after his stunning victory, this telegram certainly must have been enough to bring him back down to earth.

At noon on Thursday, November 4, Quill arrived at the TA headquarters building in downtown Brooklyn to present formally his demands; "requests so light" according to the smiling union president, "we hope the gentlemen of the Transit Authority will have no trouble granting them by early December."[2] Sitting at a long table in the TA's thirteenth floor conference room, Quill spent more than an hour explaining his proposals to the representatives of the print and broadcast media. The principal TWU demands were a four-day, thirty-two-hour work week with no loss of pay; a 30 percent across-the-board wage increase; a guarantee of no layoffs; six weeks of vacation after one year of employment; a 10 percent differential for night work; and the right to retire at any age at one-half pay after twenty-five years of service.

Quill further stated that, in somewhat of a departure from its previous negotiations, the TWU would place increased emphasis on detailed economic arguments to bolster its demands. "The old order changeth," he said. "We don't just pound the table and say we've got to have this and that any more. Now we're bringing in people who can prove their points."[3] Hired as a consultant by the TWU to facilitate this new approach was Leon Keyserling, who had served as chairman of the Council of Economic Advisers under President Harry Truman.

Further, Quill indicated that he was disappointed that Mayor-Elect Lindsay had not sent a representative to this initial meeting. The union president suggested that all public officials who could potentially subsidize the deficit ridden TA should send representatives to the negotiations; including Governor Nelson Rockefeller; Robert Moses, chairman of the Triborough Bridge and Tunnel Authority; and Austin J. Tobin, executive director of the Port of New York Authority. Quill suggested that the Triborough Authority and the Port Authority, which had been "piling up millions of dollars" in profits, should help meet some of the costs of operating the city's transit lines.[4]

Finally, Quill noted that although his contract with the Transit Authority actually expired at midnight on New Year's Eve, the TWU had set a 5:00 a.m. strike deadline. "Our union realizes that a lot of people will be out celebrating at midnight," said Quill, "So we've decided to take them home and put them to bed." The union's proposals, however, certainly did not have a soporific effect on Joseph E. O'Grady, the chairman of the TA. In his remarks to the assembled media representatives, O'Grady said that he was "flabbergasted" by both the scope and potential cost of the union's proposals. The TA chairman characterized the package that he estimated would cost more than $250 million as "absolutely impossible and far beyond anything we could be expected to pay. There isn't enough gold in Fort Knox to pay this bill," he said.[5]

The Amalgamated Transit Union (ATU), which represented 1,750 bus employees in the New York City boroughs of Queens and Staten Island, presented their demands at the same time as the TWU. They were virtually the same as those of the larger TWU, which represented 33,000 transit employees.

Asked to evaluate the possible effects of the unions' demands on an increased subway fare, O'Grady replied, "I don't know but it may be necessary to raise fares unless we can find some new money somewhere."[6] The TA had already forecast an operating deficit of more than $62 million in the fiscal year ending June 30, 1966.[7] A substantial increase in labor costs, due to a new labor agreement, would undoubtedly make this deficit even greater. Under the state law that established the bipartisan TA in 1953, its operating expenses had to be met out of its revenues. Any deficit could only be funded by either a fare increase or a subsidy by the city that was approved by the state legislature. Analyzing the financial picture of the TA, O'Grady said that on the basis of present income and outgo, his agency did not have a cent with which to satisfy Quill's demands.[8]

In spite of his own dire conclusions with respect to the TA's financial position, O'Grady nevertheless took exception to Quill's suggestion that outsiders who could potentially subsidize the Authority be brought to the bargaining table. He said that the TA was an autonomous agency and that its three commissioners did not intend to abdicate their responsibility for negotiating a contract.[9] At the conclusion of their public statements to the media, the first formal bargaining session, which lasted a scant forty-five minutes, took place.

The Transit System

The transit system in New York was extremely large and complex, operating twenty-four-hours each day, and carrying more than 1,836 billion passengers each year. The facilities for subways and elevated trains cost $2 billion to build and the cost to replace them in 1965 was an estimated $6 billion. Its 6,827 subway cars carried passengers over 720 miles of track, and its 2,200 buses traversed a total of 554 surface miles. With approximately 35,000 employees, the TA had more workers than thirty-eight of the fifty states. In addition to the operations conducted by the TA at the time of the agency's creation, in March 1962, the city seized two private bus companies, the Fifth Avenue Coach Lines Inc. and Surface Transit Inc. These formerly private bus lines were established as a subsidiary of the TA called the Manhattan and Bronx Surface Transit Operating Authority (MABSTOA). These additional bus operations employed 20 percent of the TA's total work force and carried one million more passengers each day. The MABSTOA used 2,000 buses to carry passengers over its seventy-five routes.[10]

Employees of the Transit Authority performed extremely varied tasks, as evidenced by the fact that the contract between the TWU and the TA covered fifty-five different job titles. These jobs ran the gamut from rather unskilled work such as railroad porters, watchmen, caretakers, and clerks, to highly skilled tasks, located mainly in the operating and maintenance departments. A maintenance electrician, for example, repaired equipment using as much as 21,000 volts, and subway motormen were responsible for the safe operation of ten or eleven car trains carrying several thousand passengers. Those employees who maintained subway trains, buses, or facilities did welding, carpentry, plumbing, and painting. Although the skill level of these employees varied tremendously, the wage structure of the TA was rather compressed, ranging from $2.57-1/4 per hour for a railroad watchman to $3.59-1/2 per hour for the six workers who maintained electronic equipment. Ignoring the very small number of employees (fifty-one) who earned more, the top pay for transit employees was $3.46-1/4 an hour, which was paid to the more than 4,900 bus and subway maintainers as well as 2,425 subway motormen. The hourly pay of the other significantly large groups of TA employees was $3.22 for the more than 5,000 bus operators, $2.95-1/2 for the 2,554 subway conductors, $2.74-3/4 for the clerks who made change and sold tokens in subway stations, and $2.64-3/4 for the almost 1,200 porters who cleaned the 482 subway stations.[11]

Partly because of the generally hard and unpleasant work, and partly because of the extremely low wages that prevailed under private management, transit employment was considered low-status work.[12] Motormen had to be constantly alert as they guided their trains through dark, dank, and incredibly noisy tunnels. Bus drivers had to maneuver their vehicles through the legendary New York City traffic while at the same time making change for passengers. Maintenance-of-way employees often were required to make repairs under hazardous conditions. In addition, the hours were long and irregular and many operating personnel were required to work a split-shift in order to work an eight-hour day.

The TA, established in 1953, was the most recent in a long series of attempts to transport New Yorkers efficiently, at a minimum cost to passengers. The previous attempts at achieving these goals had all ended in failure. In 1904, the Interborough Rapid Transit Company (IRT) began operating subways in New York City, which had previously relied upon horse-driven surface lines, electric trolleys, and elevated train lines. Nine years later, a second subway line, the Brooklyn-Manhattan Transit System

(BMT) came into being. Although these were private companies, a low fare soon became "a basic article in the creed of every New York politician."[13] As a result, the city established the Transit Commission in 1921 to control the rate of fare charged. To enable the companies to operate on a 5¢ fare, they were given tax exemptions and other subsidies by the city. Despite this aid, the transit operators could not remain profitable. They permitted their equipment to deteriorate, and in 1932 the IRT went bankrupt. In 1940, the city purchased the IRT and the BMT for $317 million and unified the subway system.

When the Transit Commission was abolished in 1943, the job of running the subways fell on the Board of Transportation, which had been established by the city in 1924 to build and operate the independent subway system. Under the supervision of the Board of Transportation, the system was operated profitably until 1946. But with World War II over and gasoline rationing no longer in effect, the system again began to lose money. In the postwar years, "the subways were run inefficiently, and the equipment became obsolete, labor output was bad, and huge deficits" were incurred.[14] In 1948, with a yearly deficit approaching $31 million, the fare was raised to 10¢.[15] The financial situation improved for a year, but then losses began to again mount. Equipment had been allowed to deteriorate to such an extent under private management that the proceeds of a $500-million bond issue, approved in 1951 by voters who expected a new subway line to be built, were spent on replacements and repairs. By this time, the city was spending approximately $50 million each year to subsidize the 10¢ fare.[16]

In 1953, the New York State Legislature enacted a law introduced by Republican Governor Thomas E. Dewey, which created the New York City Transit Authority. The TA was established as an independent agency charged with running the subways and buses on lease from the city. This new arrangement was to take the operation of the subway system out of politics and put it on a business-like basis.[17]

A key provision of the legislation required that the TA be self-sustaining; it would have to charge a fare that would cover its operating costs. Under the law the only money the TA could receive from the city was to pay for capital costs and interest and principal on outstanding indebtedness. The city could subsidize new subway cars, stations, buses, power plants, and other capital costs, but not operating expenses. Based on the fact that the city could no longer subsidize its operating costs, the TA was forced in the summer of 1953 to raise the fare to 15¢. The city, however, continued to pay for the TA's capital expenditures and indebtedness. In existence for a little more than a decade by the mid-1960s, the Authority had already received more than $1 billion from the city for capital improvements. In addition, the city was paying more than $100 million annaully to cover the TA's debt payments.[18]

In spearheading the creation of the TA, Governor Dewey felt that this new arrangement would prevent the city's transit system from becoming a continuous drain on municipal revenues. The governor hoped that the new financial set-up of the TA would avoid the perennial budgetary crises created for the city by large transit operating deficits.[19]

In 1955, significant changes were made in the organizational structure of the TA. As it was originally constituted, the task of managing the transit system was entrusted to five unpaid members, whose duties were limited to attending a brief weekly meeting. "The result was absentee management that turned the system's headquarters into a cauldron of executive rivalries, backbiting and confusion."[20] In order to remedy this situation, the legislation enacted in 1955 made the direction of the transit network a full-time, salaried job. The law prescribed that the TA be directed by a three-member board, of which one member was appointed by the governor and another by the mayor. The third member, who served as chairman, was selected by the two appointees. Because the TA, as a matter of law, was created as an independent agency, it had the legal responsibility to conclude any agreements with unions representative of its employees.

At the time of the 1966 transit strike, the TA comprised Joseph E. O'Grady as chairman; John J. Gilhooley; and Daniel J. Scannell. Soon after he graduated from law school, O'Grady became active in Democratic politics, and eventually joined a law firm that included Edward J. Flynn, the leader of the Bronx Democrats.[21] In the 1940s and early 1950s, O'Grady served first as deputy director and later as the director of the New York City Division of Labor Relations. In 1954, he was appointed by Mayor Wagner as the city's first commissioner of labor.[22] A year later, O'Grady was chosen by Wagner to become a member of the newly revamped TA. In 1962, after serving as a member of the TA for seven years, O'Grady was appointed by Mayor Wagner to the bench of the Special Sessions Court. However, when the first Authority chairman, Charles L. Patterson, died in October, 1962, O'Grady returned to the TA as chairman.

Governor Rockefeller's appointee on the TA was John J. Gilhooley. In 1953, James P. Mitchell, President Dwight D. Eisenhower's Secretary of Labor, brought him to Washington as an executive assistant. He served in the Labor Department until 1960, the last three years as assistant secretary of Labor-Management Relations. In 1961, Gilhooley ran unsuccessfully for city controller on the Republican ticket. Despite his defeat, Gilhooley continued to harbor political aspirations, and most observers felt he wanted to seek elective office in the future.[23] Scannell was appointed a member of the TA in 1962 by Mayor Wagner, filling the vacancy created when

O'Grady was made a judge. Scannell began his career as a New York policeman. Then, for eight years he served as an assistant corporation counsel for the TA, serving in this capacity until he was made a member of the transit governing body in 1962. Scannell was for many years an important figure in the Queens Democratic party.

The one common thread in the backgrounds of the three TA members was their strong political ties. This is hardly surprising, because appointment to the Authority was a reward for faithful party service. As a result of their conflicting political allegiances, considerable friction existed between the Republican Gilhooley and Democratic members O'Grady and Scannell.

At a November 5 news conference, Mayor-Elect Lindsay declined the invitation extended by Quill to participate personally or to send a representative to sit in on the transit negotiations. In rejecting Quill's offer, Lindsay, who during his campaign pledged to preserve the 15¢ fare, stated, "I'm not mayor until January 1, and I do not have the power or responsibility as mayor. The period of transition at City Hall is not easy, and the best role I can play is to be kept informed."[24]

Meanwhile, the *New York Times* was editorially advocating a complete repudiation of the way in which public sector bargaining had historically been conducted in New York City, and the implementation of a totally new approach, beginning with transit negotiations. It must be "made plain, from the outset," the *Times* asserted, "that the old days of economic bludgeon and political blackmail are over." Quill should not be permitted, the *Times* continued, to "... bulldoze his political allies at City Hall into extravagant settlements through his artful blend of bluff, bluster and muscle...." "The course of wisdom," the *Times* concluded, "is to create a wholly new peace mechanism now, with new faces and a new charter of authority based on a conception of the primacy of the public interest."[25]

Bargaining in the "Old Days"

Prior to the election of Robert Wagner in 1954, labor relations with New York's municipal employees were primarily handled in an informal manner. The formal procedure dictated that wage adjustments be proposed by the Bureau of the Budget, discussed with employee unions, and then approved by the Board of Estimate. In fact, however, union officials would deal informally and politically with elected and appointed officials at both the city and state levels. As David Lewin, Raymond Horton, and James Kuhn have observed, "Certain groups such as teachers, police and firefighters found the state legislature a more receptive forum than the municipal government for realization of their interests, while others such as transit workers, maintained close political ties with the mayor."[26]

After his election, Wagner attempted to bring coherence to the city's labor relations process based on his belief that "it has been generally demonstrated that when employees through their chosen representatives are accorded a reasonable and orderly opportunity to present their proposals to their employers regarding the terms and conditions of their employment and are assured adequate machinery for the redress of their grievances, it can result in a better and more efficient functional operation and entity."[27] Wagner asked the city's newly created Department of Labor to formulate a uniform city policy on labor matters and to devise a long-term program of labor relations for city employees designed to implement that policy.

In March 1958, Mayor Wagner signed Executive Order 49, which formally committed the city to a policy of collective bargaining with its employees. The order provided that the right of employees to organize and bargain collectively through representatives of their own choosing was ensured, as was the right not to do so. The union selected by a majority of the employees in the appropriate units would then become the exclusive representative of all of the workers in that unit. The executive order also required the establishment of a grievance procedure for each city department.

However, the most interesting provisions of the executive order, and in the long run the most troublesome, concerned the role it prescribed for the Department of Labor. It provided that if the parties were unable to reach an agreement on a new contract themselves, the Commissioner of Labor could enter the dispute either at the request of the parties or on his or her own volition. The commissioner was charged with the duty "to take such steps as he may deem expedient to effect an expeditious adjustment and settlement of differences between the parties."[28] Although the Wagner order did not specifically list any unfair practices, it granted the commissioner of labor the power to handle charges of violations of the general rights accorded to employees by the order. In addition, the Department of Labor was authorized to interpret the executive order and to advise the mayor of any willful failure on the part of agency heads to comply with its provisions.

The basic problem with this arrangement was that it expected the commissioner of labor to simultaneously play both a partisan and an impartial role. On the one hand, the commissioner was the mayor's advisor on labor matters, and in this capacity was supposed to counsel the mayor on how to deal with unions that were bargaining with the city. In this sense, he or she was a part of the city's management team that was responsible for collective bargaining. On the other hand, the commissioner was supposed to provide impartial mediation services in case the parties could not reach agreement. Difficulties were inherent in this structure because the same individual was expected to be both a neutral and a representative of one of the interested parties.

In the procedures set forth by the city to operationalize the mayor's executive order, the director of the budget and the personnel director were named as the city's representatives in collective bargaining. Based on these structural changes established by Executive Order 49, the focus of union activities shifted from the legislative branches of the city and state to the executive branch of city government.[29] Thus, rather than depoliticizing the collective bargaining process, all the Wagner order did was to cause municipal unions to increasingly concentrate their political efforts on the mayor's office. As Cook has described the city's labor relations practices of the early 1960s, "The expanding unions perceived the system as manipulable by political pressures and reacted on the whole with political allegiance to the Democratic Party and Mayor Wagner. . . . The Mayor's reputation in labor matters rested to a considerable degree on his political power to find solutions satisfactory to his labor supporters."[30] In a sense, the bargaining structure established by Executive Order 49 was geared to the specific strengths of Wagner, who "took an intensely personal interest in the process. The organization of the system under one of the Mayor's departments made it easier for him to do this. He could not be accused of interfering with an impartial agency. He relished the role of mediator, and he played it with great skill. . . . He never hesitated to intervene openly or furtively in the process of the city Department of Labor."[31]

Employees of most mayoral departments and agencies were included under the original coverage of Executive Order 49. However, employees of the public authorities such as the TA did not come under these procedures. Regardless, of the formal structure, however, to be successful, the mayor of New York City clearly had to be able to deal effectively with the city's municipal employees. In 1965, 250,000 people worked for the City of New York, making it the largest employer in the metropolitan area. The three city-related authorities, the Housing Authority, the Triborough Bridge and Tunnel Authority, and the Transit Authority, employed almost 50,000 more, most of them working for the TA. One of every twelve members of the city's labor force was involved in providing municipal services. The wages and salaries of municipal employees and those of the city related authorities comprised about 10 percent of the total income from wages and salaries of all city residents. And in terms of governmental expenses, more than 60 percent of the city's budget went to pay the wages and salaries of municipal personnel.

On Sunday, November 7, 1965, Theodore W. Kheel, who had

mediated many previous negotiations between the TWU and the city's rapid transit system, suggested a possible way of reaching an agreement on a new transit contract while at the same time maintaining the 15¢ fare on subways and buses. Kheel urged that tolls on the city's bridges and tunnels be doubled and that the extra money be used by the transit system. He proposed the creation of a Transportation Policy Board that would take over many of the powers of the TA, the Triborough Bridge and Tunnel Authority, and the Port of New York Authority, with the profits earned by the latter two authorities being used to subsidize the TA. Kheel conceded that legislation would be required to permit the interchange of authority funds and that such a law might be challenged in the courts. However, he felt that a new approach to the mass transportation problem was necessary because of the TA's huge deficit.[32] When asked to appraise Kheel's proposal on a public affairs program later in the day, TWU President Quill said he really did not care where the money came from. Most of it, he said, should come from the Triborough Bridge and Tunnel Authority's surplus funds, but the Port Authority, the city, the state, and even the federal government must contribute if necessary. "We'll take money from anybody," Quill said, "from President Johnson and from his namesake, Howard Johnson."[33] Quill also called upon Mayor-Elect Lindsay and Governor Rockefeller to confer immediately on ways of finding money to pay for the transit package. "Mr. Lindsay belongs to the same party as the Governor," he stated. "They should get together to find the money."[34] Further, Quill warned that the two Republican elected officials might find averting a New Year's Day strike impossible if they waited until December 31 to intervene in negotiations. "If Lindsay waits until December 31 to get into this, I'll have a pair of motorman's handles for him," said the union president.[35]

Kheel totally agreed that Lindsay had to get involved in transit negotiations if he hoped to preserve the 15¢ fare. "We have to get to that pretty quickly," Kheel said, "because if we don't—if this is allowed to drift through January 1, 12:01 a.m., and the opportunity is then presented to try and deal with the complex problems which may involve legislation—then it may be too late to save the 15¢ fare."[36]

In another comment on November 7, Theodore Kheel said he believed that Mayor-Elect Lindsay should have his own advisors for transit matters. In 1960, Mayor Wagner established a special Transit Labor Board composed of Kheel, and two other mediators, David L. Cole, former director of the Federal Mediation and Conciliation Service, and Professor George W. Taylor of the University of Pennsylvania. "Speaking for myself," said Kheel, "and, of course, this is a committee of Mayor Wagner's and I have no right to abolish it—but I think that we should consider this committee not to be in existence for this purpose."[37]

The following day, Kheel's suggestions for preserving the 15¢ fare were supported by Mayor-Elect Lindsay, who said he hoped to present proposals to the state legislature to integrate transit facilities in the city under one authority and to pool all transit revenues. "I have said throughout the campaign," stated Lindsay, "that mass transit in New York has to be integrated ultimately."[38] The mayor-elect said he realized that such a merger would not be easy; that there would be "a massive legal problem in attempting to link the city's subway, bus, commuter railroad, and highway traffic in a single unified system."[39] Difficulties could be expected because similar proposals to establish a "super authority" had been made in the past, but all had died before reaching the floor of the state legislature. However, Quill, who one day earlier had voiced his support for Kheel's plan to use subsidies from the Triborough Bridge and Tunnel Authority and the Port Authority to preserve the 15¢ faire, now indicated he "totally disagreed" with the Kheel proposal. Never one to be publicly conciliatory for long, Quill returned to a position he had long advocated; that all transit facilities, including subways, buses, tunnels and bridges, be free.

Monday, November 8, was also a day for contemplating the approach to be taken in negotiations over a new transit contract. Outgoing Mayor Wagner indicated that although he would officially remain in office until the end of the year, concluding a new transit agreement would not be appropriate because, "I can't commit the new city administration to anything."[40] For his part, Quill warned that he would not postpone his union's strike deadline "for one hour" even though "a lot of do-gooders" are suggesting that the TWU "give the new man in City Hall a chance." "Our answer," said Quill, "will be to tell them to go to hell. We don't give a damn who's in City Hall. We have the strength to take what we're entitled to."[41]

As negotiations proceeded toward mid-November, the necessity of preserving the 15¢ fare was voiced from several different quarters. In an editorial, the *New York Times* stated that the fare "must be preserved if it is humanly possible" because "the low fare is basic to sound transportation and traffic policy." The low fare is necessary, the *Times* continued, "if the city is to encourage rail traffic into it from the perimeter, and thus avoid clogging arteries and city streets. . . ."[42] A virtually identical position was advocated by John J. Gilhooley, one of the three members of the TA, who noted that a fare increase was inconsistent with national transportation policy, which favors getting people off the highways in urban centers and on mass transit. "We must recognize," Gilhooley stated, "as past history informs us that raising the fare might mean the loss of 90 to 100 million riders every year. . . ."[43] The possibility that a fare increase would drive away large numbers of transit riders would also, of course, dramatically reduce the additional revenues that a fare increase might be expected to generate.

On November 14, Theodore Kheel, chairman of Mayor Wagner's special Transit Labor Board, made official a remark he had made earlier, speaking only for himself. This time, acting as the spokesman for the mediation board, which also included Cole and Taylor, Kheel stated that the panel should be considered nonexistent as far as negotiations between the TWU and the TA were concerned. Because the board felt that negotiations probably would run past 12:00 p.m. on December 31, when Lindsay assumed office, they believed that the incoming mayor should have a say in appointing the board members. "Any mediation board that gets involved now should be by the joint invitation of both Mr. Wagner and Mr. Lindsay," Kheel said.[44]

Kheel's statement put a damper on a suggestion made earlier in the day by the TA's Gilhooley, who said it was essential for the three-member panel or another board to enter the negotiations immediately in order to avoid a New Year's Day strike. "The mediators entered the negotiations two years ago on November 13," Gilhooley pointed out, and "the problem is even graver now with the 15¢ fare at stake. It is up to Mayor Wagner," Gilhooley concluded, "to make sure that the transit board gets involved quickly."[45]

This difference of opinion between Kheel and Gilhooley regarding the proper roles for Mayor Wagner and Mayor-Elect Lindsay to play in negotiations was undoubtedly politically motivated. Kheel, who had long represented Wagner in dealing with the city's employees and who was also a close political advisor of the mayor, was obviously articulating the Wagner position in his public pronouncements. In fact, the position of Mayor Wagner regarding the appropriateness of his special transit mediation board getting involved in negotiations was indistinguishable from that of Kheel. A spokesman for Wagner said that the mayor "would be delighted to have his board take part in the transit talks," but that decision would have to be a voluntary one by the three mediators. In view of Lindsay's election, the spokesman added, the mayor did not feel he should take the responsibility of asking them to act now.[46] Gilhooley, in turn, as the sole Republican on the three-member TA board was publicly advocating the Lindsay position; that it was Wagner's responsibility to negotiate a new agreement.

Returning from a four-day vacation in the Virgin Islands on November 16, Mayor-Elect Lindsay seemed as critical as ever of the way in which transit negotiations were being handled. Calling the current methods of bargaining "archaic and way behind the times," Lindsay asked for a broad reform of "the whole bargaining process" between the city and labor unions. "What is needed," he said, "is a system of arbitration that is completely and totally independent." The mayor-elect noted that there was "plenty of talent" in the universities and suggested that professors be used in settling disputes because they had "no ax to grind."[47] Lindsay placed responsibility for averting a strike with the Wagner Administration saying that an agreement had to be reached before January 1, 1966. "When January 1 comes and I am Mayor," Lindsay stated, "I expect that the Mayor, Mike Quill and the Transit Authority will have had the good sense and the good judgement not to have made the people suffer and would have settled things in the public interest."[48]

By the following day, however, Lindsay began to soften his position that the negotiation of a new transit agreement rested solely with outgoing Mayor Wagner. Although he still maintained that the power to designate a mediation team lay with Wagner, Lindsay conceded that he was ready to consider the position advocated by Kheel, that a new board be named jointly by himself and the outgoing mayor.

On Thursday, November 18, after insisting since his election that he would keep himself "intimately informed" on the transit talks but not take an active part in them, Mr. Lindsay changed his position. Michael Quill's explanation of Lindsay's change of heart was simple—"We goosed him a little bit this morning, so he came in."[49] Whatever the cause, Lindsay said he would confer with Mayor Wagner as soon as possible regarding the composition of a neutral panel to resolve the labor dispute. Later, when asked if he felt the strike deadline on January 1 should be postponed, Lindsay replied, "I have a right to ask for a cooling-off period if necessary, but I hope we won't get to that."[50] Quill, however, reacted strongly. "A cooling-off period," he said, "is an old union-busting, strike-busting gimmick.... He'll not get away with it in this town." Quill then added caustically that the people of New York City needed "less profile and more courage" from the mayor-elect.[51]

Lindsay stated that he was delighted that Mayor Wagner had indicated he would be willing to select a mediation board jointly with him. The mayor-elect made his remarks after Mayor Wagner, earlier in the day, indicated that his own mediation panel of Theodore Kheel, David Cole, and George Taylor once again told him that they were "extremely reluctant to serve under present conditions." In his statement read at City Hall, Wagner stated that the mediators, "point out that as a fundamental principle of labor mediation that mediators must have the full support and confidence of all parties to the negotiations. They feel," Wagner added, "that the mayor-elect is one of the parties involved [and] consequently they are declining to function in these negotiations." As to what role he himself would play in negotiations, Wagner said, "The mayor's only direct role is not that of a super-mediator, but rather it is to agree—or not—to include sufficient subsidy money in the budget to enable the Transit Authority to reach an acceptable agreement with the union. I cannot make such a commitment. Only the incoming mayor who will submit the budget which must include the subsidy can make the commitment."[52]

Although agreement was reached on both the desirability of a neutral panel to help settle transit negotiations and the fact that such a group should be jointly proposed by Wagner and Lindsay, the specific role for such a panel was far from resolved. Lindsay referred to the panel as an "arbitration board" and said he favored "advisory arbitration," which he defined as fact-finding with nonbinding recommendations. TWU President Quill, on the other hand, indicated that he would welcome a mediation attempt by a neutral panel, but that he was completely opposed to advisory or binding arbitration.[53]

The following day, Mayor-Elect Lindsay submitted ten names to Mayor Wagner from which it was hoped a three-member panel of neutrals could be drawn. Lindsay suggested to Wagner that he submit the names of the candidates to the union and the TA for their approval. Lindsay's office continued to refer to the proposed transit board as a "fact-finding arbitration panel" despite Quill's protestations that the only form of third-party intervention he would accept was mediation.[54]

In a radio program broadcast on Sunday, November 21, Quill sought to allay the fears that were increasingly being voiced: that he appeared to be a totally intransigent negotiator. Quill indicated that his union would be quite willing to make concessions once serious bargaining began. "All requests, every one of them from top to bottom are for the bargaining table," he said. "Anybody who reads anything else into them is making a mistake," he added. "We are very reasonable people."[55]

The first full bargaining session between the TWU and the TA took place on Tuesday, November 23, at the Americana Hotel. The closed session, which lasted seventy-five minutes, saw nine union representatives sitting across two green-clothed tables from the four spokesmen for the TA. At the conclusion of the meeting, the Transit Authority announced that the cost of the new two-year contract demanded by the TWU would be $680 million rather than the originally estimated $250 million. The new figure was reached as a result of two weeks of study by the authority's staff on each of the requests item by item, as compared with the original estimate made by TA Chairman O'Grady, after a cursory examination of the demands. Gilhooley, a TA member and acting chairman of the authority at the time because O'Grady was on vacation, said, "$680 million is stratospheric. There can be little fruitful negotiations under such circumstances," he declared.[56] Scannell, the third member of the three-man TA, asserted that "this is an impossible figure to bargain against."[57]

Asked to comment on the negotiations, the usually effusive Quill refused to make a statement. A television reporter attempted to coax some remarks from Quill, saying, "people will be watching tonight on TV," and they will be disappointed if you have no statement. However, rather than delivering a disarming one-liner as he typically did on such occasions, Quill replied acidly, "Tell them to turn the set off."[58]

On Wednesday, November 24, subcommittee negotiations took place primarily over working conditions, but discussions between the principals were not due to resume until the following Monday. It was typical in transit negotiations for various subcommittees of TWU and TA representatives to get together early in bargaining to try to resolve issues such as working conditions, that involved a relatively small expenditure of money. This would enable those individuals most familiar with a particular problem to work out an appropriate solution and allowed the chief negotiators to concentrate on more significant issues.[59] Meanwhile, the union's enlarged joint executive committee unanimously adopted a resolution instructing its international and local officers to abide by their long-standing policy of "No Contract-No Work." A contract extension was inappropriate according to the resolution because "there is more than sufficient time remaining between now and year's end for arriving at an acceptable contract across the collective bargaining table...."[60] In a comment made before leaving for Puerto Rico on a vacation, however, Lindsay said he did not believe the time remaining before the expiration of the existing contract was being used as productively as it could. Lindsay indicated that negotiations between the TA and the TWU "ought to go into continuous session. There must be no charade here, no play acting," the Mayor-Elect asserted. "Let them get on with the job full-time, weekends and nights."[61]

By November 27, the maneuverings surrounding transit negotiations were becoming increasingly politicized. First, Mayor Wagner met with Daniel T. Scannell, one of the three members of the TA to discuss the progress being made in the ongoing talks with the TWU. Although John J. Gilhooley was acting chairman of the TA while Joseph O'Grady was on vacation, Wagner apparently felt more comfortable discussing strategy with fellow Democrat Scannell rather than with the Republican Gilhooley. Later in the day, the mayor placed the retention of the 15¢ fare squarely in the lap of his successor, John V. Lindsay. "It's future depends on how willing the next administration is to give money to preserve it," Wagner asserted.[62] In past contract settlements, Wagner had always received permission from the state legislature to grant the TA financial aid, because in the whole time he had served as Mayor expenses could not be met out of transit revenues. Gilhooley, the sole Republican member of the TA, then issued a statement saying he was "surprised to hear Mayor Wagner attempt to divorce himself from the problem of preserving the 15¢ fare." Gilhooley declared that the responsibility for obtaining a fair agreement in the current negotiations rested with "the TA, the TWU, and the present Mayor, the Honorable Robert F. Wagner."[63] Scannell, as might be expected because of the political bond he shared with Wagner, was much more sympathetic to the mayor's statement. Mr. Scannell indicated that the retention of the 15¢ fare would be a "real problem" in view of the fact that the TA anticipated a $62-million deficit before it even attempted to meet the cost of a new contract. "We'll have to have a new source of revenue," he added. "Whether it's from a fare increase or other sources is something to be decided in the future."[64]

Although the TA was created to make certain that the transit system would pay for itself and not prove to be a continuous drain on municipal revenues, in actuality it had been unable to achieve its stated objectives. By the 1966 subway strike, the Authority had operated in the red for eleven of the thirteen years of its existence. Despite these losses, the TA did not raise the fare, as it was obligated by statute to do. The TA was able to maintain the 15¢ fare, in the face of recurring deficits, because "the Wagner Administration which had an even greater interest than the Authority in preserving the fare, helpfully provided a variety of indirect subsidies," which permitted the TA to maintain the fiction that it was self-sustaining.[65]

In 1959, the city sold the power plants used to generate electricity for running the subways to Consolidated Edison on the grounds that the city could not justify a large capital outlay for this purpose and also that the city could not maintain these plants adequately.[66] The $50 million received from this sale was used to subsidize transit operating expenses.[67] Immediately after the city sold the power plants, the TA announced that the rates Consolidated Edison was charging for electricity were more expensive than what it had cost the city to produce an equal amount of electricity. Consequently, the city paid the TA the difference between the two rate schedules, and the Authority applied this money toward meeting its operating expenses.[68]

In 1960, the city took over the Transit Police Force, and the $16.8-million operating expense that went with it, on the grounds that the city should assume the responsibility of protecting its citizens from criminal activity whether they were on the streets or in the subways. The logic of the city's argument was so persuasive that no legislation was required to permit the city to assume this cost. Legislation would be needed only if the city was unable to convince the courts that it was not subsidizing the TA.

State legislation was necessary in 1964, however, when the city sought to reimburse the TA to provide cut-rate transportation for school children.[69] In that year, the city began paying the TA the 10¢ per ride difference between the regular fare and the 5¢ fare the school children paid. With 349,000 children taking public transit to school, this amounted to a subsidy of more than $12 million each year.[70] Although the state had on several occasions granted the city the right to give subsidies to the TA, it had never given funds to the TA itself, or paid any of its costs.[71]

By the time the transit negotiations began in the fall of 1965, the law requiring the TA to be self-sustaining clearly was honored more in the breach than in the observance. By 1965, Daniel Scannell observed, "the Transit Authority believed they had reached the limit of indirect costs they could pick-up from the city."[72] "The Wagner Administration, ingenious and thorough, had apparently exhausted all possible sources of hidden aid that could have...provided the basis for a settlement" in the 1965 negotiations.[73] If a subsidy was needed after the 1966 settlement, it would have to be a direct one, requiring the legislative permission of New York State.

On November 28, Quill rejected the ten people Mayor-Elect Lindsay had suggested as possible members of a transit mediation board. The TWU president made it clear that he did not consider Lindsay's nominees qualified to deal with transit problems. None of them, he said, "speak the lingo of the transit industry."[74] Quill suggested that either Mayor Wagner or TA Chairman O'Grady submit ten names of their own for the union to consider. He said he might even consider recommendations made by Lindsay if they contained "two or three persons who know transit." The ten names turned down by Quill had been submitted to Wagner ten days earlier by Lindsay so that a new mediation panel could be selected to replace the one that had recently resigned. As for his evaluation of the ten names he submitted, Mayor-Elect Lindsay characterized them as being "outstanding people."[75]

In other comments, Quill repeated his previous statements that transit rides should be provided free as with other city services such as police and fire protection. In a final remark, Quill was highly critical of Lindsay for taking a vacation at a time when the transit situation was so tense. "There's so much stupidity in the present situation," Quill said, "that we are apt to stumble into a strike...and I don't think a visit to Puerto Rico will solve it."[76]

The next day, the TA approved Lindsay's list of mediators. "These ten people are outstanding in labor relations," Gilhooley, acting chairman of the TA, stated, "There could be an acceptable panel chosen from them."[77] In a news conference at the Roosevelt Hotel, Mayor-Elect Lindsay appeared to be irritated by Quill's refusal to accept a panel of mediators. In answer to reporters' questions, Lindsay said he would be willing to meet with Quill to try to reach a settlement—"but not until Mr. Quill sits down and starts bargaining in good faith. Mr. Quill hasn't even taken the trouble to call me. He's not doing his people any good with his pyrotechnics on television. I'll meet him around the clock—on the subways, anywhere. In a problem like this, I think it's the role of the Mayor-elect to act as a catalyst."[78] Lindsay's irritation with Quill appeared to sharpen as he progressed from interview to interview, until he stated grimly, "When the time comes, I'll sit down with him around the clock for as many days and nights as are necessary and we'll see who lasts longer."[79] Asked to comment on Lindsay's charge that he had not been bargaining in good faith, the TWU president replied, "He wouldn't be in a position to know, because he hasn't attended any of our sessions."[80]

With only one month remaining before the expiration of their existing contract, the TA and the TWU met for one and one-half hours on November 30. Quill described the talks, however, as making "absolutely no progress."[81] Meanwhile, the relationship between Mayor-Elect Lindsay and TWU President Quill, which was always cool, was becoming even more acrimonious. Commenting that "there are only so many shopping days left before Christmas and it's time somebody moved off center," Quill sent a telegram to Lindsay which read in part, "We have learned from your public announcements of your desire to meet with us on the problem of negotiating an acceptable labor contract. . . . We will be happy to meet with you at whatever time and place you designate."[82]

Lindsay, however, declined the invitation. In a telegram sent to the union's headquarters on December 1, the mayor-elect wrote:

> It is regrettable . . . that you found it necessary to summarily reject the outstanding panel of labor mediators. . . . I need not remind you that the current negotiations are between the Transit Authority and the Transport Workers Union.
> However, when it is evident that the parties are prepared to engage in good-faith collective bargaining, I, as Mayor-elect, will do all I can within my limited powers to assist the parties in reaching a fair and rapid settlement.[83]

Negotiations Broken Off

Upon receiving this telegram, the TWU broke off contract negotiations with the TA. TWU President Quill charged that Lindsay had "shot to hell" any hope of an agreement. "It's all in the lap of Mr. Lindsay," he said agrily. "We won't move an inch. His telegram is the height of stupidity." In reply, a spokesman for the mayor-elect said, "Mr. Lindsay stands on his telegram." Quill's counter was quick and biting. "He can stand on the telegram, sit on it, or do anything else with it that is handy," he declared.[84] Later in the day on a radio call-in talk show, Quill used the word *coward* several times in describing Lindsay's refusal to meet with TWU representatives. He used the phrases *overgrown coward* and *a common ordinary coward* to characterize Lindsay's behavior. In addition, he consistently mispronounced the mayor-elect's name, calling him Mr. *Lindsley* and accused him of "double-talk" in declining to join in negotiations.[85] "He is an ungracious sourpuss," Quill concluded. "Let him run the trains and buses after the first of the year."[86]

Quill continued to maintain that Lindsay's ten nominees suggested as a basis for a mediation board were unacceptable to the union because they were not familiar with transit matters. The ten rejected men included Former Solicitor General Archibald Cox; Professor Walter Gellhorn of Columbia University, a former chairman of the New York Regional War Labor Board; Ewan Clague, retired commissioner of the Federal Bureau of Labor Statistics; Nathan Feinsinger, a member of the University of Wisconsin Law School faculty; Clark Kerr, former chancellor of the University of California; Ralph J. Seward, former president of the National Academy of Arbitrators and an impartial arbitrator in the steel industry; Eric J. Schmertz, former director of the New York State Board of Mediation; Lloyd Bailer, arbitrator and former consultant to the U.S. Department of Labor; Professor James J. Healy of the Harvard University Graduate School of Public Administration; and George P. Shultz, dean of the Graduate School of Business at the University of Chicago.[87]

On December 2, the TWU announced that it would break off negotiations with the TA and threatened to call a subway and bus strike at 5:00 a.m., December 15 instead of waiting until their contract expired on New Year's Day. Quill contended that the existing contract had been "broken" when "Mr. Lindsley" sent a telegram the day before charging that the union was not bargaining in good faith.[88] "His words . . . are tantamount to a charge of a criminal act against all of us," the TWU president stated.[89] His contract with the TA no longer considered valid, Quill cheerfully contemplated a transit paralysis. "I'm as happy as a pig in—well I don't want to mention it," he told a news conference, in a reference to his possible jailing for calling a strike. "Let Macy's, Gimbel's, Bloomingdale's and all the rest worry about the man they elected," Quill intoned. When asked if the public would suffer, Quill replied, "Let them do their Christmas shopping early." Indicating that a membership meeting had been set for 7:30 p.m. on December 14 to take a strike vote, the TWU president said he was sure of its outcome. "I've been taking soundings," he said, "and I'm confident they'll seize the opportunity of this blunder of Mr. Lindsley [sic] to go on strike December 15."[90]

Quill dared the TA to seek an antistrike injunction under the state's Condon-Wadlin Act, which prohibited strikes by municipal employees. "Let them call out the militia. Let them call out the Army," he stated. "If Mr. Lindsley [sic] wants to put 36,000 men and women in jail, it will be his responsibility. The militia can't run the subways." If he was sent to jail, Quill seemed to relish his possible martyrdom. "I would immediately recommend to my associates that we go on a hunger strike," he said. "The first five days will be the worst, and after that we will get used to it."[91]

Saying he had nothing against the mayor-elect personally, Quill indicated that he had never even met him. Nevertheless, the TWU president consistently continued to deride the mayor-elect by pronouncing his name as Lindsley. Asked why he persisted in the error, Quill replied, "Lindsley? That's a good Irish name." And he further observed that a subway strike would not aid Lindsay's alleged ambition to seek the presidency. Recalling that Calvin Coolidge had been catapulted to the presidency by smashing the Boston police strike, Quill observed, "that was forty-five years ago, and it may not work today."[92]

Although his words were as caustic and biting as in previous years, physically Quill appeared frail and drained by the confrontation, frequently leaning on his ever-present blackthorn walking stick for support. Now sixty years old, he had long suffered from a heart ailment. In November 1954, while waiting at LaGuardia Airport to board a flight to Washington, D. C., to attend a conference of Congress of Industrial Organizations (CIO) officials, Quill suffered a heart attack. Although he had just turned forty-nine, he was considerably overweight and was under constant pressure because of his almost limitless commitments. Many of his close associates thought his career had ended. However, within three days, without apparent regard of his health, he left the hospital and headed for Chicago, where the CIO convention was getting under way. Two years later, in 1956, Quill suffered a major heart attack that caused him to spend six weeks recuperating.[93]

Over the next decade, Quill was not in particularly bad health, but he continued his incredibly hectic schedule and put on additional weight. By about 1960, however, his health began a rapid deterioration. "The heart attacks came with frequency, and [he] had lost fifty-five of his 200 pounds by 1963" as a result of his declining health.[94] In May 1962, Quill was presiding at a conference of the International TWU Executive Board, in New York City, when he had a fainting spell and had to be rushed by ambulance to Mt. Sinai Hospital. He was now forced to rest between meetings and speeches, and this did not suit Quill's personality. "I'm not delighted about my inactive role," he observed at the time.[95] He had not lost his sense of humor, however, "I keep busy between running the union and keeping a warm bed at Mt. Sinai. . . . I have a new method of transport. I use an ambulance going and coming."[96] In negotiations in the winter of 1963, the TWU president "used a portable oxygen tank and fistfulls of pills to keep him going." Despite these precautions, "after two or three hours of frenzied conferences he would appear close to collapse. Quill's heart did not improve, and by late 1965 he remained under constant medication, and he slept with an oxygen tank beside his bed.[97]

Several hours after Quill threatened to strike in mid-December, the Transit Authority began preparing two courses of action. Daniel Scannell, said the TA would go before Theodore Kheel, the permanent arbitrator for the transit industry, and demand that the union abide by the no-strike pledge of the existing contract.[98] The TA also announced plans to seek an antistrike injunction under the state's Condon-Wadlin Act, which prohibited strikes by public employees.

Although Quill had spoken very highly of Kheel on many previous occasions, he denied that his latest ultimatum was a bluff designed to pressure Mayor-Elect Lindsay into naming Kheel as a mediator. Quill, however, did concede that he might reconsider the December 15 strike if Lindsay submitted a new panel of mediators "thoroughly acquainted with rapid transit."[99]

In a December 2 editorial, the *New York Times* articulated its belief that the TWU's December 15 strike threat was indeed an attempt to have Kheel named as a mediator. "Since things are rarely what they seem in the political morass that Mr. Quill has made of transit labor relations," the *Times* wrote, "the probability is that the union chief is less interested in tearing up his old agreement than he is in getting a familiar face back into this year's contract talks. His advancement of the strike date has given Mayor Wagner the opportunity to call in Theodore W. Kheel. . . ."[100] Concerning Kheel's consideration of the merits of the TWU's position that a December 15 strike would be permissable under the existing agreement, the *Times* was unequivocal; "This is a task that should not require more than a minute's study, since the basis for Mr. Quill's nullification is so patently non-existent."[101]

On Friday, December 3, acting TA Chairman John Gilhooley publicly voiced the identical analysis the *Times* had offered editorially a day earlier. Gilhooley referred to the TWU's December 15 strike threat as a "rather thinly veneered gimmick to spring Mr. Kheel back into the picture." "Now it seems to me that the judgement Mr. Kheel will be called upon to make," said Gilhooley, again echoing the *Times*, "should take him at most about five minutes and that then his services under the contract would be at an end."[102] Kheel's role as permanent arbitrator empowered him to settle all disagreements under the existing contract and would therefore expire on New Year's Eve.

Upon hearing Gilhooley's remarks, Theodore Kheel became angered and said he would turn down any request to mediate the subway and bus negotiations. "I'm positively, unquestionably, irrevocably out of it," said Kheel. "From now on, they are on their own," he added. Kheel, of course, was only removing himself from the transit crisis as a prospective mediator. If the TA would choose to have the threatened December 15 strike declared a violation of the existing contract, Kheel would hear the case in his capacity as permanent arbitrator. Told of Kheel's anger, Gilhooley praised Kheel as "one of the ablest mediators in the country" and said his only concern was that some people might get the idea that the TA was bowing to Quill's wishes by approaching Kheel. "We are not puppets to anybody," the acting TA chairman added.[103]

The disagreement concerning Kheel's possible involvement as a mediator contained considerable political overtones. Daniel Scannell, a Democratic member of the TA had approached Kheel soon after the election of Lindsay to see if Kheel was willing to mediate the transit negotiations. This approach was natural because Kheel had long served as fellow Democrat Robert Wagner's chief advisor and representative on labor matters. Mayor-Elect Lindsay, however, was insistent that his incoming administration not be perceived as following in the footsteps of his predecessor. Gilhooley, a Republican and a personal friend of Lindsay, was therefore trying to represent the mayor-elect's interests in having Kheel excluded from a mediation role.

For its part, the TWU maintained its public militance, indicating that it was preparing for a December 15 shutdown. The union is dreaming of a white Christmas, said Matthew Guinan, executive vice president of the TWU's international union, in hopes that the total paralysis of the city would bring about a quick agreement on a new contract. "A blizzard would be very helpful," said Guinan.[104]

On Saturday, December 4, John Gilhooley continued his efforts to establish a transit mediation panel that did not include Theodore Kheel. The acting chairman of the TA proposed that Secretary of Labor W. Williard Wirtz head the group of mediators. If Wirtz were unavailable, former State Supreme Court Justice Samuel I. Rosenman, currently the president of the New York City Bar Association, would make a good chairman, said Gilhooley. Gilhooley also suggested several other individuals who would be acceptable to fill out the proposed three-member panel. Conspicuous by its absence was Kheel's name. When specifically asked whether he would accept Kheel as a mediator, Gilhooley responded, "I'm sorry he misinterpreted my statement. But he has taken himself out of the picture." Asked to comment on Gilhooley's list of prospective mediators, TA member Scannell made it clear that this group was "distinguished," but that "any decision as to who would be acceptable would have to be made by the authority, and not by any one member." "They would," as Scannell pointed out, "also have to be acceptable to the union."[105]

On Sunday, December 5, Michael Quill rejected Secretary of Labor Wirtz as the suggested chairman of the transit mediation panel. "Mr. Wirtz is a good and experienced man," said Quill, "but he doesn't know anything about transit problems." Quill was willing to accept former State Supreme Court Justice Samuel I. Rosenman, who Gilhooley had suggested as an alternative to Wirtz to head the mediation panel. "I think Judge Rosenman, who has had experience in transit disputes, would be a good choice," said Quill. "A good mediation panel," said Quill, "would be composed of Judge Rosenman, Mr. Kheel and anyone else Mr. Lindsay wants." Quill added that if Lindsay provided a mediator with transit experience, the union would accept any other two persons selected by the mayor-elect.[106]

In other Sunday action, Lindsay sought to reduce the perception of crisis surrounding transit negotiations, while TWU President Quill sought exactly the opposite effect. The mayor-elect called for a halt in public discussions of the transit situation in newspapers and on television and radio because "It's too sensitive. The public interest is at stake." Lindsay indicated that the moratorium should include both himself and Mayor Wagner. Hardly one to support a decrease in the decibel level, Quill continued his public posturing. "This is war," said the TWU president, indicating that if the courts tried to enjoin his union from striking, "I will not be available for a subpoena—I will not be available for arrest."[107]

And on the same day that Lindsay was calling for a media moratorium of discussions of transit negotiations, the New York Times editorially asked for steadfastness in not allowing TWU President Quill to have undue influence in naming a mediation panel. "The deplorable fact," wrote the Times, "is that behind all Mr. Quill's maneuvering is a desire to name the mediation panel.... It would be tragic," the Times added, "if for the hundredth time, the fruit of his recklessness is municipal capitulation."[108]

On Monday, December 6, with the TWU's new strike deadline only a little more than a week away, actions took place on a number of fronts to help thwart the December 15 walkout. In his first direct intervention in the transit talks, Mayor Wagner called on both the TWU and the TA to meet with him on Wednesday morning at City Hall. In a telegram sent to both the TWU and the TA, Mayor Wagner reminded them, "The current transit contract which I helped to negotiate does not expire until January 1, 1966.

Any stoppage of the mass transit system of New York City is intolerable and I anticipate your cooperation to assure uninterrupted service throughout the city."[109] The December 15 strike threat had thus succeeded in precipitating Mayor Wagner's involvement in transit negotiations. The mayor had said repeatedly that he did not believe he should participate in negotiating an agreement that would have to be paid for by the incoming administration. Lindsay, in contrast, had insisted that he could not become personally involved in the talks until he assumed office on January 1. Later in the day, the TA obtained an order in State Supreme Court directing the TWU to show cause on Friday why it should not be enjoined from striking in violation of the state's Condon-Wadlin Act. The show-cause order named Quill, nine other TWU officers, and all other employees who planned to strike as defendants. If, after the arguments before Justice Samuel Silverman on Friday, an injunction was issued, Quill and his aides could be jailed for violating the court order.

On still another front, the TA called on Theodore Kheel in his role as impartial arbitrator of the existing contract to forbid the TWU from striking in violation of the agreement's no-strike clause. Kheel immediately ordered both sides to appear before him at his Park Avenue office on Wednesday afternoon. As permanent arbitrator of the existing agreement, Kheel was empowered to make binding decisions arising out of the interpretation of the contract.

December 7 was a day for discussing one of the central elements needed to settle the transit crisis: money. Having finally returned to the city after an extended six-week vacation, TA Chairman O'Grady was willing to discuss his agency's precarious financial position: "We are in a very tight financial bind," he said. "The fare will have to be raised or we will need extra funds to help us avoid a rise." O'Grady added, "So far, no one has offered us any additional money." At a news conference, Mayor-Elect Lindsay restated a campaign promise, "The 15-cent fare should be maintained and I'm going to do my utmost to see it's maintained." Lindsay did not, however, indicate how this could be achieved. When asked to comment on reports that the fare would be increased to 25¢ in the near future, Lindsay was short-tempered and showed annoyance. "Who made such a report?" he asked, bristling at the questioner. "What responsible city agency made such a report?" In addition, the mayor-elect indicated that before possible subsidy money would be made available he wanted to "examine the arithmetic of the TA" to determine their true financial position.[110]

While the mayor-elect and the TA chairman were thinking about maintaining the 15¢ fare, TWU President Quill was preparing for a December 15 strike. "The union will definitely defy a court order, and we will go to jail," he declared. "The court order on Friday is important, but what is more important is our 36,000 members. We owe our allegiance to them, and not to any judge."[111] Referring to a real or perhaps fanciful involvement with the Irish Republican Army (IRA) in his native Ireland, Quill added, "We may be put in jail, but that won't be the first time members of my family were in jail." As the occasion demanded, Quill was known to weave dramatic accounts about his rebelious activities in the IRA. Quill discussed his strike plans at Kennedy Airport, after returning from a Nevada trip in which he helped negotiate a contract for a TWU local at a government rocket installation. Asked where in Nevada he had been, Quill smilingly replied, "Jackass Flats."[112] Incredulous as it seemed, Quill, who in a previous set of negotiations had maintained he was in Ireland communing with a leprachaun about a pot of gold to subsidize the TA, was in fact returning from Jackass Flats, Nevada.

At 10:00 a.m., on December 8, Quill, accompanied by his top aides and sixty members of his negotiating committee, arrived at City Hall to meet with Mayor Wagner and thre three members of the TA. Asked for a comment by a reporter, Quill replied jokingly, "We came up here to move City Hall up to Canal Street." On a more serious note, the sessions to head off the threatened December 15 strike lasted for six and one-half hours. In a brief news conference at the conclusion of the closed meetings, Wagner announced, "There has been some progress made, but some points remain to be ironed out." Quill, standing at Wagner's side was asked if there had been progress. Quill replied, "If the Mayor said there's been progress, there must have been." O'Grady added quietly, "We have nothing to add to what the Mayor said." When Mayor-Elect Lindsay was asked if he would have liked to be present at the sessions, he replied with a shrug, "That's academic, because I was not invited."[113] Lindsay, however, could not help but be constantly reminded of the stalled transit talks. In his transition headquarters in the Roosevelt Hotel, several of the mayor-elect's staff began wearing red and white buttons reading "Lindsley button."[114]

With the December 15 strike deadline one week away, public resentment against Quill and the TWU continued to surface. A sixty-three-year old Manhattan printer offered 500 free two-color posters to anyone willing to post the anti-Quill signs. The huge posters, which measured 28" x 41", contained such slogans as: "War! Quill vs. We The People"; "Is Quill King of the Road?—Let's Find Out"; and another posed the question, "Is Quill Really the Supreme Being?" Ben Murray, whose unionized print shop normally produced posters for the philharmonic, the metropolitan Opera, and the circus explained his motivation, "This is my way to fight the arrogant, illegitimate and flagrant tactics that Mr. Quill is using in the subway dispute." In addition, Murray announced the formation of the

"Straphangers Guild," an "underground" organization that included the "Make Them Walk Division." This unit, he asserted, was restricted to teenage school pupils, the physically handicapped, and senior citizens who do not possess "automobiles, airplanes, boats, floats, bicycles, roller skates, or skate boards or any mechanically propelled device that might make them independent of the New York City transit system."[115]

Mayor Wagner had the parties back at City Hall the following day in his attempt to diffuse the December 15 strike threat. By that afternoon, Quill finally withdrew his threat of a strike after Mayor Wagner and Mayor-Elect Lindsay had persuaded Theodore Kheel to join a three-man mediation panel. Quill quickly indicated publicly that this choice was "fully acceptable" to him and went on to observe, "I want to thank Mayor Wagner and Mayor-Elect Lind-es-ley for their statesmanship in bringing an end to the threatened strike."[116] Kheel's presence on the panel was believed to be especially desired by Quill, although the labor leader had said he would settle for "any one man or woman who understands the subway system." Kheel, who earlier had said that he wanted no part of the mediation effort, reconsidered after he was approached by both Mr. Wagner and Mayor-Elect Lindsay. "I couldn't very well refuse the joint request of the two Mayors," he stated.[117] The other members of the three-man mediation panel announced jointly by Mayor Wagner and Mayor-Elect Lindsay were Sylvester Garrett of Pittsburg, who was the permanent arbitrator for the United Steelworkers Union and the United States Steel Corporation, and Nathan Feinsinger, a professor of law at the University of Wisconsin and arbitrator for General Motors and the United Auto Workers Union (UAW).

As a masterful manipulator of the media, Quill had structured the situation to achieve his desired goal. His early strike threat had garnered front page news coverage, and compelled the intervention of Lindsay and Wagner in the naming of Kheel as a mediator. In the terminology of the model, Quill had been successful in "activating" a number of individuals and groups to become involved parties in the negotiations.

In appointing Kheel to the mediation panel, Quill certainly fulfilled his desire for a man who knew transit. At the time that the maneuvering over the selection of the panel was taking place, A. H. Raskin wrote, "In the bizarre world that is New York labor, Kheel is a jewel of great price. He has the strongest labor-management contacts, the most intensive experience, the best average."[118] At the conclusion of the strike, Feinsinger concurred, observing that, "Theodore Kheel, of course, has as much experience as any mediator in the history of this country."[119]

When permanent arbitration of transit grievances was instituted in

New York City in 1949, Kheel was the first arbitrator to hold the position. Kheel left this post for a while, but returned in 1956 and had served since as the impartial arbitrator for the TA and the TWU. He had also served on Mayor Wagner's special Transit Labor Board, on which he functioned as a mediator. Kheel himself estimated that "I've spent more New Year's Eves with Mike Quill and Joe O'Grady of the Transit Authority than with my own wife."[120] After the strike settlement, Nathan Feinsinger succinctly summarized what he thought Kheel knew about the problems of transit labor in New York City: "Ted Kheel," he said, "knows everything...."[121]

Kheel not only had a great deal of experience in transit labor matters, he was also highly regarded by both the TWU and the TA. Douglas MacMahon, a top TWU official, stated his opinion of Kheel: "It was our judgement that Lindsay should have included him on his list of mediators. Kheel is the most knowledgeable man in New York on city transit."[122] Daniel Scannell of the TA was equally flattering in his estimation of Kheel; "We have always found Kheel to be good to us," he stated, "he is a good catalyst. He knows the transit system and its problems."[123]

Combining the high regard the TWU and the TA had for him with his long experience in transit labor, Kheel seemed to embody the attributes that make mediators ideally suited to help settle a particular collective bargaining impasse. Because Lindsay himself had no experience in transit labor matters, he would appear to have been highly desirous of obtaining the services of a man such as Kheel, who could provide the experience he lacked. However, this was certainly not the case.

Although Kheel may have been ideally suited to mediate the dispute from a collective bargaining perspective, the decision to exclude him from Lindsay's list of mediators was a purely political judgement. "The reason Lindsay didn't want Kheel as a mediator," stated TWU attorney John O'Donnell after the strike, "was purely political. He was advised by the Liberal Party that Kheel was too close to Quill and that Kheel was a Democrat."[124] Lindsay, of course, was not worried that because Kheel was a Democrat and had dealt with Quill for many years, he could not serve the Lindsay administration properly. Lindsay's Deputy-Mayor Timothy Costello described what did concern the Mayor, "Lindsay wanted to establish a new image. He felt that with a new administration there should be new names. Since Kheel had long been associated with Wagner he was hardly someone the new administration would want to be linked with."[125] Mr. Kheel also believed that this was the reason he was not chosen by Lindsay. "He wanted fresh faces," said Kheel, "he didn't want to be associated with the same old crowd."[126] It would not be a very astute move politically, of course, for a man who wanted to establish a new image and who had built his campaign by being critical of the "Democratic bosses" to ally himself, even before he took office, with a man who was closely associated with the very people he had attacked.

This attempt to establish a bargaining style that was consistent with the image Lindsay wanted to portray in his new administration was developed by his two closest labor advisors: the Liberal party leaders, David Dubinsky, president of the International Ladies Garment Workers Union (ILGWU), and Alex Rose, president of the United Hatters, Cap and Millinary Workers Union. In this new approach to bargaining, according to one description, Lindsay:

> ... wants to substitute genuine collective bargaining for what is referred to as the "deal" or the "fix." His critics ... dismiss such distinctions as phony and a little naive. They argue that it requires compromise to work out a contract. The result is the same they say, whether it is called an agreement, a deal, or something else.
>
> But the Lindsay Administration sees things differently. The old way, the Lindsay men say, is the deal worked out not on the basis of any merits of the dispute but on the basis of friendship and political relationships between members of the power elite involved.
>
> What Mr. Lindsay is trying to subsitute, they suggest, is genuine collective bargaining. Under his definition ... the first thing that is done is to spell out the various differences over working conditions. The issues are then translated into dollar proposals and counterproposals. Finally, a bargain is struck. There is a world of qualitative difference, it is argued between this method and the so called backroom deal or fix.[127]

The two Liberal party leaders believed that Lindsay could succeed with this new approach because they were convinced the TWU would not strike. "They in effect advised Lindsay and the Transit Authority that Quill is just a 'loud talker' and [had] never yet called a strike, and that his union as in all past cliffhanging situations would back down at the last minute."[128] Once the possibility of a strike was eliminated in the minds of Rose and Dubinsky, their advice was greatly different from what it would have been if they feared a work stoppage. The political benefits to accrue to Lindsay if he took a principled stand were rather clear, as were the drawbacks of not taking such a position. Raskin quoted a "prominent labor leader" who, although not identified, was obviously either Rose or Dubinsky, as having advised Lindsay some weeks before he took office, "If Quill forces you into a corner where you accept peace at any price, you will be labeled a paper tiger on your first day in office."[129] As for the benefits to be gained from taking a hard nosed position, Rose said, "If Mr. Lindsay succeeds in resolving the crisis, he will leave an indelible imprint on the minds of the voters and gain greatly in prestige."[130]

Kheel's close ties to the Democratic party in New York City dated back to the 1940s. His critics complained that he had so "politicalized" labor relations in New York that "the Central Labor Council has become an adjunct to City Hall—or vice versa."[131] Kheel's admirers pointed out, however, that the links between politics and labor in New York were no Kheel contrivance, but instead dated back to the earliest days of Tammany Hall and were necessary to be a successful mediator. Using his political connections, Kheel proved to be an extraordinarily successful mediator in New York City. "Ted is so ideally suited to the peculiar realities of the New York labor-management scene," said a fellow mediator, "that if there were no Ted, you'd have to invent him."[132]

Kheel was acceptable to the TA and the TWU; what difference did it make if he was unacceptable to Mayor-Elect Lindsay? As Timothy Costello explained, "It was not important that the mediator be someone that both the TWU and the TA liked. The actual parties to the negotiations were the TWU and the city. Therefore, the mediators had to be acceptable to the city because it was they who had to deal with the union, not the TA."[133]

In addition to his transit experience, Kheel had considerable background in other labor relations contexts as well. He joined the legal staff of the National Labor Relations Board (NLRB) in 1938 and later became regional director and national executive director of the War Labor Board. In 1947, Kheel was named director of labor relations for New York City by Mayor William O'Dwyer. His deputy director at the time was Joseph O'Grady, who later became the chairman of the TA. Mr. Kheel was a partner in the law firm of Battle, Fowler, Stokes, and Kheel.

Sylvester Garrett had been chairman of the board of arbitration for United States Steel and the United Steelworkers Union since 1951. During World War II he served successively as chairman of the regional War Labor Board in Philadelphia, and chairman of the National Wage Stabilization Board in Washington. He had also served as coordinator of labor relations for the Libbey-Owens-Ford Glass Company in Toledo, and as a professor of law at Stanford University. In addition, he was a past president of the National Academy of Arbitrators.

Nathan Feinsinger had been a professor of law at the University of Wisconsin since 1928. He was a public member, associate general counsel, and then director of national disputes for the War Labor Board in Washington. He was chairman of presidential fact-finding boards in steel, meat packing, and airlines disputes in the late 1940s and served as chairman of the National Wage Stabilization Board from 1951 to 1952. He was later an impartial umpire for General Motors and the United Auto Workers Union.

After the naming of the mediation panel, Kheel predicted that the coming negotiations would be the most difficult in his twenty-year involvement in transit bargaining. "For one thing time is short," he said. "For another, the issues appear to be complex. There is also the problem growing out of the change in city administration in the course of negotiations. . . ." he added.[134] After Quill indicated that there would be no December 15 strike, O'Grady said that the TA would withdraw its anti-strike injunction action scheduled to be heard in State Supreme Court the following day.

One extremely important fact surrounding the lifting of the December 15 strike deadline, was publicly ignored until it was discussed in a *New York Times* editorial. The neutral panel established jointly by Wagner and Lindsay was strictly empowered to provide mediation services. As the *Times* observed, "this panel will not have the advisory arbitration powers that Lindsay initially desired. Indeed," the editorial continued, "there is no evidence that it will even have authority to make recommendations in the public interest if the TWU head refuses to scale down his demands."[135]

Chapter 3

Lindsay Enters Talks

Negotiations over a new transit agreement resumed on Sunday, December 12, after being suspended since December 1, when the TWU broke off bargaining when Mayor-Elect John V. Lindsay suggested that they were not bargaining in good faith. Throughout this hiatus, Lindsay tried to maintain the fiction that he was actively seeking a solution to the impasse, having his press secretary regularly report, "The Mayor-Elect is in touch with the Wagner Administration and both sides in the dispute." However, according to the press secretary, Woody Klein, he "was uneasy" with this statement, "because I knew that as a matter of fact, no negotiations had taken place...."[1] Despite Klein's reservations, however, such a course was standard for press advisors to government officials. The "briefing" of the media is a typical pseudo-event, conducted solely for the purpose of structuring news coverage in a particular way.

After a ninety-minute meeting with the mediators at his Congressional office at 30 West 44th Street, Mayor-Elect Lindsay said he considered the conference a "good beginning." Although he still maintained that a contract settlement was primarily a matter for the TA and the TWU to work out, he made it clear that he would attempt to help them reach an agreement. "I have informed the mediators that I would like for them to keep me informed on all developments," Lindsay said after the meeting, and "I will receive their advice, suggestions, and be kept up-to-date."[2]

Following Lindsay, Nathan Feinsinger, who walked with the aid of crutches because of a hip ailment, sat at a makeshift table and observed wryly, "I have been designated chairman because of my age and my infirmities. We are old friends," he continued, pointing to Sylvester Garrett and Theodore Kheel who flanked him. "We hope to achieve a reasonable settlement and before the strike deadline. We would like to get the pressure off and avert a cliffhanger. If everyone is normally reasonable, I think we'll get along all right."[3] The actual negotiations between the principals resumed at 10:00 a.m. on December 13 in the Americana Hotel with Feinsinger telling the negotiators at the forty-five minute session that the mediators would not only try to settle the present dispute, but would also seek to devise a method of avoiding last minute crises in future negotiations. The only thing the parties really discussed at this initial mediated session was the procedures that would be used in their future talks.

On another front, Mayor-Elect Lindsay announced the formation of a permanent Mayor's Council on Transportation, to devise a plan to integrate the city's transportation system. The purpose of such a plan, as of numerous similar proposals advanced in recent weeks, was to provide adequate revenues to subsidize the 15¢ fare. The three mediators, however, made it clear that their sole concern was with a contract settlement and not with the fare. Mediation Chairman Feinsinger, however, conceded that if a "reasonable settlement" was made it could have an effect on the fare.[4]

On December 14, Mayor Robert F. Wagner called upon Governor Nelson A. Rockefeller to "include some provision...in his January budget" to give financial help to the city's hard pressed transit system to enable it to preserve the 15¢ fare. "Such assistance," the mayor added, "is necessary and in heroic amounts." Because the state government was granting financial aid to the commuter railroads, Wagner maintained that there was no justification for a reluctance to help the mass transit systems within the cities. The mayor's proposal, however, was quickly rejected by Governor Rockefeller, who said that the maintenance of the fare was a city problem. Later in the day, Rockefeller, a Republican, suggested that the mayor's plan "might be a last-minute maneuver of his last days in office" designed for "diverting attention."[5]

Although the governor ruled out direct state aid, he indicated that he would be receptive to other suggested measures to help the city out of its transit dilemma. "If enabling legislation is needed for the city to put together in a larger package some of the solutions to the transit problem," he said, "I'm sure there would be supportive legislative action."[6] Enabling legislation would be required from the state to merge and pool the revenues of the TA, the Triborough Bridge and Tunnel Authority, and the Port of New York Authority, as had been proposed by Mayor-Elect Lindsay and others. Statutory changes would also be needed if the city wanted to give a direct subsidy to the TA. Wagner was certainly not encouraged by the Rockefeller position, noting that in view of the very strong opposition to taking funds from profitable transit agencies to aid the subways, he did not believe this could be done in time to save the 15¢ fare.

Actually, Rockefeller had three very good reasons for refusing Wagner's request for aid. First, no precedent was found for such help. Although state legislation had, on occasion, been enacted to permit the city to subsidize the Authority, the state itself had never granted any money to the TA or paid any of its costs. Second, Rockefeller was fearful of the precedent such a direct subsidy would set. "If you gave the subways a direct subsidy," Rockefeller explained, "Then you would have to do the same for every municipality throughout the state that has transportation problems."[7]

Finally, and most important, even if Rockefeller had intended to subsidize the New York City transit system, he would not have done so while Mayor Wagner was still in office. If state aid was to be forthcoming, it would be only natural for Rockefeller to withhold it until a fellow Republican took office.

A very different perspective on the status of negotiations can be gleaned, not from the maneuverings of high-ranking officials, but by examining the perceptions of rank-and-file union members. Publicly, Michael J. Quill had long been characterized as an intransigent negotiator who had extorted exhorbitant concessions from the city because of his "public be damned" attitude, and his close alliance with incumbent Democratic office holders. TWU members, however, hardly considered their pay and benefits to be excessive, in fact a considerable amount of opposition had surfaced concerning Quill's performance as a union leader. Many rank-and-filers believed that Quill was "all blow and no show." "There will be no strike," said a white haired motorman in mid-December. "The past record shows that. They'll scream and holler and then we'll settle for half of what we should get."[8] "You know what's killing us?" asked a conductor rhetorically. "It's the victories. Every contract we win we take a beating. Today we make less than sanitation workers. If we keep winning we'll be the lowest paid workers in the city." A motorman with sixteen years TA experience summarized the dissatisfaction with the current union leadership; "Quill makes noise, but he doesn't deliver," said the man with his motorman's handle jammed into a pocket of his striped overalls. "And I'm not the only one who thinks this way." Asked if he agreed with this assessment, a porter responded, "Well, I don't know. The pay ain't that bad." With the porter out of earshot, a more highly skilled employee explained another major dissatisfaction with the Quill regime. "Until a couple of years ago we got across-the-board increases. Why shouldn't he be happy? We've got the highest-paid porters and the lowest-paid conductors and motormen in the country."[9] In an across-the-board pay increase, the same number of cents per hour is given to all employees, regardless of their current wage. On a proportional basis, such an approach is most beneficial for the lowest-paid workers. An across-the-board increase of 10¢ per hour, for example, represents a 5 percent increase for a worker making $2 per hour, but only a 2-1/2 percent increase for a worker currently earning an hourly wage of $4.

Substantive discussions in the negotiations resumed on December 15, after a two-week suspension caused by the controversy over the naming of the mediation panel. Virtually all of the two-hour sesesion was taken up by a discussion of a twelve-page position paper submitted by the TA, which analyzed the economic impact of the TWU's proposals. Granting the union's demands, the Authority asserted, would, in the absence of a subsidy, require that the fare be raised from 15¢ to 47¢. Such a fare increase in turn, said the TA, would lead to such a loss of riders that the reduced use of the system would be financially catastrophic. The TA also contended that a substantial wage increase was unjustified because its employees already received wages that equaled or exceeded those of transit workers in other parts of the nation. Nathan Feinsinger, the chairman of the mediation panel emerged from this first session and said things were going so smoothly it was "almost too good to be true."[10] Union President Quill, in turn, expressed optimism that a settlement could be reached by Christmas Eve. Joseph O'Grady, however, wryly observed that he was skeptical of Quill's assessment. "It would be unique for Mike Quill to act as Santa Claus," noted the TA Chairman.[11]

On December 17, Mayor-Elect Lindsay announced that he was having a bill prepared that would consolidate all forms of transportation in the city under a single agency. The agency would exercise municipal jurisdiction over buses, subways, taxis, and private cars and would include the Triborough Bridge and Tunnel Authority. Lindsay said he did not anticipate opposition from Robert Moses, the chairman of the Triborough Authority. Moses, in reply, said he would "of course" cooperate with Lindsay. "The problem," he said tersely, "is that the Lindsay plan is unconstitutional."[12]

On Sunday, December 19, Michael Quill charged that "outside meddlers, meeting secretly, have been slowing down the negotiations" for a transit settlement. Quill said that the meddlers were trying to break his union by getting it to extend the strike deadline beyond January 1. "They have been haunting the areas of the negotiations and the mediations for several days," he said. "They're trying to gain influence, like Rasputin over the Czarina," the union president added.[13] Quill stated that he had evidence implicating the meddlers, but that he did not want to reveal it until the time was right.

In less spectacular action that day, Mayor-Elect Lindsay disclosed that he had informed mediation Chairman Feinsinger that he was available personally to help avert a strike whenever Professor Feinsinger requested such aid. Both TWU President Quill and TA Chairman O'Grady indicated that they would welcome Lindsay's participation. "The history of negotiations with Mr. Quill," said O'Grady in a television appearance, "has always required that the Mayor or the Mayor-Elect take part since they have to supply some funds to help defray the cost of the contract."[14] The rationale for Lindsay's involvement was stated with considerably more assertiveness by TWU attorney John O'Donnell, "Never in O'Grady's history did he ever give out one dollar unless he was certain the TA could meet it out of revenues, or offset it from another source, namely City Hall."[15] Lindsay was described by O'Donnell as "the one man whose presence could give meaning to the meetings of the TA and the union representatives with the mediators, the one man with the ultimate power and responsibility" to negotiate an agreement.[16]

At the same time that Quill was making his charges about meddlers, pressure was mounting to strip the financially sound Triborough Bridge and Tunnel Authority of its autonomy so its funds could be used to help the deficit-ridden mass transit system. State Senator Thomas J. Mackell, a Queens Democrat, said that he would prefile legislation to consolidate the Triborough Bridge and Tunnel Authority, the TA, and the ferryboat operators of the Department of Marine and Aviation into a new five-member New York City Transportation Authority. The proposed authority would have complete jurisdiction over trains, buses, bridges, tunnels, parkways, parking lots, and ferry service. The Mackell measure also would establish guarantees against any impairment of the interests of bondholders and creditors of the Triborough and Transit Authorities. Senator Mackell called "absurd" the stand Robert Moses, Chairman of the Triborough Authority had taken, that in creating the Triborough agency the state had bargained away its right to ever change the obligations owed to bondholders of the TA.[17] Mackell contended that the actions of one legislature was not binding on another.

Mayor-Elect Lindsay also said he disagreed with Moses that any mergers of the Triborough Authority would be unconstitutional and said he was optimistic that the state legislature could work out a bill that would satisfy the bondholders and permit consolidation. Questioned about the Mackell proposal, Joseph O'Grady said he would support any plan that would ease the burden of the transit agency, and Quill emphasized that he had "always been for a merger of all transportation facilities."[18]

On December 20, the TWU tried to sway the TA and the mediation panel with the economic soundness of its demands. The case for the TWU was presented by Leon Keyserling, former chairman of the Council for Economic Advisors under President Harry S. Truman, who was serving as a consultant for the union. A substantial part of the Keyserling report tried to show that by all intelligent comparisons, New York City transit workers were underpaid.[19] He contended that while the Community Council of Greater New York deemed an adequate health and decency budget for a family of four to be $6,715 per year, the average annual earnings without overtime of all hourly rated TA employees in fiscal year 1965 was $6,229. Keyserling also pointed out that the average earnings of transit workers was below the "adequacy" estimate of the U. S. Bureau of Labor Statistics for New York City, which was $6,542 annually. The report further indicated that when the wage rates of employees of local transit systems were adjusted for differences in the cost of living in their city, that in four cities, Chicago; Washington, D.C.; St. Louis; and Detroit, wage rates were somewhat higher than in New York. In another section of his eighty-one-page report, Keyserling contended that through proper use of its tax resources the City of New York could easily meet the just demands of the TWU members.[20]

As described by mediation Chairman Feinsinger, the current status of the negotiations was "typical of the framework of the ordinary labor case. It's what I call the turkey dance. Courting procedure. The way the male bird goes after the female."[21] "First," he said, "there's the joint session with the mediator. At this point, nothing is expected, nothing happens." Then, according to Feinsinger:

> I say, Gentlemen, we don't know anything about this dispute—in a nice, disarming voice—and therefore let us start from scratch. Even though Ted Kheel knows everything and Syl Garrett and I have been studying the issues for days. Then we get some talk from the union: "No, Mr. Mediator, you are not correct in stating that we are asking a twenty-five-cent increase; we are asking a sixty-cent increase!" That's par for the course. Some remote goal is fixed. We flutter around a few times, and then we start talking to the parties separately. You get back to the joint session only when in your judgement you think it would be productive to do so."[22]

With just ten days remaining before the city's subways and buses were to be struck, Mayor Wagner participated directly in the negotiations for the first time on December 21. Wagner met with the negotiators and the mediators for about ten minutes and, as he reported later, "told them it would be intolerable to have a strike."[23] Wagner also said that there had been no shutdown of the transit system in the twelve years he had been mayor and that he hoped none would take place. In the actual negotiations, the TWU and the Amalgamated Transit Union spent the entire day explaining why their demands were justified.

At a December 22 news conference, Nathan Feinsinger summarized the negotiations to date. "We've been listening to some official presentations of the Transit Authority and the two unions," Feinsinger explained. "The next stage is mediation where we get down to brass tacks."[24]

Feinsinger said that the mediators had reached the end of Phase One in the negotiations. Speaking somewhat facetiously, he said that so far it appeared the unions were asking for an increase of "about $10 a second" and indicating that it would cost nothing. The TA, he continued, had indicated it "might squeeze out a penny or so over three or four years." "This is par for the course," the mediation chairman noted.[25]

The real work of the mediators, Phase Two, is beginning, Feinsinger said. In this phase, as he described it, the mediators would try to get the TA and the unions to give a more realistic statement of their positions and what might provide a basis for a settlement. The mediator acknowledged that the postures of both parties to date had been "completely unrealistic," but he emphasized that this was the reason the panel of neutrals wanted to move into Phase Two, where they could carry out "intensive mediation efforts" to lay the foundation for a settlement. Phase Three of the negotiations, Feinsinger noted, will come at about 5:00 a.m. on New Year's Day. By that time, he said, he expects the mediators to be able to recommend a "fair settlement."[26]

Feinsinger's comments came at the end of a day of routine negotiations during which Harvard University Professor John B. Meyer and Stuart Rothman, a former chairman of the National Labor Relations Board, defended the TA's bargaining position. The economists retained by the TA presented a forty-two-page book of statistics indicating that financially, transit workers in New York City were generally ahead of others in the transportation field. The figures presented by the two economists showed, among other things, that in a comparison of top wages in twenty major bus systems, TA employees earning $3.22 per hour were making 30¢ per hour more than the median. The Authority's figures also showed that the averge annual earnings of TA hourly paid employees was $6,986 at the time of the study, as compared with an annual median of $6,557 for full-time male workers in the northeast in 1964. The TA's figures also showed that while the wages of average transit workers increased by 15.9 percent from 1960 to 1964, the consumer price index (CPI) for New York City increased by only 6.3 percent during the same period.[27]

As Feinsinger indicated when he said that Phase Two of the negotiations was just about to be entered, there was not any evidence yet that real bargaining had begun. "To be truthful," Quill stated, "we're not getting anywhere." To this, O'Grady added that he and his colleagues had not made any definitive proposals as yet.[28]

In a brief speech, Quill returned to his theme of "meddlers" who, he said, were trying to influence the negotiations. "We are working at the negotiations in the daytime," he said, "and fending off meddlers and interlopers during the night." Later, when questioned, he charged that banking interests were putting pressure on Mayor-Elect Lindsay and Governor Rockefeller in favor of a "cheap contract" because they want to protect the bondholders of the Triborough Bridge and Tunnel Authority and the Port of New York Authority. Asked about Quill's charge, Mayor-Elect Lindsay said "I haven't any idea what he is talking about."[29]

Wages—Were They Fair?

Whether the wages of the TA's employees were fair or too low depends on your perspective and the basis of the comparisons being made. One point is clear, however, Michael Quill had allowed the wages of transit workers to fall behind those of other New York City employees, particularly in the skilled categories. Perhaps most significant, the rank-and-file members of the union were well aware of this unfavorable comparison, and it had created considerable dissention within TWU ranks. It had long been the norm in public sector bargaining in New York City for unions to base their demands on what workers in other city departments received. The TWU had never been greatly concerned with what transit workers in Boston or Chicago were earning; the wage contour for all municipal employees was primarily what workers in other city departments were earning. If certain wage increases, extra vacation days, or some pension concession were granted in one city department, it was very difficult for the city to prevent other unions from trying to achieve the same gains.

One reason for the importance of such comparisons in New York's municipal labor relations is that some jobs were common to all city departments, as well as some of the so-called independent agencies, such as the TA. Thus, for the job of auto mechanic, one civil service examination was given for all city departments, including the TA; a list of eligible candidates was certified; and all departments then drew on this common list for their supply of auto mechanics. An obvious basis of comparison therefore existed: someone who passed the civil service test could just as easily have gone to work for one department as for another. Matthew Guinan, the executive vice president of the TWU was highly critical during negotiations of the fact that "the City of New York pays its automotive mechanics—in the Parks Department, the Police Department, Sanitation Department—in all departments, $4.56 an hour. The TA pays its automotive mechanics—off the same civil service list $3.46-1/4 an hour—$1.09-3/4 less."[30]

In other instances, particularly in the area of pensions, the comparisons between TA employees and those in other city departments were even stronger. Shortly before the negotiations began, the New York State legislature amended the rules governing the New York City civil service retirement system. Under the civil service pension plan, the family of a worker who had reached the retirement age but preferred to continue working received lower benefits upon his death than the family of a worker who retired at the normal date. The new state legislation eliminated the so-called death gamble and prescribed uniform payments to the survivors of a worker, regardless of whether he retired.[31] However, because transit workers were technically employees of the TA and not the city government, they were exempted from the provisions of the new legislation.

To give the transit workers the same benefits that the new legislation accorded other civil service workers was estimated to cost the TA about $9 million over the contract's two-year period. Despite the substantial amount of money involved, however, this item was not really open to serious bargaining during the negotiations. It was simply assumed by both parties that the TA employees would receive the same increases that the other city employees had been given by the state legislature.[32] In essence, then, the degree to which transit workers were satisfied with their wages depended on how they compared with other municipal employees rather than comparisons with transit workers in other locations.

In such a comparison with other city workers, TA employees did indeed receive lower wages. Lower pay for transit workers began during the days when the transit lines were in private hands. Although this wage gap gradually narrowed under public control, by the early 1960s the trend began to reverse, with TA employees falling further behind their counterparts in other city departments. The TWU's Douglas MacMahon, explained why these wage disparities began to again widen at this time:

> The inequities developed over a short period of time. Other city unions gained substantial gains in the last three years, creating a large gap. Although a gap existed before three years ago, it was not as great.
>
> The union made an effort in previous negotiations to correct it, but the city had always complained about the lack of money. Faced with the alternative of a strike the union partially accepted the argument of a lack of funds. But when the gap began to continuously widen, the workers began to question whether their leaders were delivering what they should. The union, faced with the workers crying poverty, could not put the burden of carrying the Transit Authority on the workers any longer.
>
> The wage gap became intolerable... the members were becoming more militant, and the leadership was worried. The minority voting against ratification of the contracts the leadership had negotiated kept getting larger. The union leaders were worried about remaining in power.[33]

The inequities MacMahon spoke of did, in fact, exist and in some instances they were substantial. The greatest disparity in wages was between the TA's skilled workers and comparable people employed by other city departments. The workers who repaired and maintained the TA's buses were paid $3.46-1/4 per hour, compared with auto mechanics in the city's police, fire, public works, and other departments who received $4.56 per hour. A TA worker whose job included welding, painting, carpentry, and other tasks received $3.46-1/4 per hour. Although there was no comparable job in other city departments, in those departments carpenters received $5.37; painters, $4.50; and welders, $4.49. Even laborers who performed work comparable to the lowest classification of work done by car maintainers received $4.00 per hour when employed by other city departments.[34] The discrepancy between what the TA's skilled people were paid and what comparable employees of other city departments earned was not really subject to dispute and was admitted by Mayor Lindsay and his aides during the negotiations.

In addition to the skilled workers, other employees of the TA also received less money per hour than comparable workers employed by other public agencies in New York City. Motormen on the city's subways received an hourly wage of $3.46-1/4 while motormen employed by the Port of New York Authority's Trans-Hudson Corporation, which operates subways between New Jersey and Manhattan, received $3.95. Although the TA pointed out that differences in contributions to the respective pension plans of the two agencies narrowed the gap, the Port Authority's motormen still maintained an advantage of 27¢ per hour. During the negotiations, Quill was fond of comparing his transit employees' wages with those of a "garbage man." The top pay for sanitationmen, an official job title which included truck drivers and handlers of garbage cans for the Sanitation Department was $3.59 per hour at the time of the transit strike.[35] In comparison, subway motormen received $3.46-1/4 per hour and bus drivers $3.22.[36]

For its part, the Transit Authority admitted that differentials existed between what TA workers earned and what employees of other city departments were receiving. Their only defense was an attempt to show that the differences were not as large as the TWU had contended. The bulk of the TA economic argument centered on comparisons between the pay of transit workers in New York City and those in eighteen other cities. The TA's findings showed that earnings in New York City were above the median for the other cities.[37] The TWU, in turn, claimed that when differentials in the cost of living were taken into account, the wages of New York City's transit workers fell considerably below the median.

Perhaps most significantly, the wages of transit employees would be considered low when one takes into account the number of jobs the TA had eliminated in recent years. For unions operating in industries where technological change is rapid, labor leaders have generally adopted either of two approaches. In some cases, such as the typographical industry, union leaders attempted to slow the adoption of labor saving devices as a means of protecting workers' jobs. In other industries, such as coal mining and longshoring on the West Coast, unions permitted the rather rapid introduction of technology, in return for substantial increases in wages.

Although "featherbedding" (the use of a greater number of employees than management would prefer, as a way of a union preserving workers' jobs) had been considered almost *de rigeur* on our nation's railroads, such restrictive work practices did not characterize the relationship between the TWU and the TA. Very much to the contrary, the TWU was "a model of cooperation in raising standards of operating efficiency by permitting the squeeze out of thousands of jobs in the deficit ridden system."[38] In fact, according to Raskin, a long-time observer and critic of the TWU, "this cooperation extended to such lengths that the transit system fell into a perilous state of undermanning."[39] In the twelve years since the TA was established in 1953, more than 10,000 employees had been trimmed from the original complement of 45,820 workers, a reduction of more than 20 percent.[40] In return, the Authority guaranteed that no one would be laid off.

Despite his occasional public posturing to the contrary, TWU President Quill had allowed the Transit Authority a virtual free reign in eliminating jobs, as long as they did it through attrition. For example, although Quill publicly and vociferously attacked the TA in 1961 for testing a crewless, automatic shuttle train, he had previously granted them the right to automate their equipment in "clear and unambiguous" language.[41]

Quill permitted the TA to save substantial amounts of money on other labor costs as well. Long before the term was coined, Quill agreed to a "give-back" in which TWU members would no longer receive pay for the first day of an illness. This produced a considerable savings for the Authority which, in turn, increased the total number of sick days granted to its employees.[42] In sum, the Transit Authority had always found Quill to be a reasonable negotiator who was quite willing to allow the TA to institute major labor saving changes in return for very modest wage increases. For example, in 1960 it was initially estimated that the contract won by the TWU would cost the TA $35 million over its two-year life.[43] As a result of labor saving changes permitted under this contract, however, the additional labor cost during this period amounted to only $9 million. The following settlement, which was initially estimated at $36 million over two years, actually cost only $24 million as a result of the reduction in force. Although each of the contracts negotiated between the TWU and the TA since the Authority was established in 1953 was in the range of $33 to $35 million, the annual increase in labor costs during this period rose by an average of only $6.6 million per year.[44] Thus, the TWU had very willingly accepted labor saving changes, but in contrast to most other unions, had not won high wage increases in return.

Back At The Bargaining Table

Phase Two of the negotiations did not begin as mediation Chairman Feinsinger had expected. When Feinsinger arrived at the Americana Hotel two days before Chistmas for the mediation session, he was met by an "angry Michael J. Quill," who "leaning on his cane and shaking with emotion," denounced him for a statement he had made the day before.[45] The cause of Quill's anger was Feinsinger's remark that the union was demanding $10 per second and the TA was offering 1¢ per hour squeezed out over three or four years. "Doctor, it's all yours now," Quill said. "We're not going into any conference until this statement is withdrawn by you." "It was a flippancy," Feinsinger said, in attempting to explain his remarks. "I cheerfully and willingly withdraw this statement. It has taught me a lesson not to be flippant." The mediation chairman also made it clear that he wished to withdraw his comment regarding the TA.[46]

When the mediation session finally began, Feinsinger, visibly irritated by the incident, cleared the room of all but the principals and then delivered a no-nonsense lecture. He told the negotiators that he was not there to serve Quill or O'Grady, but rather as a public servant. He said that he did not mind eating "humble pie" on occasion but emphasized he was not going to do so as a steady diet. He also indicated that he had been "bored and frustrated" by some of the presentations made to the panel and that he wanted both sides to knuckle down and do some real bargaining.[47]

Later in the day, two of the union lawyers questioned whether the neutral panel, originally established as a mediation board was going to become a fact-finding panel as had been suggested in an editorial in the previous day's New York Times. The panel told the union negotiators that its role was solely one of mediation. When the TWU representatives continued to pursue the matter, Feinsinger, who was obviously upset, said he had "eaten enough crow already" and refused to continue the discussion. Always one to have the last word, Quill then asked Feinsinger if he had ever been in a famine. The wary Feinsinger said he had not. "In a famine," Quill offered, "sometimes even crow tastes good."[48] The mediation chairman then departed to spend the holiday weekend with his family in Colorado.

The Old Scenario

The overall style of bargaining between the TWU and the mayor of New York City originated in 1948, during the administration of William O'Dwyer. The process of bargaining was so consistently followed over the years, that by the 1965 negotiations, *New York Times* labor writer A. H. Raskin referred to the parties as still following "the old scenario." This process, according to Raskin, "had more to do with politics than orthodox collective bargaining." In the practice of the old scenario, as described by Raskin,

> Quill, a showman on a par with Jimmy Cagney or John Wayne, put on a great exhibition of bellicosity in every negotiation. All of the conventional trappings were there—a mammouth rank-and-file negotiating committee, distinguished mediators to assist in the climatic phases—but when it came to the clutch Quill and [the mayor] would meet in total privacy to hammer out a settlement. Eureka, the trains would run.
>
> Behind the hippodroming was a sustained exercise in palmanship that carried explicit dividends for both mayor and union leader."[49]

For the mayor, Quill's performance as "public monster number one" amply demonstrated to the electorate that the city administration was attempting to be as fiscally prudent as possible in dealing with a "madman." And, if the transit fare had to be raised, the blame fell on Quill rather than the mayor. Contrary to what has generally been reported, however, the TWU did not receive particularly good contracts as a result of following this well-worn script. Instead, the major advantage to Quill of his public militance was to demonstrate to his members that he was doing everything possible on their behalf. In a union in which factionalism was rampant, Quill needed an external enemy to bring some measure of cohesiveness to his organization. At its core, then, this relationship between the mayor and Quill was essentially "political"; it enabled the mayor to maintain his standing with the voters, and it allowed Quill to increase his stature among his "constituents," the rank-and-file TWU members.

In 1948, both Michael Quill and William O'Dwyer had political problems. "Mr. O'Dwyer needed a politically palatable excuse for dumping that holiest of New York holies, the nickel subway fare, before the operating deficits it spawned bankrupted the city."[50] For Quill, the issue was considerably more involved. As a long-time activist in the U. S. Communist party, Quill was philosophically in accord with the party's position that the 5¢ fare should be preserved. Quill broke with the

Communists in 1947, however, when he was forced to choose between their opposition to an increase in the fare and the loss of huge segments of his members because of the union's inability to get a raise for them without an increase in the fare. While ideologically opposed to the increase, Quill said that his members should not be expected to subsidize the 5¢ fare through their own low wages.

The Communists had hoped to elevate the 5¢ fare to a point where it would become the city's most burning issue in the 1949 mayoral election.[51] O'Dwyer, fearful that the Communists might be successful, sought to dissipate the threat. The mayor instructed Theodore W. Kheel, then serving as director of the city's division of labor relations "to give Michael Quill whatever help he could within the limits of his legal powers to break the influence of the [Communist party] in the city's transit system." The strategy that was developed "would enable Quill to oust those Communists who had entrenched themselves in key posts in the TWU, strengthen Quill's position in the union, emphasize to anti-Communist labor leaders the necessity of a fare increase to raise wages, and then put the fare boost across together with the pay increases." Quill told Kheel that a substantial wage increase for his members would be the best way to weaken Communist influence in the union. O'Dwyer agreed, and asked Quill:

> How much . . . would the hourly pay increase have to be? Quill thought for a moment and replied: "Twenty-four cents an hour, Mr. Mayor." "And why do you say 24 cents?" asked O'Dwyer.
>
> "Well you see," answered Quill, "the men are now getting $1.26 an hour, and 24 cents more would bring them up to $1.50. That's a nice round figure and even the Commies could never persuade them they were getting gypped at that price."
>
> O'Dwyer agreed, also OKing a dues checkoff for its members. . . .[52]

This private accord was then played out for somewhat more public consumption:

> . . . O'Dwyer invited TWU leaders, most of them in the anti-Quill camp to a closed door meeting at City Hall. Sitting in as observers [was] the full, negotiating committee. . . . The Mayor, pretending he was discussing the strike threat for the first time, asked Quill what he wanted as the price of a no-strike pledge. Quill immediately mentioned 24 cents an hour. The anti-Quill men were trapped. . . . A 24 cent pay increase was considerably more than any transit union anywhere in the U.S. had received in years.
>
> The leftists hated to see Quill achieve such a triumph. To their surprise O'Dwyer said—"It's yours!"
>
> Quill then casually mentioned the dues checkoff. . . . "You want a

checkoff?'' asked O'Dwyer. ''Well, you've got it.''

The 300 men on the . . . negotiating committee, excepting the anti-Quill leftists, jumped up and cheered. That short session . . . marked the beginning of the end of Communist influence in the TWU.[53]

Shortly afterward, the fare was raised to a dime. Quill's position in the TWU was solidified, and Quill rather than O'Dwyer was blamed for the fare increase.

Facilitating this quid pro quo arrangement between Quill and O'Dwyer was a close personal and political relationship between the two men. When O'Dwyer ran for mayor in 1945 he was endorsed by the TWU, and Local 100 established a ''Transport Workers Committee of One Thousand for O'Dwyer and Quill.'' Quill was running for reelection to City Council at the time. Because of an internal dispute, Bronx Democratic leader Edward Flynn did virtually nothing to aid his party's mayoral candidate. O'Dwyer's candidacy was successful, mainly because of the support he received from Michael Quill and the TWU. Quill received the highest number of votes of any city council candidate and because he was a resident of the Bronx, he provided O'Dwyer with support where he needed it most. O'Dwyer was deeply appreciative of the TWU's efforts, and as Joshua Freeman has pointed out, ''the election results gave the TWU considerable political capital.''[54]

Soon after O'Dwyer assumed the mayor's office, his relationship with Quill became still closer when the mayor's wife, Kitty, died. As Quill's wife, Shirley, described her husband's rapport with the mayor:

> [After Kitty died] Bill rattled around in his new home. Gracie Mansion was large, formal and unfamiliar. Busy as he was setting up a new administration, there were long, lonely nights, and Mike was one of a small group of friends who visited him often at the mayor's official residence.
>
> There was a deep affection between these . . . Irishmen. . . . Fond as they were of a bottle of scotch, and as they downed a quart, the mayor from Mayo grew ever more sentimental, while the thrush from Kerry warbled only slightly off-key, the familiar songs of Ireland's noble struggles.[55]

Under Mayor Wagner, the old script continued to be acted out. Quill persisted in his public militance, which still served to diffuse internal dissention within the union. And Wagner used Quill's public antics not to excuse a fare increase, but rather to try to gain political capital by preserving the fare.

In his early campaigns for mayor, Wagner was extremely solicitous of organized labor, but not beholden to union leaders. Initially running for mayor in 1953, Wagner courted labor support, but civil service unions were not a decisive factor in his victory. His majority in 1957 was the largest in the city's history, "and he enjoyed solid backing from organized labor without making special concessions." Unions initially supported Wagner because his father, Senator Robert F. Wagner, was quite pro-labor, and the author of the Wagner Act, which legally protected the rights of workers to join unions. Although he "owed" nothing to the city's public sector unions, Wagner's strong family ties to organized labor led him to the conclusion that he needed a formalized labor relations process to deal with the city's unionized employees.[56] In 1954, Wagner issued an executive order granting employees the right to organize, establishing a grievance procedure, and creating labor-management committees to discuss working conditions and to foster cooperation between management and unions. The city also created a Department of Labor: to certify unions, to determine the appropriateness of bargaining units, and to aid in resolving disputes. At this point, however, the municipal unions were only "consulted" by the city about matters that would effect them; they did not engage in true collective bargaining. This shortcoming was remedied in 1958 when Wagner issued his Executive Order Number 49—hailed by organized labor as the "little Wagner Act"—which granted unions the right to bargain collectively for their members. New York City thus became one of the first jurisdictions in the nation to adopt an essentially private sector model for municipal labor relations.

Despite these changes,

> the unions were still very weak and much more absorbed in organization and survival issues than bread-and-butter problems of pay and working conditions . . . Wagner did what he could to keep them that way. Instead of having the city labor department establish broad bargaining units as the basis for certification contests, the initiative was left to the employees to petition for recognition. The inevitable result was small, highly frag-mented units, a multiplicity of competitive units, a multiplicity of competitive unions, and a maximum of raiding. Wagner also kept a firm political hand on the certification process so when leaders did win recognition, they were likely to feel some personal debt to the mayor.[57]

During this period of excessive fragmentation, with a number of different unions and factions within the same union seeking to represent the same workers, the ascendency of one particular group or individual required the intervention of the mayor. Extremely sophisticated in labor issues because of his family background, Wagner recognized that in certain situations the city would benefit from playing one union group against another. However, in other instances where factionalism got out of hand and created chaos, Wagner was perfectly willing to back one faction as a stabilizing force. Such was the case in the transit industry.

When the situation demanded the propping up of a particular faction in order to achieve stability, Robert Wagner was exquisitely sensitive to the "political" needs of the union officials he sought to support. As A.H. Raskin aptly observed:

> ... Wagner was always at pains to give the union hierarchy a feeling of importance, even if he did not give their members as much money as they wanted at contract time. No union function was official without a visit from the mayor. The duty round did not stop with conventions, testimonial dinners, luncheons, funerals, weddings, and installation of officers. It ran right through the weekend to unveilings, confirmations, and bar mitzvahs for sons, daughters, nephews, nieces, and even grandchildren.[58]

In some cases, the support by Wagner was a little more heavy handed. In 1957, Quill's control over transit workers was shaken by an eight-day strike by dissident motormen and skilled craftsmen. Wagner quickly went to Quill's aid. The TA paid bonuses to nonstrikers and threatened mass reprisals against the strikers. The strike leaders were jailed, spies were planted in strike headquarters, and strike meetings were bugged. When the bugs were discovered, Wagner threatened reprisals. Despite the fact, however, that "the evidence was unmistakable that the Transit Authority and the police were up to their eardrums in the electronic eavesdroppers," disciplinary action never materialized.[59] Thus, it was advantageous to both Quill and Wagner, for Quill to be strongly in control of the TWU.

The Negotiations of 1961

With Mayor Wagner calling for a "new approach to transit labor relations," talks in 1961 were conducted under the auspices of a newly created Transit Labor Board. The committee was expected to enter negotiations on December 1, and if an agreement was not reached by December 23, they were to make public their findings and recommendations for a new contract in a report to the mayor. Although the recommendations of the board were not binding on either side, it was hoped that the prestige of its members and the public expression of its findings would exert strong pressure for acceptance. Composed of David Cole, its chairman, and Theodore Kheel and George W. Taylor, the mediation panel expressed optimism that it could find a way to eliminate the last minute New Year's Eve settlements that had long characterized transit labor in New York City.[60]

The 1961 negotiations got under way on November 8, the day after Robert Wagner was reelected mayor of New York City, with substantial support from the TWU. It soon became apparent that the promised new approach to bargaining would not materialize. The members of the mediation panel indicated that they would not make public recommendations on December 23, as provided in the original plan because their objective was "to help both sides reach an agreement before December 31," rather than "writing a contract for them."[61] In essence, bargaining would be conducted as it had in the past.

Also, as was typical of previous negotiations, Quill developed a strategy for insuring that negotiations would become front page news. The TWU president threatened a citywide subway and bus strike unless the TA cancelled plans to begin operating a crewless, fully automated train on the Grand Central Station-Times Square shuttle on December 15. Quill expressed the fear that, if it spread to the entire system, such automation could cost the jobs of 6,600 motormen and conductors, as well as being a threat to the safety of the riding public.[62] Although the existing contract between the TWU and the TA contained a no-strike clause and the Authority had the "clear and unambiguous" right to automate its equipment, Quill used this nonissue to rivet the attention of New Yorkers on transit negotiations.[63] The strike was averted when a compromise was worked out in which the TA agreed to delay the labor saving plan until contract negotiations were completed.

Although ostensibly the three major sticking points in negotiations were wages, the union's demand for a four-day work week, and problems arising out of the impact of automation, the latter two demands were clearly introduced as bargaining chips to trade away for an acceptable wage increase. On Wednesday evening, December 27, members of the TWU voted to authorize a complete subway and bus strike on New Year's Day after they unanimously rejected the TA's first money offer, which amounted to 16¢ per hour over a two-year contract. The rejected offer called for an increase of 3 percent, or 8¢ per hour in each year of the agreement, and was contingent on the TWU's withdrawal of its demand for shorter hours.

On Thursday, December 28, at the request of Mayor Wagner, negotiations moved to City Hall, the place where transit crises were traditionally settled as a strike appeared imminent. And indeed, this was again the case, as an agreement was reached that evening on a new two-year contract. Although the TA had the legal authority to conclude an agreement with the TWU, in fact, the mayor was the key to bargaining. The mayor assumed the central position because he determined how much of a subsidy the TA would receive.

Although Mayor Wagner was normally present as negotiations went down to the wire so that the parties could approach him, he was not involved in the actual give and take of bargaining. Instead, Wagner would speak in terms of a total money settlement and would not get involved in negotiating specific provisions. For example, he would say, "You have 18¢ for the first year and 6¢ for the second," and leave it up to the principals to work out the details.[64] According to Raskin, at the crucial stage "the actual dollar figure of the settlement was worked out in complete privacy between Wagner and Quill; not even Matty Guinan was present."[65]

The agreement provided that the Authority's 28,070 employees, who earned between $2.25 and $3.01 per hour, would receive an hourly increase of 12¢ the first year and 10¢ the second. In addition, the TA assumed an additional 5 percent of each employee's pension payments, something that would cost 11¢ per hour. The TWU lost its battle to obtain a shorter work week, as the new contract again provided for a five-day, forty-hour week. On the issue of automation, the union won a contract clause guaranteeing that there would be no lay-offs for the duration of the contract. However, this provision was of little real significance, because the union and the TA already had an unwritten agreement to that effect for several years. Under this understanding, the TA had reduced its workforce by 7,500 in six years through a process of attrition. Another provision gave employees four weeks vacation after fifteen years experience, instead of twenty. Finally, the Authority agreed that during the trial run of the automated shuttle, it would station a union motorman on board. Presumably, after that the TA would be free to operate the shuttle without a crew.[66]

Joseph O'Grady, the chief negotiator for the Transit Authority estimated the cost of the package at $36 million over two years. However, he indicated that the TA would be able to retain the 15¢ fare, at least through 1962.[67] Once again, the public villification of the mayor and the TA by Quill had served the "political" needs of both Wagner and Quill. In the eyes of the electorate, Wagner emerged as the protector of the 15¢ fare. Quill, in turn, had publicly demonstrated the lengths he would go to protect the jobs of his members from being eliminated by automation, something he hoped would placate the members of his union.

The Negotiations of 1963

The next set of negotiations began in the early fall of 1963, when the TWU announced the demands it would submit to the Transit Authority in the upcoming talks. As in the negotiations two years earlier, the union asked for a 15 percent wage increase and a thirty-two-hour, four-day week, without a loss in take-home pay. In addition, the union asked for fifty-two guaranteed pay checks each year; retirement at one-half pay after twenty years of service, instead of waiting until the minimum age of fifty-five; twenty-seven days of paid vacation after one year's service instead of four weeks after nine years; and twelve paid holidays each year instead of nine. Also, they requested an increase of 5¢ an hour over the existing payment of 2¢ by the TA to improve the health and welfare program and to provide medical care for retired employees, and a union shop, all to be incorporated in a two-year contract.[68]

The demands, which the TWU estimated would cost $165 million, were called "not only unrealistic, but out of this world" by Daniel Scannell, one of the two new members of the TA.[69] And Joseph O'Grady, now the chairman of the TA, said that any "substantial" wage increase won by the TWU would make a higher fare "inevitable." O'Grady explained that the TA's existing $11 million in surplus funds would be exhausted by January 1, when the existing contract expired, and that they could not afford any wage hike at all. However, the TA chairman pointed out that he was exploring "avenues to obtain additional revenues which might absorb some wage increase and still avoid a subway fare rise" as long as the union made reasonable demands.[70]

In mid-October, the city voted to increase its subsidy to the TA for the transportation of school children on its subway and bus lines by $6.8 million. Although the money was technically supposed to defray the costs of school children who rode at reduced rates, the director of the City Council's legislative finance unit testified that the $6.8 million was, in fact, "designed to help preserve the 15¢ fare for the general public."[71]

With only one week remaining on the existing contract, Mayor Wagner intervened directly in the contract talks for the first time and urged both the TWU and the Authority to give New Yorkers a "Christmas present" by moving toward a quick and reasonable contract settlement. Wagner said he wanted to maintain the 15¢ fare and indicated that the city was prepared to give monetary assistance to the TA to achieve that end. But he warned that "we do not have printing presses at City Hall—there are not unlimited funds available."[72]

When, on December 27, the TA continued to refuse to make a wage offer, Quill walked out of the negotiating session and said he would not return until given assurances that the Authority was prepared to make an offer on wages and the union's demand for a shorter work week. "There is enough stupidity in the negotiations at the moment to warrent a strike," Quill declared.[73]

At a mass rally on December 29, the transit workers overwhelmingly approved a New Year's Day strike. In his speech before the rank-and-file, Michael Quill alternated between threats and humor. He began by threatening that "before any contract is signed we'll make a breakthrough on the shorter work week." He criticized the antistrike Condon-Wadlin Act and indicated that the union would be willing to defy or circumvent it. "There's a terrific amount of laws you can get around," said Quill, as he shifted to a lighter vein. He added that the union leadership would be willing to go to jail if they called a strike, even though none of the union officials wanted to become "the Bird-Man of Alcatraz."[74]

After being served with a court order upon the completion of negotiations on December 30, Quill immediately announced that he was breaking off talks with the Transit Authority until after his court appearance, scheduled for the following day. The order was obtained by the TA and directed the TWU to show cause why they should not be enjoined from striking the city's subways and buses. In the actual discussions between the two sides, very little was accomplished because the TA still refused to put an offer on the table. At this point, with the strike imminent, Mayor Wagner was at the hotel where the negotiations were being conducted, meeting intermittently with the members of the TA and then separately with the members of his Transit Labor Board. The TA, of course, had to depend on the city for additional funds to meet any higher labor costs or it would have to raise the fare, something the mayor had precluded.

It was not until 5:00 p.m. on Tuesday, December 31, with the strike deadline a scant twelve hours away, that the deadlock in the negotiations was broken and hard bargaining began. At that time, the members of the Mayor's Transit Labor Board told the leaders of the TWU that they could not hold off much longer in making public their own recommendations for a settlement. The mediators said they had already prepared their package and that it did not include a provision for shorter hours because the cost of this item would be too much for the Authority. David Cole, the chairman of the mediation panel, then told the union leaders that he preferred to have both sides reach an agreement through direct talks rather than resorting to recommendations by his group. When the union leaders agreed to drop their demand for a shorter work week, and bargain on wages and other benefits, the mediators dropped out of the talks to allow the parties to negotiate directly.

Having achieved its primary objective of eliminating the shorter work week as an issue in the negotiations, the TA finally put its first money offer on the table. Authority chairman, O'Grady offered Quill a 25¢ per hour package incorporated in a two-year contract. Quill, according to insiders, immediately rejected the offer, saying that the union wanted a 40¢ increase.

O'Grady said the TA could not pay it. Bargaining on these terms continued for hours, with Mayor Wagner periodically meeting with Quill and O'Grady in his suite in an effort to break the impasse.[75]

Despite the fact that he had privately abandoned the shorter work week and was now negotiating on other items, Quill continued to make public statements that the four-day work week "was still on the table." Throughout the evening, Quill made brief visits to the Versailles Room of the hotel, where the union's 100-man wage-policy committee was waiting. There, he posed for television cameras, said a strike was unavoidable, denounced the Supreme Court Justice who had enjoined the union from striking, and generally painted a gloomy picture of the negotiations.[76]

At 2:00 a.m., with the strike deadline only three hours away, O'Grady increased his offer to 30¢. Quill responded by reducing his demand to 35¢. However, movement stopped there, and for the next hour both sides refused to budge.

At this point, Harry Van Arsdale, the president of the New York City Central Labor Council, arrived at the Americana Hotel. First, he conferred with the mayor, and then he went to see Quill. Between 3:30 and 4:45 a.m., Van Arsdale worked with TWU attorneys John O'Donnell and Louis Waldman to devise a formula to break the deadlock. Then, with only fifteen minutes left before the strike deadline, they gave O'Grady a counteroffer that was acceptable to the TA. The compromise proposed was for a 35¢ increase that was payable in such a way that it added up to the same money package as was contained in the Authority's 30¢ offer.[77] This was accomplished by giving the union 11¢ per hour the first year of the two-year contract, and having the additional 24¢ take effect at later dates. Of the total increase of 35¢, 11¢ were to begin immediately, 8-1/2¢ were to be added on January 1, 1965, and another 8-1/2¢ on July 1, 1965. In addition, 7¢ per hour was to be paid beginning January 1, 1965, for future allocation for health, welfare, and pension benefits. Afterwards, Cole, the chairman of the mayor's mediation panel, called the negotiations "a good example of the kind of thing we call crisis bargaining, which is not the best way to settle problems."[78]

Within hours after the announcement of the settlement, Mayor Wagner and Governor Rockefeller jointly proposed a plan that would enable the TA to maintain the 15¢ fare for at least one year and "hopefully for two." The two men proposed state legislation to permit the city to pay interest and amortization on certain TA bonds; to accelerate reimbursement for a rise in power costs for the Authority that followed the city's sale of the power plants to Consolidated Edison several years before; and to give the TA materials and supplies now leased to it by the city. It was estimated that the total subsidy from the city would add up to $41 million. Because state legislation would be required to permit the city to subsidize the TA, Wagner and Rockefeller agreed that the mayor would provide the money, and the governor would support the legislation needed to implement the plan.[79]

This time, however, Michael Quill's public display of militance was not sufficient to pacify restive elements within his union. Several days after the agreement was reached, more than 1,500 TWU members picketed in front of their union's headquarters asking for Quill's ouster, denouncing the settlement as a sellout, and charging that they had been left in the dark regarding the terms of the agreement. In addition to dissatisfaction over the total amount of the increase, the pickets were particularly critical of the TWU acceptance of an increase of 7¢ per hour, or $5 million in fringe benefits, without deciding how this money would be allocated. A substantial number of the pickets, for example, were skilled craftsmen who felt they should receive wages equal to those prevailing in private industry for members of their craft and believed that part of the $5 million should be used to correct these inequities.[80]

In the wake of theses demonstrations, the TWU and the TA went back to the bargaining table to allocate the $5 million for fringe benefits that had been agreed upon. Among the options considered were nightshift differentials, sick pay and sick leave provisions, additional holidays, and inequities within wage rates for mechanics.[81]

Although some of the fringe benefit money was used to increase the pay of mechanics, they remained dissatisfied with the amount. They were joined in their dissatisfaction by other workers who felt that the 35¢ per hour package fell far short of the demands originally presented by Quill. While a wildcat strike called by the dissident elements failed to materialize, the membership vote in favor of ratifying the contract was 4-to-1: the narrowest margin the union had achieved in many years.[82]

Christmas 1965

On Christmas Eve of 1965, Michael J. Quill expressed dissatisfaction with the progress being made in negotiations, and indicated that the union was in the process of establishing fifty-nine sites throughout the city to be used as strike centers. When it was suggested that the strike threat was not very cheerful news on the eve of Christmas, he replied, "That is as cheerful as the powers that be are making it for us."[83]

Although previously the mayor-elect had confined his involvement to conferences with members of the mediation panel, on Christmas Day the mediators asked Lindsay to speak directly to the TA and the TWU. Feeling that little genuine progress was taking place, the neutral panel believed they had to do something to get the talks moving.

Considerable difficulties were obviously being created by the change in administrations. Theoretically, three courses of action were available to Wagner and Lindsay to deal with the transition. First, outgoing Mayor Wagner could have reached an agreement with the TWU before the existing contract expired and without Lindsay's aid. Second, Wagner and Lindsay could have worked together and established some sort of bipartisan bargaining front. Finally, Lindsay could have assumed the responsibility of negotiating an agreement without any help from Wagner.

For what appear to be very sound reasons, Robert Wagner refused to negotiate with the TWU prior to the expiration of the union's contract. The mayor's only role in transit negotiations was an unofficial one. The TA had the legal power to bargain, and the only reason it gave up this authority was because it lacked the money to reach an agreement. Because Lindsay would have to provide this money, he alone would have reason to assume the TA's bargaining position.

Lindsay appears to have had a vital stake in ensuring that Wagner did not reach an agreement that he would have to finance. Yet, in what seems like a total role reversal, Lindsay was demanding that Wagner reach a settlement before he left office, and Wagner repeatedly held that this would not be proper. The reasons Lindsay and Wagner assumed the postures they did were wholly political. As a City Hall source related after the conclusion of the strike, "Certainly there were political motivations involved in his [Wagner's] decision. If Wagner had settled before December 31, as Lindsay was hoping, then Lindsay could have characterized any agreement as a 'pay-off' to Mike Quill. Then, if the fare had to be raised, Lindsay would have been able to blame it on Wagner.[84] This assessment appears extremely plausible. Throughout the negotiations Lindsay had characterized previous contracts between Wagner and the TWU as "deals," which he charged were not in the public interest. Having already laid the foundation for the accusation, it would not have been too difficult for Lindsay to charge that the latest agreement was the worst in the long line of deals which had already been consummated.

From a collective bargaining standpoint, the most effective way to have handled the transitionary period at City Hall would have been for Wagner and Lindsay to have established a common front. They could have worked together to obtain subsidy money for the TA. They could have jointly selected a mediation panel acceptable to both unions and the TA. Because Wagner had previously worked closely with the Authority and had appointed two of its three members to their positions, once subsidy money was secured, he could have told the TA how much money was available so they could guide their negotiations accordingly. Wagner had obviously enjoyed a close bargaining and political relationship with the TWU as well. As a Republican, Lindsay would have found a receptiveness from Republican Governor Rockefeller, which Wagner could not hope to achieve.

Despite the potential such cooperation held for bargaining purposes it was not carried out because a united front was intolerable from a political perspective. Neither Wagner nor Lindsay was desirous of collaborating with the other. As Deputy-Mayor Timothy Costello commented after the strike, "Wagner was no more interested in joining Lindsay in a common front, than Lindsay was in joining Wagner."[85] Wagner's refusal to become involved, and his eventual departure from the city, compelled Lindsay to become the central figure on the management side.

On the day after Christmas, 8,000 shouting transit workers voted unanimously to strike the city's subways and buses at 5:00 a.m. on January 1 if they did not have a satisfactory contract by then.[86] The large downstairs ballroom and a smaller seventh floor room were jammed with standees at the Manhattan Center building, and an overflow crowd outside on 34th Street heard the proceedings over a microphone. At the mass meeting, Quill, as international president of the TWU, told his members that with only six days left to negotiate before the strike deadline, the TA had not yet made a money offer. After hearing this many of the militant members of the union started chanting, "Strike Now! Now!" Quill, however, advised against an immediate walkout telling the transit workers, "If you're against the leadership, you'll stampede now, break your contract and look like a bunch of damn fools." Quill, informing his members that striking at that time would be a violation of their contract, then added, "When the TWU signs a contract, it lives up to its contract."[87]

At the Manhattan Center meeting, Quill identified the "meddlers" he had spoken of several times previously. He said that one was John B. Oakes, the editorial page editor of the *New York Times*. He said later that "Mr. Oakes, the publisher of the new Bible, has been trying to advise Lindsay on the direction of his programs, his appointments and the amount of money he should spend." Quill added, "I know exactly how much money Mr. Oakes has told Mr. Lindsay to O.K. for a settlement." In response, Oakes said, "I have no comment on Mr. Quill's fulminations except to say that whatever advice the *New York Times* has had to give to Mayor-Elect Lindsay about transit or any other matter has been openly expressed in its editorials."[88] Refusing to identify the second "meddler" by name, Quill said only that he was a "would-be pollster who can tell you who to be a dog catcher, or who to be Mayor or Governor or let you know how to get to Washington." Afterwards, the union's Douglas MacMahon explained the import of the Quill remark, "Lindsay was convinced by his advisors that if he would successfully stand up against Quill, 'the big bad man' and hammer him down, the next step would be the presidency." Asked specifically if he felt the suggestion that a pollster was interfering with negotiations was Quill's way of "implying that Lindsay was acting according to the way that would benefit him most politically," MacMahon replied, "Yes, I think that's what Mike had in mind."[89] Quill said the third meddler was "Mr. Doyle, a Wall Street bond manipulator," but declined to identify him further.[90]

In urging the rank-and-file to authorize the strike, Quill warned them that they were closer to walking out than they had been at any time in their history. The reason, he explained, was that "Mayor Wagner, experienced in mediation, is getting out; John Lindsay is coming in with new faces we are not keen about."[91]

While the TWU members were voting to authorize a strike, TA Chairman O'Grady appeared on a television program and sounded an equally pessimistic note about the possibility of arriving at an agreement. O'Grady said he "never had less reason to be optimistic about reaching a settlement" because the union is "asking for more money than in the past, and the TA has never had less money to give." The chairman of the TA asserted that unlike previous negotiations, when he had had advance commitments from public officials that the agency would receive financial aid to enable it to reach a settlement, he had received none from Lindsay or Rockefeller. When O'Grady was asked if he felt the mayor-elect and the governor were dragging their feet, he replied, "The Governor has said this is a city problem," and "Mr. Lindsay has not been in touch with us to offer us anything." "We're like players in a stud poker game facing an opponent without knowing what's in our hole cards," one TA member commented.[92]

In the autumn of 1965, the financial exigencies that had led to the city's participation in previous transit negotiations were still very much in effect. The operation of the subways and buses in New York City continued to be an unprofitable venture. In November 1965, the TA forecast an operating deficit of $62 million in the fiscal year ending June 30, 1966.[93] Including an anticipated $19-million surplus from the Manhattan and Bronx Surface Transit Operating Authority the city's two transit operating agencies expected to show a combined deficit of $43 million. The deficit, of course, would be expected to increase substantially when the new contract went into effect on January 1, 1966.

Faced with this bleak financial picture, the TA, according to law, had no alternative but to raise the fare. As a practical matter, however, the Transit Authority refused to take such action. From the standpoint of what they considered the public interest, the Authority felt the fare should not be increased. Such an increase, they maintained, "would be inconsistent with national transportation policy, which favors getting people off the highways in urban centers and on mass transport." From a selfish standpoint, the TA was also against a fare increase because they felt it would be counter-productive—that it would turn customers away.[94]

Throughout the negotiations the TA maintained that it had not abdicated its authority to raise the fare. Even in a private conversation after the strike, Daniel Scannell insisted that during the bargaining the TA considered raising the fare along with many other alternatives as a source of revenue. Scannell maintained that the "reason the TA was created was to end the subsidization of the authority."[95] And the only way to do this was to raise the fare. But in what appears to be a much more plausible statement, TWU attorney John O'Donnell said after the strike, "If you think a Democratic-controlled Transit Authority is going to relieve a Republican mayor-elect of the responsibility of a fare increase by raising it themselves, you're crazy." As O'Donnell continued, "O'Grady is a Democrat. Scannell is also a Democrat, and an important figure in the Queens Democratic organization. Both were appointed by Wagner. Why should they raise the fare to make Lindsay look good?"[96]

In addition, the TA would not have been expected to raise the fare because of the manner in which previous negotiations had been conducted. Despite the legal requirement that the TA raise the fare to eliminate its deficit, the unwritten law of New York City politics dictated that the price of a subway token remain at 15¢. Robert Wagner had never failed to provide the money to ensure that the fare would be preserved. Throughout his mayoral campaign, John Lindsay strongly advocated the maintenance of the 15¢ fare, and after his election his view remained unchanged. The TA could assume only one thing from Lindsay's pledge to maintain the fare: that he intended to provide them with a subsidy. For if it did not raise the fare, the TA was legally proscribed from taking any other course of action.

Mayor Lindsay's desire to maintain the 15¢ fare and the huge deficit that the TA faced both dictated that the city become involved in providing the TA with assurances of subsidy money. As Theodore Kheel explained, "Although the Transit Authority has the legal power to raise the fare, in fact, it is an operating agency and not a policy agency. It can't make a deal that would raise the fare. The only way to bridge the gap is for the two to work together, as had been the case between Mayor Wagner and the Transit Authority. The lack of the guarantee of a subsidy froze the Transit Authority."[97]

Reflecting an equally pessimistic appraisal of the status of negotiations, mediation chairman Feinsinger cut short his Colorado Christmas vacation and was en route back to New York. Feinsinger felt it imperative that he be present on Monday morning, December 27, when negotiations resumed after their weekend recess. Feinsinger then phoned Mayor-Elect Lindsay and asked that he be present at these sessions.[98]

In his first direct participation in the talks, Lindsay met alternately with the mediators, the TA members, and the union leaders. In an hour-long session with the TA, Lindsay learned that its members were hoping for a settlement of 3.2 percent—which was the limit on increases set by the federal government's anti-inflation program. "The settlement should be 3.2 percent," said Authority Chairman O'Grady. "It's within the frame-work of Presidential guidelines. That's all there is to it."[99] In dollar terms, such a settlement would cost between $35 and $40 million over two years. Lindsay replied, "Yes, that's fair and reasonable. But Mike is going for a bundle. He's asking for $45 to $50 million over two years." After a brief discussion, the other TA members, Scannell and Gilhooley, agreed with O'Grady that a package in the range of $35 to $40 million was appropriate. The three TA members were also in agreement that all of the increases should be in wages, that there should be neither pension improvements nor a reduction in the work week.

Only one question remained: how would the TA raise the $35 to $40 million? John Gilhooley argued that some of the necessary money should come from the consolidation of all city transportation agencies, including the profitable Triborough Bridge and Tunnel Authority. "We can preserve the fare by moving rapidly to amalgamate all these agencies," said Gilhooley.[100] "We can put it through this session of the Legislature—with the maximum cooperation of Albany—by the latest April 1," he added. Someone else present reminded Lindsay that in his transportation white paper prepared during his recent election campaign he had suggested using the city's gasoline tax and license fees to aid mass transportation. Such a move, however, would also require legislation. Then the question of a potential union lawsuit was raised if the TA should decide to wait until the legislature passed the necessary law to combine all city transportation departments. As a Lindsay aide summarized this session with the TA members, "the more we discussed the problem, the more tangled it seemed."[101] With so little time remaining before the strike deadline, it could not have been very comforting to the TA to observe such disarray on the part of the Lindsay people.

Transit Consolidation

During the course of negotiations, a plethora of transit consolidation plans emerged that proposed merging the disparate elements of the transit system in the New York metropolitan area under some form of unified control. While their specifics differed somewhat, all contained one common element: they would require that the deficits incurred by the TA be absorbed by those components of the unified agency that were profitable. The implementation of any of the proposed merger plans would have permitted the maintenance of the 15¢ fare on the subways and buses.

Despite all of these professions of interest in transit consolidation, these plans clearly were suggested mainly to shift the burden for raising the fare, rather than from a belief that they could be implemented in time to preserve the fare. At the time John Lindsay was elected mayor, the State Senate Committee on the affairs of New York City was already considering legislation to regulate the authorities dealing with transit matters and to establish a "super authority." In addition, similar proposals had been made previously, and all had died before reaching the floor of the legislature.[102] All of the participants in transit negotiations were aware of this history and should have concluded that consolidation was not likely.

The main impediment to consolidation, both historically and in 1965, was Robert Moses, the chairman of the Triborough Bridge and Tunnel Authority. The seventy-seven-year-old Moses, described as a man ". . . who in nearly a half century of embattled public life had taken on Mayors, Governors and Presidents. . ." believed the unification plan was "fantastic and destructive" and attempted to see that it was not attained.[103] Lindsay was certainly no match for Moses, who despite the diminution of his influence in recent years, was still the preeminent "power broker" in the city.[104]

After Lindsay's election, Moses was initially apprehensive, not knowing what to expect from the man who had promised to eliminate the influence of the "power brokers" from his administration. After meeting with the mayor-elect, however, Moses came away reassured; "If you elect a matinee-idol Mayor," he told aides, "You're going to get a musical comedy administration." Shortly thereafter, when a Lindsay aide broached the subject of consolidating the Triborough Bridge and Tunnel Authority with the TA as the mayor-elect had proposed, Moses bristled, "I wouldn't cooperate with that goddamned whippersnapper no matter what he did! He'll come and go; Triborough is going to be around for a long time!"

By any standard, Moses was a formidable opponent. He introduced and popularized the concept of public authorities in the United States and was a master of their use and, some would argue, misuse. Begun in England during Elizebethan times, these authorities were established to construct public improvements by selling bonds and to pay off these bonds by charging the public for the use of the improvements. Once the bonds were paid off, under the traditional model, the user fees would be ended, the improvement would pass to public ownership, and the authority would cease to exist. During its life, however, the public authority enjoyed unheard of independence for a public body: it was responsible only to its bondholders.

A man of tremendous ego and ambition, Moses realized that he could wield considerable power if he could modify the way in which public authorities were operated. When the Triborough Bridge and Tunnel Authority and the Port of New York Authority, which were both controlled by Moses, proved to be extremely profi̇ ɔle, these agencies should have paid off their bondholders sooner than anticipated and gone out of existence. Instead, Moses was able to push through changes in the way these agencies were structured to allow them to use their revenues for additional public projects. This was the basis of the Moses empire: he had control over the huge profits generated by the Port of New York and Triborough Authorities, with virtually sole discretion over how this money should be spent. And by continuously issuing new bonds to pay off obligations to existing bondholders, Moses assured that the agencies would never pay off their bondholders so they would never cease to exist.

Robert Moses's half century of controlling public authorities evidenced a lifelong affair with the automobile. He built roads, bridges, tunnels, and parks that people would drive to reach. He was not interested in public rail and bus transit and would not use the Triborough Authority's profits to finance such a venture.

In contrast, the philosophy of the incoming administration was militantly pro-mass transit and antiautomobile. The Lindsay people felt that taking away the Triborough Authority's profits would serve two purposes: it would improve the subway facilities, which would encourage train ridership, and it would siphon off money that otherwise would be used by Moses for more projects to encourage automobile use. All the Lindsay people were doing was to propose legislation that reformers such as the Citizens Union and the City Budget Commission had been advocating for years.

The "good government" forces that backed the Lindsay merger proposal were no match for "power broker" Moses. Armed with legal opinions from all the leading bond lawyers, the Triborough Authority head convinced state legislators that a merger of the TA and the Triborough Authority would violate the obligations to Triborough bondholders and would thereby contravene provisions of both the U.S. and New York State Constitutions. Finally, and perhaps most important, Moses had a lifetime of political IOUs outstanding to ensure that a merger would not be approved by the state legislature. He had given public projects to politicians who wanted them; he modified proposals to placate other politicians; he dispensed thousands of public jobs; he was the darling of the building trades unions because of his massive expenditure of construction funds. In addition, he enjoyed the unbridled support of the banks and bondholders because his machinations had produced lucrative investments over the years. Knowing of Moses opposition, the New York State legislature never even took the Lindsay merger proposal seriously.

Although John Lindsay was obviously disappointed that consolidation could not be implemented, the proposal nevertheless was politically beneficial to the incoming mayor. By stridently opposing a merger, Moses, in many people's minds, would become the man responsible for the inevitable fare increase.

Lindsay also attempted to shift the burden of a fare increase to Washington, D.C., when he announced just a few days before the expiration of the existing transit agreement that he would seek federal funds earmarked for the highway system to subsidize the operation of the city's subways and buses. As one of Lindsay's top appointees said, "What's the sense of making it possible for people to move between our cities if they can't move once they arrive at their destination. We feel it would be quite proper and in keeping with the spirit of the program, if it were broadened to include the needs of the urban complexes."[105] The change in the road building program advocated by Lindsay would, of course, have required legislation modifying the $41-billion program. Such action was not likely because a Democratic Congress and a Democratic President had no reason to assign a high priority to legislation designed to rescue a floundering Republican. Nevertheless, the suggestion that federal aid was appropriate also had the tendency to shift blame for an eventual fare increase away from the city administration.

Lindsay and Quill Meet

The long-awaited initial encounter between Lindsay and Quill took place in a dimly lit hallway outside the mediators' thirty-ninth floor suite at the Americana Hotel. The mayor-elect asked the TWU president, "Did you have a nice Christmas?" Quill said nothing. "Was Santa Claus good to you?" Lindsay persisted. "There's been a running dispute between Santa Claus and myself," Quill replied, in an obvious reference to Lindsay's role in providing subsidy money for the TA.[106] With only Deputy Mayor-Elect Robert Price at his side, Lindsay spent twenty minutes after lunch at his initial meeting with the top TWU leadership.

At the conclusion of his first day of direct involvement in the transit negotiations, Lindsay appeared tense and uncharacteristically restrained.

After emerging from the sessions, the mayor-elect said he expected the parties to negotiate a "fair and equitable settlement." "I am neither optimistic nor pessimistic about a settlement at this point," Lindsay said. "I am a realist. I am not an expert in labor matters. There are involved human problems here." The cause for Lindsay's concern was not readily apparent. After a cordial interchange with Quill as photographers snapped pictures, the union president offered a parting, "We'll be seeing you as we go along. . . ."[107] As he jumped into the back of his waiting limousine, however, Lindsay's mood was somber. After staring out of the window for several minutes, he finally broke the silence; "This is going to be a bitch," he said.[108]

On Tuesday, December 28, with the tension mounting due to the approaching strike deadline, Michael Quill indicated that there still had been no offer by the TA and that the situation was becoming more critical. "We're shuffling our way into a strike on Saturday morning," Quill asserted. Quill said that the state and federal governments, as well as the city, would have to become involved if adequate funds were to be made available to avert a strike. Both Quill and Joseph O'Grady emphasized that outside financial help would be required to reach an agreement. "It would take a lot of pennies," Quill declared. "I don't think the Transit Authority has enough." O'Grady said he had not, as yet, received any specific assurance of help and indicated that unless financial aid was forthcoming the 15¢ fare could not possibly be maintained.[109]

Also on Tuesday, Lindsay appointed a seven-man committee, headed by Timothy W. Costello, Deputy-Mayor designate, to develop emergency plans for use if a strike materialized. Among the courses of action considered at the initial meeting of this group was a suggestion that doctors ride with radio dispatched police cars to respond to emergency calls. Other ideas included staggering work hours for city personnel and reassigning city employees to areas near their residences. Mayor-Elect Lindsay told the committee he wanted the city-run radio station WNYC to prepare to send out information to the general public. An emergency telephone number was maintained to enable the public to receive strike information. Lindsay also encouraged both private industry and the Board of Education to stagger their hours to avoid everyone being on the roads at the same time. Lindsay told his Traffic Commissioner Henry Barnes to insist publicly that all "nonessential" driving be avoided and that every car on the road "be filled up." Other suggestions kicked around by the committee were that charter buses could be used to transport large groups of workers to and from work, and the possible complete shutdown of the school system. As a Lindsay aide described the initial deliberations of the committee, "The meeting seemed almost unreal. We were trying to prepare ourselves for a crisis [for] which none of us had any previous experience."[110]

After day-long discussions on December 29 over economic issues and working conditions, mediation chairman Feinsinger reported that "an awful lot of ground" was covered. However, with the TWU not willing to modify its original demands estimated by the TA to cost $680 million over a two-year period and with the TA not yet having made an offer, the situation was becoming increasingly ominous. "We're headed for a strike," said Quill, "and the people might as well know it."[111]

Meanwhile, the Transit Authority confirmed that it intended to go into State Supreme Court on the following day in a move to prevent the work stoppage. Sidney Brandes, counsel for the TA, said he would seek a show cause order, asking why an injunction forbidding a strike should not be granted. Brandes indicated the request would be based on both the Condon-Wadlin Act, which forbade strikes by public employees, and on applicable common law of New York State, which also did not permit strikes by employees of a government agency. Quill, however, made it quite clear that the issuance of an injunction would not block a strike. "Injunctions make very poor trackwalkers," he said. "I'm ready to go to jail, if necessary, and" Quill added, "my associates are ready, too."[112]

Clearly, however, the major stumbling block to reaching agreement on a new contract was the question of where the money would come from to pay for a settlement. Although the TA and the TWU were nominally the parties in the dispute, both apparently were looking over their shoulders at Mayor-Elect Lindsay and Governor Rockefeller for commitments of money to help defray the extra costs necessitated by a new contract. When Nathan Feinsinger was asked whether anyone was moving behind the scenes to obtain government aid, he replied, "I'd be mighty surprised if someone was not."[113]

Also on Wednesday, the mayor-elect's Committee on Transit continued to discuss ways to cope with a strike if it materialized. Mayor-Elect Lindsay gave the committee a considerable amount of direction. "I want to assure New Yorkers," he told the group, "that provisions have been taken by the city and all of its departments to handle the situation. I want city government cut back to essential agencies. I want to be certain that only essential industries send their people to work—that would include food, fuel, medical, banks, communications and perhaps one or two others." And even in those "essential industries," Lindsay indicated that as few people as possible, perhaps 50 percent of all personnel should report for work. He also said that taxi companies should be asked to cruise along bus routes and that private car owners should be permitted to use parks for parking areas. Finally, he said he would urge all people who normally drove into the city to use commuter rail and bus lines, instead.[114]

In addition to the attempt by top city officials to formulate an overall plan to cope with a possible strike, individual city departments, private companies, and even groups of citizens were likewise planning their courses of action. The New York City Police Department announced that if a strike occurred, officers would work twelve-hour days, rather than their regular eight, and would be on-duty six days each week. And, anticipating the effect the increased traffic would have on the already legendary demeanor of New York City drivers, police were cautioned to "exercise patience, tact, good judgement and courtesy" and to "allow for extenuating circumstances when dealing with the travelling public." The Department of Hospitals indicated it was ready to cancel all nonemergency functions, such as outpatient clinics, nonemergency surgery, and visits to home-care patients. "This is in the disaster category for us," said a Department of Hospitals' spokesman. "We would be the worst hit by a transit strike," he added. "We're dealing with lives not money."[115]

Chase Manhattan Bank, with 9,500 employees at its main office in downtown Manhattan scheduled seven bus routes in the metropolitan area to transport their employees to work. The bank also planned to ask key employees to sleep on "the many sofas we have in private executive offices" and on cots the bank keeps on hand for civil defense emergencies. In addition, the bank organized car pools, offering to pay drivers 12¢ per mile and reimburse them for tolls. Realizing that parking would not be adequate to absorb all these additional cars, Chase Manhattan instructed drivers who were unable to park to return home and come back at the end of the day to pick up their riders.[116]

The commuter railroads announced that they would add additional service, although they already operated at near capacity during the rush hours. On at least one of the commuter lines, however, the implementation of this plan was uncertain, as the Brotherhood of Railroad Trainmen, representing the Long Island Railroad's employees said it would not engage in "strikebreaking of any kind." Also on Long Island, groups of commuters began chartering buses to bring them to the city, if the strike occurred.[117]

For its part, the New York Times continued to editorially excoriate the TWU and Michael Quill and to offer its suggestions for handling negotiations. As it had done consistently since the naming of the mediation panel, the Times argued that the group should engage in fact-finding. "The only way [Wagner and Lindsay] can get a trustworthy measuring rod is by turning to the three mediators who have steeped themselves in all the intricacies of the dispute and asking them for a report on where equity lies on each issue." However, the Times continued, "the City should be prepared to take a strike rather than capitulate to the unbridled exercise of union power in defiance of the Condon-Wadlin Act and a court injunction.

Mr. Quill cannot be allowed to triumph over the rights of the people of New York."[118]

With just one day remaining before the strike was scheduled, the city's two transit unions walked out of negotiations with the TA and said they would not return until Mayor-Elect Lindsay joined the talks on a continuing basis. TWU President Quill said, "We've terminated the negotiations because nothing has happened . . . we're sick and tired of nonsense. . . . We're demanding that Mayor-Elect Lindsay be seated at the negotiating table for a full eight-hour day," Mr. Quill continued, "and if he doesn't do this the whole transit problem will be solved in the streets of New York."[119] "It's now his baby," concluded Quill. The TWU president was also angered by the fact that the Transit Authority still had not made an offer.

After Quill and the other negotiators walked out, the three members of the TA began what they called a "sit-in" in the bargaining room at the Americana Hotel. They said they wanted to dramatize their willingness to negotiate a fair contract despite what Quill had said. Authority Chairman Joseph O'Grady emphasized that the TA intended to discharge its obligation to bargain in good faith, but that it did not intend to be "blackjacked" by Quill into an unreasonable settlement. "We're prepared to put a money offer on the table when Mr. Quill comes down from that space ship he's in in the clouds," said O'Grady. "It's absolutely ridiculous to expect us to make a proposal against a $680 million demand." The three TA members occupied the vast Albert Hall West in the basement of the Americana Hotel in shifts, sitting at a green-clothed table amid the empty water glasses and pitchers. John Gilhooley seemed particularly pessimistic: "The public doesn't yet realize how serious it is. In the past the cry of 'wolf' was always quieted. The people don't realize that this time it may be the real thing." Gilhooley left at 10:00 p.m. and was replaced by the most recent appointee to the TA, Daniel Scannell, who was to keep the vigil until 4:00 a.m. "I'm the low man on the totem pole," he explained. Scannell brought with him a copy of *The Greek Way* by Edith Hamilton. "Maybe I can find something in mythology," he said, "which will give me a clue to dealing with Mr. Quill. You know, leprechauns and all that," he said, mixing his metaphors.[120]

At a news conference following Quill's ultimatum, Mayor-Elect Lindsay stopped short of capitulating to the demand that he join the bargaining sessions on a regular basis. Instead, he announced only that he would meet with the mediation panel on Friday morning, December 31, and that he would decide on his course of action at that time. Quill, however, interpreted the Lindsay statement somewhat differently, suggesting that the incoming mayor had been dragged into the negotiations by the union's action. Until that time, said Quill, Lindsay had acted "like a babe in the woods" in the dispute, but he added that he was looking forward to regular meetings with the mayor-elect.[121]

In a public statement issued on December 30, the mediation panel, summarizing the course of negotiations to date, was highly critical of both the TA and the unions. They said, "Despite two months of bargaining, not one single change has been made in the original positions of the parties on any issue involving the expenditure of money.... The Unions cannot expect to achieve the totality of their demands. The Transit Authority cannot refuse to come forward with a money offer. The time for fencing has passed. The time for action is now."[122]

The mediators were genuinely concerned about the lack of progress being made in negotiations. Traditionally, Michael Quill and Joseph O'Grady worked out a settlement privately, but this time things were different. "I don't know what's going on," O'Grady told one of the mediators. "I can't get a thing out of Quill." The TWU president, however, reassured the mediator, "We've never had a strike, what are you worried about?" During the negotiations, however, Quill did not seem to want to settle the dispute. "On the last days before the strike," said the mediator, "we couldn't get a damn thing out of Quill. He would sit there without saying a word to us, except that the union wasn't deviating from its position."[123]

Meanwhile, Mayor Wagner removed himself from the strike controversy with the explanation, "From now on, it's the responsibility of the Transit Authority, the mediators, the unions, and the mayor-elect."[124] Earlier in the day, the TA obtained a show-cause order in State Supreme Court calling upon TWU President Quill and other officers of the union to explain why an injunction forbidding a strike should not be granted. The order was returnable the following day. The TA's petition asked the court to restrain Quill, the TWU, nine other union officers, and "all other persons acting in concert with them" from "instigating" or "carrying on" a work stoppage or otherwise interfering with transit operations. The TA argued before Supreme Court Justice Owen McGivern that a transit strike would have a "chaotic effect" and cause "irreparable loss" and charged that the threatened strike would violate both applicable common law of New York State and the Condon-Wadlin Act.[125]

When he heard of the court action, Quill quickly brushed aside the possibility that a strike might be blocked by a court order, recalling that the TWU had previously struck the Pennsylvania Railroad in defiance of an injunction.[126] Later in the day, before a huge television audience, the TWU president dramatically ripped up the show-cause order and announced that it would have no effect. "We have respect for the law," Quill stated, "but we are not going to have our union destroyed. If we rot in jail, our second line of leadership will come up."[127] Although Quill's behavior was startling and served to indicate his view of the court's action, it was not contemptible in the legal sense. He could have incurred a possible contempt citation only if he failed to appear for the scheduled hearing, or if he would have refused to comply with any restraining order issued against him as a result of the hearing.

With an apparent lack of progress being made in negotiations, the city stepped up its preparations to deal with the impact of a strike. Mayor-Elect Lindsay urged New Yorkers not to drive their cars into the city in the event the strike materialized. He also asked key business executives who lived in the suburbs to move into the city for the duration of the strike. "It is vital," Lindsay said, "that the flow of people into and within the City of New York be reduced to a minimum pending observance of the effect of the transit stoppage on traffic conditions."[128] He asked further that deliveries to the business districts be made during the night and off-hours and that employers work out "reasonable" staggered working schedules.

In some cases, employers were making plans to have their workers sleep at their places of business so that commuting would not be necessary. Columbia University said it had prepared a student dormitory for its maintenance men, and Hertz Rent All indicated a large bank had rented fifty roll-away beds. In other instances, enterprises decided simply to close. Most of the colleges within the city university system concluded that because virtually all of their students were commuters, attempting to stay open during a strike would be foolhardy.[129]

The mediators spent most of the day on December 31, as they had the previous two, attempting to get the unions to lower their demands and to get the TA to make a formal offer. But both sides held off during the day, apparently waiting for Lindsay to disclose how much money was available to subsidize the TA. Early in the day, Lindsay visited the Americana Hotel for discussions with the mediators. Then, at 12:38 p.m., the mayor-elect sat down for a joint session with the TA and the two unions. The atmosphere could certainly not be described as cordial. At the outset of the meeting, the mayor-elect, according to an aide, "looking strained but stern," urged both parties to "settle the dispute in the public interest." "The union has waited until the 11th hour," Lindsay charged.[130] At that point, as Quill charac-terized his own remarks, "We spoke to him in very strong language. . . . You wanted this job and you're here for the duration," Quill quoted himself as saying to Lindsay. "I told the Mayor to grow up and cease being a juvenile, and I don't think he appreciated that. Running New York City is a man-sized job," Quill stated.[131] "That's a lie that we waited until the last hour," Quill added. "We still haven't got a legitimate offer from the Transit

Authority. I say you are telling us a deliberate lie."[132] Then indicating that
he held Lindsay responsible for the TA not having made an offer, Quill
bellowed, "We'll take no more bubkes from a schmuck like you." The
Yiddish obscenity, brogue and all, caused Lindsay to seethe but he "kept his
cool." After sitting quietly through Quill's denunciations, Lindsay replied
simply, "Well, that was a nice statement from the union. Now let's hear
from the other side."[133]

About forty minutes after it started, Quill left the meeting briefly to
hold a hallway news conference in which he heaped further abuse on
Lindsay. Before he left the meeting, however, Quill cautioned mediation
chairman Feinsinger not to let "that pipsqueak" leave the building,
referring to the man who twelve hours later would be the mayor of New
York City.[134]

In Quill's absence, Lindsay engaged in talks with the mediators and the
TA members as they had lunch together in the mayor-elect's suite on the
forty-ninth floor of the Americana Hotel. During this encounter, Lindsay
for the first time indicated to the TA that about $7 million would be
available to subsidize transit operations.[135]

At 3:30 p.m., a considerably more subdued Quill, accompanied by the
rest of the negotiators for the TWU and the Amalgamated Transit Union
joined the talks in Lindsay's suite. At this session, Feinsinger asked the
TWU to make the first move and reduce its demands as a way of getting
discussions moving, but Quill refused. Quill indicated that there had been
"absolutely no progress" and that there was still no offer to the union from
the TA.[136]

With no headway being made in negotiations, Lindsay announced that
he had to leave for a while to go down to City Hall to be sworn in as mayor.
The ever-combative Quill told Lindsay, "You can get any kind of judge to
come up here and swear you in. There's enough people here to swear in
anybody."[137] Quill threatened to break off the talks if Lindsay left the
room. Despite the threat, Lindsay departed from the Americana at
5:10 p.m. to go to City Hall. There, in a private ceremony at 6:04 p.m., in
the presence of Mrs. Lindsay, their children, and a few close friends,
Lindsay was officially sworn in by Supreme Court Justice William C.
Hecht, Jr. Viewing the ceremony, which lasted a scant six minutes, were two
top officials in the Liberal party and Lindsay's closest advisors in the transit
negotiations: David Dubinsky, president of the ILGWU, and Alex Rose,
head of the United Hatters Union.

In his brief remarks following the swearing in, Lindsay said New York
"was a very great city" and indicated that he looked forward to the job of
mayor. After expressing gratitude to those who had helped him he said that
he would immediately return to the transit negotiations with the "hope that

the best interests of the city" will be served.[138] Before returning to the negotiations, however, Lindsay was required to sign an official registry after which he was asked for the usual 15¢ fee that goes to the city. Embarrassed, Lindsay realized that he had no money. He turned to Robert Price, one of his two deputy-mayors, who also was penniless. They finally borrowed the 15¢ from a reporter.

John Vliet Lindsay

> Lindsay's face, stature, accent—even his faint trace of stiffness and the lack of visceral pleasure in the human pursuits of his profession—give most observers an impression of aristocracy. His presence suggests that they see before them the scion of a family of great wealth and longstanding social position—another of those financially-free young questers for public office who have been seeking preferment because they can afford to live without earning money, and to devote themselves to others.... It must be recognized, however, in any fair account of Lindsay, that while he looks wealthy and acts wealthy, he is not wealthy; and he most definitely does not find himself financially free to do whatever he wants.[139]

Although not personally rich nor descended from a long-established *Social Register* family, John Lindsay was raised in the world of Manhattan aristocrats and came to share many of their attributes and perceptions of the world. The grandson of a brick manufacturer who emigrated to the United States after his business on the Isle of Wight went bankrupt, Lindsay was born on Manhattan's West Side in 1921. Lindsay's father did not finish high school and at age fifteen he became a runner on Wall Street.[140] Continuing to work in the financial district during the day, George Lindsay eventually attended New York University Law School at night. Like many lawyers of his time, he did not attend an undergraduate college.[141] He eventually became a vice president of Bancamerica-Blair Corporation, a firm which failed during the 1920s. At that point, George Lindsay turned his attention to international finance and international insurance operations, becoming president of the Swiss America Corporation. In addition, he was a member of the boards of a number of insurance companies and was elected chairman of District 13 of the National Association of Securities Dealers (NASD), a governor of NASD, and a governor of the Investment Bankers Association. When he died in 1961, George Lindsay left an estate of approximately $750,000, which was divided among his four sons and one daughter.[142]

Although he had received a relatively modest inheritance and obviously had to work for a living, John Lindsay had enjoyed a financially comfortable and very privileged boyhood. As his father achieved financial success, the elder Lindsay was able to move his family to the prestigious East Side, to send his children to the most highly regarded schools, and to be included in the *Social Register*. Perhaps overcompensating for his own lack of educational distinction, George Lindsay enrolled his children in the very best schools. Lindsay was initially sent to the Buckley School, regarded by many as the best, and certainly the most exclusive, of New York's private East Side schools. From Buckley, Lindsay went to St. Paul's, an exclusive preparatory school in Concord, New Hampshire. He then matriculated at Yale University in 1940. However, with the entry of the United States into World War II, Lindsay accelerated his studies by taking seven or eight courses at a time and graduated in fewer than three years. He majored in history and wrote his undergraduate thesis on Oliver Cromwell.

Outside the classroom, Lindsay's closest contacts were with members of the social elite. Six fraternity houses, for eating only, were present at Yale, and Lindsay became a member of the Fence Club, "which Yale cognoscenti agreed was the most desirable socially." He was also asked to join the Scroll and Key, one of the two principal senior societies, "whose activities are so secret that only their members are reputed to understand whether or not they are significant."[143] Of Lindsay's five roommates at Yale, one was a Rockefeller.

Receiving his bachelor's degree in 1943, Lindsay entered the U.S. Navy where he served as a gunnery officer and later executive officer of the destroyer, *Swanson*. He saw action in the Mediterranean Sea, where he took part in the invasion of Sicily, and he also served in the Southwest Pacific and the Western Pacific. Lindsay was discharged early in 1946 as a full lieutenant with five battle stars. Immediately after discharge, he entered Yale University Law School; and by staying in school through two summers, Lindsay was able to graduate in two years.

Lindsay met his wife, Mary, when he was in law school, and she was a student at Vassar College. Before their marriage in 1949, she taught first grade at private schools in Providence, Rhode Island, and in New York City. By 1965, they had four children: Katherine, 14; Margaret, 11; Anne, 9; and John, Jr., 5. As a family, their interests reflected the Ivy League-Sister Schools backgrounds of the parents: they went to the theater and ballet, and played tennis, skied, and sailed together. The children all attended private schools and continued to do so, despite the criticism engendered when Lindsay announced his candidacy for mayor. The Lindsays were hard pressed to understand why working people would perceive sending your children to private schools as being elitist. As Mary Lindsay explained, "I said at the very beginning—and I even said it on the *Today Show*—that our children have always been in private schools, and when we came back to New York, there was never any question that they'd stop going to private schools."[144]

In a similar vein, the Lindsays could not understand why most working-class New Yorkers who had never seen a Broadway play would criticize them for being theater buffs. "Do you know," Mary Lindsay asked incredulously, "that we get letters criticizing John because he goes to the theater once in a while?" Mrs. Lindsay could not understand the criticism; "It's not only a pleasant respite for us, but everytime he goes, it shows people in the theater how interested he is. . . . Why, the theater industry is one of the largest contributors to the city's economy—and there are also the taxis and restaurants. I think it's important that the mayor is interested in the theater."[145] It was, of course, this image of rich people in elegant dress, taking taxies to the theater and then going to eat in a swank restaurant, that caused resentment in many working-class New Yorkers.

Also reflecting his background, Lindsay was most comfortable with his social "equals" and with those he perceived to be "worthy" of his help. This latter sensitivity puzzled many, including some close Lindsay observers: ". . . he has another quality that impresses but puzzles me—the fact that he cares very deeply about things you wouldn't have expected him to care about. Like civil rights and what it's like to be poor. He didn't grow up in East New York or Bedford Stuyvesant. . . . Anyway, I've watched him with people, and that concern of his is real. That's why he can communicate with Negroes and Puerto Ricans on a nonverbal level."[146] Likely the product of his rigorous Episcopalian upbringing and the sense of social responsibility associated with this background, Lindsay was truly concerned about the plight of blacks and the poor. In accepting the Bishop's Cross for Distinguished Service from the Episcopal Bishop of New York, Lindsay was particularly at ease, talking "somberly of the alienated poor and called on his fellow Episcopalians to show the way in humanitarian conduct."[147]

Lindsay tended to be brusque and insensitive, however, to those who did not share his concerns. As a Lindsay supporter said, "I've . . . been disappointed—amazed, really—at the attitude of Lindsay and some of those immediately around him. I mean self-righteousness, arrogance, claims to omniscience. He comes on as if he's bearing the white man's burden. With him, it's a matter of noblesse oblige rather than facing people as people."[148]

In a particularly perceptive analysis, Richard Whalen caught the messianic basis of the Lindsay personality: "He is wholly in earnest. A rather tense, tightly wound activist, he frequently cracks jokes, but his humor is studied and merely underlies the intensity of his determination. He is moved by a moral impulse, which is at once a source of his appeal and a potential weakness."[149]

This tense personality, not infrequently, exploded. To a television reporter who was interviewing him outside a church during the 1965 campaign in a manner Lindsay considered offensive, he replied, "You don't know what you're talking about, you son-of-a-bitch. Don't try to interview me again."[150] At a rally in Queens, Lindsay was heckled and called a Communist. He shouted back, "You're finks. You're fairies. Fairies!"[151] And finally, also during the mayoral campaign, Lindsay, told by his twin brother, David, that he was giving unsatisfactory answers to public questions, snapped, "Only the candidate has the right to shout in this room. Do you want to sit in my chair Dave? Will you take my place Dave, and explain what you will substitute for the sales tax? Will you?"[152]

For graduates of Yale Law School in the immediate post-World War II years, two career paths predominated. Some gravitated toward government employment, while others took jobs with large Wall Street firms.[153] Following the path of his older brother, George, who had graduated from law school a year earlier, Lindsay decided on a career in private practice. In the fall of 1948, he joined the New York law firm of Webster, Sheffield and Horan. The senior partner of the firm, Bethuel Webster, was extremely interested in politics and was a sort of "senior advisor" to the Manhattan Republican Party. Webster was known as a "political thinker of incorruptible principle," and, in a sense, Lindsay became his protege.[154]

Soon after Lindsay became affiliated with the law firm, he also joined the Republican Club for the Ninth Assembly District of New York County. This was an area on the East Side of Manhattan known as the Silk Stocking District, an appelation given when silk stockings were associated with wealth and status. He also became a member of the Young Republican Club in 1948, and four years later he was elected president of the organization. Lindsay was one of the founders of the Youth for Eisenhower movement and then became extremely active in the Eisenhower campaign against Adlai Stevenson in 1952.[155] As a result of this involvement, in 1954, Eisenhower's Attorney General Herbert Brownell, whom Lindsay had known from his days at Yale, asked him to become his executive assistant. Lindsay spent 1955 and 1956 in this capacity, where he was in charge of the preparation of a voting rights bill and other pieces of legislation. He also served as the Justice Department's liason with Congress, the White House, and the Cabinet. In addition, the young lawyer argued cases before the Supreme Court. In December 1956, however, Lindsay resigned from the Justice Department to return to his New York City law firm.

Having had a taste of political life in Washington, in April 1958,

Lindsay decided to challenge the incumbent, Frederic R. Caudert, for the Republican nomination for the Seventeenth Congressional District. Caudert, a six-term Congressman had had close races in 1954 and 1956 in what had been considered to be a safe Republican District. In announcing his candidacy for Congress in the federal Silk Stocking District, Lindsay was quite critical of Caudert: "We have not seen the type of agressive leadership needed in Congress to carry forward the Eisenhower program."[156] Caudert, however, decided not to run again, and the "regular" Republican organization put up Elliot Goodwin to meet Lindsay's insurgent candidacy. Lindsay defeated Goodwin in the primary, and in the general election defeated Anthony B. Akers, the man who had almost beaten Caudert in 1954 and 1956. Lindsay beat Akers by 7,718 votes, a considerably larger margin than the 312 vote edge Caudert had enjoyed over Akers in 1956.

Lindsay was then returned to Congress with increasingly larger margins. In 1960 he defeated his Democratic opponent, William Vanden Heuvel by 26,148 votes (59 percent). Then, despite a redistricting that produced a Democratic edge in registrants, Lindsay in 1962 defeated his Democratic-Liberal opponent Martin Dworkis by a 53,296 vote margin (68.7 percent). In 1964, Lindsay beat his Democratic-Liberal oppoenent Eleanor French by a 91,274 vote margin (71.5 percent). Lindsay's plurality in this election was the greatest of any opposed Republican Congressional candidate in the country. The victory was even more significant because Democratic presidential candidate Lyndon Johnson carried the 17th District by receiving 71.8 percent of the votes.

On his election to Congress, Lindsay was named to the House Judiciary Committee, which allowed him to play a major role in the drafting of civil rights legislation. In the first week of his Congressional career, Lindsay introduced a set of bills to deal with crimes of violence aimed at intimidating federal officers in the performance of their duties. Such legislation was intended to protect such officials in enforcing civil rights laws. In 1960, he supported the Civil Rights Act and the Constitutional amendment banning poll taxes in federal elections. He criticized the latter, however, for not covering state and local elections; "If we're going to have a constitutional amendment, let's have a meaningful one," he argued. Lindsay frequently urged President John F. Kennedy to sign an Executive Order ending discrimination in federally assisted housing and later was one of the House floor managers for the 1964 Civil Rights Act.[157]

Lindsay's two other main Congressional concerns were civil liberties and the arts. In 1959, he opposed a bill to grant the Postmaster General the power to impound allegedly obscene material. He opposed an administration supported bill in 1962 that dealt with "security risks" because he felt it did not provide for fair hearings or adequate appeal to the courts. He also

consistently opposed the use of listening devices, lie detector tests and
similar means used by the government to obtain information. In 1963,
Lindsay introduced a bill to establish a federal Council on the Arts.
President Kennedy, however, established such a council by Executive
Order before the Lindsay measure could be acted upon.[158]

Such positions made Lindsay extremely popular in the 17th Congressional District, as the increasing margins of his victories attest. The Silk
Stocking District and John Lindsay were a perfect match. The district was
generally conceded to be the most "elegant" in the United States,
encompassing the United Nations, Times Square, Central Park, Rockefeller Center, Greenwich Village, the Empire State Building, as well as the
city's principal theaters, hotels, shops, and restaurants. In addition, it
served as the home of the nation's advertising, publishing, and television
industries. The residents of the district certainly did not represent a cross-
section of America. Nearly one-half of the households consisted of single
people; four out of five homes contained only one or two people. Five out
of six residents were older than twenty-one, and nine out of ten were white.
The district included many of the nation's most familiar names in literature,
the arts, entertainment, finance, philanthropy, and politics. "I represent
brains," Lindsay had observed.[159]

As only one member of Congress, his constituents did not blame
Lindsay if his own views did not prevail. To enhance his popularity, it was
enough that he supported the "correct" positions. As one Lindsay watcher
pointed out, "Living in a section of New York City which was proud of its
sophistication, his constituents were happy that their Congressman stood
up against reaction. Lindsay's important contribution was made primarily
in standing up and discussing the issues. . . ."[160] Furthermore, as a member
of the minority party, he was not needed by his leadership to provide crucial
votes in favor of issues to which he was indifferent or possibly opposed. As
the "representative of one of the most favored districts in the nation,
needing nothing from Washington in the form of a military base, crop
supports, or special treatment, he did not require favors in return for favors
he might have had to grant over his scruples."[161]

Chapter 4

"A Juvenile, a Lightweight, and a Pipsqueak"

At virtually the same time that John V. Lindsay was being inaugurated as mayor, State Supreme Court Justice George Tilzer temporarily enjoined the TWU and the Amalgamated Transit Union from striking. In his ruling, Judge Tilzer said:

> This threat hangs ominously over the lifeline of all the citizens of the City of New York, and should a strike actually be called at 5:00 a.m., as threatened, general paralysis of the activities of the inhabitants of this city will ultimately ensue.
>
> The effect of a strike of these essential services would tragically and disastrously affect the people of the City of New York. . . . The staggering effects of a strike at this time on the inhabitants of this city by far outweigh the rights of these defendents.[1]

Sidney Brandes, the counsel for the TA, in arguing the case said that the strike would be illegal and would do "irrevocable damage to the people of the city." The union lawyers, Louis Waldman and John F. O'Donnell, contended that the Condon-Wadlin Act was no longer in effect because Governor Rockefeller had vetoed legislative proposals to amend the law. The union lawyers also charged that the transit workers were the victims of "submission to political pressures." Judge Tilzer commented during a recess in the hearings, "If the fear of God was as great as the fear of Quill and his union, we'd have a better world."[2]

Shortly after 9:00 p.m. on New Year's Eve, Quill emerged from what he said was the final meeting of his 1,000 member committee in the Americana Hotel with the warning: "Only a miracle can bring about a settlement tonight, and I personally don't believe in miracles." Then, using a transit metaphor, he emphasized that the "wheels of the strike" were already in motion and that it would be difficult to stop them. He also reaffirmed his intention of defying the injunction against striking. "If they want the body in jail," Quill said, "they can have it. We have five teams to carry on the strike."[3] Asked if his personal dislike for Mayor Lindsay had contributed to the lack of progress in negotiations, Quill replied, "I have no dislike for him. But I don't think he knows what it's all about. In our talks with him he sits and stares and looks over my head."[4]

While Quill was meeting with his committee, the TA, with Lindsay's promise of a $7-million subsidy now in hand, fashioned a $25-million package.[5] The total package included wage increases of 3.2 percent for each of the two years of the contract, the limit under the guidelines established by the president's Council of Economic Advisors. At 8:00 p.m., the package was disclosed to the mediators, but the TA refused to present the offer to the unions until the TWU reduced its demands. At this juncture, Lindsay asked the mediators for a recess to caucus with the TA members, who appeared to be unwilling to make their offer public. Moving to an adjoining conference room, the mayor-elect told Joseph O'Grady, "We have to have your offer. We have no alternative."[6] After conferring with his two colleagues on the Authority, O'Grady agreed to offer the $25-million package to the union. When the TA chairman finally put the package on the table, it was immediately met with an outbreak of derisive laughter from Quill and the other union negotiators.

Now close to midnight, Quill turned hostile. Leaning on his blackhorn cane, with his face a bright red, he pointed his finger at Lindsay and shouted, "You are nothing but a juvenile, a lightweight, and a pipsqueak. You have to grow up. You don't know anything about the working class. You don't know anything about labor unions."[7] As Quill delivered his scathing attack, an aide sitting next to him observed Lindsay's face pale, and his jaw tighten and begin to twitch slightly. When Quill had finally vented his anger and sat down, Lindsay rose slowly. "I don't mind your words about me personally," he said, "You are entitled to your own opinion. But I will not have you addressing the office of the mayor that way. It is an affront to the people of the City of New York."[8] With the clock having just struck midnight, Lindsay was indeed now officially the mayor.

"Mr. Quill, distinguished New Yorkers," Lindsay continued, looking now at the crowd of union members and their wives sitting behind the TWU president,

> I call upon you and all of your members not to walk out on your city. This is a city which is on its knees. We have obligations. You have an obligation to your members. I have an obligation to eight million people. A strike will create great personal hardships for everyone. It will have a disastrous

effect on the city's major life functions. I am inheriting a bankrupt city with a multitude of problems. I therefore call upon you in the public interest to respect the city in which you live and all of its eight million inhabitants. I am asking you to extend this contract long enough for me to pull the show together. I am asking you to come to my suite of rooms and spend the night negotiating this matter. We have an obligation to stretch ourselves.[9]

Quill's response was relatively calm: "We do not agree with you that the city is bankrupt. We do not think that the city is as bad as you say it is. I would urge you to stop campaigning. The election is over, Mr. Lindsley [sic]. I am not going to turn it down here. Although I can tell you I intend to recommend that it be turned down. We are not going to stay here all night. This is lunacy." Quill then rose, saying that "It is after midnight. And I tell you as the Mayor of New York that there is a transit strike. As far as I'm concerned, the strike is as good as on." Quill then left the room. Lindsay, apparently stunned by the turn of events sat quietly for a full minute after Quill's departure.[10]

Quill, by this time, was in front of the television cameras, telling reporters, "The strike is on." Someone shoved what appeared to be a legal paper in front of him. He glanced at the paper briefly and said, "If this is the injunction, I might as well go all the way." Then he tore the paper into pieces. Finally, before leaving the Americana Hotel, Quill said, "We've worked a long day today. At 10 o'clock in the morning we'll look at the peanut package that was put on the table at this late hour and after that—if we're not in jail—we'll discuss the situation."[11] Joseph O'Grady, the TA chairman, said he was "flabbergasted" by the sudden collapse of negotiations. He indicated that he felt the $25-million offer was a good one and certainly was the basis for further bargaining until the previously announced 5:00 a.m. deadline. Concerning possible efforts to operate the transit system in spite of the strike, O'Grady was unequivocal. "It would be most dangerous and foolhardy," he said. "Any accident could cost many lives."[12]

Nathan Feinsinger, who appeared as stunned as Lindsay by the sudden collapse of negotiations said that the mediation panel would continue its efforts to get the disputants back to the bargaining table. "It is a tough situation," Feinsinger said, "but I think with God's help we will get this thing back on the track."[13]

Some observers were of the opinion that a strike would have been called regardless of the size of the TA's final offer. As the TA's Daniel Scannell observed, "There were serious internal problems in the union that led to the strike. The members were restless. Quill had been labeled a paper tiger by the newspapers and television reports. He believed that a weekend strike would help deal with these problems."[14]

The TWU may indeed have "needed" a strike, but, in the final hours, Lindsay certainly did nothing to diffuse the volatile situation. Rather than attempting to quietly get together with top TWU leaders at this time to try to work out a settlement, Lindsay instead chose to lecture them in front of the union's bargaining committee. There is no question that by this stage in negotiations, the TWU leaders deeply resented both Lindsay's personal style and his lack of sophistication in labor relations matters.

The top TWU negotiators viewed Lindsay's lecture to be indicative of his overall condescending attitude toward them. As the union's Ellis Van Riper observed, "He just couldn't get away from his 'I am God' attitude" and telling us we "had to settle because it was in the public interest."[15] Edward Herlihy, who would later become one of Lindsay's top labor advisors, confirmed this assessment, "Lindsay looked down on blue collar workers, and Mike Quill picked up on this right away."[16]

In addition, Lindsay was completely insensitive to the "political" needs of the union leadership and failed to recognize that a major function of negotiations was to "sell" the contract to the union's bargaining committee. "Lindsay is not aware of the need for face savers," observed one expert. "The idea of making a union leader look good is anathema to him."[17] Instead, the mayor lectured the leaders in front of their 100-member stewards group. As the TWU's John O'Connell described Lindsay's lack of sophistication in labor matters, "He had a smattering of knowledge about labor relations from his college studies," but he was "as green as the grass in front of City Hall.... He was like a guy who had read a book about swimming," O'Connell continued, "but had never gone in the water."[18]

The TA's Daniel Scannell described the way he felt negotiations should have proceded in the final hours. "Quill's technique was brinksmanship. He would go to the eve of the strike deadline and then in a private meeting he would let the mediators know what he wanted.... The only real function of the public sessions," added Scannell, "was to blunt the appetites of the stewards."[19] Rather than attempting to prop up the union leadership in front of their bargaining committee, Lindsay sought to publicly undercut them. As the TWU's Matthew Guinan explained why such an approach was doomed to failure, "You can't negotiate with a 100-man policy committee. When it comes down to it, you must conclude the package behind closed doors.... It's the same with diplomatic negotiations," Guinan added, "in the sense that everything can't be done above board." Guinan summed up Lindsay's attempt to avoid closed door meetings as being "immature."[20]

Although from a bargaining perspective, Lindsay may well have been naive, he viewed transit negotiations primarily from the perspective of an image conscious politician. And from this vantage point, events were going relatively well. Negotiations were receiving considerable media coverage, locally and nationally, and in Quill, Lindsay was squaring off against a protagonist who had spent a lifetime alienating the "public." In the cursory news accounts being presented, Lindsay was portrayed as a white knight, standing up against an unreasonable union. For a media-oriented politician who needed to attract supporters to his image rather than relying on party "regulars," this was a stunning achievement.

In a brief televised appearance at the Americana Hotel, Lindsay, now the mayor of New York, made it clear that he would do his utmost to reconvene the negotiating sessions. Described by the *New York Times* as looking "haggard and shaken,"[21] Lindsay read a brief statement:

> As you may know by now, negotiations between the Transport Workers Union and the Transit Authority have broken down. It appears certain that there will be a subway strike beginning at 5:00 a.m. this morning. It is my hope that this dispute can still be speedily resolved and normal transit service soon restored. I have urged all parties in the negotiations to continue vigorous efforts toward achieving a prompt and reasonable settlement to get on with the job of constructive collective bargaining. I must also ask the public's cooperation in surmounting the hardships that will now be imposed.[22]

By 1:40 a.m., Lindsay had arrived at City Hall. Twenty minutes later, before a barrage of television and radio equipment set up in the Blue Room across the hall from the mayor's office, he conducted his first full-scale press conference. The primary thrust of Lindsay's comments was to outline a series of emergency measures aimed at lessening the impact of the strike. He requested the cooperation of the public in overcoming the hardships of a strike, and asked that all "nonessential automobile trips" into Manhattan and the business districts of the other boroughs be curtailed. When the full brunt of the strike was felt on Monday, Lindsay observed, "Under the best of circumstances, only 25 percent of those who normally come to Manhattan will be able to do so." The mayor defined "essential" employees as those who provide food, medical services and other essentials; those requested by employers to come in for essential work; and those individuals who would suffer "extreme hardship" if they did not report for work. For those employees who did need to report for work, Lindsay requested that they try to arrive before 8:00 a.m., "fill up the cars," and arrange to have someone take the cars out of the conjested areas quickly. Finally, appealing to the "spirit of self-control and cooperation" of New Yorkers, he pledged to do his utmost to settle "this unfortunate disruption as quickly as possible."[23]

Despite all the requests for cooperation and forbearance, however, it was clear, even before the transit system screeched to a halt, that New Yorkers attempting to deal with the impact of the strike were caught between the proverbial "rock and a hard place." Most Broadway theaters, for example, announced on New Year's Eve that in keeping with theater tradition the show would go on during the strike. Any patrons unable to reach the theater, however, would not be issued a refund or permitted to exchange their tickets for a later performance. Similarly, the Metropolitan Opera and Lincoln Center indicated that unless a performance was cancelled, in most instances, those unable to attend would not receive a refund.[24]

Conspicuous by his absence as the strike deadline approached was Robert F. Wagner, who on the morning of his final day as mayor boarded a flight for Acapulco, Mexico. At Kennedy Airport, Wagner insisted, "There's nothing I can do at this stage, . . . what they need the Mayor for is commitments beginning tomorrow, particularly in money." Later at the Mexico City airport, Wagner noted that in his talks the previous evening with Joseph O'Grady, the TA chairman had indicated that the settlement hinged on "where the money is going to come from." Wagner observed, "The principal role of the Mayor is to provide the money, and I can't commit the next administration. I assume they are sitting down to negotiations now, and I hope the two sides can arrange a settlement."[25]

In its final editorial written before the beginning of the strike, the New York Times continued its unremitting castigation of Michael Quill, writing, "The holiday weekend delays the calamitous impact of his [Quill's] irresponsibility for a little while; but it makes no more conscionable the vesting in one union czar of such power to damage the community in defiance of law and court orders." Then, returning to the advice it had consistently offered Lindsay, the Times called for a "demonstration by Mr. Lindsay that the city will not capitulate to such tyranny by granting such wage increases and other concessions beyond those justified by economic reality." The Times concluded by implicitly urging the conversion of the mediation board to a fact-finding panel: "the recommendation of the three expert mediators . . . represent the only dependable guideline to a fair settlement. Anything more would be appeasement."[26]

Early on New Year's Eve, Quill appeared on a radio station owned by the Times to answer the stations editorials, which were also highly critical of the TWU. Quill charged that since Lindsay's election on November 2, the Times had printed seventeen editorials on the transit situation, more than had appeared on Vietnam. "We are not going to allow the editor of the

Times, John B. Oakes, to make policy for us," he said.[27]

By this point in the negotiations the "angle" the news media were using to portray the reality of bargaining was that Lindsay had the guts to stand up to Quill and not appease the TWU as was the case in previous negotiations. To succeed politically, all Lindsay need do was to make sure that this good versus evil condensation symbol continued to be reflected in the media.

The job of putting the transit system "to bed" in the early morning hours of the new year, was accomplished very smoothly. The last train brought to a halt was an IRT Seventh Avenue express which arrived at the 241st Street terminal at 8:02 a.m., more than three hours after the strike officially began. A spokesman for the TA said that the striking motormen, conductors and bus operators had "cooperated completely" in taking their trains and buses to designated storage locations. Most of the subway cars were stored in stations and tunnels rather than in storage yards to avoid "the danger of freezups in the yards should a winter storm strike," explained a TA spokesman. With all of the subway stations closed, a transit police lieutenant wondered about the fate of "all the ladies with shopping bags" who depend on the subway system to take care of their most basic human needs. "There's one who does her laundry in the ladies room in the IND station at Lexington Avenue and 53rd Street," explained the lieutenant, adding, "she complains when too many people come in."[28]

After concluding his 2:00 a.m. news conference at City Hall on New Year's morning, Lindsay took a nap on a couch in the basement beneath his City Hall office. At about 6:00 a.m., the mayor was told that the media would appreciate some comments about his plans for dealing with the strike. The strike story had unquestionably become a major media event, with more than fifty members of the press and electronic media present. Complementing the local group of newspaper, radio, and television news people were a significant number of national, and even some international, correspondents. When asked what his plans were, Lindsay replied, "I'm going up to the Roosevelt Hotel [where he was currently living] to shave and shower, have some cornflakes, see my children and kiss my wife."[29]

The transit negotiations reconvened on New Year's Day, but after a full day of bargaining they adjourned without any report of progress. The mediators met separately with the unions and the TA, adjourning for the day at 6:30 p.m. Quill said later that he had received no further monetary offer from the TA beyond the $25-million package previously put forth. As he emerged from the talks, Quill was served with a court order directing him to appear in State Supreme Court on Monday, January 3, 1966 to show cause why he should not be punished for violating an injunction against the strike. The order had been signed about an hour earlier by Justice Owen McGivern, at the request of the Transit Authority. At a news conference afterwards, Quill said, "No matter what judges and juries do, we will not withdraw one penny from our demands."[30] Even if he and the other top union leaders were jailed, Quill maintained, second-line leaders would take over the direction of the strike. "Our loyalty," the union president continued, "is to 36,000 dues paying members. Outside of that we have no further loyalties." Despite the injunction, Quill emphasized, the strike would remain "in full force and effect" and the union was "strengthening our picket lines for Monday morning."[31]

Speaking at the very time that Mayor Lindsay was delivering his inaugural address on the steps of City Hall, Quill blamed the strike on Lindsay and on the man who was "dictating" to him, identified by Quill as the editorial page editor of the *Times*, John B. Oakes. "He [the Mayor] made such an ass of himself yesterday for 15 hours," said Mr. Quill, "that between him and John B. Oakes, the people of New York City now have a strike."[32] The role of Oakes in negotiations was discussed at some length by Edward Costikyan: "Day after day Oakes publicly instructed Lindsay, whose election was largely the result of the *Times'* daily editorial support, on how to deal with the threatened strike. Some say that Abe Raskin, another *Times* editorial writer (who has been called the unofficial Secretary of Labor of the Lindsay government) is the author of the *Times'* labor views. But whoever is author, Oakes has adopted and declared them."[33]

Later, Quill said that he saw no reason to have Lindsay participate in the mediation sessions. "We explored his mind yesterday," he stated, "and we found nothing."[34] The TWU president then predicted a long strike unless the TA increased its "peanut package." "Our strikes usually run 28 or 29 days," he said, basing his estimate on his union's recent experience in Philadelphia. "I don't think a strike for a couple of weeks would be a catastrophe," said Quill, unable to suppress a slight smile, recalling that "London withstood the blitz."[35]

After a ninety-minute respite at his temporary residence at the Roosevelt Hotel, Mayor Lindsay was back at City Hall, preparing for an 11:00 a.m. news conference and his inaugural speech to be delivered that evening. As he worked, Lindsay's spirits were buoyed by a number of telegrams of support, one of which read, "Roses are red, pickles are dill; let us hail our new mayor, and the hell with Quill."[36] After crossing the hall from his office, Mayor Lindsay could barely squeeze his way into the Blue Room, which was jammed with reporters. In a prepared statement, the mayor indicated a dual orientation; he would concern himself with settling the strike and running the city during the crisis. "My primary interest, as your Mayor," he said, "is to restore your city to normalcy as quickly as possible with as little inconvenience as possible to you and your families." Lindsay restated that beginning on Monday, January 3, no one should travel into Manhattan or the business districts of Brooklyn, Queens, or the Bronx unless "he is engaged in the critical activities of providing food, fuel, or medical services" or "has been requested to do so by his employer because his presence is essential to a highly important business activity." The mayor also said it would be okay for workers to report to their jobs if they would "suffer unusual and severe economic hardship were you to stay away from your work."[37] In order to make it more attractive for nonessential personnel to remain at home, Lindsay asked employers to pay their employees if they were unable to get to work.

With respect to the conduct of negotiations, Lindsay asserted, "I remain committed to the principle that the public interest must be served."[38] The actual negotiations, Lindsay maintained, should be conducted by the TA and the TWU. "They must find a reasonable dollar figure," he said, "and I must find a reasonable way of financing that settlement." If Lindsay did not sound overly conciliatory toward the TWU in his statements, this was precisely the public image he sought to convey, remarking to aides afterward that "You have to be tough."[39]

Lindsay's office on his first day at City Hall was described by a close aide as "a wild, virtually uncontrollable scene." The mayor's office itself, was jammed with young aides, secretaries, people from outside government wishing to offer advice, and, at times, members of the news media. In the halls outside the mayor's office, the media appeared to be everywhere. "It was impossible for the mayor to leave his office," his press secretary reported, "without being almost accosted by a dozen TV cameramen and a mob of reporters."[40] Physically, getting into the mayor's office was difficult as members of his staff milled around, waiting for an opportunity to tell him what they thought he should do. Certainly it must have been impossible to formulate a coherent plan for dealing with transit negotiations amid such chaos.

Most of Lindsay's afternoon on New Year's day was spent in discussions with Police Commissioner Vincent Broderick concerning ways to alleviate the impact of the strike and in rewriting his inaugural speech. With the strike in force, Lindsay felt the necessity to redo his inaugural address because it "did not quite catch the spirit" of the hour.[41] In recasting his speech, according to his press secretary, the mayor relied heavily on that morning's editorial in the New York Times, which had written, "The immediate need is for a demonstration by Mr. Lindsay that the city will not capitulate by granting wage increases and other concessions beyond those justified by economic reality. . . . Anything more would be appeasement." With this statement in mind, Lindsay inserted the following passage into his speech:

> As I speak, our city is crippled by a strike against the bus and subway
> system. It is an unlawful strike against the public interest, called even

before the collective bargaining process had run its course. It is an act of
defiance against eight million people. I shall not permit the public interest
to be flaunted, no matter how severe the stress. The oath of office I have
just taken requires me to uphold the law of the land. That I shall do—in
the name of those eight million people. I say to the parties to this dispute
that theirs is the immediate responsibility for arriving at a swift and
equitable settlement and I insist that they discharge that responsibility.[42]

This statement was wholly congruent with the major thrust of the
Lindsay inaugural address in which he "affirmed a dedication to a simple,
perhaps old-fashioned concept . . . that the public interest must prevail over
special interests, the good of the community over the desires of any
group. . . . The question now before us," Lindsay continued, "is whether
men of conscience and conviction can reject ignoble intrigue and join in a
massive effort to make real our dreams for New York."[43] Emphasizing a
"Proud City" theme, Lindsay suggested that such an approach would lay
the foundation for New York to again become a Proud City. The ten-
minute speech was delivered to an audience of more than 2,500 people
amid floodlights in City Hall Plaza on a balmy evening with the temperature
unseasonably high at close to sixty degrees.

Later that evening, more than 4,000 invited guests gathered at the
Americana Hotel for an inaugural ball to honor incoming Mayor Lindsay.
Dressed in dinner jackets and evening gowns, guests arrived in taxicabs and
limousines to dance and listen to the music of the Lionel Hampton and
Meyer Davis bands. Around midnight, Sammy Davis, Jr., a Lindsay
supporter, took the microphone and congratulated the new mayor for
"eliminating crime in the subways" on his first day in office.[44] It was ironic
that such an upscale gathering would take place at the same hotel in which
just one day earlier Michael Quill had chastised Lindsay for "knowing
nothing about the working class."

Losing Its Cool

To those who love the city, New York is worldly wise, sophisticated,
and not easily awed. To those who criticize it, the city is cold, unresponsive,
and indifferent. But regardless of whether this prevailing attitude is termed
sophistication or indifference—the fact is, New York is not easily rattled.
The strike, however, certainly did cause the city to "lose its cool." "Dismay
and confusion clung to the city," on the first day of the strike, "like a New
Year's hangover that would not quite wear off." "No one seems to believe
it," observed a policeman in front of a midtown subway entrance. "They
know the subways aren't running, but they still ask you if they can take a

subway home. They can't understand that there are no subways."[45] Adding to the unreality, was the record-tying temperature of sixty-one degrees, which made the Christmas decorations seem incongruous.

Even though it was Saturday, and New Year's Day, the disruption of normal activity was massive, and seemed to permeate almost every aspect of life in the city. Many pedestrians bound for Brooklyn walked across the Manhattan Bridge despite the fact that the bridge has no passenger walks. Many cab drivers rode in the back of a taxi for the first time in their lives as the companies they worked for sent cabs to their homes to enable them to get to work. There were few difficulties obtaining cabs as approximately one-half of the city's 12,000 taxis were on the street. However, this was as expected. "We hope to limp through the weekend," said a spokesman for the Metropolitan Taxi Board of Trade, but "Monday is our test."[46]

Other alternate forms of transportation also enjoyed a resurgence in popularity. Bicycle rentals soared as many people who said they had not ridden in years sought to avoid walking. The manager of a bicycle shop on East 10th Street in Manhattan estimated that he had rented seventy-five bicycles in the previous twenty-four hours. The primary reasons that motivated the cyclists were the potential shortage of taxicabs on Monday, and the inevitability of heavy automobile traffic on the first working day of the strike.[47] However, the attempt by some New Yorkers to substitute horse-drawn vehicles for the city's mass transit system was met with some frustration. Because of the strike, about twenty-five drivers of the Central Park horse-drawn carriage fleet failed to report for work. "Only the fellows from Manhattan are making it" said one driver, creating waits for those carriages that were in operation.[48]

The strike's participants were, of course also inconvenienced by the impact of the work stoppage. As one of thirty pickets at a Broadway Independent (IND) subway entrance explained, "I walked down from Kingsbridge Hill and I'm going to walk back." The walks tended not to be too long, however, because the TWU gave its members a choice of subway and bus terminals to report to for picket duty, and most remained fairly close to home.[49] Even the three mediators, who had rooms at the Americana Hotel, the site of the bargaining sessions, were personally aware of the sweeping affect of the strike. On New Year's Day they received, as did many other guests, a note from the hotel management which read:

> Because of the unfortunate circumstances caused by the transit subway strike many of our employees have been unable to come to work, similarly the laundry is not in a position to deliver clean linen.
>
> As you are staying over we shall not be changing the linen in your room on a daily basis as we customarily do and we appreciate your indulgence.[50]

On Sunday, January 2, there was some movement in the stalled negotiations, but hardly room for optimism. Early in the evening, the TWU decreased its demand for a package estimated by the TA to cost $680 million, to a package assessed at between $180 million and $200 million. "If they want to bargain and roll the subways and buses tomorrow morning," said Quill, "they are dealing with a union that has yielded 80 percent.... The monkey is now on their back," the union president continued. "It's up to them to fish or cut bait. If they don't meet this, the strike will continue on and on."[51] Calling the union's proposal unacceptable, Joseph O'Grady indicated he was unwilling to make a new offer in view of the reduction in union demands. "On this proposal?", he asked, "I'd be out of my mind."[52]

For the first time since the strike began at 5:30 p.m. on Sunday, the mediators brought the parties together for face-to-face talks. With no progress being made, however, Nathan Feinsinger, Sylvester Garrett, and Theodore Kheel decided to meet with each side separately in an attempt to get them to modify their positions. Emerging briefly from these talks at 1:00 a.m., Kheel characterized the sessions as "dismal" and indicated that the strike would definitely not be settled by morning. The mediators continued to meet separately with the parties until 2:30 in the morning before adjourning.[53] Questioned about whether an 80 percent reduction in the TWU's original $680 million demand did not amount to $136 million, rather than the between $180 million and $200 million figure announced by the union, one of the mediators replied, "that's Irish arithmetic."[54]

Quill was in rare form when appearing on the televised interview show, *Searchlight*, on Sunday morning. He called Lindsay "a babe in the woods," a "boy in short pants," and an "apprentice in labor relations." "He's promised the sun, moon and the stars," he said. "He should stop lying to the people." Quill said the new mayor had told him, "If you want to be a good American you can't strike. The hell with that," Quill responded. "Labor unions made America," Quill quoted himself as telling Lindsay. "You'd be down in some Hooverville shack if it weren't for labor unions." Quill added that he was prepared to "rot in jail" if he was arrested. He professed not to be afraid of the courts; "I was born in the injunction age," he said.[55] In his televised appearance, the TWU president also offered a new theory for the strike. It was caused he said when out of "political spite" Governor Rockefeller refused to give Mayor Lindsay the money the city needed to meet the unions demands, because he considered the mayor a political rival. "Thirty-six thousand transit workers are caught in a squeeze play between Mayor Lindsay and Governor Rockefeller," Quill said, "because Rockefeller and Lindsay are in a death struggle for the White House."[56] Finally, Quill urged New Yorkers to defy Mayor Lindsay's plea that they stay at home on Monday, and instead to drive their cars into the business districts. "Working people can't afford to stay home," said Quill. As for those who planned to follow the mayor's instructions, Quill shouted, "Let them waddle to work."[57] In other remarks, Quill's comments can only be characterized as "unprintable" because none of the news media would directly quote them. The New York Times, for example, left it to their readers' imaginations when, after reporting some of Quill's comments concerning Lindsay, they wrote that; "he used even more expressive language to describe others who did not see the strike his way."[58] At the conclusion of Quill's performance, more than 500 viewers called WNBC-TV to complain about Quill's profanity, with many wondering why the station had not cut him off the air.

On Sunday, Mayor Lindsay's official day began at 11:00 a.m. when, after sending his attaché case downtown in his official automobile, he emerged from his temporary residence in the Roosevelt Hotel on 45th Street, to begin a walk of more than three miles to City Hall. As a result of the long strides afforded by his six-foot four-inch frame, the mayor took only fifty minutes to reach his destination. Lindsay laughed when asked if he was walking for the exercise or to show solidarity with New Yorkers during the strike. "Actually both," he replied, "I want to demonstrate that it is possible to get about by walking. And I intend to do it tomorrow, too." Wearing a topcoat, but hatless, in the now more winter-like forty-degree weather, the mayor walked briskly down an almost deserted Sunday morning Fifth Avenue. Striding through Washington Square, Lindsay spotted a boy on a bicycle and shouted to him, "That's the way to travel kid, by bike!"[59] Although he originally planned to ride from Washington Square to City Hall in his automobile, Lindsay decided to send the car ahead and to continue on foot. Near the end of his seventy-block trek to City Hall, a number of motorists, recognizing the mayor, rolled down their windows to shout, "Happy New Year, Mr. Lindsay!"[60]

At 1:40 p.m., Lindsay again set out by foot, this time to observe the transit emergency communications center set up in the Civil Defense headquarters, about a five-minute walk away. Accompanied by four aides and a horde of reporters and photographers, the mayor walked so briskly that they had trouble keeping up with him. "We're learning how to walk," Lindsay observed to his fellow pedestrians, as he moved through a now-chilling rain. The mayor spent one-half hour inspecting the work of the 104 men on duty there, who performed two distinct functions. Fifty of the employees took telephone calls from the public concerning various aspects of the strike. The remaining workers were representatives of each of the city's departments that were affected by the strike, including Police, Fire, Welfare, Health, Hospitals, and Sanitation. Each of these departmental

representatives was connected to each other as well their regular departmental colleagues, to facilitate a coordinated effort to deal with the impact
of the strike.[61]

When an assistant buyer, John Friedman, called the control center to
find out how to get from his Queens home to his garment center job on
Monday morning, he unexpectedly found himself talking with Mayor
Lindsay. "This is John Lindsay," the mayor said to the startled caller.
"Look, I have asked all employers to try and let their employees stay home
until the emergency is over. I am sure your boss will understand if you do
not come to work tomorrow. So stay home and help ease the congestion,
will you?"[62] Friedman seemed convinced; "If the Mayor told me to stay
home, I guess I should stay home then," he said.[63]

Back at City Hall that afternoon, Lindsay decided to hold another news
conference. Seated at a table in front of the Blue Room, fewer than twenty-
four hours had passed since he had taken his oath of office as mayor in the
same room. Still present on the mantlepiece behind Lindsay were flowers
left over from the swearing-in ceremony, now beginning to fade and wilt.[64]
Lindsay began by reiterating his previous exhortation that no one should
attempt to enter the city's business districts on Monday unless they were
involved in the critical activities of providing food, fuel, or medical services
and had been requested by their employer because their presence was
essential; or when the individual would suffer severe economic hardship
were they to stay away from work. He appealed to every New Yorker to be
"reasonable" and to judge for himself whether or not he should report to
work the next morning. He said absentees should not be afraid that their
employers would be "mad at them" or penalize them if they were not able to
get to work. "Don't worry about that," the mayor said. Later, a spokesman
for Lindsay said that the mayor wanted employers to pay people who were
unable to get to work. Lindsay's main concern was the potential danger of a
traffic jam in midtown and lower Manhattan. As Traffic Commissioner
Henry Barnes explained the possible consequences of New Yorkers'
following Quill's advice that they should drive to work on Monday, "It
would be catastrophic," he said. "If streets are clogged a major fire could
burn down half of New York."[65]

Prior to beginning his news conference, Lindsay huddled with aides to
discuss his public response to the increasingly intemperate personal abuse
being directed at him by Michael Quill. It was decided that the mayor
should not ignore the attacks, but that he should not get involved in a name-
calling contest either. The consensus of his advisors was that he should
respond with "restrained dignity."[66] Shortly thereafter, when Lindsay was
questioned about Quill's personal attacks, he responded as planned, "I
never mind being called names as a personal matter, but anybody who's

dealing in the public arena like Mr. Quill has an obligation to treat the office of the Mayor with respect." "Do you think he's fulfilling that obligation?" the reporter followed up. "Well, that's up to the public, I think, to judge," Lindsay replied. "Sometimes it's best to let men be subject to the highest court—the judgement of the people—and the judgement of the people will ultimately prevail here on the behavior of the parties to this dispute."[67]

Lindsay thus spent virtually the whole day on Sunday creating pseudo-events designed to capture public support by utilizing the media. His two walks were conceived solely for the purpose of allowing reporters, newspaper photographers, and television camera crews to chronicle Lindsay's show of solidarity with the beleaguered citizens of New York City. And in his news conference, the mayor sought to reinforce the good guy versus bad guy portrayal of his confrontation with Quill.

Although it was Sunday, the fact that it was the end of a holiday period led to a considerable amount of traffic congestion in the city, beginning about 5:00 p.m. Adding to the problems was a chilling rain that turned to sleet in the northern suburbs and increased to a downpour as night fell. By dinner time, the police reported vehicle density "very heavy" on all bridges and in all tunnels with the exception of the George Washington Bridge, which was described as moderate. The average speed on the Long Island Expressway was reported between five and ten miles per hour in both directions.[68] With the end of the vacation period, masses of students and servicemen sought to leave the city, as large numbers of vacationers sought to return. As one suntanned New Yorker just back from Mexico said, while her husband fought for possession of a cab at Kennedy Airport, "I hate the city more and more every time I come in."[69] With the drenching rain exacerbating the problems caused by the strike, traffic backed up for more than three miles on the Van Wyck Extension leading to the airport, causing one of the worst traffic jams ever seen there. At the Port Authority bus terminal, private cars delivering and picking up passengers who normally would have taken subways or buses created a chaotic situation. By the early afternoon, cars were three deep in front of the Authority Building on Eighth Avenue as they sought to drop and pick up passengers.

Initially under fair skies, and then under umbrellas, as a cold rain moved into the city by early afternoon, TWU pickets marched in front of key subway and bus locations throughout New York City. As the rain fell and a blustery wind blew, about fifty pickets gathered at the corner of Main Street and Flushing Avenue, the railhead of the IRT-Flushing line in Queens. An IRT power maintenance man with twenty-seven years service explained the reason for his dissatisfaction, "The Transit Authority is using the 15-cent fare to keep the workers down. Who are they to set themselves up to be the saviors of the people? Where were they when the price of milk

shot up to 27 cents a quart and a loaf of bread to 43 cents?" The picket
captain, a veteran of seventeen years as an IRT motorman added quickly,
"We feel sorry for the people who have to travel, but we are also human
beings who deserve a chance at a better living."[70]

Sunday was also a day to finalize preparations for the onslaught of
commuters that was anticipated on Monday morning, the first working day
of the strike. Police Commissioner Broderick announced that, in those
areas expected to be congested, all on-street parking would be prohibited to
ease the movement of cars. In addition, he indicated that 100 tow trucks
would be dispatched throughout the city to remove stalled cars from traffic
lanes as quickly as possible. Finally, Broderick intimated that the traffic
situation was potentially so disastrous that, if Mayor Lindsay's plans for
travel were not adhered to, a ban on all traffic into Manhattan might have to
be imposed.[71]

With the absence of the Transit Authority's operations, most of the
commuter rail lines planned to offer expanded service. Getting suburban
commuters out of their private automobiles and onto public transit would,
of course, ease the number of cars heading into the city from outlying areas.
In addition, all the commuter lines normally made a number of stops within
the city limits, so that these facilities could also be used to provide rail
service for city residents deprived of subway or bus transportation.
Initially, Harold Pryor, the head of the union representing employees on the
Long Island Railroad, said that his members would not operate inside the
city limits because he considered this strikebreaking. However, the railroad
obtained an injunction in federal court forbidding the union from
interfering with the railroad's operations; and on Sunday evening, the
union said that the injunction would be honored.[72]

The ten National Guard Armories in the metropolitan area completed
their preparations for workers who wanted to sleep in the city during the
strike. At the 71st Regiment Armory on 34th Street, for example, workers
spent Sunday preparing 500 cots for guests that were expected to begin
streaming in on Monday. "People have actually phoned and asked for
reservations," said an Armory spokesman, who explained that the cots
would be allocated on a first come, first served basis.[73] In an attempt to
ensure their places, fifteen people arrived at the Armory on Sunday.
According to David Liebman, "I was in the Marine Corps, so this is nothing
unusual for me." Liebman began his journey at his home on West 167th
Street in the Bronx, walking all the way to 94th Street. Becoming tired, he
took a taxi to midtown where he went to church. Then, after dinner, he
checked into the 34th Street Armory, from where he intended to walk to
his job on 14th Street as a printer. Liebman's motivation was rather

straightforward, "I called my boss," he said. "He told me that if I didn't show up Monday I wouldn't get paid."[74]

With the city's power blackout still fresh in New Yorkers' minds, Consolidated Edison took pains to reassure customers that, "Our stations are fully manned, and the men don't leave until their replacements show up." A spokesman for the utility added that because most of its facilities were located in "outlying areas" it should not be too difficult for workers to reach their jobs by using car pools.[75] The New York Telephone Company anticipated a more difficult problem. With about 20,000 employees in Manhattan, a fleet of 100 buses had been hired to transport workers to their jobs. Employees were instructed to go to their nearest telephone company office and wait for the buses, which were scheduled to run from 6:00 a.m. until midnight. Telephone company officials were optimistic that they had planned for all possible contingencies except one: whether the chartered buses would be able to get through the tunnel and bridge bottlenecks leading into Manhattan.

For companies with offices located at the foot of Manhattan, transportation seemed to present less of a problem. The brokerage firm Merrill Lynch, with offices in the Wall Street area, reserved rooms for employees in Brooklyn hotels where space was more readily available. If vehicular traffic was stalled at the bridges and tunnels, the Merrill Lynch employees could simply walk over the Brooklyn Bridge to work. Most companies, however, seemed to combine planning with a wait and see attitude. First National City Bank, with a contingent of about 12,500 employees in the metropolitan area, epitomized this approach. The bank hired thirty buses for its essential personnel, then took the position that "We'll see who gets in, then we'll put them where they're needed most."[76]

With the notable exception of the hotels, where business was booming, the general picture on Sunday was one of sparsely attended church services, closed museums, restaurants that were hungry for business, and half-filled theaters. At the huge Riverside Church on 122nd Street and Riverside Drive, which normally accommodates 1,800 people at its 11:00 a.m. service, only about 1,200 were present. Restaurant business was substantially reduced on Sunday evening, but not as dismal as had been predicted. Undoubtedly helping business was the fact that the hotels, which are usually almost deserted on Sunday evenings, were filled with patrons. In any event, restaurant business was reportedly off between 20 and 30 percent. At the Museum of Modern Art, usually one of the city's most popular spots on a Sunday, small groups of people stood outside the main entrance and complained because it was closed. As the director of the Museum explained, "We closed because we couldn't get enough guards to ensure security." The Museum of Natural History, which normally accommodates 8,000 visitors on a Sunday, was forced to shut when only one-third of its guards reported for work. Although the main branch of the Public Library at 42nd Street and Fifth Avenue did open, only about one-half its normal attendance of 2,500 was present. "We would have been empty," said the head of the reference department, "if some of the college students hadn't still been in the city."[77]

In spite of the fact that Mayor Lindsay had consistently been praising New Yorkers for their cooperative attitude since the beginning of the strike, apparently not everyone was considered worthy of such accolades. Steps were announced on Sunday by James O'Rourke, the head of the Police Department's Hack Bureau, to ensure that the taxi drivers did not overcharge their passengers. Although group riding in taxis was being encouraged to ease traffic congestion, O'Rourke made it clear that the cab driver was not to charge the rate on the meter to each of his passengers. Regardless of the number of riders, the fare was what the meter registered so that technically additional passengers were the guests of the person who hailed the cab, O'Rourke explained. Extra riders could either give their proportionate share to the person who hired the cab or voluntarily tip the driver, he said. In order to enforce this regulation, fifty hack inspectors in civilian clothes were scheduled to be stationed around the city. If the inspectors found cabbies overcharing, they were given orders to take away the hack license and to suspend the driver for the duration of the strike.[78]

By Sunday, with the full impact of the strike not yet in effect, most New Yorkers were already convinced that Michael Quill was to blame for the work stoppage. From early morning until late at night, tens of thousands of the city's residents called the city's emergency command number and the headquarters of the TWU to vent their anger. They called Quill a "gangster" and demanded that he be thrown in jail. Another suggestion was more comprehensive in scope, proposing that the top 150 officeholders in the TWU be jailed. A number of citizens suggested that the National Guard be called to operate the city's buses. The strongest language, however, was directed to the switchboard at TWU headquarters, which was flooded with cries of how to deal with Quill: "shoot him," "drown him," "let him rot in jail," they demanded.[79]

After five hours of arguments, on Monday, January 3, State Supreme Court Justice Abraham N. Geller ordered Quill and eight other union leaders to end the city's subway and bus strike by 11:00 a.m. on Tuesday or go to jail. Quill, five other officers of the TWU, and three leaders of the Amalgamated Transit Union were found guilty of civil contempt of court for violation of an antistrike injunction. The hearing began with TWU attorney Louis Waldman asking for an adjournment. Waldman contended that he had not had time to prepare the union's case and, also, that the paramount concern of the court should have been to settle the strike through negotiations, rather than to determine the guilt of the union leaders. Justice Geller denied the motion for adjournment and then asked Waldman if the striking unions were prepared to return to work. The union lawyer replied that they would do so "as soon as they have a fair and acceptable offer."[80]

When union lawyers declined to acknowledge that a strike was under way, the TA sought to prove, for the benefit of the court, what was all too apparent to most New Yorkers—that the injunction had been violated, and the unions were indeed on strike. Daniel Scannell, a member of the Authority, testified that Quill had told Mayor Lindsay on New Year's Eve that "the strike's still on." Scannell told the court that the incoming mayor had not been in office ten minutes when Quill rejected his request that all parties continue to negotiate and walked out. TA attorney Brandes then began to call witnesses, including a photographer who had taken pictures outside various Authority installations where there were pickets and a stenographer who had prepared transcripts of telvision shows in which Quill and other union leaders had taken part.[81] Through the use of these witnesses the TA sought to establish what was common, but not legal knowledge, that the TWU and the Amalgamated Transit Union were on strike.

In his ruling, Justice Geller held that the TA had established that the defendants had "full knowledge of the injunction." In spite of this, the judge continued, they "chose to deliberately disobey court orders" and this injured the TA and resulted in "incalculable losses to the people of New York and environs."[82] Justice Geller said that unless the union leaders purged themselves of contempt by calling an end to the strike, they would be ordered to jail at 11:00 a.m. on Tuesday.

The concept of civil contempt, under which the union leaders were to be jailed, developed historically from the belief that the legal system needed the power to aid private parties in the execution of their civil remedies. An often cited example is the case in which a man is ordered by the court to pay child support to his former wife but fails to do so. The court, on the application of his former wife, will hold him in civil contempt and send him to jail until he is ready to pay.

Although the injunction had previously been granted on New Year's Eve, it was necessary for the TA to initiate the contempt proceedings because, in a civil contempt case, courts do not bring defendants in on their own. The court must rely on the party seeking the civil remedy to ask the court to act because ordinarily the court would have no way of knowing that the required remedy had been violated. Unless informed by his former wife that a man was not paying his court ordered child support, the court would not know that this was the case.

A civil contempt citation carries with it an indeterminate sentence, which means that as soon as prisoners purge themselves by doing or undoing what they were put in jail for, they may be freed. The transit union leaders were sentenced to jail until they purged themselves of contempt, which they could do only by calling an end to the strike. Thus, it was said that the union leaders "had the keys to the jail in their pockets."

When the contempt citations were issued, TA Chairman O'Grady expressed the view that he and the two other members of the TA had received the news "more in sorrow than in anger." O'Grady continued:

> The Supreme Court has sustained our position that the eight million people of our city must be protected against the flagrant disregard of law, order, and the judicial process....
>
> The most important thing to be done at this time is to arrive at a fair and reasonable settlement with the unions—fair to the employees and fair to the people of the City of New York—and to get the subways and buses running again.[83]

John O'Donnell, a lawyer for the TWU, said that the union would immediately appeal Justice Geller's ruling on the contempt citation. The TA's action, O'Donnell said, was "an unfortunate and vindictive act.... It seems," he said, "that the Transit Authority is more interested in punishing union leaders than in getting the subways rolling."[84]

While the court case was being heard before Justice Geller on Monday afternoon, representatives of the striking unions and the TA met for a brief, and obviously half-hearted, negotiating session. It was clear that both sides were waiting to see what action would be taken to enforce the injunction before engaging in serious bargaining. The parties met for a joint session at the Americana Hotel shortly before 2:00 p.m. but recessed just twenty minutes later to permit Quill to appear on a radio program on WCBS. O'Grady, appearing somewhat annoyed as he left the session indicated that the TA did not intend to make any new offer until the TWU reduced its demands to a "realistic figure." Equally unwilling to negotiate was Quill, who said he was waiting for the TA to increase its offer before he acted. The negotiations, Quill said, appeared to still be in the "fencing stage." He stated that the mediation panel offered the only hope for a settlement, but he stressed that his union was unwilling to accept any attempt at fact-finding or arbitration by the mediators. Quill added that the concurrent court proceedings would not cause the TWU to temper its demands. "No matter what happens in any court, we will continue in mediation until we are dragged from our seats," the union president said. "Then we'll throw in our second line of leadership. The courts may have their finest hour, but they'll not break us one penny from our objectives."[85]

In his radio appearance, the TWU leader was uncharacteristically restrained. He said that the strike would continue to be effective since, "I don't think the National Guard are attuned to break a strike, and I also know they are working people." Besides, he added, ever cognizant of the realities of public life in New York, "[I] don't expect either Governor Rockefeller or Mayor Lindsay from a political point of view can call in the National Guard now." In response to a question of whether the breakdown in negotiations could be attributed to his "personal dislike" or "contempt" for Lindsay, Quill was equally low key, "I have no dislike for Mr. Lindsay. It was his remarks to us that brought this exchange...."[86]

In discussing the prospect of his going to jail, Quill seemed to be in an unusually good mood; freely combining nostalgia, fabrication, and humor. "If I go to jail my first assignment will be to strengthen the militancy of the prison keepers," the TWU president said. He then proceded to relate a story of how he had served a jail term in Ireland for political activities against the British when he was eighteen years old. "There was [sic] five of my family in jail and I happened to do a little time myself and I hear the jails here are a little better equipped." When asked about the legal proceedings and appearing before the bar, Quill said with a straight face, "The bars I passed were altogether different bars."[87] Quill particularly enjoyed telling stories about his escapades with the Irish Republican Army before coming to the United States, and even his closest associates were never sure which stories were true, which were embellished, and which were total fabrications.

At 6:00 a.m. on Monday morning, Lindsay set out by foot from his residence in the Roosevelt Hotel, for his office at City Hall. Accompanied by thirty reporters, Lindsay seemed determined to beat the fifty minutes it took him to reach City Hall on his Sunday walk. Some forty-five minutes later, the mayor bounded up the steps of City Hall, more than three miles away, telling the twenty reporters who had survived the brisk pace, "It was good for us. It brought the blood surging. Good for the circulation."[88] Despite the early hour, City Hall was already crowded, particularly in the "command post" set up by Deputy-Mayor Timothy Costello, to coordinate the mayor's efforts to deal with the impact of the strike. The atmosphere, according to a Lindsay aide was "tense" in anticipation of the day's uncertainties, "but everyone from the mayor down was buoyed by the conviction that we were handling the situation correctly."[89] Those present were particularly elated by the editorial appearing in the morning edition of the *New York Times*, which was highly complimentary. The *Times*, which had consistently supported Lindsay since the beginning of negotiations, thereby incurring the wrath of Quill, wrote: "Mr. Lindsay, confronted with this grim crisis in the first minutes of an administration committed to fight for a better city, has comported himself with dignity, courage and resolution. His conduct so far encourages confidence that the Quill demand for extortionate benefits as the price for peace on the subways and buses will be met in the spirit of Mr. Lindsay's inaugural address: 'That the public interest must prevail over special interests, the good of the community over the desires of any group.' "[90] The support of the *Times* was particularly coveted because it is one of the few newspapers in the country with a true national audience. Because it is read by opinion-makers nationwide, a favorable portrayal in the *Times* is tremendously beneficial to politicians with national aspirations.

By 7:00 a.m., with traffic reports from his command post in front of him, the mayor told radio listeners from City Hall that it would be futile to try to drive into the city, "If you're on your way to Manhattan in your car at this time, turn around and go home. Turn off the highway and head back to where you came from. Don't head for Manhattan by car—because you won't make it."[91]

With the drama that was unfolding in New York arousing national and even international interest, by Monday, City Hall was literally being overrun with media representatives. On the first working day of the strike, the more than 100 reporters present began to seriously distract Mayor Lindsay. Lindsay called in his press secretary, Woody Klein, and complained, "I can't get any work done with the press wandering in and out of my office all day and night.... The Mayor should be entitled to some privacy."[92]

Shortly before 9:00 a.m., Lindsay decided he wanted a first-hand look at how the city was responding to the crisis. In the presence of Police Commissioner Broderick, the mayor was quickly airborne in a helicopter, hovering about 200 feet over the city for almost ninety minutes. During the 110-mile flight, Lindsay broadcast some of his observations over the municipal radio station WNYC. In a nonbroadcast statement while circling the city the mayor radioed, "I'm over the Queensboro Bridge now and it looks good. Traffic is moving easily." From the roof of the Traffic Department headquarters, overlooking the Queensboro Bridge, came the voice of Traffice Commissioner Barnes, "Mr. Mayor, I believe you're over the wrong bridge. It's horrible here; cars are backed up for miles." In fact, the mayoral helicopter was over the Williamsburg Bridge. Later, trying to undo Lindsay's mistake, Barnes explained, "It's awful doggone easy to get mixed up swinging around up there. It was awfully foggy."[93]

Upon Lindsay's return to City Hall, an aide observed, "he seemed invigorated and in a much better mood." The aide continued, "His behavior depended to some extent on his public performance. If he thought he was doing well—giving off an image of the active, vigorous Mayor who cared—then he was inevitably pleased, in a good mood."[94] Jack Newfield and Paul DuBrul corroborated this perception, observing that, "Lindsay was always preoccupied with the appearance rather than the reality of things. . . . [He] often asked his aides, when making a decision, how will this be played by the *Times*? How will it look on the six o'clock news? The image of things dominated Lindsay's mind to a fault."[95] In this vein, the mayor held two more formal news conferences on Monday, for a total of three during the day. He touched almost exclusively on two subjects: how the city was responding to the impact of the strike and his role in the negotiations. At his 11:00 a.m. news conference, the mayor reported that the "city is in good shape, thanks to the cooperation of eight million New Yorkers. The reason it worked," Lindsay added, "is because there was full cooperation, and that's a measure of toughness of New Yorkers, their courage and their ability to rise to an occasion."[96] At his final meeting with the media at 5:00 p.m., Lindsay asked the public to remain home again on Tuesday and urged truck owners and store owners to make deliveries at night to ease the congestion.

With the strike only a few days old, Lindsay's use of television to aid his political stature was already evident. The mayor not only granted numerous media conferences, he also "created" events, such as his walk to City Hall, which was conceived solely to garner television coverage. As the *New York Times* television critic Jack Gould observed, "Mr. Quill is directly responsible for giving the new Mayor more coast-to-coast television coverage in a few days than Mr. Lindsay normally would receive in several years. If Mr. Lindsay survives the struggle well, he could be one of television's instant national figures." Gould graded Lindsay's early television performances very highly: ". . . Mr. Lindsay always has been videogenic, and over the difficult weekend he has projected the restless vigor of youth, a quality that should stand him in good stead. . . ." After watching one of Lindsay's news conferences, Gould observed, "a viewer could not entirely escape the impression of a knight in shining armor who was doing everything but spearing the foe." The television critic was also impressed with the mayor's "skillful exploitation of the potential of the morning walk," feeling that it fulfilled all of the requirements for a successful television performance.[97]

The Monkeys Are Just Sitting There

In a city where the unusual is commonplace, the first working day of the strike produced a number of firsts. A thirty-three-year-old Astoria man roller-skated from the 59th Street Bridge to the Olin Mathieson Chemical Corporation's office at Tenth Avenue. Tired and breathless by the time he reached his destination, he explained, "[I] just wanted to see if I could do it. It was a challenge."[98] A partially blind forty-two-year-old newsdealer walked about four miles from his home in Brooklyn to the Queens side of the Queensboro Bridge. From there he hitched a ride to his newsstand on East Fifty-Ninth Street in Manhattan. A Wall Street executive boarded a commuter train at New Canaan, Connecticut, carrying a dismantled thirty-five pound two-wheeler called a Moulton Stowaway, which belonged to his eleven-year-old daughter. When he arrived at Grand Central Station, he quickly assembled the bicycle and pedaled to his office in seventeen minutes. Even the animals in the Central Park Zoo were affected by the strike. "The monkeys are just sitting there, the gorillas are just sitting there. They miss a crowd," said John Kinsig, senior zookeeper, "They're wondering what's up." Pedestrians were everywhere. A steady stream of people walked across the Queensboro Bridge into Manhattan, and a number were understandably angered by the sight of commuting autos. "I reconciled myself to walking," complained one woman. "I knew that I could have got my son to drive, but Lindsay said to cooperate, don't take the car. But the stairs! I felt I was going to get a heart attack."[99] For others, getting to work meant considerably less sacrifice: they simply squeezed into cabs or rode in the private buses that had been arranged by their employers.

Although the transportation difficulties experienced on Monday were massive, the gridlock that had been feared did not materialize. Many traffic experts had worried that so many people would try to drive vehicles into the city that a colossal traffic jam, taking days to untangle, would be created. In fact, traffic streaming into the city was lighter than usual during the morning, mainly the result of about one-half of the city's labor force heeding Mayor Lindsay's advice that they stay home. According to estimates by Traffic Commissioner Barnes, only 300,000 of a normal weekday's 600,000 cars and trucks entered Manhattan south of 59th Street. Further easing congestion was that the normal two-hour rush was spread to four hours as drivers began leaving their homes at 5:00 a.m. to avoid the anticipated tie-ups. Combining these factors, Traffic Commissioner Barnes estimated that the morning rush of vehicles into the city was only 35 percent of normal. At the conclusion of the work day, however, most drivers buoyed by their morning success, attempted to leave Manhattan almost simultaneously, creating traffic in Lower Manhattan that was "well beyond the saturation point."[100]

The commuter rail lines all experienced considerable increases in the number of riders transported, but none were completely overwhelmed. The Long Island Railroad estimated, for example, that it carried 100,000 passengers during the rush hour instead of a normal 80,000. The New York Central Railroad, which experienced the biggest increases in ridership, brought 50,000 commuters into the city instead of 32,500. And from New Jersey, the Erie-Lackawanna Railroad reported that its travel was increased between 15 and 20 percent. In part, the situation on the commuter railroads was prevented from becoming totally chaotic by good planning. With thousands of people congregating inside and outside, the police decided to shut down Pennsylvania Station between 4:50 p.m. and 6:30 p.m. as crowds attempted to board trains that would make stops in the Bronx before heading on to suburban locations. Fearful that someone might be accidently pushed in front of a train, authorities felt that they had to temporarily close the station when 5,000 people packed together on the station's lowest level waiting to board trains.[101]

Taxicabs were readily available on Monday, except during the morning and evening rush, at the bus and railroad terminals. Between the two rush periods, according to one cabbie, "business stinks." "We're better off without a strike," observed a second driver, "there's [no] people out." As commuters got off inbound buses and trains at the terminals, however, it was difficult to obtain taxis, enabling a number of cabbies to solidify their reputations for surliness. At Grand Central Station, while several would-be riders beat on his taxi roof with their fists to protest what they felt was attempted price gouging a driver yelled at a policeman; "Go to hell.... I don't give a damn about the public, I'm out to make a dime." The Police Department's Hack Bureau, which regulates taxis, had given them permission to carry more than one rider as long as they only charged the fare on the meter to one passenger. A number of people, however, complained that drivers collected the full meter reading from each of the passengers. When one passenger complained, she was told, "the Mayor is nuts if he thinks I'm going to charge separate fares." By late afternoon, the Hack Bureau had received eighteen complaints of overcharging from the public, and its fifty inspectors had issued twenty-three summonses.[102]

Although many of the city's services and attractions remained closed, those that had sufficient staffs to open were eerily accessible. The ice rink at Rockefeller Center, which had been packed throughout the holiday season, accommodated only a handful of isolated skaters. At the F.A.O. Schwarz toy store on Fifth Avenue and 58th Street which had been besieged by Christmas shoppers for weeks, the contrast was equally startling. As one clerk observed as she gazed at the empty aisles, "Well, at least this gives us a good chance to clean up. I've never seen it as quiet as this." In other instances businesses made special preparations for customers who never materialized. At Stern's Department Store on 42nd Street an elevator operator was temporarily stationed behind the handbag counter to fill in for clerks who had not been able to reach their jobs. As she stood nervously practicing before a cash register, there were no customers to interrupt her preparations.[103] In many cases, for the first time in their lives, New Yorkers could get a haircut or make a bank deposit without having to wait for service. Even the most popular restaurants were uncharacteristically solicitous of customers.

In an unexpected development, not nearly as many people decided to stay in Manhattan in order to avoid commuting hassles as had been anticipated. The Hotel Reservation Agency, which handled room bookings for a large number of hotels, reported that it had "plenty of rooms" available in the Times Square area. The high cost of a Manhattan hotel room could hardly have been a deterrent, because even free accommodations went begging. In the cavernous 71st Regiment Armory, located within easy walking distance of the two major commuter rail terminals and close to the midtown office areas, nearly 500 cots and blankets were available for men in the drill hall on the second floor, and about forty cots for women were in the third-floor Veterans' Room and in a hallway. Although use of the cots was free, by early evening only thirty men and two women had availed themselves of the armory's hospitality. It is possible that the lack of use of the National Guard's facilities was the result of the dearth of publicity given to their availability. Afraid that they might be overrun by derelicts, the National Guard intentionally did not seek out potential users and had a sign posted at the entrance to the 71st Regiment Armory warning that "Intoxicated Persons Will Not Be Admitted."[104] For those individuals who did spend the night in the Armory, they were awakened at 6:30 a.m. and served free coffee and doughnuts by the Red Cross.

If the response of residents of one apartment building in the Bronx could be viewed as a microcosm of the reaction of all New Yorkers to the strike, then two salient facts emerge: most New Yorkers were heeding Mayor Lindsay's request that they stay home, and most employers were ignoring his urging that they nevertheless be paid. One of the residents of 2249 Morris Avenue, Anna Goldberg, received a phone call from her employer; "Anna," he said, "I'm not going to come in. I'll have no place to park. You don't come in, all right?" Not really having any choice in the matter, Goldberg, who described herself as having worked "too many years" as an embroiderer, spent the day talking with relatives on the phone, window shopping on the Grand Concourse, and thinking about her lost pay. Upstairs on the sixth floor of the apartment building, Dora Koss phoned her boss in the garment center and told him she would not be coming to work. "Even if someone took me downtown in a car, how would I get back?" she asked. "Where would I sleep—the Port Authority?" she asked, referring to the fact that a number of homeless people regularly slept on benches at the Port Authority bus terminal. On the ninth floor, Costas Paraskeva, a young tailor, also stayed home, knowing he would not be paid, and wondered, "How can I go to work on 14th Street? A taxi costs too much." With school called off, fifteen-year-old Seth Holzman spent the day studying physics because "midterms are coming...." The mood of the residents of the Bronx apartment building was "gloomy." They had lost a day's pay, and the future appeared uncertain.[105]

Despite some of the hardships, one might almost get the impression that New York's bizarrely different behavior was a refreshing change for a few days. But when looked at aggregately, the conclusion was inescapable, New York had been brought to its knees. Retail losses alone were estimated at between $35 and $40 million by Walter Pease, president of the New York City Chamber of Commerce. Stores in midtown Manhattan were virtually empty. David L. Yunich, the president of Macy's, called Monday "one of the worst business days I can remember—worse even than any of the snowstorms or blackouts we have had."[106] The view of the president was echoed by a sales clerk at Macy's Herald Square store, "I think there's more life in a morgue."[107] The assessment at Gimbels was equally pessimestic; according to a spokesman, "the few customers available wander through the empty aisles trailed by squads of clerks, floorwalkers and executives. I've never seen anything like it."[108] Yunich, who also served as head of the Metropolitan New York Retail Merchants Association, estimated that as a group if retailers did 20 to 25 percent of their expected volume of business, "it was a lot."[109] Business was so slack at all of the major midtown department stores that although they normally remained open until 9:00 p.m. on Monday evenings, they were all closed by 6:00 p.m. The financial picture for the city government was also hurt, with Deputy-Mayor Costello estimating that the strike was costing $1.5 million in overtime payments to police, sanitation workers, and 500 other employees.[110]

Only about one-half of the work force in Manhattan reached their jobs on Monday, and absenteeism was especially noticeable in the low wage industries. And despite Mayor Lindsay's appeal, the experience of the Bronx apartment dwellers was mirrored throughout the city: those unable to report for work were generally not paid. Speaking as head of the Metropolitan New York Retain Merchants Association, Yunich said that the consensus of his groups members was "No show, no pay." An informal survey of garment manufacturers indicated that they, too, were unwilling to compensate employees who did not show up for work. "How can you pay a piece worker who's not here?" asked one manufacturer.[111] The *Wall Street Journal* also reported little enthusiasm for the mayor's request that those workers who remained off the job be paid, quoting one company official as saying, "Mr. Lindsay isn't going to make decisions for the entire business community."[112]

Attendance at cultural and entertainment activities was also severely curtailed by the strike. Many museums were closed for the day, others provided limited services; and others were open as usual but had few visitors. The Museum of Modern Art, the American Museum of Natural History, and the Whitney Museum were all closed for the day. The Metropolitan Museum of Art was open, but because many of its employees did not come to work, several galleries were closed. The Brooklyn Museum was open, but received only 200 visitors, compared to its normal attendance of 1,200 to 1,500.[113]

Meanwhile, thousands of miles away, former mayor Wagner was driving around Accapulco, Mexico, in a jeep when the driver of a passing truck shouted in his best New York accent, "Hiya Mister Mayor, aren't ya glad you're not in New York City today?" "You bet I am," Mr. Wagner yelled back, smiling broadly. Wagner explained later that he was keeping apprised of what was happening in New York by having friends translate the Mexican newspapers, where the strike was front page news. New Yorkers are "ingenious and can take things like this in stride," the former mayor observed.[114]

Chapter 5

"The Judge Can Drop Dead
in His Black Robes"

At 2:30 p.m. on Tuesday, January 4, Michael Quill, seemingly for the first time in several months, was silent. Fewer than two hours after arriving at the century-old red brick Civil Jail, Quill who had long suffered from a heart ailment, "went off into a little stupor, like a deep sleep," according to Dr. Bernard Goldbaum, the prison physician. Oxygen was rushed to the sixty-year-old union leader, and he was carried on a stretcher past shocked TWU pickets into an ambulance to be taken to Bellevue Hospital's emergency ward.[1]

On the morning of his arrest, Quill was his usual acid tongued self. Shortly before 11:00 a.m. the TWU President, leaning on his silver-headed blackthorn walking stick for support, stood at his union's strike headquarters in the Americana Hotel and shouted, "The judge can drop dead in his black robes and we would not call off the strike. We will defy the injunction and go to jail."[2] "Personally, I don't care if I rot in jail," he continued, "I will not call off the strike."[3]

As he descended a flight of stairs a few minutes later while headed for a news conference in the ballroom of the Americana, Quill appeared frail and weak. His lips blue and his face pale, he was forced to lean heavily on the arm of an associate for support. Then seemingly infused with energy from the dozens of television cameras, Quill suddenly became animated, announcing that he intended to go to jail, and invited "the sheriff and his lackeys" to come and pick him up.[4] The TWU president turned retrospective in explaining the background of his current position: "We were fooled two years ago, and two years before that, and two years before that. We became labor statesmen."[5] "But," he added quickly, his approach had changed, "we're labor leaders now." He then ridiculed those "labor statesmen" who sought to be "respectable." "It is about time that someone, somewhere along the road ceases to be respectable," he said. "Many generations of great Americans before us have taken this road and if they didn't take this road half of you would be on home relief," Quill declared. Then, saying he was acting contrary to the advice of his attorneys, he indicated he did not intend to appeal Justice Abraham N. Geller's decision and would not permit "anybody to bail me out" of jail.[6]

At this point, Quill turned his wrath on his two chief nemeses, John V. Lindsay and the New York Times. "We're going to compel the Sheriff to remove us from the bargaining table as a sign of how collective bargaining is being conducted in 1966 under Mayor Lindsay with the prodding of the New York Times."[7] He then observed, "I think that our good Mayor has let the opportunity [for a settlement] pass through his fingers in not getting in in time, in not serving his apprenticeship and in not getting acquainted with our problems." Quill added that the jailing of the union leaders would not stymie negotiations because "the second-line leadership will have full powers to negotiate a contract while the strike is on." Finally, the TWU president cautioned, "Our going to jail must not mean that we will settle for one penny less than what we put on the table."[8]

Around noon, the deputy sheriff and several assistants and detectives arrived at the Americana Hotel and told Quill that he had a warrant for his arrest. Rising slowly, Quill took great care in examining the badge of Deputy Sheriff Allen Green, then turned to the television cameras and said, "The sheriff is here and has properly identified himself. The dragging arrest from the collective bargaining table is typical of collective bargaining a la Mayor Lindsay and the editorial writers of the New York Times. And now," he continued, "we'll turn our bodies over to the custody of the sheriff and we'll see how it goes from here."[9]

As Quill emerged from the Americana Hotel to be taken to jail, he was met by a booing, hissing mob. "You rat. . . . You bum. . . . Why don't you go back to Ireland," they screamed. "Let the bum walk. Hey Mike, why don't you fly," they yelled. Several men tried to grab him as he grinned and tipped his hat to the booing mob, but police shoved them back.[10] "Put him on bread and water and forget the bread."[11] "Drop dead"; "Deport him," they shouted, "Die." Again tipping his hat to the crowd, Quill and eight fellow union leaders were lead to waiting automobiles for the trip to Civil Jail. Getting out of the car in front of the five-story red brick prison, Quill briefly thought back to his militant Irish past; "Jesus Christ," he observed, "I haven't felt so good since I left the other side."[12] Such reminiscences, however, were interrupted by a woman shouting, "Drop dead." Doffing his hat to the woman and others gathered, Quill shouted back, "I've been in prison before and we're going to win this fight. . . . We'll stay until we rot if necessary."[13] Inside the building, which was constructed as a police precinct and was currently being used mainly to jail alimony violators and material witnesses, Quill was allowed to chat briefly with his wife, Shirley. Mrs.

Quill brought her husband a transistor radio and several books on Irish history to help pass the time in jail. Other TWU officials arrested with Quill were Matthew Guinan, executive vice president of the international; Frank Sheehan, organizer for the international; Daniel Gilmartin, president of Local 100; Ellis Van Riper, financial secretary of the local; and Mark Kavanagh, recording secretary of Local 100. In addition, three officers of the Amalgamated Transit Union also went to jail: John Rowland, executive board member; William Mangus, president of Local 726 on Staten Island; and Frank Kleess, president of Local 1056 in Queens.

About 2:15 p.m., while Quill was sitting in the warden's office waiting for the standard preadmission physical exam, according to the attending physician, "He just collapsed. He didn't answer me. His pulse was rather weak, and he acted like he was in a stupor. I just couldn't get him to speak."[14] Oxygen was administered and an ambulance was called immediately to take the TWU president to the hospital. Lying unconscious under a blanket, his face white, Quill was carried to the ambulance as about 200 TWU pickets marched in front of the jail. Incensed, several of the pickets shouted at newsmen, "You caused this!" A union leader walked over and calmed them down; "Don't shout," he said, "Say a prayer for Mike."[15]

Initially after arriving at Bellevue Hospital, Quill alternated between consciousness and unconsciousness. He received intravenous injections and cardiograms to determine if he had suffered another heart attack. One attending physician became enraged when a reporter asked whether he felt Quill's collapse was merely "playacting." Later that evening, his condition was considerably improved, and the hospital described his state of health as "serious but not critical." After performing further tests, doctors determined that Quill had collapsed from congestive heart failure, in which a weakening of the heart muscle is followed by a shortness of breath and the buildup of fluid in the lungs, liver, and the extremities. Contributing to his collapse, said the hospital, were factors associated with the negotiations; he ws not able to eat his prescribed diet at the specified times, he would often forget to take his medication when bargaining; and he was suffering from excessive tension and a lack of sleep.[16]

Michael Joseph Quill

Michael Joseph Quill, one of eight children of a farming family, was born in County Kerry, Ireland in 1905. From the time he was five until he left at age fourteen, Quill walked three miles to a small six-room schoolhouse to receive his formal education. After leaving school in 1919,

with the Irish separatist movement in full swing, Quill joined the Irish
Republican Army as a dispatch carrier. With the establishment of Northern
Ireland, Quill went back to the family farm to help recover the losses
incurred during the hostilities. At eighteen, he decided to learn a trade and
apprenticed himself to a carpenter in a nearby town. This career ended
suddenly, however, when the carpenter fell from the roof of a home they
were repairing and died.[17]

At age twenty-one, Quill had few economic prospects in Ireland so he
decided to emigrate to the United States. Following the footsteps of two
older brothers who had preceded him, he went to New York City and got a
job in the transit industry. He obtained work as a gateman on the IRT
subway for 27¢ an hour. "For us new men," Quill recalled, "it was night
work—twelve hours a night, seven days a week—when we got the chance to
work. Other nights I sat on a bench for seven or eight hours and then
returned home without job or pay."[18]

In coming to New York City right after the turn of the century, Quill
was part of a large Irish immigration that had begun in the 1840s and
continued until 1924. Most of these new arrivals came from rural areas in
Ireland and had few skills. As a result, they tended to obtain jobs in those
industries that required large numbers of unskilled workers, such as
utilities, construction, trucking, the docks, and transit.[19] Making the newly
arrived Irish immigrants particularly attractive as transit employees was the
fact that they spoke English, a real asset because many transit jobs required
public contact. By relying on these "country people" from the poorer
counties of southern and western Ireland, the New York City transit
industry was able to cheaply meet their manpower needs.[20]

Quill quit his first transit job, and over the next few years he held a
variety of positions, both in and out of the transit industry. He soon settled
down, however, permanently returning to the subway system, and from
1929 to 1935 worked as a change agent in subway stations, making change
for passengers who did not have the nickel required for the subway
turnstiles. During this period, Quill got to know many of his fellow
employees at the IRT because the company had the practice of rotating the
stations where the change agents worked. As was fairly typical of the period,
the workers were represented by a "company union" called the Brotherhood of Interborough Employees. In 1932, the IRT was in dire financial
straights and went into receivership. In order to help the company, the
Brotherhood agreed to a 10 percent reduction in wages and the abolition of
an existing pension system. With considerable time to read about unions
because the subways had few passengers after midnight, Michael Quill
reached the conclusion that a more militant brand of unionism was needed.
By 1933, he was actively involved with a handful of other transit employees

in trying to establish such an organization. In the spring of the following year, Quill, along with five other pro-union Irishmen, attended a secret meeting at a Manhattan cafeteria, where the TWU was established. Also present at this meeting was a Hungarian immigrant, John Santo, who was not a transit worker. Santo, an official in the Communist party, explained that the party was interested in establishing a strong union in the transit industry and would be willing to provide any aid the fledgling unionists would require. Santo also asked the Irishmen to join the Communist party. The party had previously tried to organize a transit union, with a noticeable lack of success. The Communists had virtually no Irish or Irish-American members and little experience in working within the extremely clannish Irish community. As one Irish transit worker described a Communist party overture to interest transit workers in unionism: the party was comprised of "mainly Jewish fellows... [and] the Irish are extremely nationalistic," so [I] warned party leaders that "if this thing continues, your union is going to go up in smoke."[21]

At Santo's urging, Thomas O'Shea was appointed president of the union, and Quill was awarded the titles of vice-president and literature agent. As Quill described these early days: "Three weeks after we started, our seven [the six Irishmen and Santo] had expanded to forty-five. Each of these forty-five set about building up new secret groups, and by the end of 1934 we had 560 members. We talked a blue streak.... We soapboxed at the shop gates...."[22]

During this period, the existence of the so called lead-pipe brigade made union organizing hazardous. In October 1934, for example, union President O'Shea was bashed on the head and lost several teeth during a confrontation with private detectives hired by the company and was then fired from his job. Douglas MacMahon, another of the union's founders, was also fired for his organizing efforts. In August 1935, MacMahon and Quill were hired as full-time organizers for the TWU at $18 per week. Because the union did not have sufficient funds, both were actually paid by the Communist party. By this time, it was clear that in Santo's eyes, Quill had eclipsed O'Shea, and in November 1935, Santo asked O'Shea to resign as union president. Quill was then "elected" president of the TWU, without opposition.[23] Santo was the union's secretary-treasurer.

Throughout this formative period for the union, Quill remained an active Communist. "I'd rather be called a Red by a rat than a rat by a Red," he had declared. The party's support forced Quill to walk a real tightrope because about 60 percent of transit workers were Irish-Catholics and staunchly anti-Communist. This alliance with the Communist party appears to have been primarily pragmatic in nature. As Quill described the formative years of transit unionism: "We went to the Friendly Sons of Saint

Patrick, but they would have nothing to do with the idea of organizing Irishmen into a legitimate union. We went to the Ancient Order of Hibernians and they threw us out of their meeting hall. They wanted no part of Irish rebels or Irish rabble."[24]

Other Irish and Irish-American organizations such as the Catholic Church, the Democratic party, and the Irish-American press showed a similar disinterest in the plight of transit workers. As Freeman has pointed out, these groups cut across class lines and were dominated by middle-class leaders and middle-class views.[25] The Friendly Sons of Saint Patrick, for example, "nearly hit the ceiling" when it was approached because it was dominated by businessmen, and IRT general manager George Keegan was a prominent member and one-time president of the Sons.[26] Having been rebuffed by these Irish organizations, an accommodation was reached with the Communist Party. As Quill said: "Sure I worked with the Communists. In 1933 I would have worked with the Devil himself if he could have given us the money, the mimeograph machines and the manpower to launch the Transport Workers Union. The Communist Party needed me, and I needed them."[27] Other transit workers corroborated Quill's assessment, "over and over again, pioneer TWU members of varied political outlooks credit the party's contribution of money, personnel, and guidance, at a time others were unwilling to do the same, with playing a crucial, even decisive, role in the union's success."[28]

By 1936, with Quill as president and Douglas MacMahon as financial secretary, the union continued its growth, attaining about 8,000 members by Christmas time.[29] This tremendous increase in membership was reflective of what was happening throughout the United State at this time, as groups of predominantly unskilled workers exercised their legally protected right to join unions. Ironically, however, when the TWU and IRT management approached the NLRB in 1937 and requested an election to determine if the workers wanted TWU representation, the board ruled that it did not have jurisdiction because the IRT's operations did not involve interstate commerce. Although representation elections for workers of the IRT and the other privately owned transit lines were eventually held under the auspices of a voluntary agency established by Mayor Fiorello LaGuardia to handle such situations, it was the passage of the Wagner Act that had really propelled the growth of the TWU.[30] By June 1937, the TWU claimed more than 40,000 members.

Once transit workers believed they came under the legal protection of the Wagner Act, it was not suprising that they were very receptive to the TWU's organizing efforts. During the Great Depression, pay cuts had been imposed on all subway workers, and wages for the unskilled were about 50¢ per hour. In addition, although they were only required to actually work eight hours each day, seven days each week, all of the employees in the transportation departments (motormen, bus drivers, conductors, change agents) usually spent about twelve hours each day on the job because they were not paid for four hours of "swing time" between rush hours.[31] In the shop and powerhouse areas, workers were required to spend less time on the job, but rarely fewer than fifty hours per week. Few workers had vacations or sick pay, and "accident-caused injuries and deaths were frequent."[32]

Because of the generally low pay and poor working conditions, employment in the transit industry tended to be of rather short duration. It was an acceptable entry-level job for newly arrived immigrants, until something better came along. However, with the onset of the Great Depression which essentially eliminated the possibility of obtaining a better job elsewhere, transit workers became more sensitive to the need to improve conditions within the transit industry.[33]

In the fall of 1937, at the height of his union success, Quill ran for City Council under the banner of the American Labor Party (ALP). The party had been formed in 1936 when President Franklin D. Roosevelt urged New York City labor leaders to establish a party that would help garner labor and independent support for his reelection. The Labor Party was also supported by the Communist party. Quill was elected, and as a councilman he pushed for low-cost housing and a number of other pro-worker issues. A split developed in the ALP, however, when in August 1939, Russia and Germany signed a nonaggression pact. The unions that were instrumental in establishing the ALP, such as the International Ladies Garment Workers and the Amalgamated Clothing Workers, had predominantly Jewish memberships; and they therefore urged that the United States get involved in trying to stop Hitler's activities in Europe. The ALP, dominated by these unions, condemned the Hitler-Stalin pact, and all ALP candidates were given the ultimatum of either denouncing the Russian-German pact or losing the party's nomination. The only ALP candidate who refused to endorse the stand against Russia, Quill was denied the Labor Party nomination and was defeated when he ran as an independent. David Dubinsky, the president of the ILGWU actively campaigned against Quill, arguing that he had "sold out his principles to Stalin."[34] Although Quill may have supported the party out of personal convictions, it is also possible he felt the TWU was not yet strong enough to operate independently of the Communist party and therefore had to continue his adherence to the party line.

By 1940, several factors coalesced to weaken Quill's control over the TWU. In June, the part private, part public system of transit in New York City was unified under city control. As a result, all workers were now

employees of the city and were no longer covered by the provisions of the
Wagner Act. Mayor Fiorello LaGuardia said that because transit workers
"...now have virtual civil service status and thus are protected in their
jobs,...they therefore have no need and no right to strike." One TWU
leader felt that his members' new status had definitely affected their
outlook. "They don't think they need a union," he remarked.[35] Perhaps
most important, the union security arrangements that required workers to
maintain their union membership in order to retain their jobs, would no
longer be applicable after the contracts that were negotiated with the private
transit companies expired.

The dues situation became so critical that the union began throwing
picket lines in front of the homes of members who failed to pay their $1.25
or $1.75 per month dues. At least 150 of the union's most vocal critics were
brought up on charges before the union's "trial" board. Six of Quill's most
active opponents "were assaulted on the streets; five were brutally attacked,
two with blackjacks, one with a hammer and another with a lead bar; one was
kicked repeatedly in the head and the sixth was threatened with a gun."[36]
One critic found a dead rat hung by a string above his workbench. The
intent was to make transit workers fearful not to be a member of the union.

By the 1940s, considerable Catholic opposition to the TWU's
incumbent leadership had also surfaced. Acting mainly through its
publication, The Labor Leader, the Association of Catholic Trade Unionists
(ACTU), began to assert itself; "The TWU is a great union," said The Labor
Leader, "but not because of its leaders." The Catholics sought to enter the
TWU elections but were "brutally slandered and even assaulted." Quill
established a TWU "kangaroo court" and threw the opposition candidates
out of the union. Because the closed shop still prevailed on the IRT and the
BMT, these workers then lost their jobs. Operating through labor schools,
priests told transit workers, "Don't be beguiled by a brogue. We are firm in
the opinion that the majority of the men want bona fide unionism—not the
present Communist leadership of Mike Quill and his gang." In response,
Quill grabbed a copy of The Labor Leader and ripped it up before a crowd of
transit workers, telling them the ACTU was "a strike breaking agency....
No decent Catholic would belong to it."[37]

With the contracts the TWU had negotiated with the private
companies due to expire in the summer of 1941, the City of New York also
took a number of steps to weaken the union's control over the now public
transit system. Mayor La Guardia sponsored a bill in the state legislature to
make strikes on public transit illegal. Then, he obtained a court ruling that
the TWU's picketing outside the homes of "deserters" was illegal. Also, he
ordered the Board of Transportation, which was now charged with
operating the municipally owned system, to mail pamphlets to each of the

city's 32,000 subway workers, advising them that they could leave the union at any time without fear of losing their jobs. Finally, the board unilaterally announced that all workers would receive more paid vacations, paid holidays, and paid sick leaves, as a way of weakening the TWU position.[38]

As the June 30, 1941, contract expiration approached, Quill told his members that it was worth striking to obtain the closed shop. After Germany renounced its nonagression pact and invaded Russia, however, the TWU leadership did an about-face; now arguing that the union should aid the war effort by relinquishing its right to strike.

Quill's attempt to maintain the allegiance of his members now became even more difficult. With the transit system now under municipal ownership, workers had several options. They could stop paying their dues. They might join another union. They might vote out their incumbent leadership. They might call a wildcat strike. Faced with these difficulties, Quill developed what was to become his characteristic style of bargaining:

> ...he first asked them what kind of wage increase they wanted.
> "Ask for twenty cents, Mike!", came the reply. "No, ask for thirty-five cents." "Forty cents! Ask for forty!"
> Quill waited for the pot to simmer at fifty cents and then he rolled up his sleeves. "You stingy cowards," he brayed. "I'm going to go in there and demand a dollar fifty, because that's what you deserve!"
> "Hey, that's our Mike!" cheered the crowd, and Quill walked away the unchallenged leader of the pack.[39]

His approach might be fine in the short run, but what happened when Quill could not fulfill the expectations he had raised? Again, Whittemore provides an apt observation: "He didn't explain or apologize. He simply assumed a more angry attitude than anyone. He blamed the poor settlement on the nearest victim, with veiled accusations and intriguing proclamations that would be discussed for days in the press."[40]

In a sense, Quill used the same symbolic techniques to reassure his constituents (his members) that John Lindsay used in trying to sway his potential supporters. And for a long period of time, Quill was backed by TWU members because of his noble attempts, rather than his actual accomplishments. Quill was masterful in his manipulation of the media. Long-time Quill watcher, Theodore Kheel, observed that the union leader would have been a genius on Madison Avenue. "He was one of the great propagandists," said Kheel. The mediator once showed Quill a news release he was preparing, to indicate that more than 50,000 cars were parked illegally in Manhattan every day. Quill advised him to say, "Almost

100,000 cars." Kheel made the suggested change, and the next day, as the TWU president had predicted, it appeared on the first page of the *New York Times*.[41]

In a union that was more than 60 percent Irish during most of his tenure in office, Quill went to great lengths to highlight his Irishness and Catholicism. These ties were particularly important because of his close association with the Communist party. As one observer noted, Quill "became a sort of professional Irishman, exploiting his religion to the fullest extent of the matchless Quill resourcefulness."[42] As Quill himself observed, "Many a fellow who thought me a dangerous agitator found me more to his taste after meeting with me at the Paulist fathers."[43] He regularly went to Irish patriotic rallies and cultivated County Kerry societies in New York. It was an open joke that Quill's brogue grew thicker with each passing year in the United States. He wove marvelous tales of his participation in the activities of the Irish Republican Army before he came to the United States. Although he was born with a hip defect, at one point Quill explained that his limp resulted from a bullet that smashed his hip during his revolutionary days in Ireland. Later he modified the tale by blaming the injured hip on a "fall off the mountainside with a lot of equipment" during his IRA days.[44]

During this period, the lives of Irish transit workers tended to be entwined in a variety of ways. As Freeman has pointed out:

> Many knew one another before emigrating; others met in the Irish neighborhoods of New York where they found new homes. Most were Catholic, attended church with one another, and joined the same church-sponsored organizations. The numerous Irish fraternal and social groups, such as the Ancient Order of Hibernians and the county associations, had large transit-worker memberships. Athletic events and dances—the bread and butter of New York Irish social life—likewise brought together men who worked in the transit industry.[45]

In fact, Quill's initial rise to prominence came as a result of his activity in social circles where, because of his wit, he was considered the premier master of ceremonies at Irish social gatherings.[46] Having met Quill in a social setting, his fellow Irishmen were much more receptive to his exhortations that they join the TWU when they were approached at work.

In some instances, Quill's public relations coups had a very specific focus. In November 1946, while Quill was in London serving as an American delegate to a new world labor organization, he inflamed the British by referring to Northern Ireland as a slave state. He then urged its union with the Republic of Ireland. To Quill, raising the Irish question, at a seemingly totally inappropriate time, made perfect sense. "Oh, it was quite effective," explained Quill. The story made all the front pages of newspapers in New York, "and it was helpful to our slate in the local union elections, which just happened to be held that day."[47]

Finally, of course, Quill's whole public persona was an "act" played to his union member audience. One observer referred to the "two faces of Quill": the "onstage Quill" and the "offstage Quill." At a news conference during the 1966 strike, for example, Quill "took on stage presence as the heat of the television lights brought perspiration to his almost bald head." As he walked through the doorway and spotted photographers aiming cameras at him, "his eyes lit up, his jaw became slightly truculent and he assumed an air of studied deliberation...." In a few seconds "the brogue became lilting, and there was joy in his eyes as he called Mayor Lindsay an 'ass.'..." As always, Quill was on the alert for the comment that would disarm with humor. Denying he had been thrown out of City Hall during the term of Mayor William O'Dwyer, Quill quickly added, "I have been thrown out of better places than City Hall."[48]

The basic strategy of the onstage Quill was one of dramatic confrontations on every transit problem. The intent of TWU publicity was to be intentionally imflammatory, and according to his wife, Quill "orchestrated a neverending calendar of real and contrived crises every week, every month, every year. He stage-managed his temper tantrums on television, his outbursts at news conferences, the table-pounding with employers and the fireworks on the stages of auditoriums where strike votes were taken. It was all planned and deliberate."[49] The reason for this publicity-seeking, confrontational style was simple: to constantly reassure TWU members that their union was doing everything possible on their behalf.

With the cameras off, Quill "is a good listener who speaks softly, does not make notes or speak from them, the careful administrator with an eye for details and the cool negotiator."[50] Leaders, however, who listen attentively to aides and who work without fanfare find it difficult to demonstrate to their members that they are truly fighting on their behalf. Hence, the public persona.

After a short period out of political office as a result of his split with the American Labor Party, Quill was reelected to City Council in 1943, this time as an independent candidate. By the time he eventually left the legislative body, he had completed nine years of service on council. His record evidenced the kinds of concerns one would expect from a union leader who for many years had been close to the Communist party. For example, when he ran for reelection in 1943, he supported an immediate rent freeze on all housing in the city, "full budgetary support" of the public school system, social services for children, programs to curb juvenile

delinquency, the establishment of after school care and nurseries for
children of working women, the establishment of "genuine" collective
bargaining procedures in all city departments along principles outlined in
the National and State Labor Relations Acts, as well as programs to
"combat all anti-labor, anti-Semitic, anti-Catholic, anti-Negro and bigoted
movements, such as the KKK..." and to ensure "equalization of opportunity to every qualified person to obtain employment without regard
to race, religion, color, origin, or creed."[51] In addition, council member
Quill constantly attempted to address constituent concerns. Thus, when
Leo O'Connell wrote his representative in July 1938 to complain that boys
his age (between ten and fourteen), could not afford to go to swimming
pools near their homes in the Bronx, Quill wrote back immediately,
indicating he had obtained support from Mayor LaGuardia to put a new
pool in the Bronx.[52]

One final aspect of the Quill personality deserves examination—his
social consciousness. As reflected by his councilmanic stances, Quill was
certainly not an "Archie Bunkerish" loud-mouth, concerned only with
protecting the interests of his own members while taking a public-be-
damned attitude toward social problems. Quite the contrary, he had been a
social activist concerned with issues such as economic justice, racial and
religious prejudice, and war, for all of his adult life. However, because of his
own humble background, Quill was distrustful of those well-placed
members of society who professed a concern with such issues out of a sense
of noblesse oblige.

Until 1938, black workers were restricted to the jobs of porter and
janitor on the subways and were not permitted to become bus drivers. Quill
joined forces with Adam Clayton Powell and his People's Committee in
Harlem in an attempt to break such barriers. He often spoke at mass
meetings of blacks at St. Mark's Church and the Abyssinian Baptist Church
on 138th Street, sponsored by the Powell group.[53] Such a position was
extremely difficult for Quill because of the racial and ethnic animosity that
existed in the transit industry. As Quill observed, "it was shocking to see
foreign-born transit workers wreck meeting after meeting in a hysterical
attempt to keep American-born Negro transit workers from positions of
dignity."[54]

Quill's efforts in support of racial equality were not only local in scope.
In 1936, only a few months after the New York City transit workers had
become affiliated with the International Association of Machinists (IAM),
Quill attended the IAM national convention where he urged that the clause,
"white Americans only shall be admitted to membership," be stricken from
the Machinist's constitution. Failing to change the national constitution,
the TWU nevertheless maintained racial equality in their own local. At an

appearance at the TWU's 1943 convention, Paul Robeson praised the union for having "pointed the finger at every encroachment on civil rights in government, industry, education, housing and in the trade union movement itself."[55] Perhaps most indicative of Quill's racial attitudes, however, was an open letter appearing in the TWU's official publication in response to a criticism by twenty-five TWU airline workers in Tennessee, who were protesting the union's support of the Reverend Martin Luther King, Jr., and the Freedom Riders:

> Wherever there are ignorant, racist Ku Kluxers . . . trying to destroy our country, it is the business of TWU. Whenever Americans do not have the right to vote, it comes under the heading "things of the union." . . . When America is sick and endangered by the cancer of segregation, it is cause for concern by all organized labor—and by each and every member of TWU.
>
> We intend to continue fighting bigotry and ignorance on every front with our money, manpower and moral pressure.[56]

Later, the TWU president marched in the civil rights demonstrations of the 1960s and invited Rev. King to speak before the TWU convention. At the American Federation of Labor-Congress of Industrial Organizations (AFL-CIO) convention in Florida in 1961, Quill urged President George Meany to address the problems of black workers. "The gap between white and Negro workers grows even wider," he warned, "and is reaching the proportions of an open revolt by the victims of discrimination."[57]

Quill was also sensitive to religious bigotry, and not only when it was directed against Catholics. He attended numerous meetings of Jewish groups before and after the United States entered World War II to protest Hitler's atrocities. In later years, Quill was equally sensitive to such concerns. At a strike rally in 1961, he detected a note of anti-Semitism during his speech before the workers of a private bus line in Manhattan that had recently been purchased by a Dallas businessman named Harry Weinberg. Quill immediately chastized his audience, "When it comes to the dollar," he said, "it doesn't mean a damn if the boss is Jewish, Irish, heathen or vegetarian. They're all the same." He then reminded the workers that in Dublin the much-hated boss was an Irishman named Delaney.[58]

Always, however, Quill remained cynical concerning individuals whose professions of social awareness seemed to contradict their upbringing. After Nelson Rockefeller took office as governor of New York State in 1959, he invited a group of labor leaders to his luxurious mansion for a get-acquainted session. "Now boys," Rockefeller told the assembled unionists, "we're going to have to raise the taxes, and we want to make sure the burden falls on the shoulders of those who can afford to pay." Quill looked around the mansion and whispered loudly, "What did Lenin say about the contradictions of capitalism?"[59]

Quill's beliefs during the 1960s were wholly consistant with the social protesters of the day, causing him to bemoan the fact that other labor leaders no longer shared these concerns. As Quill nostalgically recalled an earlier labor movement, "If there was only some way of keeping the crusade of the 1930s alive.... Where we used to double up in a two-dollar hotel room, we now stay where dinners cost six-fifty. The unions build Taj Mahals instead of contributing the dollars to the civil rights movement." For himself, the Quill rhetoric of the 1960s could have been that of a civil rights or antiwar protester. "... [T]he revolutionary movement in Ireland smacks awfully close to the revolutionary movement in Vietnam today," said Quill. He added, "If they want their way of life, let them have it." Then Quill linked the war to the "twenty million American Negroes who are semislaves, if not completely slaves."[60] And despite the fact that the TWU represented a number of workers in the space program, Quill opposed the U.S. attempt to send a man to the moon: "$40 billion of our money is being spent to go to the moon. But we still have on earth the great killers—heart disease and cancer—they aren't checked yet. Maybe if we spend $10 billion on research on these diseases they might be checked. But the $10 billion is called socialism and the $40 billion is called nationalism."[61]

Although they often shared his concerns, Quill nevertheless distrusted those whose positions on such issues were intellectually, rather than experientially based. Spiro Agnew had referred to them as "limousine-liberals"; Quill used the equally pejorative term, the "Shubert People," referring to wealthy theatergoers: "You should see what it's like, being in the cage [change booth] and having to deal with the Shubert People. Can you imagine having to listen to them, with their stupid questions? "Was that my train?" they ask. "If this the other-r side?" they want to know.[62] Lindsay, of course, was a Shubert Person.

The Jailing

It is clear that not only did the TA take the initiative in jailing the union leaders, but also that the Lindsay Administration concurred in this course of action. What is not so clear is why a politician with aspirations for higher office, such as Lindsay, who was proud of having "long-supported legislation in Congress . . . to improve the standing of the working man," would have taken a course which was anathema to the interests of organized labor.[63] TWU attorney John O'Donnell offered his explanation of why the Lindsay Administration asked that the union leaders be jailed:

The matter tore the administration apart before it even got started. Bob Price [deputy mayor] said to Rankin [J. Lee, Corporation Counsel of the City of New York] that it would be madness to make martyrs of them by putting them in jail. Rankin replied that he was the city's chief law officer, and that he had a responsibility to the court. Price then had some more discussions with Rankin and tried to convince him that it would serve no purpose to jail the union people. Rankin replied that if he were not allowed to do things the way he thought was right, he would resign. To stop him from resigning they did things his way.[64]

In view of Rankin's public statements, this explanation appears to be highly plausible. Named assistant attorney general by President Dwight D. Eisenhower in January 1953, Rankin argued the government's position in the landmark Supreme Court case that forced the Little Rock School Board to desegregate its schools. Three years later, Rankin, who served as Lindsay's superior when the mayor worked as an attorney in the Justice Department, was appointed solicitor general of the United States. Later, he served as general counsel and supervised the investigation and the writing of the Warren Commission Report on the assassination of President John F. Kennedy. Leaving a lucrative private law practice to become New York City's Corporation Counsel, the fifty-eight-year-old Rankin was certainly not dependent on Lindsay for a job. In an interview shortly after the contempt cases against the striking union leaders were heard in State Supreme Court, Rankin said that the TA was seriously concerned about making a martyr of Quill. However, he continued, the Authority decided to seek a judgement against the union leaders because failure to prosecute them would endanger respect for the law. "It's always a problem that you might make a man a martyr," Rankin said, "but you have to ask the question whether the country can continue to exist if its laws are not enforced."[65] During the course of his remarks, Rankin made it clear that he had been advising the TA lawyers in their prosecution.

Later, Rankin expanded on his views concerning the jailing of the union officials:

> You can't play fast and loose with the courts. If we went to the judge and got this order against Quill and then didn't have it enforced, then what would happen the next time we went to the judge for an order against somebody? Don't have to be very smart to figure out what would happen. He'd say, "Hey, those fellows didn't enforce the last order I gave them!" He wouldn't be ready to give us an order so fast would he?
>
> You can't be selective about the law. . . . Now what if we go to court to sue the XYZ Corporation and they violate an order and we go after them

for contempt and they say, "Well, you gave Quill a break, what about me?" Then what are you going to do? So you see what this city would be like without law in it. It'd be a jungle.[66]

Thus, despite the propensity of Lindsay supporters to blame the jailing of the union leaders on Justice Geller or the TA, it was clear that the action was taken at the behest of the Lindsay Administration.

Before leaving for jail, Quill named Douglas MacMahon, an international vice president and administrative assistant to Quill, as the chief negotiator for the TWU. In appearance and temperament, MacMahon presented a sharp contrast to the man he succeeded as chief negotiator for the TWU. Tall, white haired, and reflective, MacMahon presented a very different image than his volatile predecessor. The grandson of Methodist missionaries to India, the fifty-nine-year-old MacMahon was born in Brooklyn. After graduating from high school, he went to work as a clerk on Wall Street. "My ambition then," he explained, "was to become a stock broker and a millionaire." When the stock market crash of 1929 cost him this job, MacMahon said, "I began to realize this world is not all sugar and honey."[67] In 1930, at age twenty-four, he went to work for the IRT as a "dirt monkey," sweeping the tracks to keep the steel dust down. Working twelve hours each day, six days each week, MacMahon earned $22. In April 1934, MacMahon and Quill were among the handful of men who established the TWU. Later that year, MacMahon led the sit-down strike at the Kent Avenue powerhouse, which resulted in the TWU being recognized as the bargaining agent for the employees of the BMT. MacMahon later became president of TWU Local 100, which represented the New York City transit workers, and by 1941 he was also secretary-treasurer of the international. Quill was president of the international at this time. MacMahon was a "natural leader, self-assured, able, intelligent," and these attributes allowed him not only to rise in the ranks of the TWU but also to become the acknowledged leader of the Communist faction within the union.[68]

Although virtually all of the top officials in the TWU were Communists during the early to mid-1940s, a schism developed over the issue of Communism. By the late 1940s, Quill, formerly known as "Red Mike," became disenchanted with the Communist party when they refused to support an increase in the transit fare from 5¢ to 10¢. The Communists believed that such an increase would be borne by those least able to afford it, the working people of New York. While not really disagreeing with this position, Quill felt that the fare had to be sacrificed if the position of transit workers was to be improved.[69] In August 1948, perhaps prodded on by attempts by Philip Murray to purge Communist party leaders from the ranks of the CIO, Quill challenged MacMahon to discuss his Communist affiliation before a meeting of 1,500 BMT employees. "I am a member of that party," admitted MacMahon, "but in the 14 years that I have been a member I did not intrude my political beliefs on the TWU. So far as the union is concerned," MacMahon continued, "I do not take my political dictation from anybody but the rank-and-file membership of the TWU." Quill then addressed the meeting, "Well, we have finally smoked out Douglas MacMahon. He admits he is a member of the Communist party. He is a prisoner of the leaders of the Communist party and he can't get away from it." At the TWU convention in Chicago several months later, Quill succeeded in purging MacMahon from the union's ranks, along with five of six vice presidents, and eleven of the seventeen executive board members.[70]

MacMahon then opened a small candy and stationary store that, by his own accounts, did not do well. Less than one year after he had been dismissed from the TWU because of his membership in the Communist party, MacMahon abruptly resigned his affiliation. Explaining his action, he said, "I left the party in 1949 because I finally woke up to the fact that these people were not legitimate, were not honest, were not fighting for the workers as I thought they were." The following year, MacMahon sent a letter of apology to Quill, disclosing that he had cut all of his ties with the Communist party because, "their policy was one of disrupting the labor movement." In his letter, which was highly publicized throughout the TWU, MacMahon continued, "Disrupt was the slogan! Wreck was the goal! I therefore quit the Communist party because such a program offends every trade union principle.[71] Although union officials publicly stated that MacMahon could expect no reward for his action, Quill was instrumental in helping him obtain a job with a small CIO union. After ten years on its staff, MacMahon decided to run for elective office, and when he was defeated, he was again out of a job. Once more, Quill stepped in, naming MacMahon an international representative of the TWU in 1960; the following year he was selected by Quill to be his administrative assistant. Neither Quill nor MacMahon have ever explained their reconciliation.

Chapter 6

Negotiations Resume

Negotiations resumed on Tuesday evening, January 4, after they had been stalled all day by the imprisonment of the union leaders and the collapse of Michael Quill. The talks which lasted until 1:15 a.m. were confined to separate sessions between the mediators and the two sides. Essentially, the three neutrals were attempting to familiarize themselves with the new team of union negotiators and to lay the foundation for direct discussions between the parties. All three of the mediators reportedly walked out of the sessions shaking their heads. One commented that Douglas MacMahon had "tried to outdo Quill at the table." In his public position, MacMahon gave ample evidence that he intended to be an unyielding bargainer. The strike will go on "until hell freezes over," he said, unless the TA made a "legitimate, substantial, reasonable, and responsible" contract offer to the union. At a news conference, MacMahon contended that the transit workers were being treated as "second-class citizens" and were being, "deliberately [and] maliciously" excluded from gains achieved by other city employees.[1]

MacMahon also continued his union's criticism of Mayor Lindsay. "Although he ran for office on the ground that he was a great liberal, what was the first thing he did?" asked MacMahon rhetorically. "The first thing he did was put Mike Quill in jail."[2] For his part, John Lindsay spent Tuesday trying to convince the public that there was no choice but to jail the union officials and that this action would not hurt chances for a quick settlement. However, the mayor's demeanor clearly indicated that he was shaken by the day's events and unsure of its impact on negotiations. Appearing tense and nervous at a news conference, he was asked by a reporter if he thought the jailing of Quill had helped or hindered the prospect for a settlement. With a considerable amount of equivocation, Lindsay observed that "with the added pressure that is being applied [from the jailing], the chances of reaching an agreement are not diminished."[3] Then, with a tremor in his voice, Lindsay continued, indicating that he supported the action of his Corporation Counsel, J. Lee Rankin:

> You had an unlawful strike and you've got a contempt of court and the
> court was presented with a set of facts and had the obligation and the
> power, of course, to make a decision. And that decision was made.
>   And I think everyone—every New Yorker everywhere—will under-
> stand that when the court decides to protect its own integrity . . . it has to
> be supported."[4]

Throughout the day, Lindsay continued to counter the impression that
negotiations were deteriorating, by trying to foster the belief that he
personally would become more actively involved. In the early afternoon his
office issued a statement that said, "The Mayor is pressing very hard to get
this dispute on the right track in the public interest . . . that's why he's
remaining at his desk. He is talking with the mediation panel on a
continuous basis. He is using every expert at his disposal to bring the
negotiations within proper dimensions." Later in the day, additional
bulletins were disseminated indicating that Lindsay intended "to step back
into negotiations" and to "stay there until there is a settlement."
Furthermore, the mayor wanted it known that he had met with the
mediation panel on Tuesday and "the Panel under Dr. Feinsinger's
direction is driving hard to reach an agreement."[5]

Speaking for himself, Nathan Feinsinger was hardly optimistic about
the impact of the day's events on the prospects for a settlement. Described
as being "profoundly disturbed" by the jailing of Quill, Feinsinger
commented sadly that the action "may very well tighten the situation to
such a degree that the panel may have an impossible job. There's a great
danger of drifting into a situation where nobody—nobody can find a key to
the solution." Feinsinger perceived of the situation as rapidly deteriorating
because he never felt there would be a "serious" strike. "Everybody
thought, including myself," Feinsinger said, "that if a strike were called at
all, it would end after the first two days, which would be before the first full
working day." Who was responsible for jailing the union leaders?
Feinsinger was philosophical, rather than specific, "I am responsible as well
as the rest of us, of all society, responsible for a situation in which we use
power of some kind to force an end to a labor dispute."[6]

In addition to its possible impact on negotiations, mediation Chairman
Feinsinger was personally shaken by the court's action: "When Mr. Quill
and the others were jailed, for the first time in my life—and I'm pretty
hardboiled—I wept. I felt that this was the beginning of a Greek tragedy. I
was up all night. It gave me a jolt. I couldn't sleep. I had a sense of impending
tragedy. A real man was going to jail. I was sick about it. I didn't see a Mike

Quill gobbling up people ... trying to debate an issue with him. I saw a nineteen-year-old Irish rebel raising hell. And it turned out to be a near tragedy."[7]

The fear that the jailing of Quill would harden the union's position and make a strike settlement more difficult was certainly borne out by the initial reaction of TWU members. "This will make a martyr of Mike Quill," said an IRT motorman. "The men won't go back until they have a decent settlement and Mike's illness isn't going to change anything." An IND conductor was even more unyielding in his approach, stressing that there should be "no work until he's out of the hospital and out of jail." Even before they received word of Quill's collapse, his jailing seemed to galvanize the striking transit workers. "They've put Mike in jail," shouted one picket with a noticeable Irish brogue. "They aren't gonna find enough jails in this city for all 36,000 members of the union." In a very different accent, a thirty-year-old subway-car cleaner who fled Cuba in 1955 said he was "in jail in Cuba because I was against Batista. I'll go to jail here if I have to," he added. As word of Quill's jailing spread through the city's fifty-nine picket sites, about 350 pickets left their locations and converged in front of the Civil Jail on West 37th Street where he had been taken. They marched in front of the jail carrying hastily constructed signs proclaiming, "God Bless Mike" and "We'll trade Lindsley [sic] for Quill."[8]

Early Tuesday morning, the commuter crush that was, in large measure, avoided on the previous day, apparently would begin to choke the city. By 7:55 a.m., John Lindsay was on radio and television pleading with New Yorkers, "If you have left home and can possibly turn back, please do so."[9] Not nearly enough people heeded his plea, however, to avoid massive congestion on both the roads and the commuter trains. It did not take a very sophisticated analysis to realize that, once New Yorkers began to return to their jobs, there was no way to compensate for the transit services shut down by the strike. On an average working day, the city's subways carried 4.6 million riders, and TA buses transported 1.5 million more, for a total of 6.1 million passengers. Of these, about 25 percent travelled in the rush hours from 7:00 a.m. to 9:00 a.m., and approximately 30 percent rode during the afternoon peak of 4:00 p.m. to 7:00 p.m. There was simply no way for the city's already strained streets and commuter rail lines to accommodate an increase of this magnitude. With an estimated 65 to 70 percent of Manhattan's work force reporting on Tuesday, the absence of TA subways and buses caused 25 to 30 percent more automobiles and trucks to squeeze their way into the main business borough. And the situation would have been worse if not for a considerable amount of ride sharing: the average vehicle inching its way into Manhattan contained 2.5 occupants, compared with a norm of 1.5.

The added traffic, of course, led to long delays and considerable inconvenience. Mayor Lindsay proved prophetic when he tried to console commuters early in the morning, "I feel very badly that New Yorkers are put out and harassed." He then predicted, "Your nerves will be ragged by the time you have sat in a traffic jam for a long period of time." One bus, chartered by the *New York Times* for its employees, left a pick-up point on Westchester Avenue in the Bronx at 7:00 a.m. for a trip to 43rd Street that normally takes an hour. At 10:15 the bus finally arrived at Times Square in midtown Manhattan. A second *Times* bus, leaving from Flushing, Queens, did somewhat better, covering a trip that normally takes an hour in two hours and five minutes. In some instances, added problems were super-imposed on the increased number of vehicles, creating still worse delays. A sixty-four-year-old Brooklyn motorist, for example, died of a heart attack in the middle of the Brooklyn Battery Tunnel and crashed his car into an oncoming automobile. The accident took place at the height of the morning rush hour, causing service trough the tunnel to be disrupted for fifty minutes. The good-natured, holiday mood that had prevailed on Monday turned grim a day later as commuters struggled to get to work. As one Sunnyside, Queens, motorist characterized the prevailing "rules of the road" on Tuesday, "Most drivers just seem to be saying, 'let the other guy go to hell.' "[10]

The commuter rail lines were hardly an improvement over the streets, as thousands of commuters endured waits of two hours during the afternoon rush hour. The Long Island Railroad became so crowded that Harold J. Pryor, the general chairman of the three locals of the Brotherhood of Railroad Trainmen that represents the lines employees, threatened to shut down operations because the number of passengers being carried was unsafe. After being reminded, however, that a federal court order enjoining a sympathy strike by his union was already in force, Pryor did not follow through on his threat. By the day's end, the Long Island Railroad had added more than twenty-five extra trains and estimated that its passenger load would exceed 300,000, compared with normal usage by 250,000 riders.[11]

The increased number of riders also taxed the capacity of the New York Central Railroad. On Monday, the situation at Grand Central Station was totally chaotic as 25,000 persons, or eight times the normal number, sought to take the line to stops in the Bronx. This group of would-be passengers joined the 35,000 regular commuters who use the line to travel to Westchester, beyond the city limits. To avoid a repetition of the dangerous situation that prevailed on Monday, police on Tuesday posi-tioned barricades that forced commuters to stay on the street until the congestion in the station eased. Then, in groups of 500, passengers were allowed to enter the station. The number of prospective passengers waiting to use the New York Central Railroad to go to the Bronx was so great that at times as many as 6,000 persons filled the sidewalks on Vanderbilt and Madison Avenues and 42nd and 43rd Streets, before being permitted through the barricades. After the expected late afternoon rush subsided, another mini-rush hour developed on the rail lines about 9:30 p.m. Apparently, a large number of commuters had heeded Mayor Lindsay's advice to stay in the city for dinner so that not everyone would attempt to leave Manhattan between 4:00 p.m. and 7:00 p.m. By 9:30 p.m., lines of approximately 5,000 passengers waited to board Long Island Railroad trains.[12]

With an additional day to assess business losses resulting from the strike, the Commerce and Industry Association estimated that they exceeded $100 million, rather than the $40 million reported on Monday. Included in the revised estimate were wages lost by workers unable to report for work. Although Mayor Lindsay had urged employers to pay workers not reporting, the Commerce and Industry Association reported that by Tuesday few employers would pay absentee workers. As Ralph Gross, the executive vice president of the association reported, by the second day of the strike the position of virtually all businesses was, "no show, no dough." Calling the mayor's position "misguided," Gross maintained that paying workers for staying home amounted to "subsidizing the strike." Making workers get to work under adverse conditions, or forcing them to suffer the consequences of going without pay, said Gross, would generate pressure for a strike settlement. "Otherwise," he added, "people won't holler for the strike to end."[13]

In a televised appearance, Mayor Lindsay conceded that the transit shutdown was "a very damaging situation economically," but he nevertheless continued to urge New Yorkers to stay out of Manhattan. This raised the ire of most businesses, particularly those in the theater and restaurant industries. "The mayor has descended from fatuity to banality," criticized David Merrick, the successful Broadway producer. The situation involving Off-Broadway shows was so bad that Actors' Equity agreed to allow shows to be suspended for the duration of the strike without paying actors' salaries. The actors' union decided that even though their contract with the producers required that they be paid in such circumstances, such an approach would force a number of shows to close permanently. Attendance was also down considerably at night clubs, museums, and athletic events.[14] And, with many people not reporting for work and staying away from the "attractions" New York had to offer, restaurant business was also down considerably.

Undoubtedly the most substantial losses caused by the strike, however, were suffered by the retail industry. Although all of the department stores remained open on Tuesday, their business was only slightly improved from the previous day when they were virtually empty. Macy's, which normally serves 150,000 customers in a day had fewer than 50,000. A spokesman for Gimbel's was more descriptive than quantitative in his assessment: "All in all," he said, "it stinks."[15] The situation for the department stores in downtown Brooklyn was no better, with Abraham and Strauss estimating that sales were down about 70 percent. In stark contrast to the situation in other sections of the stores, however, business at the shirt, pajama, sock, and underwear counters was booming. "Most of them are planning to stay in town," reported one harried clerk at the shirt counter in Bloomingdale's, "and they need these items."[16]

Although on a dollar basis the losses suffered by the retail industry were massive, the strike occurred after its peak Christmas season. For the garment industry, however, the timing could not have been worse. According to David Zalinka, the president of a coat and suit company, the first week of the year is the peak week for spring production. In general, clothing manufacturers had agreements to complete deliveries of their spring lines by January 31, and if you lose production now, Zalinka observed, "you can't make it up."[17]

Some businesses benefitted from the strike. The airlines reported that business was brisk, with most of the additional travellers leaving the city. A large number of business people apparently decided that this was the ideal time to visit out-of-town branches, plants, or customers. Unexpectedly, for casual observers, the Metropolitan Garage Board of Trade reported that profits for parking garages would be expected to go down during the transit strike. Although garages and parking lots were jammed from early morning until well into the evening, virtually all of the vehicles belonged to commuters who were in the city for the day. Because higher rates are charged for short-term patrons, profits are actually higher when parking spaces are available and there is rapid turnover.[18]

Private employers and citizens, of course, were not the only ones to suffer economic losses as a result of the strike. According to Mario Procaccino, the Controller of the City of New York, the city was losing about $1 million each day in lost sales taxes as a result of the strike and the state's losses amounted to $670,000 daily.[19]

Most of the city's public, parochial, and private schools reopened on Tuesday, but absenteeism was high. Attendance at the elementary level in both public and parochial schools was near normal because most of those students walked to school. At the high school level, however, school policies and attendance figures varied considerably based on individual circumstances. At public high schools that had student bodies drawn from throughout the city, attendance was off by as much as 95 percent. Brooklyn

Technical High School and the High School of Performing Arts, for example, each reported attendances of about 300 out of enrollments of 5,600 and 2,000 respectively. With the exception of those on Staten Island, all of the parochial high schools in the city, which also drew from large geographical areas, remained closed. Overall, about 70 percent of the city's public school students reported on Tuesday, compared with a normal absentee rate of 10 percent. Among public school teachers, 94 percent or about one percent less than normal made it to work, causing Superintendent of Schools Bernard Donovan to praise them for "a magnificent job of getting to school today."[20] Private schools reported near normal operations.

By Tuesday, the disruptions caused by the transit strike were beginning to affect virtually all aspects of life in the city. Seven of the twenty-one municipal hospitals curtailed nonemergency operations because the strike prevented key employees from coming to work. In addition, donations of blood were curbed to such an extent that the city's supply dwindled to its lowest level in twenty years. With only 1,200 pints of blood available by noon, compared with a normal supply of 6,000 pints, the situation was considered critical. However, after an emergency plea for donations and the importing of blood from other cities, 1,800 pints were available later in the day. Dr. Alonzo Yerby, the city's hospital commissioner, was equally concerned about the inability to staff the municipal hospitals at an adequate level. Later that evening, however, the Greater New York Hospital Association reported that a compromise had been reached to allow key employees to report for work. The TWU permitted its drivers to operate a limited number of TA buses to enable hospital workers to get to and from their jobs.[21]

The court system was also affected by the strike. In probably the city's most prominent case, the first degree murder trial of three men accused of killing black nationalist leader Malcolm X was adjourned until the end of the transit shutdown. Supreme Court Justice Charles Marks decided to delay the trial because fewer than one-fourth of the prospective jurors were able to reach his courtroom.[22] In a legal case of considerably less significance, the producers of a rock-and-roll show served a complaint on eight leaders of the TWU asking for $25 million in damages because the transit strike allegedly forced the show to close. In their complaint, lawyers for Murray Kaufman, a disc jockey known as "Murray the K," charged that the union leaders "acted maliciously and willfully and illegally and with complete and utter disregard of the legal and constitutional rights and the health and safety of all the other people of New York City." Furthermore, indicating the apparently worldwide importance of rock-and-roll, the complaint alleged that the union also violated the Universal Declaration of Human Rights as approved by the United Nations in 1948.[23]

Finally, on Tuesday, January 4, the political complexities which helped precipitate the strike continued to muddy the waters. Rather than attempting to resolve the dispute, it was clear that many politicians were preoccupied with trying to assign blame to someone else in order to cast themselves in the best possible light. Although there were no plans for federal intervention, President Lyndon Johnson reportedly was "continuing to watch the situation with interest."[24] Also from Washington, Senator Robert F. Kennedy sent a telegram to Mayor Lindsay saying he was "prepared to assist... in any way appropriate to reach an early and fair settlement of the transit strike."[25] At the state level, Governor Nelson Rockefeller's administration also tried to foster the impression that it was providing crucial help when it announced that those employees unable to reach work would be eligible to receive state unemployment benefits if the strike lasted longer than a week.[26] Most significant, however, was the attempt by a number of unnamed officials in the Liberal party to blame former Mayor Robert F. Wagner for the strike. Wagner branded such criticism, "sheer nonsense and the silliest thing I have ever heard. Who are these Liberals?" the former mayor demanded. "If they are so brave, let them identify themselves and I'll answer them. No one is going to pin the tail on me," he said from Acapulco, where he was vacationing.[27] The Liberal party, which had supported John Lindsay in his recently completed mayoral campaign, had previously backed Wagner. Clearly, the Liberal officials criticizing Wagner were Lindsay's two closest labor advisors in the Liberal party, Alex Rose and David Dubinsky, both high-ranking union officials themselves.

After more than fourteen hours of bargaining on Wednesday, January 5, Mayor Lindsay announced that there had been "some movement" in the transit dispute and that both sides had made new offers. But the "gap remains wide," he added.[28] This marked the first time Lindsay had joined the talks on a full-time basis and he vowed to "stay until there is a settlement." Lindsay would not disclose details of the day's discussions, but it was learned that his first suggestion to the striking unions was that they go back to work under an interim general agreement while the specific contract terms were being worked out. But this proposal was quickly rejected by Douglas MacMahon, who stated that the TWU would hold fast to its tradition of "no contract, no work."[29] Lindsay refused to say how much money was involved in the new offers.

Although his public posture continued to be unyielding, MacMahon would later indicate that his private position was quite different. As MacMahon explained: "After Mike went to jail and I acclimated myself to negotiations, I went to the mediators confidentially in hopes that a settlement could be reached in a day or two. My purpose was to let them know they weren't dealing with a wildman and to tell them what it would take to settle this. The mediators then relayed this information to the mayor. I told them we would have to make up the inequities in two bites. We realized that 30 percent could not possibly be won, but we wanted an increase of 15 percent."[30]

On the legal front, the TA asked for a postponement of a scheduled hearing to determine if the striking unions should be fined for violating a court injunction. State Supreme Court Justice Abraham N. Geller acceded to the TA's request, explaining that he had no choice but to wait until the TA had assessed its damages from the strike and for the TA to then ask for fines based on those estimates of their losses.[31] Thus far the TA had limited its legal actions to invoking applicable common law and had not asked for enforcement of the Condon-Wadlin Act, which forbade strikes by public employees and called for the dismissal of violators. A worker discharged in accordance with the law might be rehired, but he or she could not receive a pay increase for three years and had to remain on probation for five years.

Meanwhile, on Wednesday, Bellevue Hospital officials described Quill's condition as being "markedly improved."[32] Indicative of his progress was the fact that he was propped up in bed and was able to read newspapers and listen to the radio. He was still being watched closely by heart specialists, however, and special duty nurses were required to check his progress continually. In addition, his breathing remained labored, and several times during the day he received compressed air to ease his respiratory problems. Quill's health had improved to the point that he was allowed visits by his wife, Shirley, and a few clost TWU associates.

Mrs. Quill indicated that it had taken her more than three hours to drive from her room at the Americana Hotel at Seventh Avenue and 52d Street to the hospital on Second Avenue and 25th Street. She said that her husband had received thousands of telegrams, including get well remarks from Arthur J. Goldberg, the labor attorney and former Supreme Court Justice, who was currently serving as the U.S. Representative to the United Nations and from Senator Robert F. Kennedy. Asked if she believed her husband was being "defiant," Mrs. Quill replied that he believed in the principles of industrial unionism, "and I don't believe that's defiance, that's persistance."[33]

Milling around in the corridor outside Quill's room in the emergency section of the hospital were a deputy sheriff and a detective. Wooden barricades were positioned at each end of the corridor, and several Department of Hospitals' patrolmen checked the credentials of all persons who tried to enter. The extra precautions were taken because among the many phone calls the hospital had received during the day that were critical of Quill, one contained a death threat.[34]

In Albany, on Wednesday, the transit strike was becoming more and more of a political football. Shortly after the state legislature convened for the first time in the year, Democratic state legislators denounced Governor Rockefeller for not saying anything about the transit strike in his opening day message and for not taking a direct role in the negotiations. A short time later, the Republican governor, unaware of the attack, said he was in constant touch with the situation and was "doing everything I can to cooperate and be of assistance." He said that he did not see any useful direct role he could take at the moment, but that he was "not foreclosing" the possibility of taking action as the strike dragged on. The attack on Rockefeller was led by Senator Thomas J. Mackell, a Queens Democrat, who charged that the governor's failure to discuss the strike in his annual message showed that he was "completely bereft of any concern for the transit workers or the travelling public."[35] Mackell said he did not understand why the governor could not come up with a proposal to help the New York City transit system, considering that the year before the Legislature had approved Rockefeller's proposals for $5 million to help the New Haven Railroad and $65 million to enable the state to buy the deficit ridden Long Island Railroad. Mackell called on the governor to support a bill he intended to introduce to merge the TA with the Triborough Bridge and Tunnel Authority. As would be expected, the Republican minority leader, Senator Earl W. Bridges, defended Rockefeller, saying, ". . . there is no one in the state more deeply concerned with the transit strike than the Governor. . . ."[36] Rockefeller might not have mentioned the transit strike in his opening day remarks to the legislators, but it was apparent that he had the situation on his mind. As he addressed the combined session of senators and assemblymen, the governor began a sentence with the words, "Mayor Lindsley," as waves of laughter swept through the Assembly Chamber. Realizing his mistake, Rockefeller said with a wide grin, "It shows the pressure we're all under."[37]

After experiencing extremely heavy traffic and railroad congestion on Tuesday, the Lindsay Administration decided to begin a voluntary system for staggering arrival and departure hours for Manhattan motorists on Wednesday. The staggered driving experiment divided lower Manhattan into four sectors, and vehicles were expected to leave each of these quadrants during stipulated half-hour periods. Inbound motorists were urged to allow two hours travel time from the city's limits so that they would also arrive in each of these sectors on a staggered timetable. For example, commuters bound for the northwest sector were urged to arrive between 7:00 a.m. and 7:30 a.m. and to leave between 3:00 p.m. and 3:30 p.m.

After examining traffic leaving Manhattan on Wednesday afternoon, the first time the staggered plan was put into effect, Traffic Commissioner Henry A. Barnes said things "worked better" than they had during Monday's and Tuesday's monstrous traffic jams. He indicated, however, that further study would be required to determine the effects of the staggered hours plan. Overall, traffic entering and leaving Manhattan on Wednesday was about 5 percent heavier than on Tuesday, or 35 percent heavier than on a normal working day. After Commissioner Barnes announced his plan very early Wednesday morning, a number of major employers, including the Chase Manhattan Bank, Standard Oil of New Jersey, McGraw-Hill, and General Electric said they would comply. Both Traffic Commissioner Barnes and Police Commissioner Vincent Broderick expressed their hope that voluntary restrictions on transit into Manhattan would be successful so that mandatory controls could be avoided. Another element in the system of voluntary restrictions on travel, the use of car pooling was proving only moderately successful. A survey by the Traffic Department during the outbound rush on Wednesday revealed that 40 percent of the vehicles were occupied only by the driver, 22 percent had one passenger, 12 percent two passengers, and only 23 percent had three or more passengers.[38]

Some of the complexities involved in the transit crisis became apparent on Wednesday as a number of business groups took sharply contrasting positions concerning the approach that should be taken to resolve the dispute. The Fifth Avenue Association, comprised of department stores, banks, and other businesses on Fifth, Madison, and Park Avenues in Manhattan, urged President Johnson to intervene in the dispute because of the lack of progress being made locally. Frank E. Conant, president of the Fifth Avenue Association, told President Johnson that "the losses suffered run into untold millions of dollars, and, if allowed to accrue, could well spell bankruptcy for some of our business concerns which are operating on a narrow profit margin." Conant said his group was deeply pessimistic concerning the efforts of the three-member mediation team and felt that relations between the TWU and the TA had become so embittered that White House involvement was necessary.[39] Specifically, the group asked that the president urge the members of the TWU to return to work while the negotiations continued. Later in the day, a spokesman for President Johnson said that he wanted to do what he could to assist in the strike and would consider any specific requests for aid made by the city administration.[40]

The New York City Chamber of Commerce said that, while it would support the effort to get transit workers to return to their jobs while the negotiations proceeded, it would oppose any attempt by the president that would supersede the efforts of the mediation panel. In a statement that sounded as if it were written by a speech writer for Mayor Lindsay, the Chamber said the "resources and mediation machinery of this [city] are more than adequate to deal with the transit strike emergency." An "economically viable" strike settlement, the Chamber said, was essential to "local and nationwide confidence in the city's strength and ability to deal firmly and fairly with its labor problems." The Chamber endorsed what it characterized as "Mayor Lindsay's nonpartisan stance" and added that the whole country was watching to see if he would react strongly" in the face of the ruthless tactics being employed by the Transport Workers Union." The Chamber of Commerce then went on to criticize as "not defensible" the "no show, no dough" policy that another business group, the Commerce and Industry Association said was being implemented by most businesses. Employers should pay workers not able to reach their jobs, the Chamber asserted, because this supported Mayor Lindsay's position and represented a "valuable contribution to the city's future economic health."[41]

Although it was still too soon for a sophisticated analysis, the city administration was attempting to disaggregate the strike loss figures, in order to determine the extent to which different groups were being adversely affected. According to the New York City Department of Commerce and Industrial Development, the ability of workers to reach their jobs varied tremendously by industry and by skill and income levels. On Wednesday, attendance in the printing trade was 80 percent; banking, 70 percent; restaurants, 60 percent; insurance industry, 55 percent; and clothing industry, 35 percent. The City Department said the hardest hit segment of the labor force were blue collar workers who lived in the city and were forced to rely on subways and buses to get to work. The 1960 census indicated there were 1,070,000 persons in this category. The garment industry, with its work force comprising mainly blacks and Puerto Ricans living in distant areas within the city limits, was therefore hit hardest by absenteeism. As Deputy-Mayor Timothy Costello added, "The people who are hit hardest by this crisis, as in any other, are those who can least afford it. There are far fewer hourly workers able to get to work than professional sales and clerical employees."[42]

For its part, the TWU was well aware that their strike was causing particularly acute suffering among the economically disadvantaged. As the union's MacMahon explained, "We knew the impact would be mostly on the poor and that others would find some way to get to work." But, he quickly added, "We had to strike because of the circumstances."[43]

On the sixth day of the crippling strike, President Johnson, acting at the request of Mayor Lindsay, sent Secretary of Labor W. Willard Wirtz to New York City to lend whatever help he could in trying to settle the walkout. The mayor's call for Wirtz was his first appeal for federal assistance. Earlier, the president had indicated he was willing to consider intervening in the dispute, but only if he was asked to do so by Mayor Lindsay. The secretary was asked upon arrival if there was any possibility of getting federal funds to help pay for a settlement. "No, I think not," he replied. "The federal interest here is that the largest city in the country is crippled right now," he added. "Anything that hurts one big city hurts the country."[44] Asked why a Democratic administration in Washington would be helping a Republican, Wirtz replied, "There's no good reason why good Democrats and good Republicans can't work together." In fact, the political relationship between Johnson and Lindsay was complex. Certainly, the president did not want to provide support for an up-and-coming star in Republican politics, particularly someone who was already being viewed as a possible opponent for Johnson in 1968. On the other hand, the president could not ignore the plight of the nation's largest city, whose voters were overwhelmingly Democratic. For his part, Lindsay would have preferred to resolve the strike without the president's intervention, but at this point he considered that he needed a settlement more than anything else.[45]

Mayor Lindsay conferred for nearly an hour with Wirtz and Assistant Secretary James Reynolds. Then the three men met with the executive board of the New York City Central Labor Council, headed by Harry Van Arsdale, Jr. And finally, the three mediators arrived at City Hall to meet with the mayor, Wirtz, and Reynolds.[46]

The executive board of the Central Labor Council also met privately with Lindsay during the day. At this meeting, Van Arsdale told the mayor that the imprisonment of the union's first team of negotiators was delaying a settlement of the dispute. More specifically, the Central Labor Council asked Lindsay to permit the release of Matthew Guinan, who as Quill's second in command, also served as vice president of the one million-member central labor body. Later, when asked if he was sympathetic to Van Arsdale's request, Lindsay replied, "I want to do anything that will assist a speedy, fair and equitable conclusion."[47] When asked how the union leaders could be released, Lindsay replied, "That's a matter for the Transit Authority to decide . . . they having taken the initiative in this matter."[48] Despite the fact that his Corporation Counsel J. Lee Rankin was instrumental in having the union leaders jailed, Lindsay implied that the TA was solely responsible for the action. To obtain the release of the union leaders, the TA would have to go back to State Supreme Court Justice Geller, who issued the contempt citation for having violated the antistrike injunction. Although Justice Geller found the labor leaders guilty of civil contempt, it was the TA that asked for the execution of the judge's order and the arrest of the labor officials. The TA could, because this was a civil contempt case, go before the judge and ask for the prisoner's release on the ground that their release would permit them to purge themselves of contempt.

In the marathon bargaining sessions which ended at 1:30 a.m., Mayor Lindsay reported new offers by both sides, but he asked them not to disclose details of their new positions. However, the parties were still so far apart that any rapid movement toward a settlement appeared impossible. Complicating negotiations, of course, was Michael Quill's absence from the bargaining table, with early reports indicating that his replacement, Douglas MacMahon, had been an unusually tough and unyielding negotiator.[49]

At Bellevue Hospital, Quill's condition regressed somewhat from what it had been on Wednesday, but reports that he had suffered serious reverses and complications were labeled by hospital officials as an "exaggeration." The major reason for the confusion regarding Quill's condition was the hospital's position that it would not disclose details of his case unless his family gave permission to make details public. That permission was denied. Commissioner of Hospitals Yerby did, however, flatly deny the suggestion that Quill's illness might have been a hoax. "There is no question in anybody's mind," said Dr. Yerby, "that Mr. Quill is ill. This is not a fraud."[50]

In other action, the mediators asked the TA to request another twenty-four-hour postponement of a hearing in State Supreme Court to determine whether the striking unions should be fined and the amount to be levied. Asher W. Schwartz, a lawyer for the TWU, joined the Transit Authority in asking Justice Geller for the postponement, saying that the negotiations were proceeding "constructively and quite actively."[51] With both the TWU and the TA jointly asking for the postponement, Justice Geller granted the request.

The numerous effects of the strike on the noncombatants, the general public, continued unabated. Automobile travel into Manhattan experienced what Traffic Commissioner Barnes called "the longest rush hour in the city's history."[52] The crawl, which started at 4:45 a.m., lasted for six and one-half hours. The bumper-to-bumper traffic into Manhattan had barely subsided when, at 3:15 p.m., the homegoing crush began. The traffic jam in the afternoon was not as bad as the one in the morning, however, it lasted only three and one-half hours. The homebound tie-up was described by the city's Traffic Department as "the worst evening in Manhattan" in the six days of the strike. Although traffic volume on Thursday was not appreciably higher than it had been on Wednesday, an unrelenting rain was the straw that broke the back of an already overburdened vehicular traffic system. With the rain wetting ignition wires and causing cars to stall, a chain reaction was precipitated. Once cars began to break down, causing lengthy delays, other cars began to overheat, also becoming inoperable. This, in turn, caused still more cars to stall and overheat, resulting in roads being completely shut down for extended periods of time. As one Brooklyn motorist described the almost surreal vision, "They sat there with their motors running and the cars heated up. I never saw that before in January."[53]

On Third Avenue in the Bronx, a truck that was being used to transport workers to their jobs was stuck in traffic for forty minutes between 146th and 145th Streets. As one passenger described the situation, "Someone got out for five containers of coffee and danish pastry and when he got back, the truck hadn't moved one inch." It took the truck four hours and fifteen minutes to complete a route that normally takes one hour. As traffic ground to a halt, some drivers became "creative." One, barely moving through Central Park, pulled off the road and proceeded down the pedestrian path. For their part, pedestrians were equally assertive. "Every time we stopped for a light, they'd bang on the windows," one motorist said. "We kept the doors locked all the way down."[54]

The city's attempt to avoid such congestion by staggering the times commuters entered and left Manhattan proved to be totally ineffective. Most individuals and employers simply ignored the plan. Asked if her company was attempting to comply with the 7:00 a.m. to 7:30 a.m. arrival and 3:00 p.m. to 3:30 p.m. departure times established for the sector in which her insurance company was located, the personnel manager responded, "Are you kidding?" she asked, seemingly astonished. "When they get here they get here. They'd have to get up in the middle of the night to get in at that time. They're already complaining about getting up an hour or two early to get here at all." It was hard to fault private employers for ignoring the staggered timetable, however, when the city administration itself disregarded the system. A spokesman for Mayor Lindsay acknowledged that the mayor had not asked department heads to have their workers comply. "I think everyone's getting in on his own," the spokesman observed. At City Hall itself, located in an area where commuters were asked to arrive between 7:30 a.m. and 8:00 a.m. and leave from 3:30 p.m. to 4:00 p.m., the Lindsay spokesman conceded that civil service employees were still coming in at 9:00 a.m. or as early as they could get in and were not leaving by 4:00 p.m.[55]

Another element in the city administration's plan to reduce vehicular congestion in Manhattan was also failing, as commuters seemed unwilling to accept car pooling. A Traffic Department check of cars entering Manhattan during the early morning rush period indicated that they contained 1.75 riders per car, the prestrike norm. Traffic Commissioner

Barnes was appalled by the lack of cooperation with the ride pooling concept and indicated that restrictions might have to be imposed to force drivers to fill their cars.[56]

Also on Thursday, the city administration revised its previous estimates and stated that the strike was costing the city government almost $6 million per day in overtime pay and lost taxes. According to Roy M. Goodman, the city's Director of Finance, approximately $4 million of the loss was attributed to overtime payments to city employees who would be required to work overtime either during the strike or at its conclusion. In addition, Goodman estimated the city was losing $950,000 daily in sales taxes; $630,000 in business gross receipts taxes; $100,000 in corporation stock transfer taxes; and $200,000 in real estate taxes as a result of the virtual halt in new construction. The $5,880,000 total was a minimum estimate, Goodman stressed, because there were other losses that were currently inestimable that would be felt after the strike.[57]

During the day, Mayor Lindsay also received a preliminary report on the impact of the strike on the private economy from Donald F. Shaughnessy, the executive assistant to Goodman. The report showed that retail trade was the hardest hit and that absenteeism was highest among unskilled and low-paid workers. Shaughnessy reported, for example, that in the garment industry, while 75 to 95 percent of the elite workers were getting to their jobs, among machine operators, most of whom were blacks and Puerto Ricans, attendance was from zero to 30 percent.[58] Similarly, the report showed that in a Brooklyn print shop 85 percent of the lithographers and typesetters had reported for work, but that only 10 to 15 percent of the unskilled workers had done so. Finally, the Shaughnessy report indicated that in spite of Mayor Lindsay's request that workers not reporting be paid, many businesses were either not paying their employees or were deducting lost days from sick leave or vacation time. In a rather unusual development on Thursday, the TA began docking the pay of about 2,500 of its 5,000 nonstriking employees who had not reported for work during the strike. Refusing to comment on Mayor Lindsay's request that business not penalize those employees not showing up for work, the TA's general manager said, "We have no different policy than we've ever had, anybody who doesn't show up for work and has no excuse doesn't get paid."[59]

Other surveys indicated that small businesses were being hit particularly hard by the strike; and, unlike their larger counterparts, they were fearful of their ability to withstand the strike losses. A Dun and Bradstreet study of small retail business revealed that 67 percent reported "a significant drop in sales," and only 8 percent reported an increase in sales, and one-half of those were service stations taking advantage of increased automobile and truck traffic. Retail furniture stores and liquor stores were hit hardest, according to the survey, with more than one-half of such establishments reporting business declines in excess of 50 percent. Although 70 percent of the small businesses felt they could weather the strike and remain viable establishments, 15 percent said that, if the strike continued, they would be driven from business in one to eight weeks. And of this marginal group, more than one-half believed they could not withstand a strike of longer than two weeks.[60]

Lacking the economic resiliency of their larger counterparts, these small retail establishments were, according to a *New York Times* survey, "caught between a precipitous drop in sales and high fixed rentals." As a result, the *Times* concluded by agreeing with the Dun and Bradstreet study, "some midtown shopkeepers face financial disaster or indebtedness unless the transit strike ends quickly." In a variety of retail establishments sampled on both the east and west sides of Manhattan, sales volume was found to be off from 40 to 85 percent. "In fifteen years in business, this is the absolute abyss," said Mrs. Isi Fishgang, the owner of a diamond shop on West 47th Street. "There's nothing more to say," she added, "except that maybe we should have stayed in bed all week." Sam Levine, the manager of the Benhill Shirt Shop on Times Square agreed. "It's a ghost store," he said, "the worst business I've seen in 30 years in the retail trade."[61]

In addition to the effect of the strike in highly visible and well-publicized areas, the impact continued to permeate virtually every aspect of life in the city. As a result of Mayor Lindsay's request that all nonessential personnel stay out of Manhattan during the course of the strike, about one-third of the men ordered to report for induction into the Armed Services apparently decided they were not essential and stayed home.[62]

Although the strike continued to cause minimal disruptions in public elementary and junior high schools, by Thursday more than one-half of the 212,689 students enrolled in the city's sixty academic high schools and more than 90 percent of the 42,000 students normally attending vocational high schools were absent. Because the high schools were not neighborhood schools, students typically relied on the subway and bus system to transport them to and from school. The Board of Education therefore announced that if high school students were unable to reach their regular schools, they could attend the school closest to their homes until the end of the strike. The board also indicated that approximately 400 high school teachers who were unable to reach the specialized schools in which they taught would be used to augment the teaching staffs in the neighborhood high schools. The move, which was expected to affect more than 150,000 students, was believed to be the first time in the system's history that students and teachers were asked to attend other than their regular schools. Although Superintendent of Schools Bernard Donovan said that this move was implemented because "both the parents and we are concerned about the absence of instruction for such a large number of pupils," it was not clear how instruction could be effectively achieved with such an ad hoc collection of students and teachers.[63]

Perhaps the best way to discern the impact of the strike on "regular" people is to examine the telephone calls that were flooding into the city's emergency control center at the rate of about 2,500 calls per hour. The calls were handled by seventy-three TA employees working in twelve-hour shifts. "Some are really pathetic," said a man who usually acts as a train dispatcher. "They want to know if they'll get paid if they can't get to work. Some have heart conditions and want to know how to get to doctor's appointments." A second worker handling the phone inquiries added, "The old ones, and the sick ones, they make your heart heavy."[64]

The plans that Mayor Lindsay had for his first days in office were also turned topsy turvy by the strike. Originally, the Lindsay Administration had planned for a whirlwind first week in office that would foster images of accomplishment reminiscent of Franklin Roosevelt's first 100 days as president or Fiorello La Guardia's first days in office in 1934. Instead, Lindsay did virtually nothing that was not directly or indirectly connected with the strike. Even the nonstrike related functions performed by the mayor tended to be nuts and bolts oriented activities absolutely necessary to keep the city from grinding to a halt. For example, on Sunday evening, January 2, Lindsay took the time to swear in nine Criminal Court Justices, who otherwise would have been unable to begin work the following day. However, planned appearances by Mayor Lindsay to focus attention on what were expected to be major themes in his new administration did not materialize because of the strike. Lindsay had expected to spend time attending a meeting of his antipoverty study group and to be at a hearing on a rent strike law to be considered by the city. Other cancelled activities, that Lindsay had planned for his first week in office included: the opening of a New York City office in Washington, D.C.; the appointment of a permanent council on transportation; the naming of the fifteen members of the committee on judiciary selection; and the announcement of one task force dealing with health issues and a second dealing with social welfare.[65] In sum, Lindsay intended to spend the first weeks of his administration creating what he considered an appropriate image.

The mayor's staff was also preoccupied with the strike. Deputy-Mayor Costello, for example, spent virtually every waking moment directing the emergency control board established to cope with the impact of the strike on the city. He devoted no time to his principal assignment, the direction of a plan to reorganize the city government. A number of Lindsay aides had not even settled into offices by the end of the first week of his administration because the mayor wanted to allocate office space himself and had not had the time to do so. As a result, moving boxes and files remained unpacked in the corridors of City Hall, adding to the air of confusion.[66]

On The Legal Front

On Friday, January 7, New York City ended a week without subway and bus service. The actions and events of this day were as diverse and complex as the issues facing the negotiators.

On the legal front, after postponing the action for forty-eight hours, the TA asked the State Supreme Court to assess the two striking unions money damages. Sidney Brandes, the counsel for the Transit Authority, told Supreme Court Justice Geller that the agency was seeking about $322,000 a day in damages, in addition to a lump-sum payment of more than $100,000 as the "extraordinary cost of putting the system to bed" when the strike began. If Justice Geller did set a figure for damages, the TA would have the option of seeking payment, just as it had the option of asking for execution of the order for the arrest of the union leaders. Because this was a civil and not a criminal contempt case it was not the court's concern whether any damages were collected, even if a specific dollar figure was established.[67]

It was not immediately clear why union leaders were held in civil rather than criminal contempt. Certainly, as required in a criminal contempt proceeding, the transit strike had all of the requisites of "an active interference with the crown [government] or its acting official agents" because the TA was a governmental agency. It was equally true, however, that as the concept developed over the years, governmental bodies as well as individuals were allowed to seek civil contempt relief. The TA thus had the option of pursuing the strike through criminal or civil contempt procedures. A major advantage of utilizing the civil contempt option was that it granted the TA considerably greater flexibility than would the criminal procedure. Criminal contempt, for example, is punishable by a set prison term or a set fine or both, which is determined by a judge. Civil contempt, in contrast, involves an indeterminate sentence: as soon as the individuals purge themselves of contempt by doing or undoing what they were put in jail for, they may be freed. Thus, the jailing of the union officials and the potential fine against the unions were essentially under the control of the TA and the striking unions.

Not only were these legal moves deeply resented by the TWU, they also served to complicate negotiations. On the one hand, said the union's chief negotiator, MacMahon, the TA is trying to "wreck the union" and, on the other, attempting to negotiate a contract settlement. "As a result," he declared, "negotiations are now at a standstill." Similarly, union attorney John O'Donnell told the court, "The union cannot negotiate at the Americana while trying to defend itself against efforts by the Transit Authority to destroy the union in court."[68] Then, as if to prove his point, O'Donnell left the court proceedings to his associates as he headed for the Americana Hotel where the negotiations were taking place.

Compounding these problems was the fact that everything in the TWU revolved around Michael Quill, and he was not available for consultation. ". . . When Quill suffered his heart attack," lamented one of the mediators, "I thought we'd never get a settlement. Even though he was in the hospital, every decision had to be approved by him at his bedside." And when his condition improved to the point that his doctors would permit someone to speak with him, Mrs. Quill came into the picture and became extremely protective of her husband's health. "[She] wouldn't let us come within shouting distance of him," the mediator related. "She said he was too ill to talk. That was the kind of impossible conditions we were faced with."[69]

After meeting for more than three hours with Harry Van Arsdale, the president of the New York City Central Labor Council, and other members of the council's executive board, Governor Rockefeller said that it was the responsibility of the TA to decide whether releasing the imprisoned strike leaders would increase the chances for a settlement.[70] The Labor Council's officers were reportedly at the governor's Manhattan office to ask him to use his influence to release the jailed TWU and Amalgamated union leaders.[71] Mayor Lindsay, who met Thursday night with Van Arsdale and the others, said early Friday morning that he had passed along their request on freeing the union leaders to Joseph O'Grady without recommendation.

In the absence of any public guidance from either Rockefeller or Lindsay, the TA was forced to assume the onus of determining the fate of the jailed union leaders. The Authority decided not to take the necessary legal steps to release Quill and the eight other union leaders. In justifying their decision, the TA said: "Michael Quill and his fellow leaders are in jail for violating the law and flouting the injunction of the court not to strike. The members of the Transit Authority, as responsible public officials, sworn to uphold the Constitution and the law, cannot now in good conscience ask the court to release Mr. Quill and the others until it is clear that they are acting to call off the strike."[72]

Despite his public statements to the contrary, union negotiator Douglas MacMahon had concluded by this time that from a tactical standpoint it was beneficial for the first-line negotiating team to remain in jail. Unaware of MacMahon's position, however, Van Arsdale approached the TA's O'Grady to seek the unionists' release. Van Arsdale told the TA chairman that they were against the imprisonment of the union officials and believed that their release would help end the walkout. O'Grady reportedly replied, "Why don't you ask the TWU how they feel about it?" O'Grady was aware by this time that the TWU felt it was advantageous to have their first line negotiators remain in jail. Although Mr. O'Grady refused to deny or confirm the freedom story, his silence was eloquent. "It was a private discussion we had," the TA chairman said. "I haven't discussed this with anyone. I don't think it is appropriate to talk about it."[73]

Initially, a spokesman for MacMahon denied that an offer to free the union officials was made. "It's another of the many lies that are now being told," the spokesman asserted. After the strike was settled, MacMahon was considerably more frank in discussing his reasons for wanting his colleagues to remain in jail:

> An effort was made by Harry [Van Arsdale] to get an arrangement where Matty [Guinan] would come out of jail. I objected because in order to obtain the release, an effort would have to be made to get the Transit Authority to appeal to the judge. The union feeling was that they [the Transit Authority] should not be reached. We felt that the membership might have looked at this in the wrong way. The workers would say that if the men had stayed in jail they could have gotten a better settlement. It would have been viewed as a sellout by the members. The workers would have felt that some of their bargaining power had to be given up to get the release; that the only way the Transit Authority would agree to release them would be to get something in return.[74]

In fact, the continued incarceration of the union leaders was instrumental in rallying the support of organized labor behind the striking unions. New York, the labor leaders felt, "must not become injunction city."[75] The initial public reaction of organized labor in the New York area to the transit strike was hardly an expression of "solidarity forever." The first public statement on the strike by a union official was made by Edward Swayduck, president of Local 1 of the Amalgamated Lithographers of America. Swayduck termed the strike "sabotage" and said he was looking into the possibility of suing Quill and the TWU for any wages lost by members of his union due to the strike. He added: "I don't know of any union that will help Quill. Other union leaders feel as I do, but they won't take him on. He could easily have extended negotiations two weeks to let the new Mayor get into the job. Retroactivity is not a dirty word in the union movement. Many leaders have used retroactivity to avoid a strike. No union leader wants strikes."[76]

The only other comment by a labor leader to appear during the first weekend of the strike was attributed by the *New York Times* to an important union leader who had supported Mr. Lindsay. The labor official reportedly said: "We know that Quill is giving the labor movement a black eye. This is a strike against millions of workers who have to work for a living—and many of them earn less than Quill's members get. If the strike runs a while they may start bringing pressure on their own union leaders and then Quill may be looking for someone to save his face."[77]

When the injunction prohibiting the strike was granted on January 3, however, those unions more representative of organized labor in New York began to break their silence. That day, thirteen union leaders pledged their support to the TWU, and as the *New York Times* reported, "One point made very strongly by some of Mr. Quill's backers . . . was their opposition to the use of courts as a means of fighting unions." Among those announcing their assistance to the TWU was Harry Van Arsdale, president of the New York City Central Labor Council, which comprised 500 local unions with a combined membership of more than one million. The telegram from the Central Labor Council said, "That the Transport Workers Union could not achieve a contract without a strike is nothing short of scandalous. We call upon the TA to immediately negotiate a just contract and we pledge you our support."[78] A telegram from the president of the New York State AFL-CIO, Raymond R. Corbett, stated: "All the irrelevant charges and smoke screens with which you are confronted cannot hide or confuse the simple issue that the 36,000 members of Local 100 of the Transport Workers Union and the Amalgamated Transit Workers Union are entitled to an equitable increase in wages and improvements in working conditions and that has not been offered by the Transit Authority or anyone else."[79]

Among the union leaders who spoke out strongly against the court action against Quill and his colleagues were Louis Hollander, manager of the New York Joint Board of the Amalgamated Clothing Workers of America; Charles Cogen, president of the American Federation of Teachers; and Michael Mann, the Regional Director of the New York AFL-CIO. Hollander said he was "hastening to advise you that you have the full support of the New York Joint Board Amalgamated Clothing Workers. . . . We must not permit New York to become a labor injunction city." Cogen, like Quill, the president of a union that represented public employees, wrote:

> We have telegraphed Mayor Lindsay to protest the use of court action as an attempt to substitute coercion for the normal collective bargaining process. There is no moral justification for the use of such anti-labor actions. All unions with members in public employment should stand

united on this point. We are confident that you will be able to withstand this attack and emerge with a contract of which you can be justly proud.[80]

Mann, in articulating his opposition to the use of an injunction, said: "Injunction and jailing of trade union leadership totally reprehensible. Smacks of slavery and marks a black chapter in history of workers' struggle for justice throughout the ages. Once again reiterate wholehearted support of TWU leadership now on the picket lines in the finest tradition of our trade union movement."[81]

On Tuesday, January 4, telegrams of support continued to flow into TWU headquarters. The Communications Workers of America pledged their aid and accused the TA of attempting to "substitute the courtroom for the collective bargaining table."[82] Albert Shanker, as president of the United Federation of Teachers, issued a statement asserting that the imprisonment of the union leaders, "will undoubtedly prolong the strike."[83] Max Greenberg, president of the Retail, Wholesale, and Department Store Union, sent a telegram to Quill stating that he backed the TWU efforts "to improve the lot of transit workers. Injunctions won't run trains or feed transit workers' kids," the telegram continued. "If we can help in any way call us."[84] The unanimity of support for the TWU from their fellow unionists was broken by a resolution adopted by the ILGWU, which was critical of both the bargaining tactics of the TWU and the jailing of the union leaders. The statement said: "Regrettably, tactics and methods employed in present situation, and the atmosphere supporting it, have been such as to frustrate traditionally and accepted processes of collective bargaining. Jailing of union leaders not only adds to the unnecessary complications, it is also a futile gesture."[85]

The telegrams of support continued, seemingly interminably, until the end of the strike. At that time the only union leaders to fail to pledge their support to the TWU were Swayduck and the several unnamed labor leaders quoted in *New York Times* articles and editorials. In a telegram to Quill, another fiery Irishman who was head of a New York City civil service union, John J. DeLury, the president of the Uniformed Sanitationmen's Association, caught the feeling of most of the statements of support and left little doubt as to who he felt were the unnamed labor leaders to whom the *Times* had alluded. DeLury's telegram read:

> Our city press is hell bent on drawing blood—labor's blood—and in this instance—your union's blood. The pack is already in full hue and cry for the use of the Condon-Wadlin Act; injunctions, jail sentences, and the appropriation of workers' dues by fines. These people still hunger for the days of 1919 and Coolidge. We scorn the position taken by Swayduck. In

days gone by, he would have been termed a fink. Other unnamed labor leaders characterized by the Times as "pro-Lindsay" have obviously never had the unique experience of bargaining with city officials. Until they do, they should confine their energies to raising the standards of their own depressed millinery or garment industries.[86]

The only two union leaders of consequence to support Mr. Lindsay in his campaign for mayor were ILGWU President Dubinsky and Rose, president of the United Hatters, Cap, and Millinery Workers' Union—both leaders in the Liberal Party, which supported Lindsay's candidacy.

In addition to their statements, organized labor in New York also took concrete action in response to the use of legal sanctions. On January 4, Joseph Curran, the president of the National Maritime Union, called upon Van Arsdale, as president of the New York City Central Labor Council, to convene an emergency meeting of the labor group to plan assistance for the strikers.[87] On Thursday of the same week, the executive board of the Central Labor Council met in emergency session to discuss the transit strike and the jailing of the nine union leaders. Although the union officials did not wish to be set free, the actions by their fellow unionists in seeking their release generated sympathy for the striking unions among all union workers and solidified the support of transit unionists behind their leaders.

Secretary of Labor Wirtz, who spent Thursday night in New York conferring with Mayor Lindsay and the mediators, returned to Washington on Friday. Wirtz clearly stated that, after investigating the situation in New York, the federal government did not intend to intervene as long as negotiations were progressing. Thus, rather than providing aid to New York, the Wirtz visit was, as characterized by the New York Times, "primarily a gesture by the Johnson Administration to demonstrate the government's concern."[88]

In other action from Washington, New York's Democratic Senator Robert F. Kennedy said it was clear that the strike had become a "catastrophe to the people and to the City of New York." He urged the negotiators to go on a "24-hour basis" without recesses until they reach a "fair and reasonable settlement. It is imperative," Kennedy said, "that the strike end by this weekend."[89]

In the actual negotiations, the three mediators held separate sessions with each side seeking to narrow the differences on the central issue of wages. After the sessions ended at 1:20 a.m., one of the mediators, Sylvester Garrett, using "mediators language" to obscure the fact that significant progress was not being made, reported that the meetings "were fruitful in contributing to a narrowing of the gap between the parties and clarification of the remaining areas of dispute." TA chairman O'Grady was considerably more frank in his public assessment of the status of negotiations; "I think we are a long way from a settlement," he said.[90]

MacMahon reported at a news conference that his union was no longer asking for an immediate increase in wages of 30 percent. Instead, the TWU was pressing for a 15 percent increase retroactive to January 1 and an additional 15 percent on January 1, 1967. Although the increases still amounted to 30 percent by the end of the contractual period, the TA would save a considerable amount of money because only one-half of the increase would take effect during the first year of the proposed agreement. For his part, O'Grady was also willing to sweeten the pot a little bit. The TA chairman said that while the wage component of his offer should stay at 3.2 percent, that all seventy-five other items were open for discussion. Initially, the TA proposed that increases in all areas of the contract be limited to 3.2 percent. O'Grady clearly stated that the TA's substantial budget deficit was not an impediment to a contract settlement. "I have never pleaded poverty," he observed. Likewise, he maintained that the failure of the city and the state to guarantee subsidies was not causing difficulties. "I want to emphasize again," he said, "that if we had a billion dollars in our treasury, we would not give these people a cent more than we consider equitable and reasonable."[91]

With the family of Quill still refusing to grant Bellevue Hospital permission to discuss his condition publicly, the hospital's sole public comment regarding his health was an extremely terse, "The doctors for Mr. Quill report that he had a restful night and is somewhat better." Later in the day, the union leader's wife, Shirley, who had kept him up to date on the progress of negotiations during her daily visits to the hospital, was considerably more expansive in her remarks. Mrs. Quill said her husband was "very much better" and was the "favorite darling" of the nurses at the hospital. In addition to receiving reports on the strike from his wife, Quill was well enough to follow events in the newspapers and on the radio. The TWU president occupied a private room in the hospital, and because he was still technically in jail, a deputy sheriff was stationed in the hall outside his room.[92]

The Traffic Department reported on Friday that more cars, carrying more people entered Manhattan than at any time in the city's history. "It's been a hell of a day for the city," said Traffic Commissioner Barnes, "but we were still a long way from reaching the saturation point." The probable cause for the massive influx of vehicles, experts guessed, was the desire of many employees to pick up their Friday paychecks. The movement of vehicles into and out of Manhattan was facilitated by the decision to increase the number of lanes on the Queensboro and Williamsburg Bridges used to take commuters into Manhattan in the morning and out of the business district in the evening. In addition, the Queens Midtown Tunnel was closed to Manhattan bound traffic at 4:00 p.m. for two hours and forty minutes, so that all four lanes of the tunnel could carry cars away from the city. For those motorists attempting to go against the flow, however, the delays were monumental. As one of the hundreds of horn-tooting, cursing, motorists headed for Manhattan in the late afternoon said as he was diverted from the closed tunnel, "It's very frustrating to see the lights on top of the Empire State Building shining just across the river and not be able to get there."[93]

Although traffic was better on Friday than the previous day, it was still horrendous. Traffic on the major north-south avenues and on the crosstown streets near the garment district was heavy and slow moving. And even with the improvements to whisk cars out of Manhattan, tunnel and bridge approaches started to jam at 3:30 p.m. In one, somewhat typical case, a driver reported it took him two and one-half hours to drive from 13th Street and Fifth Avenue to First Avenue and 48th Street.[94]

For the Long Island Railroad, Friday was also a record setting day. "We probably handled the largest number of people out of Pennsylvania Station in our history—125,000," a spokesman said. The railroad, which normally carries 260,000 riders per day from all of its locations, had about 350,000 passengers. Most of the Long Island's additional riders took advantage of the newly initiated Queens shuttle service, which carried passengers from Pennsylvania Station to various stops in Queens. Two unions representing the Long Island Railroad's employees, the Brotherhood of Locomotive Engineers and the Brotherhood of Railroad Trainmen initially refused to provide such service because they considered it strikebreaking. However, faced with the prospect of a court order enjoining the unions from preventing such service, they agreed to operate the additional trains.[95]

With the strike one week old on Friday, Ralph C. Gross, the executive vice president of the Commerce and Industry Association of New York, estimated that the work stoppage caused the loss of 50 million man hours in the city's labor market. Taking into account those employers who did not pay their workers, he estimated that $125 million in wages were lost during the first week of the strike. Wage earners and employers, added Gross, were hit harder by the strike than by any other disruption since the Great Depression.[96] Increasingly clear by week's end was that the immediate economic impact of the strike was highly regressive: it fell hardest and most cruelly on those least able to afford it. Many of the city's blue collar workers received little or no pay on Friday because they had been unable to reach their jobs.

Although no really comprehensive study was ever completed, all of the available statistics support the fact that workers in the lowest income groups were hurt most by the strike. On the same day that Deputy-Mayor Costello estimated that 75 percent of the city's work force reached their jobs, the *Herald Tribune* wrote that only one-half of the residents of Harlem reported for work.[97] Several black leaders explained the reasons for the strike's disproportionate effect on the residents of the city's black ghettos. "Most Harlem residents had no cars," observed W. R. Cochrane, executive director of the Harlem branch of the YMCA, "and their jobs were miles away."[98] A complementary view was expressed by the Reverend David N. Licorish, the associate pastor of the Abyssinian Baptist Church, "Because our people make up the lowest economic structure, we've been hit harder by this. We can't afford taxis," he added, "This transit strike must come to a stop."[99] An equally pessimistic appraisal was given on Friday by William R. Hudgins, the president of the Freedom National Bank, which had been established by prominent blacks in the city. At his office in the heart of Harlem, Hudgins said: "There is already a great deal of economic hardship because of the strike. Unless it is settled soon it could result in economic chaos. Many of our people pay rent on a weekly basis. I predict that . . . when rents are due, there will be a lot of landlords who won't be paid."[100]

And on Friday, a lot of landlords were not paid. The office of Samuel Weisstein, who owned forty Harlem tenement buildings containing 800 furnished apartments, which normally bustles with activity on Fridays as tenants pay their rent for the coming week, was almost empty. "That means it's bad," said Marvin Cooper, a lawyer who worked in Weisstein's office. "The basic philosophy of poor people is that rent is the primary thing they pay."[101]

Although the effects of the strike were equally bad in all of the city's ghetto districts, the slump was most noticeable in Harlem. And these consequences were most apparent on the first pay day after the strike began, Friday, January 7. Normally, 125th Street, the center of life in Harlem "starts to swing on Friday afternoon, when factory workers, domestics, porters and other people who work downtown get off the subway with money in their pockets."[102] But the transit strike had made things different; no one got off the subway, and 125th Street was almost deserted. William Taylor, who was the only customer in a large Harlem liquor store, bought a half-pint of whiskey and explained the problems the strike had created for him: "I'm a porter. I haven't been to work all week. There's no point to it. Cost you $4 or $5 a day just for the taxi. My wife does housework out on Long Island. She can't get there. We got $100 laid by. When that's gone we going to just have to rough it. The whiskey? That takes the sting out."[103]

A nineteen-year-old black man, Lamont Smith, who was able to reach his job pushing dress racks in the garment district, described his plight: "I have to get up at 4 a.m. and walk to work or else I shoot half my day's pay on catchin' a ride. Then I have to push this damn cart all day for my $1.50 an hour. You think I feel like gettin up the next morning to work for Mr. Goldberg?"[104]

At the Lenox Check Cashing Service, one of the few people who had a check to be cashed on Friday put the $62 he received in his pocket and told a reporter how he managed to get to work, "The boss of the laundry sends a truck for us. But it's a mean ride. Takes a couple of hours sometimes."[105]

The economic incentive of working for $60 a week and spending $25 to $40 of that amount on taxi fares was, of course, not very great. However, the barriers to blacks getting to work were not solely economic. Even in normal times, it was extremely difficult to get a taxi into or out of Harlem, and the transit strike exacerbated this situation. Several days before the strike was called, black commedian Godfrey Cambridge, all too familiar with the ways of New York, envisioned that the subway strike would leave him pleading for a taxi to stop, yelling, "I'm not going to Harlem," or forcing him to beg on bended knee for a cab, saying, "I'm not colored, I'm Jewish."[106] In addition to the difficulty with cabs, few white motorists driving through Harlem or the black ghettos of Brooklyn were willing to share their cars with black pedestrians. An example of this situation was provided by Wilhelmina Banks, an administrative assistant at the Urban League's Brooklyn office, who related that while she was walking to work she observed a black man walking toward the Brooklyn Bridge, trying to thumb a ride. "There was a stream of cars coming down the avenue, headed for the bridge. Most of them had space and most of them were operated by white motorists," she noted, but "nobody picked him up."[107]

The first really mass movement out of Harlem took place on Friday, January 7. The reason for the exodus, and its results were described by a barmaid in the Baron Lounge in Harlem that evening: "Lots of them managed to get downtown today. They thought the Mayor asking their employers to pay them," she noted, "was, like, law. Did they get a surprise."[108]

Business in Harlem was also hit hard by the strike. Al Doby, the manager of the large Davega sporting goods store on 125th Street, told a reporter who was the only person in the store, "You know what we did yesterday, a big fat $400. We can take it for a while," he noted, "but the small businessman is ready to jump off a building." Burke Horne, the treasurer of the Apollo Theater, which was forced to cancel a blues show that "figured to be very big," estimated his losses at more than $8,000 for the first week of the strike.[109]

Harlem and the other black and Puerto Rican ghettos were hit hardest by the strike because as marginal members of economic society, their residents were forced to bear the brunt of the many dislocations that occur. As William Hudgins, the president of the Freedom National Bank said, "They live a hand-to-mouth existence up here." Al Doby, the Harlem sporting goods store manager, explained that this kind of life made it impossible to prepare for the contingencies created by the transit strike: "What can you save," he asked, "when you get maybe $65 a week and have a wife and a kid and you have to pay half of it for rent. . . ?" Perhaps an even more telling effect of the strike on Harlem was pointed out by Claude Barrow, the proprietor of the Harlem Food Market, who recognized that, "It's gonna get worse, too. Once you get behind, it's hard to catch up." Emerging from the difficulties the people of the ghettos had to endure and from the disastrous effects on business in these areas was one "bright" spot. At least one man's business was good—Bernard Fisher reported that business at his Tri-Lex Pawn Shop was up at least 10 percent. "Redemptions are down, too," he added.[110]

On Friday, close to 20,000 high school students took advantage of the Board of Education's plan that allowed students who were unable to reach their regular schools to attend the high school closest to their home. Although School Superintendent Donovan said he was gratified with how well "the new approach to education" had worked, a number of hitches did develop. A long-haired youth entered Hunter College High School, an all-female school at Lexington Avenue and 68th Street and asked to be assigned to a class. After looking carefully to make sure he wasn't a girl, the principal, Bernard Miller told him, "You're in the wrong school—we admit no boys." Hunter High School, however, did admit twenty girls from other schools. At Stuyvesant, an all-male high school on First Avenue and 15th Street, twenty-five girls were included among the eighty students who said they were unable to reach their regular schools. However, Leonard Fliedner, Stuyvesant's principal told the young women, "We have no facilities for girls," and directed them to Washington Irving High School.[111]

It was clear, however, that while the Board of Education's plan enabled high school students to physically attend school, little of educational value was being achieved. The Music and Art School on Convent Avenue and 135th Street was inundated with more than 1,000 students who normally attended other schools. The school offered their guests an improvised science program and a concert in the auditorium, with the regular students playing the harp, the viola, and the flute. Florence Flas, president of the United Parent Association, was extremely critical of the board's plan, saying the school administration had failed to make any "serious effort" to aid strike stranded high school students. School administrators acknowledged the shortcomings of their plan from an educational standpoint, admitting that the main reason for the school shift plan was concern that the strike might encourage students to loiter in the streets, which they felt would be more harmful than a loss of instruction. The Roman Catholic school system, in contrast, did not encourage its 30,000 absentee students to attend other schools while their own were closed. The Very Reverend Monsignor Eugene Malloy, the Superintendent of Schools in Brooklyn and Queens announced that on Monday a home-study program would begin in which students would be sent assignments by mail and telephone. Msgr. Malloy also urged parents to make sure that high school students not attending classes stay at home during normal instruction hours.[112]

Governor Rockefeller's first direct act during the transit strike came on Friday when he attempted to come to the aid of the hard-pressed small businesses and homeowners of New York City. With many small businesses already in dire straits and facing the beginning of the second week of the strike, Governor Rockefeller phoned President Johnson and urgently appealed for help. Within hours of the governor's call, Johnson announced that the federal government would grant low-interest loans and other aid to individuals and small businessmen. Specifically, the president agreed to two measures requested by Rockefeller. He indicated that the Small Business Administration (SBA) would provide direct loans totalling up to $20 million for small businesses in the city and that it would grant delays in the repayment of loans. In addition, the Veterans Administration (VA) arranged to get lenders to postpone the collection of monthly mortgage payments on home loans guaranteed by the VA, in those instances in which the borrowers' earnings were reduced by the strike. Governor Rockefeller also took some action on his own at the state level, ordering a moratorium on the payment of New York State unincorporated business tax, a move that would benefit approximately 30,000 businesses.[113]

Chapter 7

Membership Control

Even though the TWU president had not been participating in negotiations for several days, the transit strike still tended to be viewed by the public as "Mike Quill's strike." In truth, by the second weekend of the strike, TWU leaders were acutely aware that they could not try to sell a mediocre contract to their constituents and hope to remain in office. As Lee Trotman, a thirty-six-year-old black bus driver observed, "We are 100 percent for this strike and we won't go back until we get a decent increase. We won't accept a settlement from Mike Quill or the negotiators unless they get us what we need, not just what we want. Showdown time has come. Everyone I know in the union is united on this 100 percent." Trotman then voiced the threat that TWU leaders, lacking the protection of any form of union security, greatly feared, "If Mr. Quill and the others don't get us a satisfactory increase, we'll get out of the union. There is no use paying $4.50 a month in dues if we can't get any benefits." Then, reiterating the often sounded criticism that Quill had not produced in previous negotiations, Trotman concluded, "Sometimes you hear that Mike Quill didn't do enough to get wage increases in the past, that he didn't get as much as he should, but he's definitely reflecting what the workers want now."[1]

One of the biggest mistakes made by the media and by officials of the Lindsay Administration in analyzing transit negotiations was their failure to appreciate the degree to which the TWU's rank-and-file members influenced the union's policies. Despite Michael Quill's portrayal in the media as an iron-fisted leader who was in absolute control of his union, the TWU had a long history of leadership repudiation by its members. Because of this history, Quill, Douglas MacMahon, and other TWU officials were running scared and felt that certain actions had to be taken during the 1965-66 negotiations to placate the restive elements within the union.

How do union leaders use negotiations to diffuse rank-and-file criticism? Victor Gotbaum, the head of another group of New York City public employees discusses this point:

> The collective bargaining table is the union leader's seat of power. This is
> where he makes it or breaks it. . . . This in the final analysis, is where his
> election is ratified.
>
>   The labor movement is an institution of people. The leader is
> supposed to represent the hopes, the aspirations, the needs of these
> people. In order to deal successfully with a public service union, public
> service management must understand the relationship between the leader
> and his men.[2]

Gotbaum goes on to explain why an extremely militant public posture is
necessary, even if it has the undesirable side effect of alienating the general
public:

> Good public will is of little help to a leader whose union is poorly
> organized and whose opposition grows troublesome. [For the union
> leader] it would be nice to bring the public over to his side, but it [is] much
> more important that in an open shop situation [the workers are] 99
> percent organized.
>
>   In an open shop situation[3] you do not want your contract just
> ratified; you want it overwhelmingly ratified. The opposition does not
> need a majority, all it needs is to keep the leadership off guard. If you lose a
> point at the bargaining table it is not considered by the opposition to be
> part of normal bargaining. "You sold out" becomes the rallying cry for the
> opposition. In addition you never know how many members you are
> going to lose because you did not satisfy their specific desires. So you
> become an "irresponsible union boss. . . ."[4]

If TWU members did become disenchanted with their leaders, this
disatisfaction could manifest itself in any of five ways: first, in the absence
of any contractual requirement that they join the union, transit workers
could simply choose to stop paying their dues; second, all workers could
collectively select a union other than the TWU to represent them; third, a
particular subgroup of workers, such as motormen or carpenters, could
select a different union to bargain for them; fourth, the union members
could vote their incumbent leaders out of office; and finally, the members
might refuse to ratify a contract negotiated by their union officials.
    The ability of workers who were dissatisfied with their union's
performance to cease paying their union dues had been a significant
problem for the TWU for twenty-five years. During the period that the
New York City transit system was in private hands, the Transport Workers
Union negotiated a contract in which union membership was required as a
condition of employment. However, when the city took control of the
system in 1940, Mayor Fiorello LaGuardia refused to allow compulsary

unionism, forcing the TWU to become constantly solicitous of its members views because the workers could leave the union whenever they chose. During the 1943 negotiations, the TWU unsuccessfully tried to get the city to agree to a maintenance-of-membership clause, as a way of at least partially stabilizing union membership. Under the union's proposal, workers could relinquish their membership only during periodic escape periods (every two years), but if they did not leave the union at this time, they were required to wait for the next such period. Unable to obtain this provision, TWU leaders resorted to any means possible, including misrepresentations, in their attempt to retain members. At the conclusion of the 1943 negotiations, for example, MacMahon, then president of Local 100, implied that only dues paying union members would receive wage increases, although this was not the case.[5]

In 1948, the TWU continued its quest to stabilize its membership and was able to achieve the voluntary dues checkoff. Under this arrangement, union membership remained voluntary, but workers could authorize their dues to be automatically deducted from their wages. Although workers were still able to leave the union whenever they wished, the process was now more formalized and disgruntled members could no longer simply refuse to pay their shop stewards when they became dissatisfied.

To what extent did this lack of "guaranteed" members really have an impact on the TWU? In late 1954, Quill agreed to a contractual change in which transit workers received an increase in their total number of sick days, but they would no longer be paid for the first day of an illness unless the illness lasted for nine days. A number of TWU members viewed this change as a "sellout" to management, and as a result there was a sharp decline in the number of workers authorizing the deduction of dues from their wages. In December 1954 and January 1955, the number of dues cancellations doubled their usual number, and in the next two months the figure redoubled.[6] Then, as the extent of the dissatisfaction gained momentum, 1,000 TWU members stopped paying their dues in April alone.

In September 1958, the TA agreed to a maintenance-of-membership clause in its contract with the TWU. Under this agreement, if a worker did not leave the union during a brief "escape" period at the beginning of the contract, he was required to remain a member until the contract expired. At the time that he won this concession, Quill claimed that the New York local had 28,000 members. In fact, records indicated that only 17,000 workers had authorized a dues checkoff. When, on one occasion, Quill was asked about this apparent discrepancy, he wove a long and involved tale of how "thousands of old-timers still come in to pay their dues over the window—and very loyal members of the union they are." When it was pointed out that it was against the union's bylaws to pay dues in person, Quill asserted with a straight face that "the old-timers had special dispensations."[7] In truth, with 17,000 dues payments, only about one-half of the eligible transit employees were members of the union. While providing some stability for the union, the maintenance-of-membership provision continued to allow dissatisfied TWU members to leave the union during the stipulated "escape" period.

Although union leaders were not sure how the dissatisfaction might manifest itself, at the onset of the 1965 strike, TWU leaders were primarily worried about two sources of unrest within their ranks: the skilled workers felt that the union was primarily interested in the concerns of the unskilled employees, and the newly hired black and Puerto Rican workers did not have the same personal affinity for the predominantly Irish union leadership that had characterized their Irish predecessors.

Of these two main sources of rank-and-file dissatisfaction, by far the most serious was the restiveness among the skilled workers. According to Theodore Kheel, probably the leading expert on New York's transit labor relations, one of the greatest barriers to a strike settlement "was the narrowed pay differential between skilled and unskilled workers in the TWU, which had been produced by the across-the-board increases of the preceding contracts."[8] Because they were numerically in the majority and because the traditional strength of the TWU had come from the unskilled station and stockroom employees, union leaders not surprisingly pursued a wage policy primarily concerned with the interests of such workers.

By the time of the 1965-66 negotiations, the resentment of the skilled transit employees had been simmering for decades. In fact, the only previous work stoppages on the transit system since the city assumed control of its operation were called by insurgent groups of more highly skilled employees. The dissatisfaction of the skilled employees was in large measure the result of the city's takeover of the transit system and of the labor policies pursued under municipal control. Under private management, both skilled and unskilled transit workers overwhelmingly selected the TWU to be their bargaining agent. In a series of representation elections conducted by the National Labor Relations Board in 1937, the employees of the city's two private lines, the IRT and the BMT, were subdivided into craft groups, with each group voting separately for the union they desired to represent them. Among IRT workers, who were split into twelve separate craft groups, the TWU won each of the elections, receiving 10,638 votes out of 11,585 cast, to get the right to represent 13,500 IRT employees. Although support for the TWU was also extremely strong among BMT workers, with the union receiving 6,269 votes of the 8,401 cast in the NLRB elections, two groups of craft workers, the motormen and the signalmen and covermen selected other unions as their representatives.[9]

When the city assumed control of the two private lines in 1940, however, it refused to recognize the TWU as the bargaining agent for its employees. The city could, of course, legally assume such a posture because as public employers, the IRT and the BMT no longer came under the jurisdiction of the NLRB. Although the TWU continued to "discuss" wages, hours, and working conditions with transit management, they did this as "invited guests," because public management was under no legal compulsion to bargain with the representatives of its employees. Because the TWU was not officially recognized as the representative of transit employees, any group of craft workers was free to directly petition management for changes they considered desirable. Under this arrangement, the existence of dissident groups, each purporting to represent the interests of particular subgroups of employees, proliferated. As one observer commented, "in refusing to recognize the TWU for many years, [the city] so emasculated the union's status as to weaken its internal political structure and encourage the formation of splinter unions."[10]

When considerable uncertainty surfaced in 1953 as a result of the creation of the Transit Authority, Quill decided to take the offensive in his quest to obtain representation rights for transit workers. What Quill wanted was for one election to be held among all transit employees so that they might select a single union to represent them. There was no question that if such an "industrial" union approach was taken, the TWU would win bargaining rights for all employees. Quill considered two options to be intolerable: the existing situation in which no union officially represented transit employees, and the possibility of holding separate elections for the different groups of craft workers. Under such a "craft" union approach, the TWU could potentially lose some elections among the TA's skilled employees, where their support was weakest. By 1953, for instance, about one-half of the city's motormen were members of the Brotherhood of Locomotive Engineers, and this group was militantly anti-Quill. In addition, eleven other craft unions which also opposed the TWU had considerable strength. "Transit," said Quill in a 1953 reference to the craft unions, "is at a turning point." According to the TWU president, the craft unions "cause confusion and roadblocks and slow down the bargaining process. We are tired of them and we're going to drive them out."[11]

Considerable speculation existed at the time that Quill entered into an unholy alliance with then Manhattan Borough President Robert F. Wagner, to gain exclusive rights to bargain for the city's transit workers.[12] Tammany Hall wanted Wagner to challenge the incumbent mayor, Vincent Impelleteri, in the city's Democratic mayoral primary. Seeking labor support for the primary fight during the summer of 1953, Tammany Hall leaders

approached Quill, who in addition to his TWU position also served as head
of the 500,000-member New York CIO. "Some writers have proclaimed
flatly that a secret, backdoor deal was arranged with the leader of the
Transport Workers Union: that Mike would throw the support of his
union and the CIO behind Wagner and that once Tammany got into City
Hall, Quill would receive exclusive bargaining rights . . . covering every
worker on the municipal transit system."[13]

Regardless of whether such a deal actually was struck between Quill
and Wagner, the incoming mayor was certainly not in a position to grant the
TWU exclusive bargaining rights. The newly formed TA, which was legally
empowered to run the city's subways and buses, was definitely not
controlled by Wagner. Of the five members serving on the Authority, two
were selected by Republican Governor Thomas E. Dewey and two were
appointed by Wagner's predecessor and opponent in the Democratic
mayoral primary, Vincent Impelleteri. The final member, as provided by
statute, was selected by members of the Port of New York Authority. Based
on the composition of the TA, when it finally did agree to a representational
election in June 1954, it was hardly on the terms that were dictated by Quill.
The Authority's employees were subdivided into ten units for election
purposes, rather than the single unit preferred by Quill. And rather than
having the right to represent all of the employees in the unit for collective
bargaining purposes, the winner of each of these elections was limited to
representing employees in the processing of grievances. The TA emphasized
that the election in no way permitted any union to be the exclusive
bargaining agent for negotiating wages and working conditions. Despite
these limitations, the TWU did surprisingly well in the ten elections,
winning eight, and receiving 25,198 of the 29,017 votes cast. The TWU
decided not to contest two elections among bus workers in Queens and
Staten Island, where the Amalgamated Association of Street, Electric
Railway and Motor Coach Employees was traditionally strong, and
conceded the elections to this AFL affiliated union. In the only contested
election in which the outcome was close, the TWU received 1,752 votes
from subway motormen, compared with 1,344 for the independent
Brotherhood of Locomotive Engineers.[14] The TWU had shown that
dissident elements among transit workers were not as prevalent as had been
believed, but the union still lacked the unifying force of being able to
represent workers for collective bargaining purposes. Those employees
who were critical of the TWU's leadership could continue to bypass the
union and try to directly affect the TA's policies.

For his part, Quill tried to cast the TWU victories in the representation elections in the best possible light, declaring that the elimination of

"splinter groups" in these elections and the ensuing negotiation of a new agreement by the TWU promised greater stability in dealings between transit labor and management than had been known in years.[15]

Although criticism of TWU leadership was somewhat quieted by the union's election victories, it was far from eliminated. Because the TWU's preeminent position as the bargaining agent for most of the TA's employees resulted from an *ad hoc* arrangement formulated by the Authority it was subject to criticism on a number of fronts. While the TA had negotiated contracts with the TWU for those workers in the eight units in which it had won representation rights, the TA had made it clear prior to these elections that their outcome would determine who would process their grievances, not who would negotiate their contracts. In the absence of any laws governing the conduct of representation elections and collective bargaining in the public sector, the status of the TWU's position was unclear. Nevertheless, when a newly constituted three-member Transit Authority replaced the Republican dominated five-member TA in July 1955, it immediately took steps to solidify the position of the TWU. Realizing that the recognition of one strong union would tend to stabilize labor relations, Joseph O'Grady, the new TA commissioner in charge of labor matters agreed to deal with the TWU as the exclusive bargaining agent for transit workers in the eight units in which they had won representation rights for grievances.[16] Although transit workers had never selected the TWU to be their agent for collective bargaining purposes, O'Grady declared that this would be the case. Furthermore, he indicated that the TA would no longer entertain direct dealings with unions claiming to represent factions of transit employees because the TWU was now considered the exclusive representative for workers in the eight units in question.

Within weeks after this new arrangement was announced by the TA, a new contract was reached that was due to run until December 31, 1957. The agreement, which provided for across-the-board wage increases of 17¢ per hour, was overwhelmingly supported by cheering workers at a victory celebration. However, because the skilled workers received the same 17¢ increase as the unskilled, dissatisfaction began to mount in the ranks of the skilled craftsmen. By October 1955, the dissatisfaction manifested itself in a brief work stoppage by nearly 150 motormen, which interrupted service for thousands of passengers. Although Quill had in the past staged a number of half-day stoppages and slowdowns without reprisals, this time the motormen taking part in the walkout were suspended. One craft union leader, feeling that Quill was working with the TA to drive out dissident workers, called the TWU a company union. As dissatisfaction among the skilled workers began to proliferate, new craft unions among towermen, signal electricians, conductors and motormen were organized in defiance of the TWU's leadership. Quill denounced the rebels as "criminal mis-leaders."[17]

The dissatisfaction among the skilled craft workers continued to grow, and when Quill visited the Harlem IRT shop in April 1956, he was confronted with an array of placards proclaiming, "Quill the Stooge," "Quill the Traitor," "Quill Sold Us Out," and "Judas Quill." When the TWU president told his supporters to tear down the signs, a fistfight developed and eight policemen had to be called in to separate the combatants and escort Quill to safety.[18] Several days later, Quill paid a visit to a bus garage where disgruntled workers had challenged him to appear. "[He] was greeted with a mixture of boos and cheers, shouts, horn blowing and other noises—and a great deal of pushing and shoving." Then several hundred hostile workers shouted him down and threw firecrackers at him. Finally, when fighting broke out Quill was forced to leave but promised to return. As he left Quill reassured his worried supporters, telling them that "he had been holding such abnormal social gatherings for twenty-six years and 'we're too old to give up the habit now.' "[19]

As the dissatisfaction among the craft workers grew, a number approached City Hall to demand a new election to select their own unions for collective bargaining purposes. One of these organizations that claimed to represent skilled workers, the Motormen's Benevolent Association (MBA), began to threaten a strike unless they could present their case to Mayor Wagner. Initially receiving a cold shoulder, the motormen were able to arrange a conference with Nelson Seitel, the city's new labor commissioner. When Quill heard about the conference, he immediately led a CIO delegation down to City Hall to confront Wagner. Claiming that his labor commissioner had acted without his authorization, Wagner assured Quill that the city would not allow the craft groups to bargain separately with the city. The mayor then publicly rebuked Seitel for even agreeing to talk with the motormen. Said Wagner, "It was an honest error."[20]

Thus, although the MBA claimed to represent 2,400 of the 3,200 drivers of the TA's subways, no mechanism was available to allow them to demonstrate their alleged majority status. The MBA set a June 19, 1956, strike date to impress upon the Transit Authority and Mayor Wagner the seriousness of their concerns. In anticipation of such a walkout, the TA assigned dispatchers with experience as motormen to sit in subway cabs for several days, so they would be able to replace the motormen should the strike materialize. When two motormen refused to take the dispatchers out on the refresher runs, they were suspended from their jobs. Within hours of the TA's disciplinary action, approximately 400 motormen walked off the job. The nine-hour wildcat strike stranded some 750,000 commuters and indicated that the insurgent group of motormen could paralyze the city's transit system. MBA President Theodore Loos urged his members to return to work, but publicly defended the basis of their action; "this stoppage," he said "was a spontaneous reaction of outraged men against the operation of trains by dispatchers who have not operated trains for years." After protracted departmental hearings, Loos and twenty-five other MBA leaders were suspended from their jobs.[21] In protesting the TA's disciplinary actions, the MBA president pleaded, "We are looking only for what we believe are our rights." Throughout the disciplinary procedures, TWU president Quill strongly supported the TA's stance, and "guaranteed" the public that he would break any future wildcat strikes.[22]

During the summer and fall of 1956, the motormen continued their efforts to obtain a union of their own choice to represent their interests. Correctly perceiving that Robert Wagner and not the TA would be responsible for making such a decision, Loos repeatedly wrote the mayor, warning him that the motormen were becoming uncontrollable. Despite considerable pressure, however, Wagner still refused to respond to the entreaties of the motormen. When Wagner became the Democratic candidate in an unsuccessful Senate race against Jacob Javits, the motormen were a constant thorn in his side. Together with other dissident groups of craft workers, the MBA organized a number of mass demonstrations at Wagner campaign stops in order to pressure him to meet with their leaders. On several occasions a group of motormen followed the mayor to Buffalo and Rochester, where they attempted to speak to him at campaign gatherings. At an Elks Club meeting in Rochester where Wagner was scheduled to speak, motormen posing as Democratic supporters bought $5 tickets to a fundraising dinner. Then after the speeches, they approached the startled mayor to request a hearing, which he denied.[23]

Quill, of course, was even more strongly opposed to granting craft workers the right to select their own union than was Mayor Wagner. Quill frequently explained that his entire adult life had been devoted to the cause of industrial unionism. "Every victory," wrote Quill, "every gain, every right established on the road was through industrial unionism. Craft divisions have always meant divide and go down to defeat." Quill was aware that such an approach would deny minority groups their rights, but believed that their interests had to be sacrificed to achieve unity and strength. "American tradition," wrote Quill, "commands that the majority shall rule. This system is the key to our democracy."[24]

Despite the combined opposition of Mayor Wagner, the Transit Authority, and the Transport Workers Union, the Motormen's Benevolent Association continued to press for craft union representation. Throughout the first six months of 1957, the MBA as well as a number of smaller craft unions siezed upon a series of minor issues to dramatize their cause. Loos, still suspended from his job as a motorman, worked full-time on behalf of the separatist sentiments in the dissident group. Loos spent his time travelling between subway terminals, articulating his belief that all workers needed "Freedom . . . freedom to join, or refuse to join, any organization, union or association."[25] Already having lost his job, Loos added that he would rather go to jail than see motormen forced to join the TWU.

Faced with this unrelenting pressure, the TA tried to placate the motormen. In August, the TA agreed to reinstate Loos as a motorman and to hold a new representation election among Authority employees if he would agree not to call another strike. In addition to its fear of a strike, the TA was being constantly criticized in the press for trampling the interests of the motormen. Seeking to regain its legitimacy in the minds of the press and the public, the TA agreed to have the issue of craft versus industrial representation decided by a panel of experts. The Authority asked the American Arbitration Association to name a distinguished panel to hear the contentions of the various parties and to make a determination regarding the proper unit for a representation election. The three-member panel was chaired by David L. Cole, a former director of the Federal Mediation and Conciliation Service, who had also served as a labor advisor to Presidents Eisenhower, Truman, and Franklin Roosevelt. Other members of the group were George W. Taylor, a professor at the University of Pennsylvania, who had served as chairman of President Franklin Roosevelt's War Labor Board and President Truman's Wage Stabilization Board; and Aaron Horvitz, a long-time arbitrator, who had recently completed a term as president of the National Academy of Arbitrators.

On December 1, 1957, the panel issued its report which following standards that were generally applied in deciding questions of representation elections in the private sector, decided that TA employees should not be accorded separate elections based on their craft. According to the AAA panel, "If each dissatisfied segment were free to secede and create a competing organization whenever it wished to do so, then the organization would be split, next fragmented, and finally pulverized. There is no way," the panel continued, "of avoiding in a collective activity of this kind some loss of freedom of action on the part of the individual or the smaller group when opposed to the common interest of the larger group."[26] Specifically, the panel recommended that three representation elections be held, one each among Queens and Staten Island bus employees, and one big unit for all remaining TA workers. The two groups of bus workers were accorded separate elections because of their long history of being represented by a union other than the TWU, a group then called the Amalgamated Transit Union. There was no question that the decision to hold elections on an

industrial union basis would result in victories for the Amalgamated
Transit Union in the two small bus units and for the TWU for the
remaining unit of more than 30,000 workers.

Faced with certain failure in the representation elections, which were
scheduled for December 16, 1957, a number of craft groups, led by the
motormen, struck the transit system. With more than one-half of the
subway system shut down, the MBA said they would not return to work
until the TA agreed to a representation election on a craft union basis. In
addition to the motormen, the craft groups joining in the walkout included
conductors, towermen, signal electricians, repair shop mechanics, coach
workers, and a group representing plumbers, carpenters, electricians, and
other subway platform repairmen.[27] Estimates of the number of workers
actually on strike varied widely: the craft unions estimated that between
4,000 and 5,000 workers had walked off the job, while the TA estimated
500 motormen and a total of 450 from the other crafts.[28] The dissident craft
groups, nevertheless, claimed to represent more than 11,000 members.[29]
Of these craft groups, the motormen operate the trains; the conductors
close the doors and supervise the station traffic; and the towermen, working
in towers along the tracks, route trains by controlling signals and switches.
The signal electricians maintain and repair all signal equipment, and the
mechanics maintain rolling stock. The coach union represented a small
group at subway power installations. In addition to the seven striking
unions, fifteen other craft groups representing transit workers also
protested the plan to hold representation elections on an industrial union
basis.

TWU president Quill quickly described the strike as "a dying kick"
from motormen disgruntled by the Transit Authority's adoption of the
American Arbitration Association panel's formula for conducting representation elections. "The strike-call issued by the leaders of the splinter
groups is an act of desperation," said Quill. "It is an attempt to blackmail
the majority of the Transit Authority employees and the people of the City
of New York into submission."[30] Reiterating his belief in industrial
unionism, Quill maintained that "in fifty years of bargaining, transit
employees have never been able to win anything on a craft basis."[31]

Disagreements with respect to a craft versus an industrial approach to
unionism were, of course, not limited to the transit industry. The AFL had
long been dominated by adherents to the craft philosophy, while the
industrial approach had come to the forefront during the tremendously
successful organizing drives in the mass production industries during the
1930s. Feeling that their interests were being ignored, the skilled craft
workers who were members of industrial unions began to rebel. By the post
World War II period, dissention, wildcat strikes, and secession movements

became so prevalent among craft workers in the mass production industries, that the industrial unions that represented them were forced to make concessions to their demands for preferred treatment. The United Auto Workers, for example, rewrote its constitution to give skilled workers the right to have bargaining representatives of their own choosing sit in on the union's negotiating committees. In addition, the craftsmen were granted the right to vote separately on whether to ratify a contract negotiated by UAW leaders.

Implicit in the drive by the TA's craft workers for separate representation was the belief that their interests had suffered under TWU leadership. If the craft workers had received acceptable wage increases while in an industrial union, it is doubtful that they would have been clamoring for separate representation. The motormen, however, contended that under TWU leadership their wages had not been keeping pace with those of other civil service workers. "At one time, about ten years ago, we were getting about $100 a year less than policemen and firemen," said an official of the striking Motormen's Benevolent Association. "Today they are getting almost $1,300 more than us. We used to earn $700 a year more than Department of Sanitation drivers. Today we earn about $300 less." And finally, added the MBA official, "In 1939, we earned twice the salaries paid to transit system porters. Now we get $2.32 an hour to their $1.79."[32]

Although MBA leaders initially held that they would not return to work until they were granted a separate representation election, they modified their position after it became clear that neither the TA nor Mayor Wagner would accede to their demands. The MBA then maintained that they would end their walkout if the union that won the right to represent all transit employees would include on its negotiating committee, the leaders of the unions that had craft workers as members. According to the modified proposal, the composition of the negotiating committee should be proportional to the number of members each union had among TA employees. In addition, the motormen's group suggested that each union have the right to process the grievances of its own members. For his part, Quill urged that no special concessions be made to the dissident craft groups. He said he was well pleased with the way he had been representing motormen and had no intention of changing his approach. However, as the wildcat strike continued for almost a week, Mayor Wagner began to make some compromises to restore transit service. He pledged that there would be no summary dismissals of strikers and urged the TA and the TWU (which was expected to win the upcoming representation election) to give consideration to the "particular problems" of motormen.[33] Finally, the mayor said he had gotten the TA to agree to allocate a sum of money for the study and elimination of inequities in the pay rates of skilled workers.[34]

Wagner steadfastly refused, however, to hold a separate election to permit craft workers to decide which union should represent them.

The MBA greeted the new Wagner position with mixed emotions. As a spokesman for the MBA articulated its position, "The Mayor's statement holds promise that the city at long last recognized the necessity of dealing with the special problems of skilled employees, but this cannot be accepted if with it goes subjugation to a union which they reject—the union of Michael Quill."[35]

On December 16, 1957, with the strike by craft workers still in effect, the American Arbitration Association conducted three representation elections among TA employees. The TWU did not contest the two elections involving bus workers in Queens and Staten Island, conceding the outcome to the Amalgamated Association of Street, Electric Railway and Motor Coach Employees, who had represented these workers for years. In the one big unit comprising more than 30,000 workers, the TWU was challenged only by a local of the International Transportation Employees Union, a relatively new group which was constantly changing its affiliations with other unions as well as its positions on issues. At the time of the representation election, James J. Donegan, the president of the local group indicated that they had broken relations with the ITEU and were an independent anti-Quill group, with hopes of granting some craft representation through an organization of semiautonomous locals.[36] The craft unions, including the Motormen's Benevolent Association urged their members to boycott the AAA-conducted election. As the executive secretary of the MBA told his members, "I know that you men do not want to be trapped by the conspiracy between Mike Quill and Joe O'Grady. If you vote in Monday's phony election, you will only be helping Quill and delivering all transit employees into his hands. Do not participate in this farce."[37]

The TWU won the representation election, but the results could certainly not be interpreted as an endorsement of the Quill regime. Of the 30,740 workers in the bargaining unit only 10,029 voted for the TWU. The International Transportation Employees Union received 2,328 votes, and nineteen different unions shared 2,554 write-in votes. Although it is always difficult to attribute motives to people who do not cast ballots, it appears that the small turn out was at least partially motivated by anti-TWU sentiments. The craft unions, of course, had urged their supporters to boycott the election. Perhaps most telling, however, was that only 51 percent of the eligible voters turned out, compared with a representation election in June 1954, when 79 percent of TA employees voted. As might be expected, leaders of the MBA and the TWU had differing interpretations of the election results. Louis Waldman, counsel for the motormen, said the vote showed "it is obvious that Mr. Quill's union, with all the backing that he had from the Transit Authority and other political sources, has completely lost the confidence of the overwhelming majority of the city's transit employees." Mr. Quill, in contrast, claimed to have won despite "the worst possible conditions."[38]

Just as it appeared the hopes of dissident workers for craft representation were being irrevocably denied, a new possibility emerged. At the very time the votes in the representation election were being counted, the strike by craft workers ended when Republicans in the state legislature announced a plan that could potentially grant craft autonomy. Essentially, the plan called for the enactment of legislation that would give the State Labor Relations Board the power to decide how transit employees should be grouped for collective bargaining purposes. Because of the heavy Republican majorities in both the New York State Senate and Assembly, passage of the proposal was ensured. MBA leaders, who had discussed the plan in advance with key Republican legislators, called off their strike as soon as the proposal was made public. The motives of Republicans in proposing the measure appeared to be wholly political. If Democratic Governor Averill Harriman vetoed the proposed legislation, he probably would be charged with undermining a key element in the agreement to get the motormen to return to work and perhaps of provoking a new walkout. If, on the other hand, the governor signed the bill and the State Labor Relations Board decided there should be a separate unit for craft workers, Harriman would incur Quill's wrath. In addition to being president of the New York City CIO, Quill was also instrumental in the statewide CIO machinery, and both groups had made important financial contributions to Democratic state and city campaigns in previous years.[39]

Publicly, MBA leaders characterized their eight-day walkout as a huge success. Their attorney, Louis Waldman, indicated that when the strike began they were virtual pariahs, but by the time they returned to work "an aroused public has become completely sympathetic with the motormen and the other workers who joined them." In fact, the MBA had little alternative to calling off the walkout. They could obtain no further concessions from the city administration and their treasury was empty. When the MBA called a membership meeting to vote on whether to end the strike, the union did not have enough funds to pay the $200 needed for renting the hall. As one MBA official observed, "It was an amateur strike all the way."[40]

At the time the motormen agreed to end their wildcat strike, only a few weeks remained on the contract between the TWU and the TA. Initially, the TA refused to negotiate a new contract with the TWU, claiming that the proposed state legislation might result in other unions representing craft workers. Eventually, however, the Authority negotiated a two-year agreement with the TWU which became effective on January 1, 1958. Although the bill granting the State Labor Relations Board the authority to conduct representation elections among TA employees was passed in February 1958, it was vetoed by Governor Harriman.[41] Some of the bitterness among the craft workers subsided in 1958, however, as a result of the large settlement negotiated by the TWU for all employees. They also received additional increments from the fund that had been promised by Mayor Wagner to eliminate wage inequities, when the motormen went out on strike.[42]

Having witnessed the havoc that could be caused by dissident craft groups and facing considerable external pressures from politicians and other union leaders, Michael Quill agreed to pursue merger talks with the dissident groups. After Mayor Wagner initially established a "harmony" committee to try to work out a peace formula between the TWU and the MBA, George Meany, the AFL-CIO president, eventually supervised the merger talks. By the fall of 1958, several craft groups including the MBA, were merged into the TWU as semiautonomous divisions. The TWU agreed to assume all of the administrative costs, but each division was allowed to have its own meetings, bylaws, officers, and organizers. Each division would represent its own members in grievance processing and had proportional representation on all committees, including the negotiating committee.[43] At the time of the 1965-66 strike, these special interest groups had maintained their autonomy, and a separate list of the demands of each division was presented to the TA at the outset of negotiations.

Even these merger concessions were not adequate, however, to placate the dissatisfaction among the craft workers. The remaining dissident craft groups, forming an alliance called the United Transit Employees Council garnered 8,784 votes to the TWU's 13,149 in a single unit representation election in May 1959.[44] And in the 1963-64 negotiations, another manifestation of craft worker dissatisfaction with Michael Quill's leadership reared its head. Some 1,500 bus drivers, motormen, mechanics, conductors, and maintenance workers picketed TWU headquarters chanting, "Down With Quill" because they felt the interests of craft workers had once again been sold out. According to a *New York Times* report, "sources close to the union said the demonstrations might presage an internal movement to oust Mr. Quill as president."[45]

With this long history of leadership repudiation, it was clear to TWU officials at the time of the 1965-66 negotiations that the continued viability of their union, and particularly their own positions, were vulnerable. Not only was it necessary to win a package that would be supported by a majority of TWU rank-and-filers, any contract would also have to appeal to the interests of each of the separate craft groups.

The problems involved in attempting to address the concerns of skilled workers in industrial unions were hardly unique to transit unionism in New York City. In fact, as the passage of the National Labor Relations Act spurred the formation of industrial unions in the 1930s, virtually all of these newly formed labor organizations were forced to balance the specialized interests of skilled craft workers against the more egalitarian views of the unskilled. As Harold Davey, et al. discuss the dilemma:

> Nearly all union leaders face difficult problems at times in reconciling and accommodating internal pressures of a heterogeneous union member-ship.... In negotiation of job rate hierarchies, significant conflicts of interest develop that must somehow be accommodated. The net result may square with one party's view of equal pay for equal work while doing violence to the other party's conception of how the goal should be achieved.... Should a toolmaker (highest skill level) receive twice as much or three times as much as a yard laborer (lowest skill level).[46]

Perceptive economists have long recognized that workers' satisfaction with their wages derives not only from their actual purchasing power, but also from how they compare with their fellow workers. In his seminal work in this area, Arthur Ross observed that workers' satisfaction with their wage was based on "an invidious comparison with the wages, or wage increases of other groups of workers."[47] And when Ross's work was elaborated on by sociologists and social psychologists, it became clear that for most workers, their most compelling comparisons were made with the wages of their fellow union members working for the same employer.[48] Because they saw these other workers daily and were aware of their skills and abilities compared with their own, these fellow employees typically served as the most compelling reference group.

An examination of collective bargaining outside of the rapid transit system in New York City illustrates the universality of union leaders' problems in simultaneously dealing with their skilled and unskilled workers. In mining, the "egalitarian predilictions" of the United Mine Workers Union leadership caused them to secure across-the-board wage increases throughout the 1950s and early 1960s. "The result," however, "was a dramatic compression of skill differentials which ultimately necessitated a special skilled trades wage adjustment in 1966."[49] An almost identical situation existed in the automobile industry, and leaders of the United Auto Workers Union were forced to negotiate an extra increase of 30¢ per hour in 1967 to placate their dissatisfied skilled trades workers. As Harry Katz explained the approach of UAW leaders: "It appears that workers...are not primarily driven by the desire to receive ever higher compensation and consequently do not possess absolute wants. Rather workers are motivated by the desire to maintain their relative position with critical reference groups."[50]

On the nation's private railroads, the sense of craft protectionism and one-upmanship has been so pronounced that industrial unionism never gained a foothold. The railroad industry has been characterized by "overlapping interests, jealousies, and...frequent conflicts and occasionally members of one organization have acted as strikebreakers in disputes involving a sister organization." One major distinction is that the so called operating employees believe their wages should reflect the superior status they enjoy over the nonoperating personnel.[51] The nonoperating personnel traditionally have been paid a straight hourly rate. The operating employees, in contrast, have been paid on a dual basis, taking into account both the number of hours worked and the mileage covered. As technological changes enabled greater distances to be traversed in a given time period, the operating personnel wanted to maintain the existing pay structure, but the nonoperating workers felt they were being unfairly treated by the continuation of the existing pay system. A major issue in virtually all railroad negotiations, therefore, has been how to divide the existing economic pie among various competing and often contentious railroad unions.

In addition to the problems created by the craft groups in the TWU, further complications were brought to bear by the increasing numbers of black and Puerto Rican workers in the bargaining unit. Perhaps most significant, the needs of the blacks and Puerto Ricans and those of the skilled craft workers were in direct conflict. The minority workers, mainly recent hires, tended to be concentrated in the lower-level unskilled jobs. Having no ethnic attachment to the overwhelmingly Irish-American leadership of the TWU, they could only be won over by substantial increases at the bargaining table. The skilled workers, of course, felt that the TWU had long pursued a wage policy that was overly solicitous of the unskilled workers and therefore detrimental to craft interests.

At the time of the transit strike, no accurate statistics regarding the racial and ethnic composition of the TA existed. The TA, fearing that a racial survey of its employees might be illegal, did not compile such figures.[52] However, based on inferences from later data, the black and Puerto Rican membership of Local 100 at the time of the strike was probably at least 25 percent of the work force.[53] More significant, perhaps, was that the TWU leadership recognized these racial changes as being significant and felt that they had to attempt to win the allegiance of these minority workers. As a leader of another union observed just after the strike, "Mike had problems. The union now has a number of Negro and

Puerto Rican members with no special loyalty to the Irish leadership. They were growing restless with the modest gains in the last few contracts. So with Mayor Wagner on the way out, and with Quill owing nothing to anyone, he made up his mind to strike if he couldn't get a contract that would fully satisfy the membership."[54]

Further contributing to the concern of TWU leaders over the allegiance of black workers was the growing tide of black consciousness and militance that characterized the 1960s. Although the TWU had been active since its inception in fighting racial discrimination, the top leadership of the union was all white. In this environment, a number of efforts emerged to express the concerns of black transit workers. In 1960, a group calling itself the Rank-and-File Committee was formed in the TWU "to promote democratic reforms within the union." The leadership of the group was predominantly black, and the organization was primarily concerned with the needs and aspirations of the union's minority group members.[55] By the summer of 1963, several hundred members of the TWU joined to fight discrimination with respect to obtaining transit jobs, gaining admission to apprenticeship programs, and having access to promotions. Called the Transit Fraternal Association, this group was also lead by Joseph Carnegie, the black subway conductor who had previously been instrumental in establishing the Rank-and-File Committee. Although the lines between the two Carnegie groups were somewhat blurred, the Transit Fraternal Association sought "to impress on all transit workers, and especially Negroes, the importance of participating actively to achieve equality of opportunity through unions."[56] According to Carnegie, the group sought to "fight the discrimination that occurs when entrance requirements and the distribution of apprenticeship and work assignments are decided by a union's white majority."[57] Not separatist organizations, the Carnegie groups sought to achieve their goals by working within the TWU. In 1965, believing that the incumbent TWU leadership was not sufficiently responsive to black members, Carnegie organized a slate of candidates to challenge the union's office holders. While soundly defeated, it was clear by the time of the strike that the restiveness among the TWU's minority workers was becoming better organized.

Chapter 8

The Second Week

The second week of the strike began on Saturday, January 8, 1966, with both sides working all day and throughout the night in an attempt to reach an agreement in time to get the subways and buses rolling again by Monday morning. The sessions, which lasted until 5:00 a.m. Sunday, involved separate private talks by each side with the mediators, with the parties never getting together for face to face negotiations. Nathan Feinsinger, the chairman of the mediation panel, indicated that wages were the main issue to be resolved. "If we get over the wage problem," he said, "the other issues will fall into place." Feinsinger indicated that the prime motivation of the mediators was "to get the subways and buses moving by Monday morning."[1]

Mayor John Lindsay, who did not attend the sessions, kept a vigil until the early morning hours at City Hall and maintained telephone contact with the mediators. Echoing Feinsinger's concerns, the mayor said that it was "critical and essential that this dispute be brought to a fair, equitable and responsible settlement this weekend." Then continuing to articulate the position that concern for the welfare of all New Yorkers was paramount, Lindsay added, "Any agreement to do so must be such that the public interest is recognized as being the first and foremost consideration...." Trying to assure New Yorkers that everything possible was being done to settle the strike, Lindsay added, "I appreciate [the mediators] extraordinary efforts. I realize that the mediation panel and the parties have been working without sleep. The city hasn't had much sleep either," he continued, "No matter how exhausted, I requested the parties to stay at the negotiating table steadily without letup."[2]

Because actions are more effective than words, Mayor Lindsay spent considerable time on Saturday attempting to demonstrate that, in his confrontations with the TWU, he was defending the interests of those people most in need, the inhabitants of the city's ghetto areas. In fact, the mayor's efforts at "working the crowd" were so politically oriented that it seemed as though his mayoralty campaign had never ended. During the afternoon Mr. Lindsay made a tour of three of the city's ghetto neighbor-hoods"; "areas of the city," as Lindsay characterized them, "that are feeling much of the pain" of the transit strike.[3] In his three-hour tour, which took him to the Bedford-Stuyvesant section of Brooklyn, the South Bronx, and Harlem, the mayor was accompanied by the two black commissioners he had appointed, Alonzo Yerby, Commissioner of Hospitals, and Robert O. Lowery, the Fire Commissioner. As the mayor walked along the sidewalks of these predominantly black and Puerto Rican neighborhoods he was met by huge crowds. Throughout the tour, Lindsay equated his actions in the transit crisis as being synonymous with the needs of these ghetto dwellers. As he walked along De Kalb Avenue in the Bedford-Stuyvesant area, the mayor kept repeating to the crowd, "I'm trying to settle this for you."[4] One woman in Bedford-Stuyvesant told the mayor, "I haven't been able to get to work all week." Lindsay asked her if she was being paid, and she replied that she wasn't. "Well, that's why we're trying to settle this thing—quick," the mayor responded.[5] "Are you getting to work all right? Are you getting paid?" the mayor asked a thirty-three-year-old construction worker. Getting an affirmative response, Lindsay said, "Good boy," then quickly correcting himself, "Good man."[6] Continuing along De Kalb Avenue, the mayor encountered Sol and Sidney Jaslow, the proprietors of the Appetizer Nut and Fruit Shop. "How about getting us out of this mess we're in?" yelled Sidney. "I'm trying to do what I can for you," said Lindsay, accepting a handful of pickles from Sol. As he walked along munching on a pickle, some of the residents were critical, one wondering why he wasn't at the bargaining table. But Rueben Montalbo, quickly came to the mayor's defense, "That's a good Mayor. It's about time. He comes to see us when we need him. No one else ever did."[7]

Moving on to the South Bronx, Mayor Lindsay was again surrounded by generally supportive residents. The Reverend Nelson C. Dukes, the pastor of the Fountain Spring Baptist Church, however, was vociferously critical, "We want action. It's nice of you to set an example by walking, but our own people are suffering. You tell us to stay home, but who's going to send us the paychecks?"[8] "We want some action—you have the power," shouted Rev. Dukes.[9] "We're trying to settle it," the mayor responded. A woman quickly came to Mr. Lindsay's defense; "Get Quill," she said. "Don't get mad at him [the mayor]. It's not his fault, the poor thing."[10] Because the Lindsay tour was a media inspired pseudo-event, the mayor was accompanied by a host of reporters and photographers who captured his movements for newspaper and television coverage.

After visiting with Quill for more than thirty minutes on Saturday afternoon, Dr. Hyman Zuckerman, his private physician, reported that the union leader was "markedly improved." Noting that Quill had a good night's rest, Dr. Zuckerman indicated that he was nevertheless still confined to his bed. Shortly before Dr. Zuckerman's arrival at Bellevue, the hospital received the latest of a series of bomb threats that began when Michael Quill was admitted. However, after a bomb squad from the 13th precinct examined the hospital, it was determined that no bomb was present.[11]

Away from negotiations, Saturday was mainly a day for rest; taking care of business left unfinished during the first week of the strike; and planning for the second week, should that eventuality come to pass. According to the Traffic Department, traffic was lighter than usual for a Saturday and no traffic jams were reported. Seemingly, people were content to stay at home and rest from their ordeals of the previous week. With only one or two exceptions, business at Broadway motion picture theaters was off by as much as 75 percent. After seven days of 12-hour tours of duty, police officers reverted to their normal eight hour shifts for the weekend. While at work the officers received a message of congratulations from Police Commissioner Vincent Broderick; "This has been a strenuous, difficult and troublesome week," he said. "In my judgement, New York City could not have remained operative without the resourcefulness, initiative, leadership and dedication which the men of this department exhibited." Members of the fire department could also relax somewhat, knowing that they would not have to circumvent traffic jams to respond to calls, as they had done 1,677 times during the first week of the strike.[12]

In the garment district, clothing manufacturers took advantage of the overall lull in activity to deliver finished spring garments to their customers. The deliveries, which were not attempted during the week were common enough that traffic congestion developed in the garment district, although no real traffic jams materialized.[13]

In planning activities on Saturday, the Reverend William James, pastor of the Metropolitan Community Church and president of the Interfaith Council of Churches, said that pastors were in the process of arranging car pools to enable parishioners to attend services on Sunday. Also, Superintendent of Schools Bernard Donovan said that school playgrounds would remain open for the duration of the strike to allow cars to park, hoping to somewhat alleviate the critical shortage of parking spaces in the city. The Traffic Department did not announce any new regulations, but it did indicate that its quadrant system to stagger arrivals and departures in Manhattan would be continued, though it had not proved effective the previous week. In perhaps the most innovative plan developed to ease commuter congestion, the Circle Line Company announced that on Monday two sightseeing boats would be used to ferry the staffs of seven hospitals to their jobs. The boats, the 1,000-passenger, Miss Circle Line, and the 600-passenger, Circle Line Twelve were scheduled to make four trips during the day, stopping at the East River piers, at Wall Street, 26th Street, and 63rd Street in Manhattan, and at the World's Fair Marina in Queens. Captain Joseph O'Hare, president of Local 333 of the National Maritime Union, which was supporting the TWU strike, agreed to provide the crews and permit the boats to operate. There would be no charge for the passengers, who would be served hot coffee in the heated cabins on board.[14]

In final action on Saturday, two prominent New York rabbis used the sabbath to assail the position of the TWU and Quill. The Reverend Dr. Louis I. Newman, rabbi of Temple Rodeph Shalom, on West 83rd Street, told his congregation that "the vituperative, archaic language of the union leaders against authority and the tearing up of court documents in the plain sight of millions of citizens can work only the most deplorable psychological and social harm. While it is true," the rabbi said, "that the right of workers to take drastic steps to insure their compensation sufficiently to meet the burdens of inflation is inviolate, nevertheless the public good should be borne in mind by all concerned. . . ." The second rabbi, the Reverend Dr. William F. Rosenblum, rabbi emeritus of Temple Israel, called it "immoral and unwarranted" for any labor group to take a "public be damned" attitude and said their activities must be curbed so that they recognize that "the public must be served."[15] The involvement of Newman and Rosenblum is indicative not only of Mayor Lindsay's success in "activating" various interest groups; it also demonstrates his success in defining "how" they viewed his participation in negotiations.

Late Sunday afternoon, Mayor Lindsay summoned the mediators and negotiators to City Hall in an effort to end the transit strike before another workweek began. As the seven police cars arrived, an air of anticipation prevailed at City Hall. The three mediators, Nathan Feinsinger, Theodore Kheel, and Sylvester Garrett, arrived first. Feinsinger, the chairman, who suffered from a painful hip ailment and had been getting only three to four hours of sleep for several nights nevertheless seemed in good spirits. "How do you feel?" someone asked him. "Fine," Feinsinger replied, "I'm not wearing a hat because someone laid a lighted cigar on it last night."[16] The talks began shortly before 5:00 p.m. and continued until 6:15 a.m. Monday without resolving the impasse. By early evening it was clear that even if a settlement was reached, another traffic nightmare on Monday could not be avoided, because the TA had estimated it would take between eight and twelve hours to resume subway service once the strike was settled.

The movement of the bargaining site to City Hall was symbolic of what was taking place in negotiations; the city government had replaced the TA as the employer representative at the bargaining table. This shift in power from the TA to the Lindsay staff slowly evolved from the time Lindsay first assumed office. Once the strike was called, TA commissioner Daniel Scannell related, "the mayor began to take a much more active role."[17] Without getting into specifics, Scannell stated that as a result of this greater participation, "things began to happen to which the Transit Authority was not privy. Things were done without our knowledge." Douglas MacMahon indicated that there were instances when this shift in authority created confusion. At times, after the mediators had helped the union and the Authority work out one part of the settlement, MacMahon related, one of Lindsay's staff members, who had no idea of what had already been done, would tell the union something else.[18] "The trouble with Lindsay," said one of the mediators, "was too many so-called advisors. I told [Lindsay] more than once," said the mediator, "I would resign if his unofficial advisors didn't stop interfering." The mediator continued:

> The people around Lindsay were too undisciplined; none of them knew what the other was doing at the negotiations. During one session, Deputy Mayor Robert Price said to the union, "Would you agree to X number of dollars on this item?"
>
> The union men sat back and considered this was what they were getting, but a few minutes later Lindsay came in and told them Price hadn't been authorized to make such a commitment. And Price would insist that what he had said was just hypothetical.
>
> Nobody negotiates like this and all that happened was that the union got sore and thought they were being double-crossed. This went on all the time with Lindsay's aides. They would give something without getting a quid pro quo from the union.[19]

Although the TA was theoretically an independent agency with the power to conclude an agreement with its workers, the City of New York had a vital concern with the terms of a settlement because an agreement reached in transit probably would serve as a basis of comparison for other city employees. It was traditional in labor relations in New York City for unions representing employees of the city government to base their demands on what workers in other city departments received. If a substantial wage increase, extra vacation days, or some pension concession was granted to one city department, or independent agency, it was very difficult for the city to prevent other unions from trying to achieve the same gains. It was likely that any concessions won by transit employees would eventually be translated into gains by other city workers.

From the TA's standpoint, asserting their independence was difficult because they were forced to accept monetary contributions from the city in order to survive. As the chief negotiator for the TWU, Douglas MacMahon, explained, "While technically the TA is the agency to deal with, the

practicality of the situation is that the city has to subsidize the TA. The TA
has been subsidized by the city for years. For this reason, the city
government was much more important than the TA in the negotiations."[20]
Even spokesmen for the Lindsay Administration, which during the
bargaining maintained, "that the current negotiations are between the
Transit Authority and the Transport Workers Union," admitted after the
conclusion of the strike that the city had played the central role in the
bargaining. After the strike, Deputy-Mayor, Timothy Costello observed,
"The real negotiations took place between the city administration and the
Transport Workers Union; not between the Transit Authority and the
Transport Workers Union. The TA had no money and therefore it could
do no bargaining."[21] The city's second deputy-mayor, Robert Price,
corroborated this observation: "The Transit Authority may be independent
legally, but as a practical matter it isn't. I'm sorry to say the Transit
Authority looked to the Mayor for leadership in the transit strike."[22] Price
contended that most New Yorkers regarded the transit system and the 15¢
fare as the responsibility of the mayor, and added, "If you don't believe me,
raise the fare tomorrow and see how many letters flow into City Hall."[23]

After the conclusion of the strike, the role of the Lindsay Administration was discussed in depth by the TWU's MacMahon. "Bargaining," he
said, "didn't start until we went to City Hall. There we began to get some
give and take. The Transit Authority stopped at a point, and said there's no
money. Then," continued MacMahon, "Lindsay stepped in, just as the
mayor did in the past."[24] In corroborating this statement, Kheel said, "It
wasn't until City Hall Sunday that the Mayor endorsed a settlement that
went beyond the 3.2 percent initially offered."[25] As the negotiations
continued into the early morning hours, a new package, including a 10
percent wage increase, began to take shape.[26] Also offered the union
negotiators were $1 million in 1966 and $1 million in 1967 to finance
improved working conditions, free uniforms, and payments to eliminate
the so-called death gamble pension provision, under which a widow whose
husband did not retire when eligible received a lower pension than if he had
retired.[27] When the wage component in this $50-million package was
rejected by MacMahon at about 3:00 a.m. on Monday, Mayor Lindsay
went downstairs to the gymnasium below his office and fell asleep on the
couch there. At this point, Robert Price, one of Lindsay's two deputy-
mayors kept the negotiations going with the union leaders who were
alternating taking naps on the floor. Then, "apparently much to the surprise
of the union and the Transit Authority, Price put on the table a $500-a-year
supplementary pension benefit to sweeten the pot." After the strike, the
TA's Scannell explained the city's reason for offering the pension, "Lindsay

said the strike should be settled and this had to be offered to achieve a settlement."[28]

The city's offer of the $500 supplementary pension was bitterly opposed by the TA.[29] Theoretically, the pension plan was actuarially sound. It was supposed to be in existence for only two years and would then be discontinued. But, as the TA's Assistant Director of Labor Relations A. Edward Schneyer stated after the strike, "It's ridiculous to believe this pension can be taken away. That's not the way collective bargaining works."[30] Daniel Scannell also did not even consider the possibility that the pension could be discontinued after the two-year contract expired. In articulating the Authority's opposition to the pension, Scannell said the TA "was against the pension because it has a pyramiding cost. It keeps getting worse. Its cost," he concluded, "wouldn't level out for fifteen or twenty years."[31] The reason for the pyramiding cost over the years is basic to all nonfunded pension plans, which by their very nature do not appropriate money until benefits have to be disbursed. For example, in a nonfunded plan of the type granted to the transit workers, 100 employees might retire the first year the plan existed. Since the yearly pension for each worker was $500, the cost to the TA the first year would be $50,000. But, if an additional 100 workers retired the second year of the program's operation, as would be expected, the TA would then be faced with providing $500 pensions for 200 retirees instead of the original 100. The yearly cost the second year would therefore be twice what it was the first year, or $100,000, and would be expected to increase until some of the pensioners began to die, causing a leveling out effect.

Why would a benefit be offered that would create such a burden in future years? As the TWU's Matthew Guinan viewed the situation, "They are human beings and just like the fellow who says I'll buy on time. They made a decision that would lighten their burden now, without worrying about what will happen later."[32] Edward Herlihy, who would later become a top labor advisor to Mayor Lindsay, saw the supplemental pension as a way of deceiving the public into believing the cost of the settlement was lower than it really was:

> By deferring the payment it became more attractive. When you get sophisticated people working with each other, certain accommodations are made. For example, in upstate [New York], school boards and teachers' unions may decide on a strike, usually during the hunting season, in order to marshall public acceptance for the tax increase that will be required for the raise. The strikes usually last about three or four days. The same things happen in the city too.[33]

Perhaps most cynical, however, was the view of Deputy-Mayor Price. After Price offered the additional $500 pension plan, one of the mediators, realizing that the deputy-mayor was a novice at negotiations, took him aside and asked him if he realized what the annual cost of the pension would be in eight or ten years. Price then replied, "Screw them. Lindsay won't be mayor then."[34] There could be no clearer demonstration that the Lindsay people were concerned more with political perceptions than economic reality.

The TWU eagerly accepted the supplemental pension, but maintained that further increases in wages were necessary to achieve a settlement. At this point, Lindsay, somewhat refreshed by his nap, returned to the bargaining table and offered a 15 percent wage increase that would bring the wages of the top rated job classifications to $4 per hour by July 1, 1967. "That," said Douglas MacMahon, obviously pleased with the new offer, "was bargaining."[35] MacMahon, however, decided to hold out for a little more. Although the size of the wage increase was acceptable to the TWU, Lindsay had again attempted to defer the cost of the plan for as long as possible. Lindsay's formula for distributing the 15 percent increase was 2 percent on January 1, 1966; 2 percent on June 30, 1966; 2 percent on January 1, 1967; and 9 percent on July 1, 1967. From a cost standpoint, the offer represented another time bomb: the total cost of the package was not nearly as significant as the eventual cost over time. The cost over the two-year life of the agreement would be kept down by the fact that most of the wage increases would only be paid for the final six months of the contract. However, by the time a new contract was to be negotiated in two years, wages would have increased by 15 percent.

Being a seasoned negotiator, MacMahon realized that he now had the 15 percent increase; it was simply a matter of trying to arrange for a distribution of the increase that was more favorable to the union. The chief TWU negotiator wanted to "front-load" the contract more; to implement a greater portion of the wage increases at an earlier time in the life of the two-year agreement. Using the same logic, MacMahon wanted all of the $2 million offered for improved working conditions to be spent in the first year of the contract.[36] Finally, at 6:15 a.m., with agreement still lacking on when the increases would be implemented, Mayor Lindsay, looking grim and needing a shave, announced, "The panel has decided to recess until later today."[37]

While MacMahon and the rest of the two union's second-string bargaining teams were attempting to hammer out a contract, eight of their predecessors remained in Civil Jail, and Michael Quill continued to be confined to Bellevue Hospital. In front of the jail, three pickets marched, carrying signs saying, "Contract Yes, Jail No" and "TWU, United and Invincible." The men decided to picket the jail on their own to show their support for their union leaders and to demonstrate to the public that "these men have to be let out.''[38] The jailed unionists were not confined to cells, but instead slept in a large dormitory with several other prisoners, mainly men who were jailed for not paying alimony. All prisoners in Civil Jail wore their own clothes and were assigned to work details in the kitchen, dining room, or dormitories. They were not fingerprinted nor were mug shots taken when they were admitted. After lunch, all prisoners were allowed to take supervised walks in an enclosed courtyard or to stay in a recreation room where there was a radio, television, ping-pong table, and a supply of newspapers. Inmates were permitted to make two phone calls each day to their families, and because Sunday was one of the three days during the week when visitors were permitted, each of the eight unionists received callers between 1:00 p.m. and 3:00 p.m.

Quill remained at Bellevue Hospital under the watchful eye of a city detective, a hospital guard, and a man from the sheriff's office who remained outside the door. On Sunday, the TWU president was visited by his wife and a number of fellow union officers. According to a spokesman for the hospital, his condition "continues to improve.''[39]

With negotiations over the weekend not proving successful, the plans to deal with the problems associated with the work stoppage took on added urgency. Preparations became even more significant when the Regional Plan Association reported that even with the maximum utilization of alternatives, 450,000 workers, or 26 percent of the normal labor force in the central business district of Manhattan would not be able to reach their jobs on Monday during usual commuting hours. A number of measures were announced on Sunday by Police Commissioner Vincent Broderick and Traffic Commissioner Henry Barnes to ease traffic congestion during the coming work week. The two commissioners asked that penalties for blocking fire hydrants, double parking, and parking in crosswalks be increased to $35 from their current range of $5 to $15. They also announced that the reversible lane system on bridges and tunnels designed to facilitate traffic into Manhattan in the morning and out of the city in the afternoon would be continued and expanded. Beginning at 6:00 a.m., three lanes of the Brooklyn-Battery Tunnel would be used for inbound traffic, and one to take cars out of the city. On the Manhattan Bridge, the Williamsburg Bridge, and the Queens-Midtown Tunnel a total of thirteen lanes would be inbound in the mornings and four outbound. At 4:00 p.m., these lanes were reversed. Commissioners Broderick and Barnes also indicated that plans had been completed to allow cars to park in certain areas of Central Park and Battery Park to accommodate nearly 3,000 cars. Finally, the two city officials reiterated their plea to encourage group riding and to stagger arrival and departure times in the four sectors of Manhattan that were designated.[40]

As promised by President Lyndon Johnson, the offices of the Small

Business Administration opened on Sunday to begin processing loan applications from small businesses hurt by the strike. By the time Ignace Tar, the elevator operator, arrived at the office building at 6:00 a.m., six hard-pressed business owners were already braving the cold on the sidewalk outside. By days end more than 600 applications for loans had been filed and the federal office had responded to several thousand phone inquiries. As Shirley Montini described the plight of her antique store, "No one came into our shop at all last week until Saturday, when two people came in just to warm up." Montini of Florence had opened about eighteen months earlier on an admittedly shoestring budget to sell antiques imported from Italy and Spain. The shaky financial foundation of the shop could not survive many more weeks like the previous one, according to Montini. "The rent is due January 15," she said, "and we just don't know what will happen."[41]

Leroy Giles, a thirty-nine-year-old former truck driver who started his own business eleven months earlier with four vehicles, seemed to have little in common with the well-dressed Montini except for the precarious financial plight of his fledgling operation. "Our trucks just couldn't move," said Giles, "and when they did get someplace there wasn't anything to haul because many of the factory workers had stayed home." According to Giles, the traffic congestion cost him about $1,100 in lost business during the first week of the strike.

By the second weekend of the strike, the disruptions and economic losses resulting from the strike clearly were not confined to the New York metropolitan area. In Detroit, for example, the national sales director for 123 K-Mart stores observed that the strike "has put a monkey wrench in our whole distribution system." Because a New York subsidiary of the Detroit-based retailing chain handled most of the ready to wear clothes they sold, K-Mart found it extremely difficult to supply their 123 stores nationwide. In Chicago, an interstate trucking company reported, "We're seriously hampered by the Manhattan tie-up. Since the second day of the strike it's been virtually impossible to operate there." Another Chicago company, United Airlines also reported substantial problems associated with the strike. A United flight scheduled to be filled with cargo from a large New York shipper had to be cancelled when an insufficient number of employees were able to get to their jobs, making it impossible to box the material and get it to the airport.[42]

The transit strike was having a number of indirect effects on the city as well, and although they could not be quantified, their long-term ramifications could prove to be devastating. Coming soon after other city crises, such as a major power blackout, a water shortage, and a projected municipal fiscal deficit, a number of business executives said they were thinking of relocating out of New York City. One high-ranking executive in a New York-based company with annual sales in the "billions of dollars" indicated that he was ready to propose the movement of its headquarters out of the city to Connecticut. And as the president of another large manufacturing company confided, "The strike is certainly accelerating our consideration of moving out" of New York. In addition, the strike was expected to make it more difficult to attract good personnel to accept jobs in the city. "New York City has been hard enough to sell to executives," commented an official of the Manhattan-based Morgan Guarantee Trust Company. "This strike is going to make it that much tougher."[43]

Mark Richardson, the executive vice president of the New York Chamber of Commerce also indicated why the strike's long-range effects on New York would be considerably worse than the immediate impact. "With New York manufacturers unable to fill orders," Richardson said, "out-of-town merchants are turning to manufacturers in other cities to supply them. Once they've got their foot in the door you can be sure those manufacturers will try to hold onto the business."[44] Sidney Prince, the executive director of the United Better Dress Manufacturers Association, said that in his industry out-of-town retailers had, in fact, been cancelling their orders in New York and reordering from manufacturers in Chicago, California, and Florida because they were fearful they would not receive all of their spring line.

Finally, on Sunday, pollster Samuel Lubell indicated the results of his survey of the attitudes of "the public" toward the transit strike. According to Lubell, when people suffered only physical inconvenience, they tended to take the work stoppage pretty much in stride. Often, he found, "they experienced a sense of personal triumph in walking from Brooklyn into Manhattan or in sleeping in the back of stores or in hitching rides through the city. In contrast, said Lubell, the cries of "Quill should drop dead" or "rot in jail" typically emanated from individual workers or business owners who were hurt financially by the strike. Regardless of how they accepted the inconvenience associated with the strike, by its second weekend, Lubell's poll indicated that a "sizable majority" were convinced that the fare would have to be raised to 20¢ or 25¢ to end the dispute.[45]

Shortly after 11:00 a.m. on Monday, approximately 12,000 striking transit workers and their supporters picketed City Hall for ninety minutes and then attended a rally nearby. Parading around City Hall, the pickets, three and four abreast, carried U.S. flags and signs criticizing the city government. One sign read, "Mayor Lindsay—Less Walk, More Talk"; another, "Till [sic] hell freezes over."[46] They shouted, "We want Quill!" and "We want money!" A stocky, middle-aged picketer with a brogue kept shouting, "Lindsay said he's put New York on its feet again and he did, everyone is walking." When asked to identify himself, the man simply glared and responded, "Mike Quill."[47] The picketers reached City Hall by chartered bus, car pools, and on foot. About 200 of those arriving by chartered bus were members of TWU Local 234 in Philadelphia, where they were employed as bus drivers and maintenance personnel. Three of the picketers from Philadelphia wore striped prisoners uniforms to protest the jailing of the TWU officials. With about 200 police with bullhorns urging the demonstrators to "keep moving," the demonstration remained orderly.

During the half-hour rally, Shirley, Quill's wife, received a thunderous ovation when, speaking from a sound-truck, she told the strikers she had "a message from Mike." On behalf of her husband, Mrs. Quill told the transit workers, "Keep your lines firm! Keep the picket lines strong! Keep your solidarity! Keep your determination to get what you deserve!" The applause drowned her out and she waited. "This is the greatest medicine anyone could ever give Mike," she said. "He asked me to also tell you that he has the greatest confidence in those now leading the negotiations." When she mentioned Douglas MacMahon and James Horst by name, the demonstrators tossed paper into the air like confetti. "What's good for the transit worker is good for every worker in America," shouted Mrs. Quill. "We shall win!"[48]

MacMahon's turn to address the crowd came next. "Let's have three cheers for Mike Quill. Come on!" he urged amid thunderous applause. "I think Lindsay could hear that," he said, pointing toward City Hall, as the crowd booed. "We spent 13 1/2 hours with that gentleman and that other gentleman Joe O'Grady," he said amid a round of boos, "and got nowhere. This demonstration might help move 'em a little bit." Referring to former Mayor Robert Wagner, who was still vacationing in Mexico, MacMahon continued, "I never met such amateurs in all my life. I tell you it was a sad day when Bob Wagner left this town. This guy doesn't know what the hell he's doing." Then continuing to stir the crowd, the chief negotiator added, "I wouldn't tell you what he offered us, but if I did, you'd go through the roof. You know what we told him? We told him to get it up all the way." The crowd cheered and applauded. "We didn't call this strike," MacMahon concluded. "It was called by Lindsay and the Transit Authority." More boos drowned out MacMahon.[49]

When Mayor Lindsay learned of MacMahon's remarks, according to his press secretary, Woody Klein, "he was furious. I have rarely seen him as angry," said Klein, "his face was expressionless, his jaws taut, his hands nervously twirling a pencil between them." Lindsay recovered quickly, however, and to break the tension phoned his twin brother, David, "Hey Dave, they just hung a guy in effigy outside City Hall. He looks like you!"[50] A little more relaxed after he got off the phone, Lindsay and several key aides decided it would be wise to take firm action. The two chief advocates of this "hard line" approach were Barry Gottehrer, a former reporter for the *Herald Tribune*, and David Garth, who were then given the task of writing the speech that Lindsay wanted to deliver to the residents of New York that evening.

The Power Brokers

In his televised address to New Yorkers at 5:40 p.m., Lindsay sought to portray the transit crisis as an old-fashioned morality play in which the forces of good must triumph over evil. He also attempted to show how his approach to the strike was part of his overall philosophy of government. Throughout his mayoralty campaign, Lindsay asserted that the problems of cities were not insoluble, that New York City was not ungovernable. Instead, he claimed, it was the way in which municipal problems had been attacked, as much as the problems themselves, that proved to be such an impediment. Throughout his campaign, Lindsay expressed the belief that under previous administrations the business of City Hall was conducted by making deals. The old-line entrenched interests had been making deals for many years on the basis of what was in their own interest rather than the public interest. Lindsay seemed to be saying that out of this old style of government in which politicians were motivated by self-interest, a new political style was emerging. This new-style government would institute rational policies in which issues were decided on merit, not who you knew or what sort of relationship you had with the powers that be. It would be a government which would treat all people equally. It would be a government presided over by a new, idealistic, young mayor, an honest man, a man who had been a fusion candidate, a man who would represent all of the people of New York. The approach was carefully crafted to portray the image Lindsay sought to convey.

In the opening statement of his televised remarks, the mayor said:

> This strike was brought about by a small group of men . . . who allowed a single interest and, in the last analysis, an unreasonable interest to supplant any allegiance to the public interest, to their fellow citizens or to their city.
> . . . A handful of men consigned a city of eight million people to paralysis. Forces bent on laying siege to the city seemed to move forward as if following a prearranged script.
> My fellow New Yorkers, the strike could be settled today if the city were willing to pay any price. The city is not, but it is willing to pay a fair

price—fair to the employees, fair to the employer and fair to the public.... I am prepared to take whatever steps are necessary to serve the people and to free them from the hold the collection of power brokers have had over our city.

When I was inaugurated I affirmed a dedication to the principle that the public interest must prevail over special interests, the good of the community over the desires of any group, and I meant precisely what I said....

Let there be no mistake about it. The transit strike is no ordinary conflict between labor and management. It is an unlawful strike which defies the dignity and usurps the freedom of every New Yorker....

The government of this city will not capitulate before the lawless demands of a single power group. It will not allow the power brokers in our city, or any special interest, to dictate to this city the terms under which it will exist in New York.

The paramount issue confronting us today, the one that threatens the destiny of our government, is whether New York City can be intimidated. I say it cannot and will not for I sought the office of Mayor to give this city leadership, not to betray its spirit in a time of crisis.[51]

Then, ignoring the ground rules under which the mediation panel was initially appointed, Lindsay said that he would ask the panel to follow one or more of the following alternatives: First, to make specific recommendations on all terms for a settlement. Second, "to agree to the appointment of a fact-finding commission to investigate and present the basis for a rational impartial settlement," with the strikers resuming work immediately pending a resolution of the dispute. Third, to arrange an agreement between the parties to accept any new procedures, other than the first two alternatives, to end the strike immediately.[52]

In a brief question-and-answer period following his speech, Lindsay explained in a little more detail what he meant by the term *power brokers*, although he declined to specify by name whom he meant. "The power brokers," he said, "is that group of special interests in New York City who, for long years, have sought to control the engines of government in our city through all of the political systems and other avenues of tentacle control around the machinery of government, and I say it's time to free our system from that. It's time," the mayor added, "for a people's government and for a people's control."[53] After the strike, however, Theodore Kheel commented that Lindsay's reference to the "power brokers sounded like nonsense. The implication Lindsay sought to give was that in the past Mayor Wagner had made deals that were excessive."[54]

Deputy-Mayor Costello explained who the mayor had in mind when he referred to power brokers, and what he was trying to achieve by referring to them. "Lindsay believed that traditionally many interest groups were able to get their way in New York City. We are speaking of whole groups of people—who are part of the establishment—and who tended to exclude other people from influencing city decisions. Lindsay wanted to create the impression that City Hall was not only open to these groups, but that it would also be open to all people. He wanted to open up city processes so that more people could be involved."[55] Asked if Lindsay actually believed that he could do away with the power of interest groups in the city, the deputy-mayor was unusually candid: "Lindsay is not naive. Of course he didn't believe this. But he wanted to create the impression that City Hall was not being dictated to by pressure groups. He wanted to put the establishment on guard that things would be done differently under Lindsay."[56] Deputy-Mayor Costello insisted, however, that there was a difference between "real" collective bargaining and the making of "deals" which had characterized the administration of former Mayor Wagner. "In real collective bargaining no outside political pressures are brought to bear," said Costello. "It is not possible to go around to the back door and make a deal."[57]

However, the critics of this position point to the differences between a "deal" and "real" collective bargaining as being more semantic than substantive. As the chief negotiator for the TWU, Douglas MacMahon said: "You can characterize any agreement reached through collective bargaining as a deal. If an agreement is reached honestly through a give and take process, then the contract has been arrived at honestly and a deal has not been made. The agreements reached with Mayor Wagner were agreed to on an honest collective bargaining basis. There were no deals."[58] MacMahon's remarks were seconded by A. Edward Schneyer, the assistant director of labor relations for the TA, "There is no difference between compromise and a deal. Things were done no differently under Lindsay than they had been under Wagner."[59] Theodore Kheel offered his opinion as mediator to the two partisan views already voiced: "There is no difference between collective bargaining and a deal. There was no difference between the way Lindsay and Wagner bargained. Every individual has his own technique, so naturally differences occur. But at some point in every dispute there has to be a quiet conversation involving the principals which is then submitted to the membership. You can call this collective bargaining or a deal, but it has to take place."[60]

Despite public statements to the contrary, as the strike dragged on, the distinction between real collective bargaining and the making of deals became increasingly blurred. After the strike was settled, union attorney John O'Donnell disclosed that Deputy-Mayor Price had met with Quill in his Bellevue Hospital room at the very time that negotiations were going on

at the Americana Hotel. Initially, Price refused to substantiate the fact that
the meeting had occurred. "Sources close to the situation said that
Mr. Price was reluctant to disclose his meeting with Mr. Quill because the
Lindsay Administration had said it opposed negotiations that were not
carried on openly."[61] Later, however, the deputy-mayor disclosed that he
had met with Quill at Bellevue, but denied that a deal had been made. Price
said:

> I visited Mr. Quill...not for any purpose of bargaining or any arrange-
> ments. This fact was told to the mediators. Mr. O'Donnell was there, and
> Mr. O'Donnell also visited with Mr. Quill separately.
>
> The fact of this visit was known to many people, including the
> mediators, the Transit Authority and the union negotiators. It was not
> designed to decide anything or negotiate anything because that was being
> done at the Americana, and we all knew that.
>
> I deny that any deal was made or attempted or that the union reneged
> on any deal. Mayor Lindsay had indicated as early as December that the
> way to resolve that dispute was through mediation, which would set an
> important pattern for future city negotiations.
>
> Mr. Quill and the union knew how strongly the Mayor felt about the
> importance of a third party, now the mediators, helping to resolve the
> dispute. I again conveyed this thought to Mr. Quill at the hospital.[62]

It appears highly unlikely, however, that Price would have made a
secret trip to visit the TWU president solely to impress upon him the
importance of utilizing the services of the mediators. Price's statement must
be viewed even more skeptically in light of a denial by the chairman of the
mediation panel, Nathan Feinsinger, that his group knew of the meeting.
"We had no advance knowledge of the visit," Feinsinger said, "we were
innocent bystanders."[63]

At the conclusion of the strike, union attorney O'Donnell, who was
present, provided what appears to be a much more accurate picture of the
"secret" meeting: "Price hoped to get Quill to agree to a lump-sum package
and on the basis of that to instruct the negotiating team to work out the
application of it. However, we have had huge problems in the past in
converting lump sums into cents per hour. The only way you can negotiate
once a strike is called, is in terms that men understand; cents per hour."[64]

Thus, the way in which his administration handled transit negotiations
seemed to belie Lindsay's contention that his election would "signal the
beginning of a fresh and rewarding era in labor-management relations."

Although he would not name him publicly, certainly the chief person
Lindsay had in mind when he referred to power brokers was Harry Van
Arsdale, the chief intermediary through whom Mayor Wagner dealt with

organized labor in New York. As president of the 1.2-million member New York City Central Labor Council, "Van Arsdale was the man to see when the union wanted action by the city, whether it involved a member in quick need of admission to a hospital or a commissioner's ruling that could imperil a thousand jobs." Similarly, whenever Mayor Wagner was contemplating a proposal that would affect organized labor he would invariably ask his advisors, "Have you cleared this with Van Arsdale?"[65]

It was particularly easy for Mayor Wagner and Van Arsdale to establish a good working relationship because they practiced almost identical styles in maintaining positions of leadership in their respective organizations. Each was a master at resolving the competing claims of different groups, and each was particularly sensitive to the need to make the leaders of the groups they dealt with "look good." Mayor Wagner was convinced that by symbolically demonstrating that he was on good terms with the city's labor leaders (and particularly Van Arsdale), his interests would be served. Wagner felt that if union members believed their leaders enjoyed a cordial relationship with him, they would accept the contracts they negotiated as being the best that could be achieved. Wagner recognized that because he was "always at pains to give the union hierarchy a feeling of importance" he could get away with paying their members less at contract time.[66]

What Wagner well realized was that he could satisfy the competing claims on the city by allocating "symbolic" as well as monetary rewards among the various interest groups. That is, by publicly demonstrating his support and commitment to the unions that negotiated with the city, Wagner was able to achieve relatively low contract settlements. Wagner recognized the essentially political nature of the job of union officials and did his utmost to make these individuals look good.

As president of the Central Labor Council, Van Arsdale was equally convinced of the need to make his constituents, the presidents of the local unions, look good:

> Van Arsdale, who has a hand in every labor settlement in the city, will purposely withdraw when the announcement of a settlement is being made. He does this, not only in order to allow the union official, whose membership is directly involved in the settlement to get the Gabe Pressman [the city's most respected television news reporter] interview, have pictures taken shaking hands with the mayor and generally be a New York power-for-a-day, but also to further solidify the official's position with the members of his union.
>
> "Everytime a local union president stands up and hears a boo," the Daily News labor editor said ... "he knows there's a guy out there after his

job. ..." The only thing that Van Arsdale wants is a group of strong local presidents whom he can depend upon. He'll do anything to make them look good, and sometimes that's hard.[67]

Thus, both Wagner and Van Arsdale realized in their leadership positions, that the heads of the various groups they dealt with could be placated by the conferral of "symbolic" rewards. Were the leaders of these various groups cognizant of the fact that they were not receiving as many tangible gains as they had hoped? Of course, but they realized that the dispensing of such symbolic rewards was extremely effective in maintaining rank-and-file loyalty.

By using the term *power broker* to refer to Van Arsdale, Lindsay sought to characterize the Central Labor Council president as a "labor boss," interested only in selfishly protecting the rather narrow interests of his constituents. The power brokers, according to the Lindsay view, felt threatened by the new mayor's recognition of the aspirations of the city's blacks and Puerto Ricans, and his attempt to enable those aspirations to be realized. Such a portrayal, however, was certainly not an accurate depiction of Van Arsdale. As a young man, "he had to slug his way into the business managership of Local 3 of the International Brotherhood of Electrical Workers in 1934 as a reform candidate opposed by both the Lepke-Gurrah mob and a Communist faction that was seeking to penetrate the building trades."[68] Once in office, Van Arsdale began "a range of union services and a degree of rank-and-file involvement in union affairs so embracing that Local 3 has been cited with almost monotonous regularity . . . as a model of enlightened unionism, a garden spot in the trackless wastes of the building trades."[69]

In 1962, Van Arsdale received national recognition and almost universal criticism when he negotiated a contract with the electrical contractors, establishing a five-hour work day. However, by utilizing the job opportunities that the shorter work schedule opened up, Local 3 was able to admit several hundred black and Puerto Rican apprentices into the high-paid craft. And, as one analyst observed, this was "the biggest breakthrough minorities have made in any construction union in New York or anywhere else." In his role as president of the Central Labor Council, Van Arsdale was equally "zealous in extending the horizons for black workers":

> His help was crucial in breaking down the resistance of the city's voluntary hospitals to the unionization of their wretchedly underpaid nonprofessional employees. He got the aristocrats of the building trades to walk the picket lines alongside the washers of bedpans and the haulers of slop. He

fought racket unions that preyed on the unskilled and uneducated. He threw his weight around in municipal departments to speed union progress where wages were lowest and organization weakest.[70]

At a news conference following the mayor's speech, Douglas Mac-Mahon rejected Lindsay's three proposals for ending the strike. MacMahon called for Mayor Lindsay "to face the issues realistically and deal with us fairly" and to "stop trying to cheat the people of New York with innuendo and talk of power blocs and other nonsense that has nothing to do with this case." MacMahon then offered a challenge to the mayor: "If you have proof . . . of a prearranged script of a strike, I challenge you to name names and take your facts to any of five District Attorneys." MacMahon emphasized at his news conference that the union wanted to settle the dispute at the bargaining table. "Our differences are not too great," he said, "and they can be settled by collective bargaining." He concluded, ". . . we will not accept Mayor Lindsay's formula."[71]

Prior to Mayor Lindsay's speech on Monday, no negotiations took place. However, after the mayor's talk and MacMahon's seemingly intransigent response, the mediation panel met separately with each side on Monday evening. By the time these discussions ended at 1:00 a.m., they agreed to reconvene on Tuesday to discuss Lindsay's alternatives. One of the mediators, Sylvester Garrett, acknowledged that the future role of the panel probably would be changed as a result of the alternatives suggested by Mayor Lindsay. Garrett indicated that, public statements to the contrary, MacMahon would at least be willing to discuss such changes.[72]

Meanwhile, the TA continued to press its claim on Monday in State Supreme Court for money damages against the two striking unions. The hearing, which began on Friday, proceeded at an extremely slow pace as the TA submitted thousands of pages of time sheets indicating the amount of time worked by supervisors as a result of the strike. TWU lawyers continually objected to the admission of the time sheets on the basis that they were especially prepared by the Authority for the hearing and were not part of the regular bookkeeping operation. Justice Abraham Geller, however, overrode each of these objections, holding that the records were maintained "in the normal course of business during the emergency." The hearing was expected to continue for days as the TA proceeded with the laborious process of trying to prove its "actual loss or damage" during the strike.[73]

The traffic situation, which was intolerable the first week of the strike, was even worse on the first working day of the second week. The largest number of vehicles ever reported to have entered Manhattan inched their way in during a morning traffic jam that began at 4:30 a.m. and lasted for six hours. Traffic Commissioner Barnes estimated that during the morning influx, traffic was 40 to 43 percent above normal and perhaps five to eight points higher than the throng on Friday. Barnes estimated that 850,000 cars and trucks entered Manhattan south of 59th Street, compared with the usual number of 600,000 commuters. Barnes attributed the traffic increase to the influx of workers who stayed home the first week but were now "beginning to feel the pinch" financially. Asked how much worse it might get, the commissioner said, "I didn't think it could get this bad. But," he added, "we survived."[74]

In the afternoon, the homegoing rush began "very suddenly" at 3:00 p.m., and continued for four hours. Things got so bad that at times hundreds of desperate pedestrians ran alongside vehicles entering the Queens Midtown Tunnel pleading with drivers to give them a ride. In some cases accommodating truck drivers were allowing thirty to forty men and women to climb aboard their steel-bed trucks. At the height of the outbound rush at 5:30 p.m., a Traffic Department observer reporting from 42nd Street and Fifth Avenue said that his car had not moved for twenty minutes. Traffic was so bad, in fact, that for a time an extreme response was planned. The police department indicated that twenty policewomen would undergo traffic training at the Police Academy so that they would be available for duty on Wednesday. This would be the first time women would be used for regular traffic patrol duty since the start of policing in New York City in 1700. Lest one get the impression that the city was moving too quickly, however, the policewomen would only be permitted to direct traffic during daylight hours.[75]

With the traffic situation deteriorating, city and state officials were receiving increasing pressure to provide alternate forms of transportation. The most emotionally charged option suggested was the possible use of the National Guard. Asked specifically about whether he had any plans to ask Governor Rockefeller to call out the Guard, Mayor Lindsay was non-committal, saying "any consideration of any remedies to supply transportation will get further consideration and examination." The idea of having the National Guard provide some form of emergency transportation was strongly supported by the Citizens Union, a nonpartisan civic group. The organization's chairman, Milton Bergerman, emphasized, however, that he was not suggesting the troops be used to operate the struck subways and buses because such a plan would certainly be considered strike breaking by the labor movement. What was proposed, Bergerman said, was the use of about 300 Guard trucks fitted with special seats or rented buses that would make runs along major routes in each borough, as a free service. A considerably stronger measure, the use of the Guard to run portions of the bus and subway system and to help maintain order was suggested by

William F. Buckley, Jr., the columnist who had just run for mayor on the Conservative party ticket. Although most observers felt that the use of the Guard to operate the subways and buses was unlikely under any circumstances, the feeling was growing that some form of emergency transport might be provided by midweek if the strike was not yet settled. Under the law, the mayor could ask the governor to send in the National Guard when there was a breach of the peace, a riot or disaster, or when such a development appeared imminent. Although some disagreement existed, the majority of legal experts were of the belief that the law was flexible enough to permit the call-up of the Guard to deal with the transit strike.[76]

In addition to traffic, the school situation also presented continuing problems. The plan developed by the Board of Education to allow public high school students to attend the school closest to their homes, regardless of where they normally attended classes, failed on Monday. A number of high schools were overrun with students and had great difficulty in dealing with the situation. At the High School of Music and Art, the building quickly filled to capacity before approximately 2,000 neighborhood students were turned away. The huge throng of young men and women milled around outside, "giving policemen and teachers an anxious time before they dispersed." The situation outside the school became so chaotic that a few students who normally attended the specialized music and art school, including one girl who said she walked five miles, were denied entrance. At Seward Park High School on the Lower East Side, 1,400 neighborhood teenagers who normally go to school elsewhere showed up in addition to the regular student body. The school normally operates overlapping sessions and when most of the "outsiders" arrived at about the same time the school was strained beyond capacity. In order to deal with this confusion, Superintendent of Schools Donovan announced that the ten high schools most affected by the influx of neighborhood students would operate a split session. They would accommodate their regular students from 9 a.m. to 11:30 a.m. and the "outsiders" would be admitted for a 12:30 p.m. to 3:00 p.m. session. All other high schools were to follow their regular schedules.[77] Dr. Donovan also indicated that once the strike was settled, tutorial help would be offered after school at those high schools where attendence had been poor because of transportation problems.

Nearly 8,000 persons filed unemployment claims forms on Monday, a 50 percent increase over the previous year, which was attributed solely to the transit strike. The law required unemployed workers to wait one week before applying for benefits. With the strike entering its second work week, those workers who had been unable to get to their jobs went into the twenty-eight unemployment insurance offices and applied for benefits ranging from $10 to $55 per week. In order to be eligible for benefits because of the strike, employees would have to prove that it was virtually impossible for them to reach their jobs. "If a person was in a reasonable walking distance from work," said a spokesman for the unemployment system, "naturally we're not going to pay them." Under the state's unemployment insurance program, payments would also be appropriate for workers whose employers had closed because of the strike. Those workers who did meet the state's eligibility requirements could expect to receive checks in about two and one-half weeks.[78]

By Monday, the striking transit workers were also feeling the full brunt of the strike. On Friday, they received their paychecks for the week before the strike began. As municipal employees, they were not part of the state unemployment insurance program, and the TWU did not pay strike benefits. How would they manage? According to Marion Jones, a thirty-year-old bus driver from Brooklyn, during the last week his family had been using nonfat dry milk, had substituted margarine for butter, and had stopped toasting bread. "The toaster uses too much electricity," he explained, as he continued his picketing of City Hall. Jones said that his $105 weekly salary had been barely enough to provide for his family of four and that he had no savings. When his picketing and the rally that followed were completed, the bus driver accompanied some other pickets to the offices of the Municipal Credit Union across the street from City Hall in the Municipal Building. There, the strikers were told that the bylaws of the credit union prohibit making loans to persons "not on full duty" at the time they apply for a loan.[79]

A second TWU member, Thomas D'Agostino, also believed he was in dire financial straits. The father of two with "one on the way" said that with pension, tax, and other deductions his weekly take-home pay was $90. He and his family lived in a three-room apartment on the fourth floor of a walk-up apartment building. "I'm in sympathy with the public," said D'Agostino, "but who's in sympathy with us? Who's going to put bread on our table?" Asked about the suffering public, the small business-owner, the low-wage earner, the striker replied, "I'm suffering as much as anybody, if not more."[80] The TWU established a welfare fund to aid the neediest of its members but by late Monday afternoon no one had asked for help.[81]

On Tuesday, January 11, the negotiations came to a halt while the mediators discussed the three procedures for settling the dispute proposed the day before by Mayor Lindsay. Although they were initially reluctant to accept the Lindsay proposal the unions agreed, after discussions with the mediators, to present a written response to the neutrals concerning the Lindsay formula for ending the strike. By 8:30 p.m., the mediators had received written responses from both the TA and the unions and tried to determine if any common ground existed. The Transit Authority was clearly willing to accept the Lindsay formula with TA Chairman Joseph O'Grady commenting, "If the unions will accept the recommendations of the panel without reservations, we should have an agreement within 24 hours." The mediators then met again with the union representatives from 10:55 p.m. until after 1:00 a.m. in their suite at the Americana Hotel, trying to convince them to agree to have the neutral panel recommend a settlement. At a news conference shortly after 2:00 a.m., however, Nathan Feinsinger indicated that agreement on how to proceed would not be forthcoming that evening.

Although neither the TA nor the unions authorized the public disclosure of their positions, the salient features of their remarks were telephoned to Mayor Lindsay at City Hall. Mediation Chairman Feinsinger said that his group hoped to have a more detailed discussion with Lindsay on Tuesday morning. "During that discussion," he said, "we shall indicate to Mayor Lindsay the procedures which the panel unanimously believes and firmly believes should be followed to resolve this dispute and bring about a resumption of work at the earliest possible moment."[82]

While the public discussions exclusively concerned procedural matters, the mediators clearly were also engaging in substantive talks with the TWU regarding the wage issue. Obviously, the union negotiators would be much more willing to allow the mediation panel to make recommendations for a settlement, if they were convinced they could not get "burned" by such an approach. If the final positions of the TA and the unions regarding the implementation of wage increases was sufficiently narrow, the unions would be assured of an acceptable recommendation by the mediators, who probably would, by mutual agreement, decide somewhere between those final positions. By late Monday, the differences between the sides over wages had sufficiently narrowed that AFL-CIO President George Meany disclosed a TWU official had told him the parties were only a fraction of one percent apart on wages and that a resolution of that issue would lead to a quick settlement.[83]

In other comments following a meeting of the AFL-CIO Executive Council, Meany was somewhat critical of the TWU and praised Mayor Lindsay's conduct during the strike. In commenting on the impact of the strike, Meany acknowledged that it might hurt labor's legislative program, but asserted that he did not think it would give the movement a "black eye."[84] When asked how he felt about Quill being sent to jail, Meany smiled and replied, "Mike is an old friend of mine and I always want my friends to have everything they desire. He wanted to go to jail and I wouldn't do anything to take away from his happiness."[85] Saying that as a general rule the jailing of a union leader would impede collective bargaining, Meany believed that in this case the TWU felt it was "some advantage" to have

Quill in jail.[86] Although it was not public knowledge, Meany of course was aware that TWU officials felt it was advantageous to have their first-line negotiators remain in jail. Adding insult to injury, the AFL-CIO president then proceded to laud Mayor Lindsay's performance. "Looking at it from a distance, I think he has handled himself very well. I think," Meany added, "he's trying very hard to settle this and is being fair to everyone concerned."[87]

Meanwhile, pressure continued to mount for a quick settlement to the strike, and if that failed, to provide alternate forms of transportation. The city's major business associations joined forces to demand that the transit tie-up be broken by using whatever resources of the city, state, or federal governments that were necessary. In a telegram sent to the mayor, Ralph Gross, the executive vice president of the Commerce and Industry Association, commended him for his "forthright identification of the major issues in this illegal transit strike and for your resolute refusal to yield to the blackmail techniques of irresponsible labor leaders." Calling the damage to the city's economy and especially to wage earners and small businesses "catastrophic," Gross said that "the grave situation in our city demands emergency measures." The Commerce and Industry Association suggested that the mayor mobilize all available public and private transportation facilities to allow workers to reach their jobs. They said Lindsay should ask Governor Nelson Rockefeller to activate transportation units of the National Guard to drive personnel carriers on Manhattan's major north-south streets, which would be cleared of other traffic. Finally, the association suggested that "tugs, boats, barges, ferries and other craft" be used to transport workers from uptown to midtown and downtown piers.[88]

A second business group, the New York Chamber of Commerce, said that immediate action should be taken to reinstitute bus service and asked that "the whole of our governmental resources be brought to bear toward ending at once this unconscionable and illegal strike...." Such action was justified said the Chamber's president, Walter Pease, because "unskilled workers are suffering most of all, being unable to get to their jobs.... Our schoolchildren are losing valuable classroom days. Small businesses are suffering unprecedented losses, which may well force many into bankruptcy." The situation, said Pease, was becoming "unbearable" and was causing "the image of the city to suffer throughout the world." Pease concluded by asking the city, in cooperation with the state and federal governments, to get the city's buses rolling "so that our citizens can get to their jobs."[89]

In a separate telegram, the Fifth Avenue Association praised the mayor for his Monday night speech, but quickly turned critical, "in our considered opinion enough words have been uttered on both sides and now we need action. The wheels must roll and quickly." The Fifth Avenue business group issued the strongest suggestion, asking for the restoration of subway as well as bus service. The group's message to the mayor concluded, "Let's get the buses and subways rolling even if it means calling out the National Guard."[90] Although the three business groups issued separate statements, they did so only after discussing their common problems and reaching the conclusions that a concerted demand for action was desirable.

Traffic Commissioner Barnes estimated that on Tuesday 780,000 vehicles entered Manhattan, a slight decline from the approximately 850,000 that made the trip on Monday. With traffic 30 percent above normal, the morning congestion lasted from 5:30 a.m. to 9:50 a.m., and the afternoon rush from 3:45 p.m. to 6:00 p.m.[91] And while there were somewhat fewer vehicles on the road than on the previous day, traffic jams were actually worse in many parts of Manhattan as well as in parts of Brooklyn and the Bronx.

With the streets virtually impassable, many commuters developed timesaving, if somewhat circuitous, methods of getting to work. Because entry into Manhattan during the first week of the strike was easiest from New Jersey, a number of commuters decided to use this route, regardless of where they lived. A Wall Street lawyer, for example, who lived in Mount Kisco, New York, drove his car each morning to Ridgewood, New Jersey, where he rode an Erie Lackawanna Railroad train to Hoboken. From there he changed to the Hudson Tubes commuter line for the trip to lower Manhattan. A growing number of Westchester commuters with downtown destinations took even more bizarre routes. The major hurdle was to devise a way to get from midtown to lower Manhattan. They initially rode commuter trains to Grand Central Station in midtown and then walked to the Hudson Tubes at 33rd Street and the Avenue of the Americas to take the Tubes to Jersey City. Once at the New Jersey terminal they boarded trains on another Tubes route bound for the Hudson terminal in lower Manhattan. A number of upper Manhattan residents opted for a rather eclectic combination of bus, rail, and boat service to replace the subways that normally transported them to their lower Manhattan offices. They were taking a Public Service commuter bus across the George Washington Bridge to West New York, New Jersey. From there, they would board other buses to take them to Hoboken, where they could take either the tube trains or the ferry to lower Manhattan.[92]

After most buses and trucks chartered by employers to take their employees to work got stuck in seemingly interminable traffic jams, a number of businesses decided to try a more nautical approach. The New York Telephone and Telegraph Corporation assembled a six-ship fleet to bring its employees to work each morning and to take them home at night.

The somewhat unusual collection of boats included a sixty-five-foot cable layer, a converted submarine chaser, a former Coast Guard cutter, two fishing boats, and the 112-foot motor ship, *Victory*. The Gulf Oil Company was utilizing a tugboat it normally rented to dock tankers, to ferry workers to their jobs from Brooklyn and Staten Island. The tug, which cost Gulf $40 per hour, carried forty employees each day, including one who could not stomach his one and one-half hour trip without taking pills to prevent seasickness.[93]

As the strike wore on, a number of advertisers began targeting their sales pitches to the crisis. Volkswagen ran a full-page advertisement that was headed, "Next time be prepared, strike back with a Volkswagen bus." The single line of copy noted that while the bus seats nine comfortably, "in a pinch you can do much better." The Scholl Manufacturing Company, the maker of Dr. Scholl's foot products tried a more pedestrian approach, running an advertisement that said, "As long as you're walking anyway . . . use Dr. Scholl's foot aids."[94]

To help ease the journey of those riding cars and trucks to work, the police department completed its one day session to train twenty-one policewomen to direct traffic. The policewomen spent the morning and the early afternoon at the Police Academy in discussions and watching training films. Then after purchasing their regulation whistles and earmuffs, they were taken to busy streetcorners for on-the-job training. "The main thing," said one of the Police Academy instructors, "is for them to build up their confidence. . . . They're timid when they go out there at first. Men are the same." Although this was the first time policewomen had been used for traffic duty, a police spokesman said it appeared to be a good idea that would probably continue. At least one of the policewomen, who during a break was rubbing her hands and stomping her feet in an effort to get warm, was not sure it was such a good idea. "This is absolutely the worst thing that ever happened to me," said Sandra Miller. "What really makes me want to scream is that my husband is one of the strikers—he's a bus driver—and he sits around all day playing pinochle."[95]

The impact of the strike on the lives of New Yorkers was succinctly summarized by a *New York Times* editorial, "Seldom in its history has New York City been through more difficult days than it has known since the transit strike began. Probably not since the draft riots of the Civil War has the normal course of life in this city been more profoundly altered for so many days than it has been by the extended disruption, last week and this, of its public transportation system."[96]

Police officers were so preoccupied with their strike duties and so exhausted by their extended shifts that a man charged with possession of narcotics with intent to sell was allowed to slip, unobtrusively, out of the front door of the Police Headquarters' Building. In monetary terms, Police Department officials estimated that overtime pay to personnel during the strike was costing $2 million per week. Still, there was simply not enough time to deal with any police matters that were not emergencies. On December 31, the nine-member anticrime task force appointed by Mayor Lindsay submitted a report to him just as he was assuming office. But because this was also the beginning of the strike, Lindsay had not had time to even look at the report, let alone use its recommendations as the basis for policy changes. In a different area, the police department's chief of planning, George P. McManus, said that the strike had delayed a pilot program in Queens that could potentially lead to complete motorization and "scooterization" of the patrol force. The strike did have some positive effects on police operations. With the exception of Staten Island, which is relatively isolated and therefore least affected by the strike, crime rates in the remaining boroughs had declined. Police officials attributed the decrease to the fact that more police officers were on the street, greater overall activity on the streets made it difficult to prey on solitary individuals, and criminals were afraid that because of traffic tie-ups, they would be unable to escape after committing a crime.[97]

With the strike well into its second week, educational officials were becoming increasingly concerned about the effects on the city's school population. School personnel agreed that those high school students who were unable to get to class would be at a serious disadvantage when the State Regents examinations were given later in the month. The passing of this series of exams was required by the state for students to be able to receive an academic diploma, which was required for admission to most colleges. For January graduates, the failure of a Regents exam in a required subject would mean that they would receive a general diploma, which would not suffice for college admission. For the majority of students planning to graduate in June, the failure of the Regents exam would necessitate either repeating the course and then passing the state test or possibly taking the exam again without repeating the course. In either case, the failure of such an exam would prove highly disruptive to college-bound seniors. Others were worried about how the strike would affect admission to the city's specialized high schools, such as the High School of Music and Art and the Bronx High School of Science, whose entrance examinations were still scheduled for the following week. One parent, whose son wanted to attend such a school, was worried that the strike would put him at a psychological disadvantage: "He is worried that he won't make it because he's been out of school, and who knows whether this will affect him on the test."[98]

At the high school level, where absenteeism was highest, about one-third of the 245,000 students were missing class. In some cases, the policy of having students attend the closest high school to their home regardless of where they normally attended classes, produced a minimal adverse impact. In other instances, such as the High School of Music and Art, a group of only 260 regular students were overwhelmed by the influx of 3,000 transients. In such instances, there was not even the pretense that normal instruction was taking place; instead they were said to be receiving "special programs" such as "current affairs" or "cultural subjects" in the school's auditorium.[99]

With the strike affecting the lives of so many New Yorkers, it was "good politics" to try to alleviate their suffering. In this vein, Governor Rockefeller moved on Tuesday to pay workers who were unable to reach their jobs unemployment compensation for the entire period, rather than requiring them to wait seven days without receiving benefits as was normally the case. The state labor law authorized the governor to grant immediate compensation if, in his judgement, an emergency existed. Speaking of the "human suffering" and the "tragic situation" caused by the strike, Rockefeller waived the waiting period.[100] Applications for unemployment insurance benefits had been running about 7,000 per day in New York City since the strike began, which was about 50 percent above normal. In an even more transparently political move, the state Senate passed a bill urging landlords, utility companies, finance companies, and other creditors to allow delayed payments from workers who had been kept from their jobs by the strike. Based on the wording of the bill, creditors were under no legal obligation to comply with the resolution, but its sponsors said they hoped it would generate moral pressure for compliance. Initially, the bill was referred to the finance committee by the Senate Majority Leader Earl W. Brydges, an upstate Republican. However, its sponsor, Irwin Brownstein, a Brooklyn Democrat, pleaded for immediate action. "There is hardship beyond belief," he said. "People don't know where they're going to get the money to pay for their support." The majority leader responded, "I think the resolution is demogogic and meaningless," but he consented to allow the Senate to vote on it immediately "for whatever it's worth." By a voice vote, the bill passed unanimously.[101]

Mayor Lindsay was forced to eat political crow on Tuesday when his own administration conceded that municipal employees would lose one sick day for each day they failed to report during the strike. The mayor had eloquently urged employees to stay away from their jobs early in the strike and had assured them "that employers will respect my wish . . . that you will not be prejudiced." The mayor approved the leave penalty, which was initially recommended by the Personnel Department. According to a spokesman for the Lindsay Administration, the reversal of policy resulted from the fact that some employees were reporting for work "under great hardships" while others chose to remain at home knowing they would not be penalized. "This we considered to be unfair," he said.[102]

After more than two months of disagreements, lawyers for the TA, TWU, and the City of New York joined forces to prevent the invocation of the state's Condon-Wadlin Act, which prohibited strikes by public employees, against the striking transit workers. George Weinstein, a lawyer who said he was acting as a "taxpayer and voter," petitioned State Supreme Court Justice Irving H. Saypol to rule that because the transit workers were involved in an illegal strike they should be dismissed from their jobs, and if rehired they should be ineligible for pay increases for three years, as provided by the terms of the Condon-Wadlin Act. Claiming that "never in the history of collective bargaining have so few brought hardships, loss and damages to so many, Weinstein told the court that if pay increases were granted and the suit sustained, Mayor Lindsay and other public officials might be subject to civil or criminal litigation. The Authority, the TWU, and the city's lawyers jointly pleaded with Justice Saypol not to issue the writ of prohibition requested by Weinstein, arguing that such action was premature. They said that no pay increases had been announced and no employees had been dismissed. Further, the lawyers contended that such action by the court would "create confusion" and make a strike settlement even more difficult to achieve.[103]

At the very time that the Weinstein suit was being heard in court, state Assemblyman Joseph Kotler, a Democrat from Brooklyn, introduced a bill to repeal the provision of the Condon-Wadlin Act that prescribed termination of striking public employees. Essentially agreeing with the Weinstein suit, Assemblyman Kotler argued that a strict interpretation of the state's antistrike law would prohibit a settlement of the strike because pay increases could not be implemented. For a two-year period ending in July 1965, the punitive provisions of the act were relaxed on an experimental basis. Under these more lenient provisions, pay increases for reinstated strikers were barred for only six months. Governor Rockefeller immediately indicated that he would be sympathetic to a permanent revision of the Condon-Wadlin Act. Asked if he would return its penalties to the less severe provisions stipulated by the experimental amendment, Rockefeller said, "I think we may have to go farther than that."[104] There was no immediate indication of when Justice Saypol would issue a ruling in the Weinstein suit.

In separate court action, the TA continued to present evidence in State Supreme Court that it was entitled to $322,000 a day in damages, and $100,000 as the one-time cost of shutting the system down. If the court assessed the fine for the eleven days of the strike so far, the total figure would be $3,542,000. However, based on reports filed with the Department of Labor, as required by the Labor-Management Reporting and Disclosure Act of 1959, the International TWU had net assets of $1,467,144 and TWU Local 100, net assets of $833,000. Thus, even if the TWU's International and Local treasuries were totally emptied, the fine asked by the TA could not be satisfied.[105] The TA's request for a fine was scheduled to continue before Judge Geller at 10:15 a.m. on Wednesday.

Chapter 9

In the Early Morning Hours

In the early morning hours of Thursday, January 13, 1966, New York City's transit strike was settled. Earlier in the day, however, the prospect for resolving the dispute did not appear bright. At noon on Wednesday, the mediation panel reported to Mayor Lindsay that consensus could not be reached regarding the alternate disputes procedures he had suggested for ending the walkout. John Lindsay, nevertheless, unilaterally asked the mediators to give their thoughts "as to the basis for a fair, equitable and responsible settlement." He indicated he was taking this initiative on his own because "As Mayor, I reserve the right to take such action as I consider best in the public interest, including release of the report to the public."[1]

Despite the fact that throughout their mediation efforts, Nathan Feinsinger, Sylvester Garrett, and Theodore Kheel had maintained that they could not make recommendations regarding a settlement unless both sides agreed, they consented to write such a report. The task itself was not that complicated because virtually all issues with the exception of wages had already been settled directly by the parties.

Perhaps the most difficult problem in composing the report involved providing a rationale for why it was being written at all, considering the consistent position by the mediators that they would not pursue such a course of action. The mediators' arguments on this issue involved considerable sophistry, emphasizing that they were not making recommendations for a settlement but were simply making a report of their views at the request of the mayor. They pointed out that the panel had been established by former Mayor Robert Wagner, with the concurrence of Mayor Lindsay, to serve solely in a mediation role and that it was not intended to make recommendations for a settlement or to be a fact-finding or arbitration board. Then, in an apparent non sequitur, they asserted that "we do not report our views as arbitrators or fact-finders, but solely as mediators, giving you our thoughts concerning a basis for resolution of the remaining differences."[2] The basic difference between mediation and fact-finding, of course, is that mediators work quietly to help the parties reach an agreement without making their own views public, while fact-finders are expected to report publicly their ideas regarding an appropriate settlement. Regardless of what kind of word manipulation they engaged in, the public declaration of their views made the neutral panel a group of fact-finders.

At 6:20 p.m., the mediation team headed for the Americana Hotel to deliver their report to the negotiators for the TA and the striking unions. Continuing the group's double-talk at this time, Theodore Kheel insisted that the panel had offered "views" and not "recommendations," but conceded that the views were significant enough that if they were rejected by the parties, the panel would be forced to go out of existence. "We would have committed ourselves," said Kheel, "and we would no longer be impartial."[3] The highly pragmatic mediation panel, of course, knew exactly what it was doing. They had a settlement; all that remained was to make the agreement appear in the best possible light to rank-and-file union members and to the New York City electorate. From the standpoint of the Lindsay Administration, it was extremely important that an impartial group of experts such as the mediation panel publicly assert that the settlement was fair in order to reduce the possibility that the mayor would be perceived as giving in to the union to end the strike. From the perspective of the union leaders, at this point, they did not care whether public recommendations were made because they were assured of a settlement that would please their membership.

On Wednesday afternoon, while the mediators were composing their report, Senator Robert Kennedy, sensing that a settlement was imminent, tried to use the situation for his own political advantage. Senator Kennedy's secretary called the mayor's office and said he might be coming to City Hall later in the afternoon to discuss the transit strike. Approximately thirty minutes later, the New York Democrat was bounding up the steps of City Hall headed for the mayor's office. After waiting outside for about ten minutes, Lindsay came out of his inner office to greet the Senator warmly. "Hello, Bob. It's good to see you," the mayor said smilingly, shaking Kennedy's hand. "Hello, John," Kennedy responded also smiling. Seated at the side of Lindsay's desk, in a pensive pose with his legs crossed and his right hand on his chin, Kennedy acted as though he knew little of the status of the negotiations. "Well, tell me what it's all about, John. How has it been going?" Getting up from his desk and pacing back and forth, the mayor discussed the issues, the union's demands, and what he felt the city would and could do. Lindsay then described what he perceived to be the major cause of the strike: that the Irish dominated leadership of the TWU was being pressured by an influx of black members and felt that a strike was necessary to remain in office. Kennedy sat quietly through Lindsay's comments and then asked about the prospects for a settlement. The mayor said that both parties were close to an agreement, that it would come within a day or two, and it would have to result from both sides accepting the recommendations of the mediators. Then, taking a more long-range view, Lindsay told Kennedy he wanted to get some legislation passed after the strike was settled that would improve collective bargaining procedures in New York City and said he might need the senator's help in getting such a law passed. Kennedy nodded in agreement and said he would have one of his aides work with the Lindsay staff on this issue.[4]

As the meeting ended, Senator Kennedy declined a Lindsay aide's suggestion that he speak first at the news conference that would ensue. Lindsay therefore made the initial comments, uttering the seemingly obligatory remarks about Senator Kennedy being "concerned and helpful" and having had a "fruitful discussion." Lindsay then added that he was "delighted to have the junior Senator from New York as our guest here at City Hall" and said he considered the visit "a sign that all good men pull together in time of difficulty."[5] Rather than returning these niceties, as protocol demanded, Kennedy seized the opportunity; he called the strike "intolerable" and "catastrophic" and urged "the union as well as the Authority to accept the findings of the mediation board. There's going to have to be give-and-take on both sides," he added. "That give-and-take must take place today. The strike really cannot go on for another day." The senator concluded by telling the reporters that he had sent a telegram to the mayor two days earlier, urging that immediate action be taken to end the strike. According to Lindsay's press secretary, Woody Klein, "Kennedy's timing had been perfect. There was no doubt in my mind," Klein observed, "that Kennedy sensed a settlement and that he wanted to try and take the credit for it himself." Lindsay was hardly pleased by the Senator's performance, remarking to an aide, "He really put it to us."[6]

Later, Senator Kennedy continued to "put it to" Mayor Lindsay, although he never became stridently critical of the mayor's performance. As he left City Hall, Kennedy reiterated his assertion that it would have been better if Lindsay had made his request to the mediators two days earlier. If the mediators' ideas concerning a settlement had been made public at that time, the senator said, the "weight of public opinion" could have helped produce a settlement if New Yorkers were aware of the differences between the parties." When asked by reporters if the idea to have the mediators recommend a settlement was his or Lindsay's, Kennedy was intentionally vague; "That doesn't matter," he said. When asked if he thought the mayor had exercised poor judgement in the negotiations, Kennedy refused to be explicitly critical, but he let the implication stand; "That sort of thing doesn't help," he replied.[7]

The strike came to an end when negotiators for the TA and the two striking unions accepted the mediation panel's proposals for settling the dispute. At 1:37 a.m. on Thursday, Douglas MacMahon, the TWU's chief negotiator smilingly announced that the union's negotiating committee was recommending acceptance of the mediators' proposals.[8] MacMahon said that the membership would vote on ratification by mail, after they had returned to work. "I am very happy to make this announcement," MacMahon said. "The union feels that this is a substantial victory...."[9] MacMahon accepted the proposal only after consulting with Michael Quill, who remained in Bellevue Hospital, and with the other jailed leaders— Matthew Guinan, Daniel Gilmartin, Ellis Van Riper, Frank Sheehan, and Mark Kavanagh.[10] The TA, of course, had indicated earlier that it was willing to accept the recommendations of the mediators as the basis for ending the strike. Nevertheless, the Authority met to formally consider the mediators' report and, at 3:30 a.m., indicated that they, too, would accept the recommendations.

In their report, the mediators took as their starting point the place where the parties themselves had left off in negotiations. Because most issues, except wages, had been settled earlier, the report dealt primarily with money differences. The mediators stated that their views were predicated on what they believed the parties would have agreed upon if the bargaining had been permitted to run its normal course.[11]

First, however, the mediators had to determine who constituted the parties to the dispute. They reasoned that:

> This is an extraordinary dispute...since the TA...and MABSTOA (Manhattan and Bronx Surface Operating Authority), as a matter of law, are independent agencies. In this sense, it is their responsibility to conclude any agreements with the unions. But as a practical matter, the Mayor, as representative of the citizens of New York, has a vital stake in the terms of such agreement, as well as in the method of financing their cost, for reasons fully known to you (Mayor Lindsay) and the public.
>
> Thus, your (Mayor Lindsay's) own view as to the terms of a settlement also must be taken into account.[12]

In its attempt to ascertain the final position of the parties with respect to the various issues, the fragmented nature of management in the dispute became even more apparent: some of the final offers were made by the TA, others were extended by the Lindsay Administration.

A number of major issues had, of course, already been settled by the parties by the time their final session adjourned on Monday at City Hall. The Transit Authority's offer to guarantee the existing health and welfare benefits, at a cost of $800,000, was accepted by the unions as was the TA offer to supply uniforms to bus operators and conductors, which would also amount to an outlay of $800,000 over the two-year life of the agreement. The Authority also agreed to finance the removal of the so-called death gamble. Under this proposal, which was offered retroactively to July 1, 1965, survivors of TA employees would not lose pension benefits because their spouses had died while still working, rather than retiring when they were eligible. Although the TA agreed to fully finance this offer, estimated to cost $2 million over the life of the agreement, it was to be financed on a pay-as-you-go basis, rather than being funded. While the total cost to the TA would eventually be identical regardless of how it was financed, the pay-as-you-go option would have the effect of deferring payment to a later date. Under a funded arrangement, money would have to be set aside immediately to finance the proposal. Utilizing the pay-as-you-go financing option, however, money would not have to be available until workers died.

The TA had also made offers on several major items of bargaining that were not accepted by the TWU. The Authority offered $1 million in 1966 and $1 million in 1967 to be used to improve working conditions. The union, however, took the position in the final set of negotiations that the entire $2 million in working condition improvements take effect on January 1, 1966. And, most important, of course, the unions had not accepted the TA's final offer with respect to wages, which amounted to increases of 2-1/2 percent to take effect every six months during the life of the two-year agreement, for a total increase of 10 percent.[13]

In addition to such offers made by the TA, the Lindsay Administration also made several "final offers" to the unions. One, to provide a $500 per year supplementary pension benefit to all employees who retired during the life of the agreement, on a nonfunded basis, had been accepted by the unions. In the area of wages, the city administration had proposed a 15 percent increase over the life of the agreement, considerably more than had been offered by the TA. Lindsay's staff, however, sought to delay the implementation of this increase for as long as possible; finally offering 2 percent retroactive to January 1, 1966, 2 percent after six months, another 2 percent after one year, with the remaining 9 percent to be paid for only the final six months of the contract's life. Because the mediators considered the city administration to be a party to the dispute, as it unquestionably was, this offer on wages was considered to be management's final offer on this issue.

The union's main problem with the city's final proposal on wages was not the overall amount, but rather when the increases would take effect. The unions' last position with respect to wages was to receive 4 percent increases during each of the six month intervals of the contract life, for a total increase of 16 percent over two years. Given their choice, all unions would prefer a completely front-loaded contract; that is, one in which all increases take effect on the first day of the contractual period. Thus, if management is willing to offer workers making $5,000, a 10 percent increase over the life of a two-year contract, the union wants the money to be paid out immediately. With each pay check increased by 10 percent, the workers would receive $500 more each year, for a total increase over two years of $1,000. Management, in turn, would prefer to back-load a contract as much as possible, to implement most of the increases as late as they could during the contract period. A 10 percent increase for workers making $5,000 a year involves a considerably smaller outlay of funds, if a contract is significantly back-loaded. Take the extreme example in which none of the 10 percent increase takes effect during the first 18 months of a two-year agreement, with the total increment being withheld until the final six months. In such an arrangement, the total cost to management would be 10 percent of the person's salary for six months ($2,500), or $250. Thus, based on when the identical 10 percent increase is implemented, the total cost will vary considerably.

In addition to the very sound economic reasons for public employers to attempt to back-load contracts, equally compelling political reasons exist. By delaying the payment of a wage increase, politicians effectively disassociate their bargaining performance from its economic consequences. It would be very difficult for taxpayers to realize that a tax increase was necessitated by a wage increase given to employees, if the increase was delayed for twelve or eighteen months. Back-loading a contract is most politically palatable, of course, if it can delay the implementation of an increase until after the current administration has left office.

In addition to the disagreement in their final positions on the wage issue, the parties were also unable to agree on when the $2 million they had agreed to for improvements in working conditions should take effect. The unions contended that the entire $2 million should take effect on January 1, 1966, while the TA offered $1 million immediately and an additional $1 million to take effect only during the second year.[14]

In sum, two issues remained for the mediators to decide: money and working conditions. On money, the city had offered 15 percent over two years; the unions finally demanded an increase of 16 percent. The mediators were able to finesse this discrepancy rather easily in their report. Although they differed over the percentage increase, in their final bargaining session the parties focused on workers currently earning $3.4625 an hour and agreed that they should receive an increase to $4.00 an hour and that all other employees should receive the same percentage increase. The mediators determined that the 16 percent increase cited by the union would produce a wage of $4.05 for the workers in question, rather than the agreed-upon figure of $4. Thus, the mediators concluded, the total size of the wage increase should amount to 15 percent. The sole wage issue to be decided, then, was how to apportion this increase. The mediators explained their reasoning:

> With regard to the steps by which the rate of increase of 15 percent should be achieved, we believe that only the minimum addition equitably necessary should be permitted over the offer of 2 percent, 2 percent, 2 percent, and 9 percent, mainly to correct the obvious disparity in the proposal for increases totally 6 percent of the wage rates during the first 18 months of a two-year contract and 9 percent for the last six months of the contract term. We do not believe that it is fair to require employees to defer for such a length of time adjustments in wage rates requiring correction. But the total cost of the package must likewise be considered because of the heavy financial obligation which the TA faces. . . .
>
> Thus, it would seem to us that it would be more appropriate to achieve an increase in the amount of 8 percent over the first 18 months . . . with the remaining 7 percent to become effective for the last six months. . . .[15]

With regard to the remaining issue of working conditions, the panel said that $1 million of the increase should be deferred until the second year of the agreement "so as to minimize the over-all cost of the package."[16]

In addition to the formal report submitted to Mayor Lindsay, the panel's chairman, Nathan Feinsinger, also provided the mayor with a separate analysis of his own, which indicated that the settlement fell within the presidential guidelines, which limited increases to an annual rate of 3.2 percent. Feinsinger said that the national guidelines provided the necessary flexibility to take into account particular inequities or injustices. Among the inequities cited by Feinsinger was the fact that auto mechanics in the police, fire, and sanitation departments received $1.09-3/4 above the rate for the TA's bus and subway maintainers. The panel chairman discussed how the TWU's long-standing practice of achieving across-the-board pay increases had resulted in the narrowing of differentials between skilled and unskilled jobs within the TA, thereby causing the skilled to be underpaid. He pointed out that the percentage increase granted to all employees would help correct this inequity. Finally, Feinsinger indicated that a *New York Times* editorial had several days earlier pointed out that previous negotiations had failed to make "an honest assessment by both sides of what economic justice required" and that Mayor Lindsay had consistently talked about eliminating "injustices."[17]

The Feinsinger memo was also intended to provide Mayor Lindsay with some support to counteract the inevitable criticism that the settlement had exceded the presidential guidelines. In fact, the settlement did not address the inequities or injustices that existed in the TA's pay structure, it simply prevented them from getting worse. The TWU had long favored across-the-board pay increases in which the same cents per hour increases were given to all workers regardless of their existing rates. In such settlements, for example, a porter making $1.50 per hour and a motorman making $3 per hour would each have received an increase of 15¢ per hour. On a percentage basis, such an approach would greatly benefit the lower-paid worker, amounting to a 10 percent increase for the porter, but only a 5 percent increase for the motorman. As a result of following this approach over a number of years, skilled TA employees wound up receiving considerably less pay than their counterparts in other city departments. An attempt to reduce the wage injustice to skilled TA employees would have required that they receive a higher percentage increase than that for the unskilled workers. Such an approach would not have been popular with the majority of rank-and-file members, however, because few occupied these very skilled jobs. Although not very accurate, the Feinsinger memo served two purposes: it argued that the settlement was permissable under the guidelines and it helped convince the long critical skilled workers that their interests were being championed by union leaders. As an experienced mediator, the panel's chairman was well aware that a settlement not only had to be agreed to by the negotiators, it also had to be accepted by rank-and-file union members.

Once the TWU and the TA accepted the mediator's report, Mayor Lindsay asked both sides to come to City Hall where he wanted to announce the settlement. The mediators, looking extremely tired, arrived first. Panel Chairman Feinsinger was limping badly and had to be helped from his car into City Hall. "The union negotiators looked equally bedraggled, unshaven and bleary eyed."[18] By the time the news conference to announce the strike settlement began in the Blue Room, opposite the mayor's office, it was almost 8:00 a.m. Thursday. Despite the fact that he had just agreed to the largest increase in the history of negotiations with the TWU, Mayor Lindsay spoke as if the union had by and large settled on his terms. First, Lindsay indicated that the dispute had been settled on the basis of a rational analysis by respected experts in the field. "The contract terms were proposed, at my request," Lindsay said, "to the parties...by a distinguished...panel yesterday as the basis for a fair, equitable and responsible settlement." The "distinguished panel of mediators," he continued, "made a judgement based upon their best considerations of what was in the public interest, what was best for the workers, best for the City of New York, best for the employer, the Transit Authority, and best for the country." Then, following a disclaimer that agreeing on the cost of a settlement is difficult, the mayor estimated the new agreement would cost $43.4 million over the two-year life of the contract for TA employees or $52 million if MABSTOA employees were also taken into account. "This settlement," Lindsay continued, "fulfills my pledge to stand fast until the city achieved an honorable settlement to the strike...." Then, at least implicitly, the mayor indicated that the days of the power brokers dominating municipal labor relations had come to an end. "I believe the successful resolution of the subway strike," he said, "may signal the beginning of a fresh and rewarding era in labor-management relations in New York City; a time in which rectitude, candor and objectivity implement the essential soundness of collective bargaining procedures." Finally, the mayor recognized the tremendous costs the strike had inflicted on the city, which he estimated at more than $500 million. These losses included more than $200 million in paychecks that were never issued; "retail sales that plummeted 50 to 75 percent"; countless hours of productive time wasted in the struggle to get in and out of the city; and $6 million losses for every working day to the city government in sales and other taxes.[19]

Earlier, on Wednesday afternoon, with movement toward a strike settlement apparent, Governor Nelson Rockefeller flew to New York City and reasserted his support for Mayor Lindsay's attempt to gain a "fair and equitable" settlement.[20] Although Governor Rockefeller had consistently maintained that he would not discuss the availability of state subsidy funds with Lindsay until after a settlement was reached, this was certainly not the case. In Deputy-Mayor Timothy Costello's words, "by the time there was a definite money settlement in sight, Governor Rockefeller had promised the money needed to back the settlement."[21] The availability of state money apparently was kept secret out of fear that its revelation would have caused the union to stiffen its demands.[22] That Mayor Lindsay must have known of the availability of state funds before the settlement was reached was also supported by the fact that the existence of such aid was publicly revealed by Governor Rockefeller fewer than twelve hours after the TA had indicated its acceptance of the pact.

With the strike settled, Superintendent of Schools Bernard Donovan announced that after-school study centers would begin operation to prepare high school students for the State Regents examinations which were fewer than two weeks away. Dr. Donovan said he was "particularly concerned" about the educational welfare of those students who had been unable to attend their regular high schools because of the strike. The tutoring sessions were scheduled to run for two hours, five days each week and were to be staffed by regular teachers. Attendence at the sessions for the 51,000 students scheduled to take the exams was voluntary.

Just as the economic impact of the transit strike was felt nationwide, the political reverberations were also felt well beyond the city and state. In his State of the Union message on the Wednesday prior to the end of the transit strike, President Lyndon Johnson said he would propose federal legislation that "will enable us effectively to deal with strikes which threaten irreparable harm to the national interest." Although the president did not refer directly to the transit strike in his address, his aides said the statement was motivated by the work stoppage in New York. The contemplated legislation probably would have involved an amendment to the Taft-Hartley Act to make it specifically applicable to strikes by public employees. The president said he was interested in being able to deal with damaging strikes "without improperly invading state and local authority." Johnson's remarks also had the effect of putting considerable pressure on the TWU to settle their dispute. Sources close to the president made it quite clear that a prompt settlement of the New York City transit strike would reduce the need for such legislation and could remove the need completely.[23]

With a strike settlement near, it was Shirley Quill who made news on Wednesday, rather than her husband. Angered by statements made the previous day by George Meany who said Quill had welcomed being sent to jail, Mrs. Quill called Meany a labor leader who knew more about the hazards of Burning Tree golf course in suburban Washington than about the discomforts of the picket line. Mrs. Quill's comments were made in front of the city's Civil Jail, where she had been prevented from visiting the still-imprisoned union leaders because she was not a relative. Commenting on Meany's remarks, Mrs. Quill observed coldly, "I don't want to be disrespectful of my elders, but I am not really surprised. Mr. Meany has boasted he's never called a strike or been on a picket line," she said. "It would be better for the labor movement if Mr. Meany practiced more with a picket sign than with a golf stick at Burning Tree."[24] As she briefly joined the hundred pickets marching in front of the jail in the freezing weather, they began shouting, "Let Mike Out!" "Let'em all out!" Mrs. Quill corrected, and the pickets began her amended version. Mrs. Quill walked the picket line arm in arm with Douglas MacMahon and James Horst, wearing a pink "I Like Mike" button pinned to her coat. Like Mrs. Quill, the two TWU negotiators had been prevented from visiting the prisoners by two police officers who had been told by the sheriff's office to bar everyone except relatives.

Later, Mrs. Quill told reporters that she had been spending much of her time attempting to handle the flood of mail that was arriving at her husband's hospital room. It was running "85-to-1" in favor of the strikers she said. In addition, she added, "over 700 cards" had been received telling

Quill that special prayers had been offered for his recovery.[25]

Restoring Service

By 12:45 p.m. on Thursday, January 13, fewer than seven hours after the official end of the transit strike, the city's subway system had returned to full operation. The speed with which the system reestablished normal service surprised and pleased transit experts, who believed it would take almost twice as long. The restoration of service followed a detailed plan worked out by the TA during the strike. Even before the end of the walkout was officially announced, supervisory personnel gathered at virtually all of the thirty terminals of the various subway lines. They boarded subway trains at these terminals, picking up subway employees along the way as they stopped at local stations. The first order of business was to transport the motormen and conductors to the terminals from which they normally began work. At their regular terminals, they were told the train on which they would be working and where it was being stored. They then boarded another "employees only" train, which took the local tracks until it reached the point where the train they were going to operate was being stored on the express tracks. Because local and express trains run along adjacent tracks, all the TA employees had to do was walk across one set of tracks and board their trains. It did not take long for the public to realize that the subways were operating, even if they were not yet accepting paying customers. At 5:30 a.m., while a group of media representatives were awaiting the official announcement of the strike's end in the basement of the Americana Hotel, they suddenly felt the floor vibrate. They cheered and the photographers scampered to the street and down into the nearest subway station to record the event.[26] By 9:32 a.m., the first train carrying regular paying customers began service.

The first real test for the reestablished service on the subway system came during the evening rush between 5:00 p.m. and 7:00 p.m., and it went very smoothly. Not only were the trains maintaining normal service, the passengers were uncharacteristically civil to each other. But, as one reporter observed, "the experts knew the situation was not quite normal." "Wait till tomorrow this time," said a subway guard at Times Square, "They'll be fighting again. Today, they're good-natured."[27]

Getting the buses operating was a much simpler procedure than restoring subway service. Before the walkout began, employees had filled the buses with fuel and left them parked in the huge garages that normally accommodated them. Drivers had remained close to the garages throughout the strike, either congregating at the union halls nearby or picketing the garages themselves. Thus, when it was obvious that a settlement would be reached early Thursday morning, more than a dozen drivers had already gathered inside the East New York garage in Brooklyn before the strike was officially settled. At 6:42 a.m., with the strike settlement just announced, the first bus rolled out of the 13.5-acre bus terminal to complete its run from New Lots to Pennsylvania Avenue in Brooklyn. The driver of this first bus, ironically named Joseph Lindsay, was greeted warmly by his initial passengers. "Honey," said a Brooklyn woman, "you're the most important man in this city." A second woman told Lindsay, who had operated TA buses for seven years, "Today you look better to me than my husband." Other passengers offered a friendly, "Welcome back," "Glad to see you back," or "Happy New Year." Several, perhaps more finely attuned to the reality of the situation, asked if the fare was still the same.[28]

With the strike settled, considerable attention focused on the various court proceedings. First, the TA dropped its claim for approximately $4 million in damages it was seeking from the TWU and the Amalgamated Transit Union. Sidney Brandes, the general counsel for the Authority informed State Supreme Court Justice Abraham Geller that, because the strike had been settled, the TA had no intention of pursuing its claim for damages. Justice Geller immediately agreed to discontinue the hearings, indicating that the court had no choice but to accede to the TA's request. "The court cannot concern itself," Geller said, "with the nature of the arrangements made in calling off the strike, but only with the fact that it had been called off." Justice Geller was obviously pleased that a settlement had been reached. "If this had gone further," he observed, "God only knows what would have happened to the extremely vital concept of collective bargaining."[29]

At the TA's request, Justice Geller also ordered the release of the nine union leaders who had been jailed on January 4. The Authority took such action, it said, because as part of the strike settlement it had agreed to end "recriminations and reprisals." The union leaders had been sent to jail for contempt of court when they called a strike in violation of a court order. Technically, by calling an end to the strike, the union leaders had purged themselves of contempt and were free to leave jail. The eight union leaders walked out of Civil Jail at 11:20 a.m. and were met by a large group of cheering supporters. The released prisoners were led through the barred and screened doors by Daniel Gilmartin, president of TWU Local 100, who was immediately hugged by his two teenage daughters who had been shivering in the cold outside. Douglas MacMahon, the chief TWU negotiator in the absence of the jailed leaders, then burst through the crowd of news reporters and hugged the prisoners.[30]

At 9:00 p.m., Michael Quill, the international president of the TWU, was quietly released from the prison ward at Bellevue Hospital. The delay in Quill's release from the hospital was the result of medical, rather than legal, reasons. Legally, he was free to leave when Justice Geller ruled the strike leaders had purged themselves of contempt by calling off the strike. It was not until Thursday evening, however, that his physician, Dr. Irene Ferrer, would permit his discharge. At the time that Quill's associates were being released from jail, sheriff's deputies were removed from the area of Bellevue Hospital where he was being held as a medical patient prisoner. However, in view of the threats to his safety that had been received, armed police guards and hospital security men equipped with nightsticks remained outside Quill's room until his discharge.[31]

Quill's release from the hospital took place quietly as a result of a diversionary tactic that had been worked out with his wife, Shirley. After visiting with her husband for about four hours, Mrs. Quill conducted a news conference as she left Bellevue. She said that her husband had expressed his gratitude to Mayor Lindsay and to the people of the city for the "union's smashing victory." Asked if her husband intended to complete his four-year term as president of the TWU, Mrs. Quill said he would, "God willing." Finally, she dismissed as "plain garbage" reports that Douglas MacMahon had been trying to "take over" during Quill's incarceration and subsequent illness.[32] While Mrs. Quill was speaking with the group of reporters, the TWU president was taken out a back door to Mt. Sinai Hospital. There he could be under the care of Dr. Hyman Zuckerman, who had treated him for his heart ailment three years earlier.[33]

The legal action that was considered most significant, however, involved the suit brought by George Weinstein, as a "taxpayer and voter" to prohibit the Transit Authority from granting any pay increases for three years. Privately, the lawyers for the unions and the TA conceded the suit was a "blockbuster."[34] The Weinstein suit was based on Article 5 of the state's Condon-Wadlin Act, which stated that the compensation of striking public employees, "shall not be increased until after the expiration of three years from such appointment or reappointment, employment or reemployment" after the strike ends. The arguments in the case had already been heard by State Supreme Court Justice Irving H. Saypol on Tuesday, and the parties were awaiting his ruling.

Assessing the Settlement

At a news conference on Thursday, President Johnson denounced the settlement as inflationary. Obviously anticipating a question on the subject (because he appeared to be reading from notes as he answered), Johnson said, "Candor requires me to say that I am quite disturbed that essential services could be paralyzed for so long, and I am equally concerned by the cost of the settlement." The president added that Gardner Ackley, chairman of his Council of Economic Advisors had informed him that the agreement violated the administration's guidelines for noninflationary wage increases. "I do not believe that any settlement that violates the guideposts to this extent is in the national interest," Johnson said. Because the wage guideposts were voluntary, President Johnson acknowledged that there was nothing he could do to force compliance, but he was nevertheless displeased. "Most of the labor organizations and most of the business organizations of this country have been willing to consider the guideposts and to take them into account in connection with their agreements," the president said, "and I am always sorry when there are exceptions that may contribute to inflation." Johnson then attempted to characterize the settlement as being contrary to the public interest, "It is not a personal matter with me; this is your inflation, our inflation, and anything that contributes to it is a matter of concern." In a separate statement, Ackley also characterized the settlement as inflationary and destructive of the public interest. The agreement, he said, was "a serious violation of the wage-price policy of the federal government designed to protect the whole nation from destructive inflation. The public interest," Ackley added, "has been adversely affected both by the strike and by the terms of its settlement."[35] The attempt by the Johnson Administration to paint the settlement as being against the public interest served a dual purpose. Certainly, the statements were designed to gain compliance with the anti-inflation program. But perhaps even more important, the politically astute Johnson was attempting to counter some of the accolades being received by Lindsay for his handling of the strike because he was aware that Lindsay was increasingly being mentioned as a possible Republican candidate for president in 1968.

Following the criticism by President Johnson, the wisdom of having the mediation panel recommend a settlement made even more sense from the perspective of Mayor Lindsay. In replying to President Johnson's criticism, the mayor said, "The chairman of the mediation panel, Dr. Nathan P. Feinsinger, prepared a memorandum at the time the panel recommended the settlement. The memorandum stated that that settlement was within the guidelines." Then, in spite of the fact that it was the city's wage offer and its proposal to establish a $500 supplemental pension that caused the package to be inflationary, Lindsay attempted to shift any blame to the TA, "Under all circumstances, the mediation panel having arrived at a firm recommendation and the chairman having stated that it was within the guideposts, the Transit Authority had no choice but to accept."[36]

The Feinsinger memo which indicated that the settlement was within the "spirit and intent" of the guidelines was, by the mediators own characterization, a "very informal, rough, and incomplete memo that . . . [was] prepared for the internal use of the panel—and possibly as background for the Mayor. . . ." Feinsinger was asked if he was mad that Lindsay had made the confidential memo public. "Not at all," Feinsinger replied, "He'll just grin over the phone and say, 'I'm sorry.' He's a politician—get it?" The Wisconsin mediator then added in obviously admiring tones, "But how do you like that Mayor broadcasting my confidential memo? I've now learned that Mayor Lindsay can be tough, but that's politics. He's a politician, after all, and this I understand and forgive."[37]

Several individuals quickly defended the settlement, arguing that it certainly fell within the spirit, if not the letter, of the wage-price guideposts. Dr. Donald F. Shaughnessy, one of Mayor Lindsay's assistants for labor matters said the settlement represented an increase in labor costs of 5.5 percent if pension increases granted to other city employees previously were not counted. While the agreement exceeded the guidelines by 2 percent, without counting the full pension increases, Shaughnessy, nevertheless maintained that, "The settlement is not so dramatically out of line" when compared to increases throughout the country and with recent contract settlements negotiated in New York City. In addition, the mayoral assistant added, Lindsay and the TA did "everything possible" to reach a settlement in line with the president's guidelines. Governor Rockefeller also came to the mayor's aid on this issue, saying, "Mr. Lindsay did everything in his power to see that the strike was settled within the guidelines."[38]

The three members of the Transit Authority also attempted to deflect the president's criticism of the settlement as inflationary. The two Democratic members of the TA, Joseph O'Grady and Daniel Scannell argued that the agreement fell within the scope of the guidelines. Chairman O'Grady observed that the settlement was made on the recommendation of the mediation panel and noted that Feinsinger had submitted a memo to the mayor in which he said the guidelines were observed. Scannell noted that the guidelines permitted the correction of injustices that had developed historically in the wage structure of TA employees. "Where inequities exist in a situation of this sort," Scannell said, "those features of the settlement are not considered in the guidelines." The sole Republican on the Authority, John J. Gilhooley, was the only member to acknowledge that the guidelines had been broken. The mediators proposed settlement, he said, "troubled me enormously." Gilhooley explained why he nevertheless supported the package: "Obviously, despite Mr. Feinsinger's assurance, I was aware that the guidelines would be fractured. But my deepest concern was with the misery that the strike was causing to 8 million New Yorkers. I finally struck the balance in favor of alleviating the people's agony. Frankly, with all due respect to the President of the United States, I would do as much again."[39]

On Thursday afternoon, Governor Rockefeller announced a $100-million plan to preserve the 15¢ fare until a possible merger of the TA and the Triborough Bridge and Tunnel Authority could be worked out. Mayor Lindsay had proposed the integration of these two agencies so that the Triborough profits could be used to offset Transit Authority deficits. Rockefeller said he anticipated no real opposition to his plan in the state legislature. "When people are in trouble—and believe me, the people of New York have been in trouble—all New Yorkers want to help the people out," he said. Most of the newspapers in the city carried headlines such as the one in the Herald Tribune, "Rockefeller: $100 Million to Save 15-Cent Fare," which implied that the governor was using state money to come to the aid of the city.[40] In fact, however, the status of the $100 million was the subject of considerable dispute. Everyone, including the governor, conceded that $51 million represented the acceleration of payments the city was due to receive from the state after April, the beginning of the state's new fiscal year.[41]

Rockefeller contended that the remaining $49 million was "new money." The city, however, had long claimed that this amount and more was owed to it as the result of deferred state aid to education. During the 1930s, when the state was short of cash because of the Great Depression, it had withheld the payment of one-quarter of the state's annual aid to the city's school system. The amount was never paid but neither was it forgiven by the city. The city had long claimed the money, contending that in order to account for inflation, an amount equal to one-quarter of the state's current payments in school aid was due the city. In 1962, Mayor Wagner put this quarterly figure at $49 million, and this was apparently the source of the amount cited by the governor when he said its payment would go toward "elimination of this item." A city official, however, claimed it would take $70 million at the current rate of state aid to education to satisfy the city's full claim.[42]

Rockefeller said that the mayor's proposal to integrate the city's transit facilities had "a great deal of merit" but indicated it was "a little too early" to tell if the legislature would support such a measure. The governor praised Lindsay for handling the strike "with great courage, with great fortitude. I think he was fighting a very difficult battle," he continued. "He hadn't had a chance even to get settled in his office before this thing hit him, I think it's extraordinary that he's been able to handle this as effectively as he has."[43]

Finally, Rockefeller insisted that the state money was not an issue until after the strike was settled, on the grounds that if the unions knew the money was available it would harden their bargaining position.[44]

The city suffered through one last commuter tie-up on Thursday morning, but by the evening rush hour period, both vehicular traffic and the commuter railroads had returned to normal. The day did not begin brightly for Traffic Commissioner Henry Barnes. Although the strike had been settled, subway service had not yet been restored, and the weather bureau had predicted snow, sleet, and rain. The strike was technically over, Barnes conceded, but the forecast made it appear that "we are jumping out of the frying pan into the fire." With traffic still 30 percent above normal and with the added weather complications, the city's streets were a mess. By 7:30 a.m., traffic delays were reported throughout Queens. In Brooklyn, cars were stalled on the Brooklyn, Manhattan, and Williamsburg bridges, and there were traffic jams on the Prospect and Gowanus Expressway approaches to the Brooklyn-Battery Tunnel.[45] In Manhattan and the Bronx, the worst delays also centered around the bridges and tunnels. Extensive delays occurred on the Cross Bronx Expressway, which served as an approach to the George Washington Bridge, and in lower Manhattan near the exits to the Brooklyn Bridge and the Brooklyn Battery Tunnel.

By evening, however, Commissioner Barnes was able to report that "this is even better than normal." Afternoon traffic, as it had throughout the strike, began building about 3:30 p.m., but by 5:15 p.m. seemed to be virtually ended. On a normal day, the traffic rush lasts until 6:15 p.m., and during the strike the congestion did not begin to subside until about 6:30 p.m. or 7:00 p.m. Barnes theorized that many people had gotten relatives or friends to drive them into the city in the morning and then immediately take their cars home, anticipating that transit service would be restored by the evening rush.[46]

The commuter railroad terminals also seemed virtually deserted compared with the chaos that had prevailed during the previous twelve days. The Long Island Railroad, which had been straining to handle an evening crowd of 100,000 out of Pennsylvania Station, returned to its normal number of 50,000 passengers. "It's just like a normal night," a railroad spokesman said. "No waits, no delays, no crowds, no anything. It seems sort of lonesome around here now." The explanation for the passenger load being halved was simple, "The subway passengers," the train spokesman said, "are back in the subways." The New York Central Railroad which had been running a special Westchester shuttle service that handled 40,000 additional daily passengers announced that there were only about 5,500 extra commuters by 6:00 p.m. "There's no waiting, and everyone has a seat," a spokesman said.[47]

With the strike settled and transit service now restored, businesses and individuals began to try to return to normal. The garment industry, New York's largest, planned to begin working nights and weekends in an attempt to fill a huge backlog of orders that had to be shipped within three weeks. Although shipments of spring merchandise are normally completed by the end of January, industry officials believed the delivery could be delayed until the first week in February without substantial cancellations of orders. Overtime schedules were still in the process of being negotiated with representatives of the garment unions, but most manufacturers believed the early February deadline could be met. A spokesman for the International Ladies Garment Workers Union also sounded a largely optimistic note, "A small segment of the industry will suffer irretrievable losses. But I predict that the spring season on which manufacturers are working, will be a good one."[48]

The second largest industry in the city, the printing trades, lost in excess of $25 million as a result of the strike, according to Paul L. Noble, president of the Printing Industries of Metropolitan New York, Inc. Noble acknowledged that some of these sales could be deferred and ultimately would not be lost. However, even this recouped business could result in significant losses, because workers would have to be paid overtime to complete the delayed jobs.[49] The printing industry spokesman also predicted a long-term consequence of the strike: customers would begin to think that New York was not a reliable city in which to place orders.

Retail business also began efforts to make up some of their strike losses. All of the large department stores announced they would remain open until either 9:00 p.m. or 10:00 p.m. on Thursday evening. "Some of the business we lost is recoverable," said William Tobey, vice president for sales at Abraham and Strauss, "but it will take a little time to assess the situation to determine what can be done."[50] Tobey indicated that his department store would run some promotions that had been cancelled because of the strike.

Collectively, there were a lot of pieces to pick up. Ralph C. Gross, executive vice president of the Commerce and Industry Association, called the strike "a calamity of huge proportions. It is already abundantly clear," said Gross, "that the city's economy was struck harder than at any time since the Great Depression." Specific dollar estimates of the strike's losses ranged from "upwards of $500 million" by Mayor Lindsay to a "conservative estimate" of $800 million by the Commerce and Industry Association. In nonquantitative terms, Michael B. Grosso, vice president of the Fifth Avenue Association declared, "The shellacking we have taken is a nightmare. We can never recover from it."[51]

Lindsay's Image

With the strike settlement only a few hours old, Mayor Lindsay had "apparently come out ... as a popular hero." From virtually all quarters, Lindsay's handling of the strike was being given rave reviews. Governor Rockefeller said that Lindsay "handled it with a great deal of courage" and added that "the people in the city appear to have supported him." Although most Democrats were not willing to speak for public attribution, they also suggested that Lindsay "had come up roses all over." One prominent Democrat, Senate Majority Leader Joseph Zaretzki, was willing to comment, "I think Lindsay came out of it very well," he said. "The public is on his side."[52] Even the city's most prominent labor leader, Harry Van Arsdale, Jr., president of the New York City Central Labor Council, believed the mayor's performance had strongly aided his political aspirations. "Lindsay is much bigger in the city and nationally as a result of his performance in this thing," he said. Asked if he believed Lindsay had gained a pro-labor image during the strike, the labor leader said, "He's got a pro-people image. I think everybody feels he made a great effort."[53] This assessment of Lindsay's performance also appeared to be shared by the general public. A sampling of twenty people in Times Square, conducted by the *Herald Tribune*, revealed that all but one were on Mayor Lindsay's side and reserved their criticisms for former Mayor Wagner and TWU President Quill.[54]

Several weeks later, a professional polling company reached a similar conclusion, finding that 75 percent of those sampled believed Lindsay had achieved a good settlement. In contrast, 90 percent of those interviewed believed that Rockefeller had done a poor job.[55]

Editorials in the New York City newspapers exhibited a similar uniformity of opinion in assessing blame and assigning praise in the transit strike. Despite the heterogenous nature of their readers and the varying editorial postures they normally assumed, their editorial stance on this issue was unanimous: they cursed Michael Quill and used superlatives to describe John Lindsay.

From the beginning of the strike, the *New York Times* editorials so closely echoed the public statements of Mayor Lindsay that there appeared to be some credence to the TWU charge that Lindsay was following the dictates of the *Times* editorials. The *Times* initially characterized Quill as tyrannical and urged Lindsay to resist giving in to the union's excessive demands. In a January 3 editorial, the *Times* equated Lindsay's actions in dealing with the strike as being synonymous with the public good, citing the mayor's inaugural address in which he said "that the public interest must prevail over special interests, the good of the community over the desires of any group."[56]

The January 7 editorial of the *Times* continued to reflect Lindsay's views, in this instance making the identical distinction between collective bargaining and deals, "The chief reason for the strike was Mr. Quill's determination to keep alive a system of transit labor relations built on backdoor deals, rather than an honest assessment of both sides of what economic justice required."[57]

Other newspapers also lauded Lindsay's concern for the public interest. The *Post*, usually considered the most pro-union of the city's major daily newspapers, wrote in its January 11 editorial, "Mayor Lindsay sounded the right note in his report to the city on the transit stalemate last night. He was firm and solemn in his warning against prolongations of a strike that is both unnecessary and illegal. He made plain that he would not cynically foresake the public interest."[58]

And on January 13, even before the final terms of the agreement were known, the *Post* heaped praise on Lindsay, ". . . it is not too early to salute Mayor Lindsay for the gallantry and steadfastness he displayed in his first great trial, thrust upon him at the moment when he took office."[59]

The *Journal American* also gave its editorial support to Mayor Lindsay, stating in its January 2 edition:

> Through the decision of this one imperious labor leader, the great City of New York has been plunged into crisis by the walkout of its 33,000 transit employees. . . . Michael J. Quill must not be permitted to force the Transit Authority and the City of New York to purchase transit peace on his own terms. The settlement terms of the new labor contract he seeks MUST be fair, reasonable and responsible to the taxpayers of this city who will pay the bill.[60]

In their evaluation of the mayor's performance in handling the transit strike, after a settlement was reached, the *Journal American* concluded, "We have learned that in John V. Lindsay we have a Mayor who can resist enormous pressures with courage, dignity, grace and common sense. He has stood his first major test at City Hall as well."[61]

The *Herald Tribune*, too, had little difficulty in assessing blame for the transit strike. In their January 2 editorial the editors wrote:

> One man, Mike Quill, has inflicted a monstrous strike on New York that defies the rights of 8 million people. One man, Mike Quill, has the arrogance to sneer at law, refuse fair settlement, and throw a great city into crisis. . . . [This] is a question of law and order, a strike against government

in contempt for public health and safety. And the only way to settle the matter is to stand on principle and refuse the customary appeasement.[62]

The *Daily News*, a "workingman's" newspaper that had long taken an antilabor stance editorially, remained consistent with its editorial tradition during the strike, "We've had enough nonsense from Quill. Let's all flatly refuse to stand for any more of it."[63] Later, the *Daily News* developed their position in a little more detail: ". . . Quill's illness does not make them martyrs either; nor his, God forbid, death. These men are persons who have declared war on the vast majority of the people of New York City, and are fighting that war by keeping the people's principal means of city transportation paralyzed. Their objective: to bleed the Transit Authority for outrageous amounts of money, which the TA does not have, in fantastic wage boosts. Such birds are not martyrs."[64]

The *World Telegram and Sun* made it unanimous; all of the major daily newspapers in New York City blamed the strike on Quill and his TWU and viewed Lindsay and his city administration as being virtually blameless. In its January 2 editorial, the *World Telegram and Sun* stated, ". . . the city's solidly allied with Mayor Lindsay in the counter-measures he has ordered. But more must be done and swiftly. . . . Quill has disgraced even himself— and shamed all decent labor leaders—with a lawless strike that disrupts the economy of the nation's greatest city, closes its schools and penalizes the interests of the "working people" whom Quill fraudulently champions."[65]

In its editorial of January 10, in which the paper attempted to answer the question, "Who's Running This City?", the *World Telegram and Sun* indicated that it, too, found it easy to separate the good guys from the bad guys in the transit dispute:

> The answer to the foregoing question is as obvious as it is galling. The answer is a pack of so-called union leaders who care nothing about law, government, the city's economy, the transportation needs of the public or, in truth, the welfare of the "working class" to whom they pledge so much spurious allegiance. . . . The arrogance of the lawless strike leaders is all the more incredible in the face of the strenuous efforts of Mayor Lindsay and the mediating panel to find a fair, honorable solution.[66]

Even the *Amsterdam News*, which mainly served the black community, was pleased that Mayor Lindsay had taken a strong stand, seemingly feeling that this was worth the price blacks were paying for this act of resolution. Its January 8 editorial stated:

...John Lindsay is not the lackey type of politician who "heels" everytime someone roars at him. And when Lindsay wouldn't "heel," Mike Quill called the strike. We think the courts acted quite properly in ordering Quill to jail and we believe that, despite their discomfort, the New York public will stand with Mayor Lindsay and the courts against Mr. Quill. In a city of laws we must draw the line somewhere. And we can think of no better place to draw it than at the point where an individual begins to flout the law as Mike Quill has.[67]

The editorial policy of the New York City newspapers was summarized exceedingly well in an article in *Editor and Publisher*, a magazine written for people in the publishing industry: "Unanimously, contemptuously, relentlessly, New York City's newspapers have dealt with the "wild little Irish leader" of the Transport Workers Union. In editorial after editorial they have scorned, condemned, and criticized the stand taken by Michael J. Quill...."[68]

The editorial comments on radio and television also exhibited almost unanimous support for the actions of Mayor Lindsay during the strike and placed the blame for the work stoppage solely on Michael Quill and the TWU. An editorial broadcast by radio station WINS amounted to a summary of Mayor Lindsay's philosophy of government:

> New York City is suffering its first mass transit strike. To his great credit, Mayor Lindsay has met the strike head-on and done his best to keep the city running, although not without hardship to many.... We congratulate him on his leadership.... We believe that one additional fact has become clear—that the head of the Transport Workers Union guessed wrong about the people of New York and their new leadership. His public profanity, threats and abuse are no substitute for bargaining, and his attempts to blame the Mayor, the Governor and even the Editorial Page Editor of the *New York Times* have fooled no one. If this one episode has proved anything, it's that this City is bigger than any of the pressure groups—which would try to strangle it. None of them is above the law or the judgement of the people. We commend Mayor Lindsay for helping us to appreciate this fact.[69]

A WABC editorial, which aired on both radio and television, also was critical of Michael Quill and supportive of Mayor Lindsay: "...Mr. Quill and his union are not above the law. No one is.... Mayor Lindsay has ... for the most part given a good account of himself. He is right to insist that negotiations continue until an equitable settlement fair to both sides is achieved."[70]

WCBS-TV, as well, had little difficulty in summoning invectives to use in describing the actions of TWU president Quill: "Michael Quill and the Transport Workers Union have committed the final outrage against the millions of people who live in New York or who work in New York. His action, and the action of his union, could not be more irresponsible or unwarranted."[71]

Public opinion can also be gauged by examining the "Letters to the Editor" in all of the major daily newspapers in New York City: the *Journal American*, the *Herald Tribune*, the *Daily News*, the *World Telegram and Sun*, the *New York Times*, and the *Post*. An analysis of all of the letters appearing on one arbitrarily selected day during the strike provides a fairly accurate portrayal of the views of average citizens. On January 6, thirty-five letters appeared in the six newspapers. They were divided into five categories: anti-Quill/pro-Lindsay, anti-Lindsay, pro-Quill and the TWU, anti-Wagner, and anti-Condon-Wadlin Act. Categorizing the letters presented few problems, because most writers minced few words in stating their position.

This categorization produced a virtual unanimity of views; revealing twenty-nine anti-Quill/pro-Lindsay letters, no anti-Lindsay letters, four pro-Quill and TWU letters, one anti-Wagner letter, and one anti-Condon-Wadlin Act letter. The majority view expressed in these "Letters to the Editor" made most of the editorials appear to be models of restraint by comparison. A letter in the *World Telegram and Sun* stated:

> How long are we going to tolerate the defiance of our courts by a blatherskite labor representative who degrades the entire labor movement in his actions and his vile insults against the duly elected executive of the people?... It is about time that the people of New York resisted being kicked around and that full support be given to our energetic and dedicated mayor who gives every promise of restoring the prestige and honor that our city deserves.
>
> There should be some legal means of depriving the pseudo labor leader of his American citizenship on criminal grounds and effecting his deportation to the great satisfaction of our loyal and suffering citizens.[72]

Another letter in the *World Telegram and Sun* suggested a somewhat different form of deportation: "They are always talking about sending a man to the moon. Why not put Mr. Quill in a nice cozy capsule and send him there? I'm sure he would have the place entirely disrupted in nothing flat!"[73]

In a letter to the *Journal American*, one man wrote: "Mike Quill has no regard for human decency, human sincerity, or for the courts of this country. His demonstration of defiance of the law, his complete arrogance and his theatrical display on T.V. by tearing up an order served on him by the State Supreme Court makes one ashamed of his country."[74]

A letter to the *Daily News* suggested that: "As a fitting punishment for Quill, and a warning to others of the same stripe, how's about adopting the old Apache Indian trick of pegging him out over an anthill and leaving the rest to the ants. They always started with the eyes, with a little sugar or honey to add vigor to their appetites."[75]

Another writer submitted a "some of my best friends" letter to the *Daily News*: "I am a union man inside and out, but I remember why unions were born—because of unscrupulous employers thinking only of large profits, by enslavement of workers who never got decent wages. But unions were not founded for pirates desiring to prey on the taxpayers and humanity. Long live unions of integrity, but Mike Quill should be put in the nut house."[76]

One of the anti-Quill letters that appeared in the *Times*, stated: "Draft-card burners are being arrested and are being required to pay fines of sizeable sums. Does Michael Quill, who tears up a court order before the eyes of a national television audience deserve less? This blatant disregard of the judicial system upon which our society has built its foundations should not go unpunished."[77]

Those letters that voiced support for Michael Quill and his striking Transport Workers Union all spoke in general terms championing egalitarian principles but failed to deal with the specifics of the transit situation. In a letter to the *Times*, for example, an assistant professor at the City College of New York wrote: "Congratulations to Michael Quill! In spite of the Square Deal, the New Deal and the Fair Deal, wealth remains unevenly distributed. The most powerful weapon of labor has always been, and must remain, the right to strike. The laboring people of New York, especially civil servants, should realize that Mr. Quill is fighting to make that Great Society a reality."[78]

A letter to the *Journal American* was also couched in general labor terms and did not treat the question of what was happening in the transit crisis: "Thank God we have some men who think of the working people as something more than a source of taxes. In the richest country in the world, the people who make it run should not need for anything."[79]

On Friday, January 14, the Transit Authority joined the Transport Workers Union in asking the New York State Supreme Court to temporarily prohibit the punishment of those workers who struck in violation of the Condon-Wadlin Act. The temporary stay was granted by Justice Abraham Geller after the TA took the unusual position of arguing that it wanted to be prevented from punishing its striking employees. The court's action, which had the prohibitive force of an injunction, was to last for one week, at which time a hearing would be held to determine the constitutionality of the state's Condon-Wadlin Act. After observing that he felt the law needed a "complete overhauling," Justice Geller scheduled the hearing for the following Friday. However, because of the state's system of rotating justices so that they consider various types of litigation, the hearing would be held before a different Supreme Court judge. The penalty provisions of the state's antistrike law provided for the dismissal of striking employees, and if rehired, they could not receive a pay increase for three years. In addition, rehired employees would be placed on "probation" for five years, during which they could face immediate dismissal. In asking that the temporary stay be granted, TWU attorney Asher W. Schwartz told the court, "I submit that any statute whose terms are so harsh, repressive and ill-conceived as to induce responsible public officials to conspire to ignore its clear requirements must be treated at arm's length in a judicial proceeding concerned with its threatened enforcement." In accepting the stay, Sydney Brandes, who represented the TA suggested that the court's action "would lend a needed period of stability during these trying times."[80]

As part of its recommendations, the transit mediation panel said that the TA should not seek to enforce the penalty provisions of the Condon-Wadlin Act. The Authority concurred in this belief but was fearful that a suit by virtually any taxpayer or voter would force it to carry out the law. Without the temporary stay, Brandes argued, the TA could not accede to any request to ignore the law if such a "citizen's" suit was filed. This possibility was hardly moot, because State Supreme Court Justice Irving H. Saypol was already considering whether to enjoin the TA from granting any pay increases to the strikers for three years. The case before Judge Saypol, which was heard on Tuesday, was brought by George Weinstein, a thirty-three-year-old lawyer, acting as a taxpayer.

The differences between the Republican-Liberal Lindsay Administration and the administration of Democratic President Johnson continued unabated. After Johnson criticized the settlement on Thursday as violating his anti-inflation guidelines, Lindsay responded on Friday morning that "perhaps the President was not as familiar with all the facts of this case as was his Secretary of Labor." The mayor said that at no time had Secretary of Labor, W. Williard Wirtz, passed judgement on the settlement terms as being within or outside the federal guidelines. Despite his outstanding reputation as a mediator, Wirtz's response was hardly conciliatory. "Your recollection and your arithmetic are wrong," said the telegram the Labor Secretary sent to Lindsay. "The costs of the settlement are variously reported as ranging from $52 million to $70 million," Wirtz added. "If the lowest of these figures is correct, this settlement exceeds the guidepost by a substantial amount. This settlement may have been necessary to release the city from unconscionable bondage," Wirtz concluded, "but it was unquestionably far outside the stabilization policies."[81]

At the same time that his performance in the transit strike was being criticized by the Democratic Johnson Administration in Washington, Mayor Lindsay attempted to blame its onset on the failure of his predecessors at City Hall to develop adequate means for resolving such disputes. Lindsay indicated that "procedures for municipal employees have got to be modernized and sanity put in them. What we must have," Lindsay added, "is the kind of thing that we had ... for the first time in New York City in connection with the transit settlement. And that," the mayor concluded, "is an independent highly qualified panel, whether you call them fact-finders or whatever you call them—in this case, they were known as mediators—being in a position to make firm and final recommendations."[82] While emphasizing that he was not proposing the use of compulsary arbitration, the mayor indicated that the use of panels of experts would bring the weight of public opinion behind a fair settlement.

In a different area, Mr. Lindsay reiterated his belief that the 15¢ fare could be retained. The way to achieve this end, the Mayor maintained was through the unification or integration of the city's transportation system. Lindsay said that state legislation creating a central agency to oversee all transportation in the city would be ready by early or mid-February. He said he did not believe there would be any trouble in getting such a measure passed.[83]

On Saturday, January 15, Governor Rockefeller announced the appointment of a five-member committee that was charged with proposing state legislation to avert a recurrence of situations like the transit strike. Such legislation was necessary, the governor said, because "as a consequence of the illegal transit strike, millions of residents of New York City and its suburbs have just gone through the most devastating experience and have suffered personal hardships and economic losses through no fault of their own." In addition, Rockefeller said, "business—large and small— throughout the area has sustained heavy losses...."[84] Rockefeller acknowledged that the task of proposing legislation "for protecting the public against the disruption of vital government services by illegal strikes, while at the same time protecting the rights of public employees" was a difficult one. Virtually everyone agreed that the state's Condon-Wadlin Act, which prohibited strikes by public employees under the threat of dismissal but provided no machinery for resolving disputes, was totally unworkable. The five nationally prominent experts in the labor relations field named to the panel included: George W. Taylor, professor of labor relations at the

University of Pennsylvania, who would serve as chairman; E. Wight Bakke, director of the labor and management center at Yale University; David L. Cole, chairman of the advisory committee of the labor management center of the American Arbitration Association; John T. Dunlop, professor of industrial relations at Harvard University; and Frederick H. Harbison, professor of industrial relations at Princeton University.

The charges and countercharges between the Lindsay Administration and the Johnson Administration grew increasingly acrimonious, but the differences continued to generate more heat than light. While Mayor Lindsay was highly critical of the Democratic administration's statements that the transit settlement was inflationary, he was content to voice his displeasure without providing any additional information regarding the size of the settlement.

In fact, setting a precise dollar figure on the size of the settlement, which was estimated as being somewhere between $52 million and $70 million, was impossible. The $52-million figure cited by the Lindsay Administration was probably fairly accurate in terms of the actual outlay of money during the two-year life of the agreement. However, if one is concerned with the ongoing increase in expenditures over time, then the $70 million figure over two years is more correct. Quite simply, many of the increases agreed to in this settlement would not have to be paid for until future years. For example, because the $500 supplemental pension plan offered by the city was not funded, its cost would not peak for about ten years. Thus, if only the cost of the settlement over the initial two-year period is measured, it would be relatively low for this item. Ten years later, however, this concession would involve a considerable expense. Similarly, the so-called death gamble was provided on a nonfunded basis. Although survivors of transit workers would receive higher benefits as a result, these increases would have to be paid only as workers died. Thus, each year the TA would have to pay increased benefits not only to the survivors of employees who had died that year but also to those who had died in previous years. The true cost would not be reflected until after the survivors began to die, causing a levelling out effect.

Finally, even the size of the wage increase could be counted in different ways. The actual dollar outlay of the settlement was greatly reduced by the fact that 7 percent of the total increase of 15 percent would not take effect until the final six months of the agreement. Thus, more than one-half of the increase granted would only have to be funded for a six-month period. However, when a new contract was negotiated two years later, all wage increases would be added to a base that was 15 percent higher than what it was two years earlier. Again, the eventual cost of the agreement would be considerably greater than the cost for the initial two-year period.

In essence, the Lindsay Administration had agreed to a generous, but not exhorbitant, outlay of money over two years, by mortgaging the future of the TA. At the time, however, the media not only failed to discuss the longer-term financial implications of the settlement, they would not even discuss the "real" size of the agreement. Instead, they uniformly reported that the size of the package was "according to different estimates, from $52 to $70 million." Curiously, this superficial presentation was dictated by the professional standards of news reporters. Reporters are trained that being objective means to get out of the way of the story and attribute every statement to a source. Because the correspondent is not overtly taking a stand, objectivity is presumed. Whenever differing perspectives exist, impartiality is demonstrated by having representatives of each side tell its story. Although such objective impartiality is more easily demonstrated, an accurate portrayal requires analysis, interpretation, and an investigation of whether assertions are accurate. This, the media did not provide.

Successful Image Politics

Although the $70-million cost of the settlement was closer to being accurate than the $52-million figure cited by the Lindsay Administration, even the lower estimate represented the largest package transit workers had ever received. How could Lindsay have "given away the store" and still be perceived as having acquitted himself with distinction in these negotiations? The explanation is centered in image politics.

Regardless of the outcome, John Lindsay's actions dealing with transit negotiations were totally consistent with the image he sought to portray. And because they found this image attractive, most observers concluded that Lindsay had performed well. As was typical of successful new-style politicians, it was a victory of image over substance. Asked how Mayor Lindsay could possibly have improved his image in view of the size of the transit settlement, Theodore Kheel replied bluntly, "A person's public image is in no way related to reality."[85]

In recent years, political scientists and psychologists have concluded that voters often make political judgements that have little or no factual basis. Most people have neither the time nor the inclination to devote several hours of study to each of the important public policy issues that arise each day. The "relatively low amount of information possessed by most persons means that most decide their political preferences on the basis of comparatively simple slogans and catchwords, since the more subtle analysis will pass them by."[86] With this in mind, Lindsay certainly provided the simple slogans and catchwords that made it possible for voters to form an opinion of his behavior during the transit crisis. Most people would have found it difficult to disagree with the philosophy of government that he publicly espoused, in which he attacked the power brokers and asserted his belief in honest government.

Another consequence of this lack of information on the part of voters is that it forces them to depend on external social referents in forming and changing their opinions. These external referents may be used as either positive or negative reference groups. If they are positive, an individual will value what they say; if negative, he or she will be disposed to act in the opposite direction of the action recommended by the group. For most people, newspaper, radio, and television editorials serve as a positive reference group, especially when the views expressed are virtually unanimous. This was certainly the case of the editorial comment dealing with the transit strike. On the other hand, after being exposed to Quill's perennial strike threats and vitriolic language for more than thirty years, most New Yorkers, even before the strike began, were highly critical of the TWU president. Consequently, Quill was a negative referent for the majority of New Yorkers, and his attacks on Lindsay merely enhanced the mayor's image.

Not only is knowledge of political actions severely limited, it is also highly selective. People do not always acquire information and then after mulling over its implications, decide which position to support. Instead, as strong experimental evidence supports, people frequently "first decide who or what they are for, and then seek information and arguments to support that position."[87] Because of his long history of militant behavior and his statements prior to the strike, public reaction was strongly against Quill even before the strike was called. Then, as a result of this initial public sentiment against the TWU and in favor of the Lindsay Administration, people became selectively attentive to those facts which supported their position.

Because most voters have an extremely limited amount of political knowledge, image politics can be quite successful. As the definitive study *The American Voter* stated: "A great deal can be explained in terms of what has and what has not penetrated the public consciousness. In the electorate as a whole the level of attention to politics is so low that what the public is exposed to must be highly visible—even stark—if it is to have an impact on opinion."[88]

This partially explains why Mayor Lindsay's image came out extremely well after the strike, and Governor Rockefeller emerged so poorly. An examination of how they each responded to the hardships being suffered by New Yorkers during the strike is illustrative. The governor lowered the requirements for receiving unemployment benefits to ease the burden of the strike. He obtained federal loans for small businesses. He was able to get payments on VA loans delayed until losses from the strike were recouped. One would expect that these actions would have enhanced Rockefeller's image; and if voters were wholly rational, they would have. The governor saw the difficulties people were encountering and competently, if quietly, sought to provide some remedy.

The only problem with this approach is that the public does not respond to quiet competence. Most people are simply not aware of the actions of public officials, nor are they in a position to judge their effectiveness. They are only aware of highly visible actions, and this is where Lindsay excelled. A successful image politician must fulfill two requisites: to penetrate the public consciousness and to appear to be doing the right thing. As Murray Edelman says:

> As the world can be neither understood nor influenced, attachment to reassuring abstract symbols rather than to one's own efforts become chronic. And what symbol can be more reassuring than the incumbent of a high position who knows what to do and is willing to act.... Because such a symbol is so intensely sought, it will predictably be found in the person of any incumbent whose actions can be interpreted as beneficent, or because their consequences are unknowable....
>
> The manner in which men have reacted in recent decades to incumbents of high political office who appear to be in command of the situation supports the conclusion that seems reasonable on a priori grounds that the public official who dramatizes his competence is eagerly accepted on his own terms.[89]

When we view the actions and statements of the politicians involved in the transit strike in this context, the surveys of public opinion become much easier to understand. If incumbent politicians are judged not only by their accomplishments but by their goals, by what they set out to accomplish, then Lindsay should have emerged from the transit strike a hero. For judging by his public statements, no one was purer of heart or nobler of purpose than Lindsay.

Perhaps most significant, however, was that Lindsay's public posturing during the strike impressed not only his constituents, but a national audience as well. By demonstrating his brand of Republican liberalism before an attentive national audience of media representatives, Republican party officials, and grant administrators, Lindsay was establishing himself as a distinct alternative to the recently rejected Republicanism of Barry Goldwater. Thus, while many of Lindsay's actions during the strike were extraneous to bargaining, they certainly served to enhance his image in the eyes of a national audience. And this was Lindsay's main concern.

Essentially, Governor Rockefeller concerned himself primarily with dispensing "material" rewards to parties affected by the strike; Lindsay was primarily concerned with the conferral of "symbolic" rewards.

In a post-mortem analysis of the strike, the TWU's Douglas MacMahon joined Lindsay in recognizing that public sector strikes had become media confrontations, but he was at a loss to explain how unions could compete in this new arena. "Lindsay did a terrific job with the media," said MacMahon. "I tried to improve our image on TV and radio but I admit I was only partially successful. I tried to show the real reasons for the strike," MacMahon continued. "The papers deliberately tried to blacken the union and Mike and portrayed Lindsay as a man on a horse."[90]

Jack Gould, the television critic for the *New York Times* saw things in considerably less conspiratorial terms, but he agreed on the importance of television to negotiations, "a viewer feels he knows Mr. Quill like the proverbial book and has not the vaguest idea about the specific grievances of the subwayworkers. In the 1960s," Gould concluded, "theatricality apparently is a major element in the resolution of disputed issues."[91]

MacMahon elaborated on the failure of organized labor to gain favorable media coverage:

> Public relations is very important. We have failed to get labor's story across. People do not understand what is good for the country. What is good for workers is good for America. Control of the press and radio is in the hands of big business and anti-labor forces. In our case we made efforts at influencing the media but they were small and unsuccessful. It takes an in depth approach which was not undertaken. The reason is the editors and owners and not the reporters.
>
> More and more labor has to become oriented toward public education and establish ties with organizations that influence people. We must establish links with civil rights and anti-poverty groups so people are disabused of the idea that labor is only self interested. Labor is interested in the country as a whole. We are our brothers keepers. Unfortunately, TV as a whole does not portray us favorably.[92]

The strike, long considered a test of economic strength, had evolved into a war between competing public relations approaches.

Amid all of the political backbiting, Authority Commissioner Gilhooley, who was in charge of the TA's fiscal affairs, attempted to assess the impact of the strike settlement on the retention of the 15¢ fare. According to Gilhooley's "unofficial figures, the situation is bleak, very bleak indeed." Assuming that the TA would get no outside aid, Gilhooley said that even if the TA cut its $50-million contingency reserve "to the bone" and initiated a 20¢ fare immediately, there would have to be another increase to 25¢ in

August 1967. If subsidy money were available, the TA commissioner estimated it would need $51 million in 1966 and an additional $115 million in 1967 in order to preserve the 15¢ fare. Although Governor Rockefeller initially proposed to make $100 million available to the city to help cushion the impact of the wage settlement, it was already clear that $31 million of this amount was in reality earmarked for social welfare programs. The remaining $69 million would enable the 15¢ fare to be retained through 1966 but would leave the Authority facing a $97-million deficit in 1967. It would require $69 million, nearly depleting the TA's emergency reserves as well as the proposed consolidation of the Triborough Bridge and Tunnel Authority, to hold the 15¢ fare through 1967. The prospect that the city could subsidize the TA's operation appeared unlikely because it was facing a deficit of $412 million in the fiscal year due to end on June 30. The Authority's precarious financial position was not solely a result of the recently completed negotiations; the TA faced an estimated deficit of $43 million before the strike settlement.[93]

On Monday, January 17, considerable political wrangling also took place with respect to the prospect of state aid to retain the 15¢ fare. On the previous Thursday, Governor Rockefeller proposed a $100-million advance to the city to enable it to maintain the transit fare until the mayor's proposal to merge the TA and the Triborough Bridge and Tunnel Authority could be decided by the state legislature. Of the $100 million, which would be paid to the city before the start of the state's fiscal year, $51 million was an acceleration of payments the city would have received eventually. This included a $31-million payment for social welfare costs and $20 million in proceeds from the stock transfer tax which the state had previously agreed to give to the city. Although the $31 million would provide cash that could immediately be used to shore up the 15¢ fare, by the end of the fiscal year this money would have to be used for social welfare costs. The remaining $49 million in the package was the quarterly payment of school aid that the state had deferred during the Great Depression thirty years earlier when it was short of cash.

The three bills which embodied the governor's $100-million aid package passed the Senate on Monday evening, with the closest margin being a 59-to-4 vote of approval. The proposal's support was hardly unexpected because Governor Rockefeller had fashioned the package with considerable political savvy. After meeting behind closed doors for two hours, Republican senators fell into line behind the proposal when they realized it involved the expenditure of no "new" money. The state's Democratic senators, who were concentrated in New York City, could hardly go on record as opposing legislation that was being touted as necessary to preserve the 15¢ fare. Although Senate Democrats were highly critical of the aid package during the two-hour debate, claiming that the money had long been owed the city, they had no choice but to support the measures. "It's a gubernatorial election year con job," said Irwin Brownstein, a Brooklyn Democrat. "It was uncalled for for the Governor to tell us this is the panacea for our transit problem," concurred Senator Samuel L. Greenberg, also a Brooklyn Democrat. "It isn't, it wasn't, and it won't be." In closing the debate, Senate Majority Leader Earl W. Brydges, a Republican from Niagara Falls said with a smile, "Little did I realize we were going to have this much difficulty forcing this much money on the City of New York."[94]

In addition to the interparty differences, the prospect of state aid for the city's transit system also generated a considerable amount of intraparty squabbling. In what was both literally and figuratively a "Dear John Letter," Governor Rockefeller indicated to his fellow Republican Lindsay on Monday that New York City had little prospect of receiving the nearly $600 million in additional state financial aid that had been requested by the mayor to meet problems in education, welfare, and antipoverty programs as well as transit. In his letter, Rockefeller reminded the mayor of several of his campaign promises, which included a reorganization of city government agencies and a suggestion that between $300 million and $400 million could be cut from the city budget by implementing economy measures. "In studying your request for increased aid," the governor said, "it would be very helpful if we could have some indication of the city's new fiscal plan, based on your contemplated reorganization of the city government, anticipated economies, new programs, estimated increases and expansions in Federal aid, and your proposed revenue structure."[95] Much more significant, however, were the political reasons for the governor's reluctance to provide substantial increases in state aid to New York City. Rockefeller was up for reelection as governor later in the year and he was well aware of voting patterns in the state. New York City was overwhelmingly Democratic, and most Republican support came from upstate. It would not be very politically astute to raise taxes statewide to come to the aid of New York City because this would alienate upstate Republicans and probably would not cause the city's residents to vote Republican. Finally, Governor Rockefeller had no intention of providing too much support for someone he viewed as a possible rival in his quest for the presidency.

On Tuesday, the State Assembly passed, and Governor Rockefeller signed, legislation to provide $100 million to help preserve the 15¢ fare. In signing the three-bill package, Rockefeller said the funds should be sufficient to maintain the fare for twelve months. Once receiving the money, however, the city was in the strange position of being unable to give or loan the money to the TA without additional state legislation. When the legislature created the TA, the city was supposed to pay for capital costs but the Authority was required to meet operating costs out of operating revenues. "In the past," said Mayor Lindsay, "the city hasn't needed legislation because they gimmicked it."[96] By *gimmicking*, Lindsay said he meant that the city had used its general funds to pay for the TA police and for transit fares for schoolchildren. In fact, in 1964 state legislation had been required to enable the Authority to provide cut-rate transportation for school children and to assume other TA expenses. No legislation had been required, however, to allow the city to cover the expenses for the transit police.

Another Strike

On Friday, January 21, the State Supreme Court paved the way for taxpayer suits to force the TA to punish workers who struck in violation of the Condon-Wadlin Act when it vacated a stay prohibiting the Authority from punishing the strikers until the constitutionality of the act had been tested in the courts.

The decision placed the Transit Authority in an extremely precarious position. As TA Commissioner Gilhooley observed, the Authority would have to "take any and all actions necessary to enforce the law, whether we like it or not" if a taxpayer suit required them to fire those workers who struck, as provided by the Condon-Wadlin Act. But as fellow Commissioner Scannell pointed out, such a course of action "raises some question about how you can operate the subways if you have some 30,000 employees who run the subways out of work." Adding immediacy to this question was the fact that such a taxpayer suit had already been heard, and a decision was pending. The TWU, the TA, and the city had hoped that the temporary stay would be continued until February 18, when a TWU suit challenging the constitutionality of the Condon-Wadlin Act was due to be heard.[97]

On Monday evening, January 24, TWU President Quill was released from the hospital where he had spent three weeks undergoing treatment for congestive heart failure. The following day, according to newspaper accounts, "smiling quizically and looking surprisingly well," he returned to the Americana Hotel for a thirty-five minute news conference. Supported by his walking stick but appearing considerably more alert and fit than he did just prior to his arrest, the sixty-year-old union leader gave a vintage Quill performance. His response to reporters' questions was a combination of disarming one-liners and outrageous overstatements. He described the settlement with the TA as a "good" and "fair" agreement that was long overdue. "The men didn't have enough money," said Quill, "and there was nobody came to their aid until they struck and after they struck people came out of the cracks." The TWU president seemed to want to begin mending fences with Mayor Lindsay. He said the mayor "did everything he could to end the strike" and seemed to excuse Lindsay's problems in reaching a settlement on the fact that he "was new on the job."[98] Perhaps most important, Quill tried to come to Lindsay's defense by minimizing the size of the settlement, now claiming that it amounted to $60 million rather than the previously estimated $72 million. Realizing that they would have to negotiate future contracts with Lindsay, it was now time to deflect some of the criticism the mayor was receiving for having agreed to an inflationary settlement.

Quill said that President Johnson "knew very well that the guidelines did not apply to municipal employees." The TWU president called Johnson's statement that the settlement violated the wage-price guideposts as being "typical of Mr. Johnson and his wheeler-dealer approach." Quill criticized President Johnson for "doing absolutely nothing" to head off or settle the strike and for "trading on the hardships of the people in the hopes that it would gain him votes at the next election. . . . Mr. Johnson has found money for countries all over the world from Pago Pago to the Khyber Pass and I'm wondering why he can't find money for transportation for the eight million people of New York City." Quill then singled out New York's Democratic Senator Kennedy as "the one man in public life that worked hard to settle the strike and relieve the people."[99] Kennedy, in fact, was only peripherally involved in the strike proceedings, and Quill did not elaborate on just what the Senator did. However, support for Kennedy, an Irish-American closely associated with the aspirations of blacks, would be popular in a union that was dominated by those two groups.

Late Friday afternoon, January 28, four weeks after he led his union out on the strike that paralyzed the city, Michael Quill died in his sleep. Quill was in his apartment taking a nap when his wife checked on him shortly after 5:00 p.m. His personal physician, Dr. Hyman Zuckerman, had ordered him to remain in bed except for meals. About 5:30 p.m., Mrs. Quill became alarmed by her husband's appearance, and she and the city detective, who had been assigned to guard Quill because of threats against him, immediately administered oxygen from a tank at the bedside. The detective telephoned for an ambulance and a police emergency unit, and they arrived almost simultaneously at about 5:45 p.m. The emergency police tried to revive Quill but were unsuccessful. As more than a dozen policemen stood around in awkward silence, a priest administered the last rights. Suddenly, Mrs. Quill cried out, "No! It can't be. It can't be."[100] Dr. Zuckerman, an internist and cardiologist, said that Quill died about

5:15 p.m. of a coronary occlusion. Quill had had at least two heart attacks
before the congestive heart failure he suffered in Civil Jail.

In the hours immediately following his death, tributes poured in, many
coming from individuals Quill had verbally sparred with during his life.
Mayor Lindsay issued a statement in which he said, "Michael Quill's death
marks the end of an era. He was a man who was very much a part of New
York. My sympathy goes to his wife and family." Former Mayor Wagner,
who had somewhat better relations with Quill than his successor, said,
"Naturally, I'm shocked. But Mike hasn't been well for a year now. . . . He
was a tough antagonist in negotiations. I have always liked him. He was a
man of his word." And although Quill had publicly attacked President
Johnson only a few days earlier, Labor Secretary Wirtz said that "Mike
Quill believed in human justice and he fought hard for the way he believed
in." AFL-CIO President Meany, who, at least implicitly, had criticized
Quill's actions in the transit strike said, "It's tragic. He was a man who
devoted his entire life to the union. He lived for it and he died for it."
Perhaps the feelings about Quill were best summed up by Joseph E.
O'Grady, the retiring chairman of the TA, who spent many days across the
bargaining table from Quill. O'Grady called the TWU President "a tough,
witty and fair opponent who always kept his word."[101]

Four days after his death, 3,000 transport workers filed into St.
Patrick's Cathedral to pay their last respects to their union president.
Draped over Quill's casket, in a final act of defiance, was the IRA flag. Then,
in an irony Quill certainly would have appreciated, his body was driven to
the cemetary despite a strike by the city's hearse drivers. In a final tribute,
the International Brotherhood of Teamsters authorized a union driver for
the trip.[102]

As was provided in the union's constitution, Quill was succeeded as
president by Matthew Guinan, the fifty-five-year old secretary-treasurer.
The next election of officers would not be held until the next national
convention in 1969.

On February 7, the TWU rank-and-file members voted overwhelmingly to accept the contracts negotiated by their leaders with the Transit
Authority and its subsidiary, the Manhattan and Bronx Surface Transit
Operating Authority. In the mail ballot conducted among the employees of
the two authorities, 15,683 voted in favor of the contracts and they were
opposed by 2,683 workers.[103]

The transit crisis, however, was still far from settled. Several days after
the ratification vote by TWU rank-and-file members, a State Supreme
Court Justice warned the TA that it would be illegal to grant any pay
increases for three years to its 34,000 employees who had gone out on
strike. "It is plain," said Justice Saypol, "that [the TA and the Civil Service

Commission] are forbidden at their peril from any course which would increase the compensation of the strikers, in violation of the Condon-Wadlin law, before January 14, 1969."[104] In his decision, Justice Saypol did not mince words. He was sharply critical of the Authority for "submitting to illegally extorted demands. If responsible officials cannot stand up in firm resistance, the court will," he said. "Submission today to this unlawful conduct under the guise of civil disobedience, grinding into the dirt the civil rights and liberties of the city's millions, is craven servility and could lead to disaster for all." With respect to the union's conduct, Justice Saypol said that "No personal reason on their part can justify the ransom they extorted from eight million citizens." Justice Saypol's decision to prohibit the pay increases came in the suit brought by Queens lawyer George Weinstein, who brought the action as a "taxpayer and voter." Several possible areas of recourse to the decision were available, although neither appeared promising. First, Judge Saypol granted the TA ten days to file an answer to his opinion before granting a prohibitive court order forbidding the wage increases. In addition, the TA could make a direct appeal to the Appellate Division for a reversal of Justice Saypol's ruling. For its part, the TWU's response to the decision was both terse and ominous: "New York's transit workers," said a union spokesman, "will insist that the Authority and the Mayor live up to their agreement which ended the strike on January 12."[105]

Leaders of the Transport Workers Union met with Mayor Lindsay on February 11 to discuss the implications of Justice Saypol's decision. Although union officials did not make any public threats, it was clear that any extended delay in implementing the higher wage rates won in their recently negotiated agreement might precipitate another crisis. "We're really walking on eggs," one union official commented. Later, Guinan, the new president of the TWU, said that unless something were done he would not be able to hold his members because they were "positively incensed" by Justice Saypol's ruling.[106]

Several days later, Governor Rockefeller announced that he would do his utmost to get legislation enacted that would permit New York City to pay its transit workers the raises they won in negotiations. Not wasting any time, Rockefeller said he would try to have a bill introduced on February 14, and passed the same day, that would forgive the transit workers for violating the Condon-Wadlin Act, without amending the state's antistrike law. After discussing his proposed measure with the leading Democrats in the Assembly and Senate, however, it was clear that the Rockefeller measure was certainly not a fait accompli. Assembly Speaker Anthony J. Travia was critical of the proposed bill for exempting only transit workers. "What about the pending actions against the ferryboat and welfare workers?" he asked, concerning recent strikes by those employees, "Their penalties are still pending in court." Travia indicated he was anxious to undertake a complete review of the Condon-Wadlin Act rather than simply avoiding a major crisis. The TA, however, indicated there there was a lot to be said for expediency. In a telegram to the governor, the Authority urged him and the Legislature to act quickly on Rockefeller's bill "in order to avoid the imminent possibility of a renewal of a strike on the New York City subways and buses."[107]

In announcing the governor's plan, his press secretary said that Rockefeller would sign the legislation immediately if it were passed. "The Governor is concerned about another shutdown on the subways and buses in New York and he wants to make certain there is no further snag in implementing the transit agreement," his spokesman explained. Included in the measure proposed by Rockefeller was the statement, "Notwithstanding any other provisions of the law to the contrary, the Transit Authority and the Manhattan and Bronx Surface Transit Operating Authority are hereby authorized to continue in employment their hourly rated operating employees and pay them the increased compensation recommended by the mediation panel appointed by the Mayor."[108] The measure would be retroactive to January 1.

Despite the fact that the proposed legislation was accompanied by a message of necessity from Governor Rockefeller that would have enabled it to be passed immediately, the Legislature was not inclined to act precipitously. Misgivings about the governor's plan were expressed by both Democrats and Republicans, who believed that the Legislature should undertake an overall revision of the Condon-Wadlin Act rather than a hastily drafted, stop-gap measure. Republican Senate Majority Leader Earl W. Brydges said his colleagues were concerned that "if we pass this bill gratuitously, Civil Service groups may feel that it's better to get a special bill every time they strike rather than seek an intelligent overhall of Condon-Wadlin." For somewhat different political reasons, a Manhattan Democrat concurred with this course of action, "If the Governor and Lindsay need this bill to save their heads then we've got them where we want them. This is the time to press for an intelligent change to the Condon-Wadlin Law."[109] During the 1965 legislative session prior to the strike, the Democrats were able to get a bill passed that softened the law's penalties, but Rockefeller vetoed it on the ground that it would have reduced the law's deterrent effect against strikes. For the most part, the Republicans in the Legislature wanted to make the law tougher while the Democrats wanted to soften the penalties to make it more "realistic." In his message of necessity, Governor Rockefeller pointed out that as he had previously promised, he would propose an overall revision of the Condon-Wadlin Act later in the session.[110]

The second major criticism of the Rockefeller proposal was that it made a "special category" out of the transit workers and treated them differently than ferryboat captains and welfare workers. Both groups of New York City employees struck during 1965; several ferry captains were discharged; and the issue of penalties for the welfare workers was still being argued in the courts. Senate Minority Leader Joseph Zaretzki said that he and his fellow Democrats would try to amend the Governor's bill to include the ferry and welfare workers, but he conceded that, if the amendments were defeated, "we won't be happy about it, but we'll go with the Rockefeller bill."[111]

As might be expected, the differential treatment did not please the welfare or ferryboat unions. A delegation from one of the two welfare worker unions, the Social Service Employees Union (SSEU), tried to see Governor Rockefeller to urge their inclusion in his exemption bill, but they were turned away. The union group was referred to one of the governor's aides, who told them that both the bill and message of necessity had already been printed and could not be amended. Judith Mage, the president of the Social Service Employees Union, was incensed by the course of events, "The only way we can view the bill is that the government gives special treatment only to public employees who can put the city in a mess, but not to those whose strikes affect only a few people." An official of the other welfare union, Local 371 of the American Federation of State, County, and Municipal Employees (AFSCME), was equally perturbed saying that, if the transit workers were exempted and penalties were imposed on welfare employees, "I promise you we will go on strike."[112]

Despite the reservations of others, TWU Local 100 President Gilmartin was in Albany to try to rally support for the Rockefeller legislation. He said the governor's bill was "the only solution," adding that his members were "very restless" over the delay in getting pay increases. "They just want to get paid," Gilmartin said of the 34,000 members in his local. "They don't want to hear anything about technicalities."[113]

On February 15, for the second straight day, the New York State Legislature refused to act on Governor Rockefeller's bill. As an indication of the magnitude of the opposition to the Governor's measure even within the Republican party, Rockefeller had been unable to find a single Republican who would introduce his bill in the Assembly. As a result, the governor went to the Senate and introduced it there through the Rules Committee, which was headed by the Senate Majority Leader Brydges.[114]

After refusing for two days to heed Governor Rockefeller's admonition to immediately pass his bill, the Legislature relented on February 16 and passed the measure. Minutes after the bill was adopted the governor said he was "gratified," and that evening he signed the bill into law in his

New York City apartment. In speeches on the floor of both the Senate and the Assembly, Governor Rockefeller's proposal was attacked by members of both parties, who characterized it as "hypocritical," "awful," and "unconstitutional." Moments later, the bill was passed overwhelmingly by both houses of the Legislature. Most of the legislators voted for the bill they had denounced because they agreed with the Governor that there was an "imminent danger" that the "restless" TWU would call a wildcat strike. As Moses Weinstein, the Democratic majority leader of the Assembly, said, "Which of you as legislators wants to take the responsibility for having another strike tomorrow? . . ." Republican Senate Majority Leader Brydges was among those legislators who attacked the bill and then voted for it. He explained, "I'm going to vote for it, but I hate every word of it. I'm doing it for only one reason, only because this emergency [the strike possibility] threatens sixteen million people and I have to weigh alternatives."[115]

Democratic Senate Minority Leader Zaretzki also joined the attack on Governor Rockefeller, denouncing him for having excluded the welfare workers from his bill, stating, "The two cases are absolutely the same. There isn't one ounce of logic in his [Rockefeller's] position—he's just being blindly stubborn. These 6,000 [welfare workers] are doing work just as necessary as the guard on a subway train or the porter in a station." Assemblyman Daniel Becker was among those legislators who expressed astonishment that their colleagues would vote for such a "bad bill. I never dreamed when I entered this house eight years ago," said the Republican from Newburg, "that I would ever hear responsible legislators get up before us and say 'Yes, we have before us an unconstitutional piece of legislation, but I urge you to vote for it.' "[116] Becker voted against the bill. Nevertheless, the Rockefeller measure passed easily, with a vote of 46-to-16 in the Senate and 118-to-39 in the Assembly.

The Democrats attempted to amend the governor's bill to include the welfare workers. But the Republicans, apparently whipped in line by Governor Rockefeller, voted along strict party lines in the Senate, and the amendment was defeated 37-to-23 in the Republican-controlled chamber. In the Assembly, where the Democrats held the majority, the amendment never reached a vote. Democratic leaders tried to get a message of necessity so the amendment could be voted on immediately. But Rockefeller refused, and when the governor's bill came to a vote, the amendment was not yet eligible to be considered.[117]

Visitors to Albany on February 16 would have been treated to an unusual sight: that of TA member Gilhooley roaming the chambers and corridors of the Capitol seeking support for a bill to pay the Authority's workers more than was permissible by law at the time. Gilhooley's presence was quite understandable; he was trying to prevent another transit strike.

Gilhooley had come at the request of his old political ally Rockefeller, who asked him "to do what he could do to help. I was told the TA bill was in trouble," the TA member said. Asked to comment on the argument that welfare workers should be included in the exemption legislation, the TA member took an understandably narrow focus. "My job," he said, "was to solve our particular problem so we could stay in business and continue to run a railroad."[118]

On February 17, the day after it was passed, the top officials of the TWU called at Governor Rockefeller's office in New York City to thank him for pushing through the bill that exempted the transit workers from the penalties of the Condon-Wadlin Act. But at the very time that this congenial meeting was taking place in the governor's office upstairs, leaders of the Social Service Employees Union carried picket signs outside the building; and on the staircase inside, they denounced Rockefeller for refusing to get a similar exemption for welfare workers.[119] What was the cause of this differential treatment of the TWU and the welfare unions? First, Local 100 of the TWU had 34,000 members and operated an extremely effective lobbying machine.[120] This compared with 6,000 members in the two welfare unions, who in addition to being small in size were politically unsophisticated. Secondly, a strike by transit workers had an impact on millions of New Yorkers, including those with a considerable amount of political power. In contrast, a strike by welfare workers had virtually no impact on the operation of "mainstream" New York, and those clients affected tended to be politically impotent.

Most important, however, as a reliable source related, a deal was struck between the TWU and Governor Rockefeller. In return for the governor's sponsorship and support of the bill to exempt the transit workers from the penalty provisions of the Condon-Wadlin Act, the union agreed that, while it would not openly endorse him in his upcoming bid for reelection, they would not oppose him and would give him their tacit approval. All outward appearances support the belief that such a deal was made.

After the meeting of TWU leaders with Governor Rockefeller at his New York City office, TWU President Guinan said that the members of his union would remember that Rockefeller had come to their aid when they needed him most. As he left the closed meeting Guinan said, "We have 100,000 members [in the international union] and we can only make a recommendation to our members. They don't have to follow the recommendation. But this action by the Governor sits well with the membership."[121] TWU Local 100 President Gilmartin described the bill exempting the transit workers from the penalties of the Condon-Wadline Act as being the result of "prompt, intelligent action by Governor Rockefeller."[122] In the March installment of a monthly column written by Gilmartin in the

TWU Express, the union's newspaper, the president of Local 100 heaped more praise on the governor. In complimenting Rockefeller for his part in obtaining passage of the exemption bill, Gilmartin wrote, "the Governor...never wavered from start to finish despite heavy political pressures that were brought to bear from all sections of the state and even the nation."[123]

In his column in the April issue of the *TWU Express*, titled "Support Those Who Helped Us," Gilmartin left little doubt that the union's half of the "deal" made with Governor Rockefeller would be fulfilled. Although he did not give Rockefeller his overt approval, Gilmartin's support was quite clear. His column began by describing the predicament the TWU was confronted with after the State Supreme Court ruled that TWU members should be made "provisional employees of the Transit Authority and barred them from wage raises for five years." At this point, Gilmartin wrote, "Governor Rockefeller acted wisely and quickly in pressing for the required piece of legislation," which was so direly needed by the TWU. Gilmartin concluded his column with a plea to "Support Those Who Support Us." He wrote, "It is...to our credit that TWU has not tied itself to the coattails of any one political party. Democrats and Republicans—when they knew and understood the facts—supported us in the crucial moment when the chips were down."[124] In the campaign for governor, the TWU adhered to its part of the deal and found itself in the unusual position of not supporting the Democratic gubernatorial candidate.

The passage of the state law exempting the transit workers from the penalty provisions of the Condon-Wadlin Act seemed to finally bring stability to a transit situation that had been chaotic for almost four months. But before anyone who was involved in these recurring crises had time for quiet reflection, another bombshell was dropped. On February 25, Robert Maidman, a real estate lawyer, filed a suit in State Supreme Court challenging the constitutionality of the special law exempting the transit workers from the penalties of the Condon-Wadlin Act. Supreme Court Justice Mitchell D. Schweitzer signed an order requiring the city and the TA to show cause why they should not be enjoined from paying the transit workers what they won in their twelve-day strike in January. In the papers filed with the court, Maidman contended that the law exempting the transit workers from the provisions of the Condon-Wadlin Act violated the equal protection clause of both the federal and the New York State Constitutions. Maidman said that the law discriminated against all other categories of public employees.[125]

On February 28, a second suit was filed in State Supreme Court, which also sought to enjoin the city from paying the transit workers the wage increases the TA had agreed to as the terms of ending the strike. This suit filed by Robert B. Blaikie, an Independent Democrat not directly involved in the dispute, argued that the special law exempting the subway and bus workers from the Condon-Wadlin Act was "illegal and unconstitutional." In his papers filed before the court, Blaikie said that although he sympathized with the transit workers, as well as with other public employees, he felt the Condon-Wadlin Act was unenforceable, which, he contended, "tends to bring about deviousness and corruption."[126] A hearing on the constitutionality of the state law exempting the transit workers from the provisions of the Condon-Wadlin Act began on March 9 before State Supreme Court Justice William C. Hecht, Jr.[127] The hearing was the result of the suits filed by both Maidman and Blaikie questioning the constitutionality of the law. After hearing almost two hours of arguments by twenty-one lawyers, Justice Hecht reserved decision until a later date. The fact that the lawyers seeking to have the two suits dismissed represented the TA, the TWU, the Amalgamated Transit Union, the New York City Corporation Counsel, and the state attorney general attested to the complexity of the situation.

Although the question of the legality of the action was still before the courts, on March 17 the TA began to pay the wage increases granted when the subway and bus strike was settled more than two months before.[128] "We have no choice," said a TA spokesman. "The contract was signed," and because there is no restraining order, he said, "we will pay the increases."[129]

On March 24, the possibility of a transit strike finally subsided when the state law exempting the city's transit workers from the penalties of the Condon-Wadlin Act was upheld by State Supreme Court Justice Hecht. In striking down the two suits challenging the constitutionality of the special law, Justice Hecht said the court could not question the "wisdom of fairness" of the legislation. In his twelve-page ruling, Justice Hecht found that other public employees were "not deprived of their privileges and immunities as citizens by the penalties of the Condon-Wadlin Law, merely by virtue of the fact that those penalties are not applied uniformly to all public employees. The problem comes down to whether the Legislature might reasonably make this distinction between transit employees and all other public employees." Justice Hecht indicated that the Legislature was not prohibited from giving the same immunity to other public employees. He added, "It has failed to do so up to this point because of its conclusion that exemption of transit employees is a reasonable classification— something which the Legislature has the constitutional right to do. This is no more the grant of an exclusive privilege or immunity to the transit

employees than the railroad full-crew law is a grant of exclusive privilege or
immunity to railroad employees, despite the fact that such regulations are
not imposed on other industries."[130]

For the first time since he had been elected mayor almost six months
earlier, a transit strike no longer hung over Lindsay's head.

Epilogue — Strike Aftermath

Image Politics

Governor Nelson Rockefeller's maneuverings in the strike aftermath epitomize the old-style politician. He weighed the political clout of the TWU and saw that not only were they politically potent, they were strongly supported by the respective city and state AFL-CIO organizations. Because the welfare workers lacked political power they could be treated in a cavalier fashion. Not particularly concerned with how he looked to the general public, Rockefeller essentially added up the votes of the different pressure groups and responded to the perceived power that these groups possessed.

In contrast, Mayor John Lindsay's behavior in transit negotiations served as a model for a new-style, image-conscious politician. He devoted considerable effort to activating various interest groups and to determining how these groups perceived his performance. By engaging in such pseudo-events as calling numerous news conferences, walking to work, and touring ghetto areas, Lindsay symbolically portrayed the strike as a contest of public interest versus self-interest, of good versus evil, of John Lindsay versus Michael Quill. Through the successful use of the media, Lindsay was able to activate or intensify the interest in the strike of such groups as: the national media, "good government" groups, national Republican leaders, private foundation executives, business groups, the clergy, and black leaders.

Once these different groups became "activated" or interested in the outcome of negotiations, Lindsay sought to satisfy their different expectations by conferring both economic and symbolic rewards. Union members, of course, were given economic rewards in the form of the largest monetary settlement they had ever received. The expectations of other groups, however, were mainly met through the conferral of symbolic rewards. Lindsay was entitled to the continued support of such groups as the

269

national media, national Republican leaders, and leaders of minority groups because he had acted heroically in the confrontation with Quill. He had demonstrated that he was principled, that he was tough, and that he would represent the needs and aspirations of all citizens regardless of their political connections.

The Taylor Law

In the immediate aftermath of the transit strike Governor Rockefeller established a committee to propose a new collective bargaining law for public employees in New York State. Chaired by George E. Taylor and also including John Dunlop, E. Wight Bakke, Frederick Harbison, and David L. Cole, each of them an industrial relations expert from outside New York State, the committee worked feverishly and issued a report on March 31, 1966. However, because of some rather serious political disputes in the legislature, a bill embodying the proposals of the "Taylor Report" was not passed until April 1967, and it did not go into effect until September 1, 1967.

The main thrust behind the Taylor Law was to shift the penalties from the individual employees to the employee organizations. Rather than spelling out specific penalties for individual workers violating the new legislation, the Taylor Law simply subjected striking employees to the penalties and procedures for misconduct that were present in the existing Civil Service Law for all offenses.

The Taylor Law provided that injunctions could be obtained from the State Supreme Court to prevent unions from striking. If a union disobeyed such an injunction, for each day of the strike the court was empowered to fine the employee organization an amount equal to one week's dues collections from its members or $10,000, whichever was less. Employee organization leaders who violated an injunction were subject to fines of not more than $250 or to imprisonment for not more than thirty days, or to both. Finally, the law provided that a striking union might lose the privilege of a dues checkoff for up to eighteen months.

As distinct from the Condon-Wadlin Law, which was solely punitive in nature, the Taylor Law established procedures to prevent impasses from developing into strikes. Rather than establishing uniform procedures for all bargaining relationships, however, the law permitted several options. First, local governments acting through their own legislative bodies were empowered to develop local procedures. If a municipality adopted its own procedures, it was free to utilize any approach it desired. The City of New York took advantage of this option and established its Office of Collective

Bargaining (OCB). In addition, all public employers were authorized to enter into agreements with employee organizations to develop procedures to be invoked in the event of an impasse.

If either of these alternatives to the State procedure was established, the Public Employee Relations Board (PERB) set up to administer the law could not become involved until the alternate procedures failed or unless they were requested to do so. If alternative procedures were not established, PERB could provide mediation services at the request of the parties or on its own initiative. If this effort was not successful in resolving the dispute, PERB could appoint a fact-finding board which had the power to make public recommendations. If either the public employer or the union rejected the fact-finders' report, the chief executive officer of the government involved was required to submit a recommendation for resolving the dispute to the legislative body of the government involved. The union was also allowed to submit its recommendations to the legislature. The decision of the legislature was final.

Office of Collective Bargaining

In addition to action at the state level, the transit strike also precipitated movement at the local level to deal with public sector labor disputes. In early 1966, Mayor Lindsay requested the Labor Management Institute of the American Arbitration Association "to facilitate through continuing informed discussions the development of an agreement between representatives of municipal employee organizations and the City of New York on improved collective bargaining procedures." A Mayor's Tripartite Panel was then established, and by mid-1966 it had produced a Memorandum of Agreement that was approved by the representatives of the city and of the employee organizations represented.[1]

Although the Memorandum of Agreement was endorsed by the labor representatives on the Tripartite panel, who were led by Victor Gotbaum, the executive director of District Council 37 of the American Federation of State, County, and Municipal Employees, organized labor was certainly not unanimous in its support of the agreement. Most vociferous in opposing the proposal was Joseph Tepedino, the president of the unaffiliated Social Service Employees Union, who in a telegram to Mayor Lindsay said the plan "discriminates against smaller unions in favor of one union in particular, and contains therefore the seeds of company unionism."[2] Tepedino's reference was to AFSCME, since the plan provided that bargaining on "citywide" issues for Career and Salary employees would be limited to the union that represented more than 50 percent of such employees. As the representative of about 60,000 of the 80,000 Career and Salary employees, the plan would enable District Council 37 to bargain for almost all issues affecting the Social Service Employees Union (SSEU) except wages. Tepedino felt that the effect of such a plan would be to squeeze smaller unions out of existence, while at the same time promoting Gotbaum and District Council 37, a view that was essentially correct. The SSEU had long been a thorn in the side of the city government, and the Lindsay Administration tried to use the situation to strip it of most of its bargaining power and to eventually force it out of existence.

John DeLury, the president of the Uniformed Sanitationmen's Association, was also extremely critical of the Mayor's Tripartite Panel, especially because the chairman of the labor representatives benefited his union (AFSCME) at the expense of others. DeLury called the panel's proposal "an engaging exercise in glittering gimmickry." "In essence," DeLury maintained, "the boss [the Mayor] handpicked the members of the Municipal Labor Committee with whom to bargain the terms of a collective bargaining bill."[3] Gotbaum was known to get along well with Mayor Lindsay, and the two men generally agreed on most issues.

Despite this opposition, a bill embodying the recommendations of the Tripartite Panel was enacted by the City Council and became effective on January 1, 1968. Basic to this new collective bargaining law for New York City was the establishment of an independent agency, the Office of Collective Bargaining, to administer its provisions. OCB was run by a seven-member board comprised of two city representatives, two designated by the Municipal Labor Committee, and three impartial members who were chosen by the other four.

The new OCB established machinery for determining bargaining units and holding representation elections. The OCB was also given the power to make final determinations of whether a subject was negotiable under the ordinance. This question of the "bargainability" of various issues had gained primacy during the city's most recent negotiations with its welfare investigators in which the city contended that many of the issues the SSEU sought to discuss were management prerogatives.

The ordinance establishing the OCB also set up a rather elaborate procedure for resolving impasses. After negotiations began, it was the responsibility of the OCB director to follow bargaining closely and to aid the parties by providing any information they requested. Then, after thirty days of bargaining, either at the director's initiative or at the request of either party, the OCB could appoint a mediation panel. Upon the request of both parties or the motion of the director, the director was to establish a dispute panel if the majority of the seven-member board of the OCB found that "collective bargaining, with or without mediation has been exhausted."[4] If the panel was unable to resolve a dispute after a reasonable period of time, it was required to submit a written report containing findings of fact, conclusions, and a recommended settlement. The report was to be made public within seven days after its submission, unless the parties agreed otherwise. During all of the negotiations, mediation, and impasse procedures, and for thirty days after the panel submitted its report, the union was prohibited from striking, slowing down, or engaging in mass absenteeism. The city law did not specifically prohibit strikes, although municipal employees would, of course, come under the strike ban of the state's Taylor Law.

In terms of coverage, the new city law covered only employees directly under the Mayor's jurisdiction. It did not cover the employees of the so-called independent boards of education and higher education or the housing or transit authorities. Since these agencies were not covered by OCB and because the Taylor Law was applicable to all bargaining relationships in which local procedures had not been established, these "independent" agencies came under the procedures set forth in the Taylor Act.

Poststrike Image Politics

About midway through Lindsay's two terms as mayor of New York, his deputy-mayor and chief political strategist, Richard Aurelio, observed, "If I were writing a book, it would be about the importance of a politician's image."[5] John Lindsay certainly concurred with this belief and acted accordingly during his tenure as mayor.

Although Lindsay ran for office with a pledge to reduce the city's public relations budget, he actually tripled expenditures for such purposes. He had a weekly television show on which he hosted people such as the mayor of Jerusalem and numerous show business types. The attempt was to showcase the Lindsay "personality" rather than to focus on the real problems facing New York City.[6]

In certain instances, Lindsay was concerned primarily with how he was perceived by voters in New York City. As Steven Weisman observed, "The Mayor's manipulation of his image reached its height during the 1969 reelection campaign when he placed hundreds of policemen and sanitation men on overtime at great cost and then pointed proudly to reduced crime and cleaner streets. Within weeks after the election, the men were pulled back, their overtime cancelled."[7] He made sanitation the highest priority of his second administration because it was the most visible of city services. "If garbage wasn't collected or snow removed," said Newfield and DuBrul, "everyone noticed." As a result, "diminishing resources were directed away from more fundamental problems—housing, heroin, jobs, education—because actual progress in those areas was not so easy to dramatize to the media."[8] Although disdained by conservative columnist William F. Buckley as "streetwalking," Lindsay's highly visible presence in ghetto neighborhoods was undoubtedly instrumental in keeping New York relatively riot free compared with other large cities. By his presence, the Mayor was demonstrating his concern for the plight of the city's blacks and Puerto Ricans.

In other instances, Lindsay was more concerned with his image among a considerably wider audience, primarily the private foundations and the national media. Lindsay's staff actively pursued private grants, not only because of their monetary value, but perhaps primarily because they marked his administration as being innovative and on the cutting edge. Faced with a deteriorating relationship between the black community and the police, a program funded by the Ford Foundation provided civilian women in police precincts to act as go-betweens to buffer relations between police and local residents.[9] Also funded by the Ford Foundation was a school desegregation plan that inflamed racial tensions in the city and precipitated violence. Despite the deleterious effect on the city, the decentralization effort was generally praised by the national media.

Despite the fact that Lindsay's policies and programs were considered by most analysts to be unsuccessful, he continued to receive favorable media coverage. As Newfield and DuBrul pointed out, "Lindsay dramatized the role of Mayor, but he couldn't do it. He was the mayor of America, but not of Queens."[10] Despite his failure to reverse New York's deteriorating relations between the races, the proliferation of municipal strikes, increased difficulties in keeping the city clean and traffic moving, and the imposition of a host of new taxes, Lindsay was viewed by many as being qualified for higher office. "While his rivals boast about what they've done," said one observer, "Lindsay may be the only politician in America to get anywhere by viewing his own record with alarm."[11] He deserved to be president, he argued, because he had been in the trenches while the other aspirants had been sideline observers.

Throughout his image conscious mayoralty, Lindsay dramatized the city's problems and presented every crisis as a morality play, and this approach proved successful. "Much of the popular writing on New York," one analyst wrote, "has mistakenly cast Lindsay in the role of an almost Homeric figure in combat with other gods, demi-gods and devils...."[12] When Lindsay began to seriously pursue the presidency in 1972, he continued his polarizing rhetoric. The problem with American society, he told a group of students at the University of California, Berkeley, was that it was dominated by the "big corporations," "the military," and "decaying political machines" and was consequently "unresponsive to the needs of the people."[13] Lindsay pledged to do battle with these nameless foes. In 1965-66, when New York City was the battleground, the antagonists who had incurred Lindsay's wrath were the power brokers. By the time of his presidential quest of the early 1970s, those who needed to be opposed were the "quiet men in business suits" who frequent and occupy the White House.

By the end of Lindsay's second term in office, his image-based house of cards began to crumble. Venturing into a solidly middle-class section of Queens after a fifteen-inch snowfall, Lindsay was villified by a group of angry residents. The mounds of uncleared snow amply demonstrated that by seeking to address national concerns and aligning himself with the aspirations of the disenfranchised, Lindsay had both ignored and blamed the middle class for the urban crisis.

As the opposition of middle-class voters in the city began to coalesce, Lindsay's advisors began to position him for a presidential run in 1972. However, despite his generally favorable notices from the national media, Lindsay was increasingly being criticized for his ineffectual performance as mayor of New York. Faced with this image problem, Lindsay needed to strengthen the way he was perceived in order to run for higher office:

> So he used the lines in the capital budget and the expense budget as bribes to this group or that group to stop criticizing him and let him run for president as the man who prevented riots, or as the man who had no strikes.... Boondoggles ... were foisted upon the taxpayers, because the pols would get the gravy. Short-term borrowing from banks was increased to finance quick-fix programs designed to inflate the mayor's popularity quickly. Excessive pension settlements were made with municipal unions to improve his image as a negotiator—by averting strikes.[14]

Newfield and DuBrul sum up Lindsay's meteoric rise in New York and national political circles as well as his eventual failure: "He was a successful candidate because he understood the power of television, but he was a failure as mayor because he could not see the limits of television as a surrogate for reality."[15]

Poststrike Bargaining and the Fiscal Crisis

With the settlement of the transit strike, the Lindsay Administration moved from one confrontation with municipal unions to another. In the spring of 1966, nurses struck, protesting the fact that their wages were so low that 60 percent of the registered nurse positions in municipal hospitals remained unfilled. Soon after, doctors at several hundred city health clinics stayed away from their jobs until the city agreed to increase their wages from $23.50 to $43.00 an hour.[16]

Most significant, however, were negotiations with police, fire, and sanitation unions in the fall of 1966, which evidenced the intense rivalries between these groups. Traditionally, police and fire employees had pay parity, and sanitation workers received 10 percent less. Police and fire union officials negotiated a two-year package with Herbert Haber, Lindsay's new director of labor relations, which provided for a wage increase of $900 and increased benefits in the amount of $465. The police ratified the offer, but the firemen rejected it and, because of pay parity between the two groups, negotiations with both started over. Meanwhile, the police were outraged by the terms announced in the settlement with the sanitation union after Haber had promised them that the one-year contract with the Uniformed Sanitationmen's Association would be worth less than the first year of the agreement with the Patrolmen's Benevolent Association.[17]

A new package was structured for police and firefighters, reallocating money from fringe benefits to wages in an attempt to sweeten the pot, but it was rejected by both the police and fire unions. The firefighters began a work slowdown, and the police picketed City Hall. A face-saving formula was eventually worked out in which the length of the contracts were changed and more money was offered the police and fire unions during the first year of their agreement in order to retain the 10 percent premium that these groups enjoyed over sanitationmen. Most significant, however, was that the sanitation union was bought off by the offer of the same twenty-year, half-pay pension that police and firefighters received.

This response was to become typical of the Lindsay Administration whenever they were faced with a ticklish bargaining situation. Pension improvements were favored because assessing their cost is difficult and defering their funding until a later date is easy. In fact, when the city and the Uniformed Sanitationmen's Association were bargaining in 1966, a considerable discrepancy existed between the two sides cost estimates of the twenty-year, half-pay pensions. The city actually insisted on including a clause in the agreement that the improvement would only be granted if the union's cost estimates proved to be correct. Practically speaking, of course, once the pension improvements were announced they would not be rescinded, even though the true cost was considerably more than the union claimed. From the city's standpoint, however, this approach allowed them to grant the sanitation union a highly valued benefit while at the same time minimizing its cost for comparative purposes when examined by the police and fire unions.

Other extremely acrimonious confrontations between the Lindsay Administration and organized labor followed. In January 1967, welfare caseworkers returned to work after a brief strike, under an agreement to submit disputed economic issues to arbitration. Several months later, however, when the city refused to negotiate nonmonetary issues such as lower caseloads, streamlined case processing, and more generous payments for clients, the caseworkers engaged in a "work-in." They reported to their welfare centers but refused to work. Later, centers were broken into and flooded; records were torn and scattered, and locks were jammed. The city held its ground and after six weeks the caseworkers agreed to resume their jobs.[18]

Perhaps the ugliest, most devisive strike during Lindsay's tenure began in the fall of 1968, when 60,000 teachers struck in reaction to Lindsay's school decentralization plan. Developed by the Ford Foundation, the plan created three largely autonomous local school districts in ghetto areas. When the local school board in the black Brooklyn slum of Ocean Hill-Brownsville dismissed ten white teachers in the spring of 1968, 100 other teachers walked off their jobs in sympathy, and they, too, were fired. Over the summer, Lindsay did nothing to resolve the dispute, and by fall teachers throughout the city stayed away from their jobs. Lindsay denounced the strikers as "lawless, unscrupulous, enemies of New York City," but the teachers returned to work only after the school decentralization plan was modified to become acceptable to the union.[19]

Sandwiched between the high-profile, violence-laden, welfare and school decentralization strikes was a less showy but more significant strike: the three-week teachers' strike in September, 1967. Rather than attempting to work with the union leaders, Lindsay laid down the gauntlet, and as in the transit crisis, paid dearly for his approach. As union president Albert Shanker describes Lindsay's failure to recognize the "political" needs of union leaders:

> I sat down with the Mayor and explained to him that I had 106 different organizations among the union members—librarians, special education teachers, vocational education teachers, you name it. To keep the union together, I needed to get special little things for some of these groups. Not all of them, but a few each year.... But the Mayor didn't seem to comprehend what I was talking about. He seemed to have this idea that unions only wanted money.[20]

Because they initially refused concessions in any other areas, the city offered a very generous wage increase. The case went to fact-finding and the fact-finders, apparently sensing the city's intrasigence in the nonmonetary areas, recommended a 20 percent increase in wages and fringes over two years but none of the union's nonmonetary demands. The union struck, eventually receiving virtually all of their nonmonetary demands as well as the 20 percent monetary increase, the largest any union had yet received from the Lindsay Administration.[21]

Taken in concert, the sanitation settlement of 1966 and the teachers settlement the following year left the city in an extremely vulnerable bargaining posture. The sanitation settlement established a pension precedent for other unions to try to achieve, and the teachers' settlement set a wage figure for other municipal unions to emulate. Of the wage and pension settlements, pensions were by far the most significant in contributing to New York's financial difficulties.

In 1965, the annual cost of providing retirement benefits to New York City employees was $364 million, but by 1974 that cost had risen to $1.21 billion. These exploding pension costs were the result of three factors: improved pension coverage for employees, changes in the "administration" of the pensions that were more favorable to employees, and the deferred payment of costs that eventually had to be assumed.

Improved pension coverage for municipal employees centered in two areas: paying workers a higher percentage of their working wage as a pension and enabling workers to receive such pensions after working for a shorter period of time. By the early 1970s, police and firefighters could both retire at full pay after thirty-five years of service or at half pay after twenty years. Sanitation and transit employees as well as corrections and housing police officers could all retire at half pay after twenty years of service. The norm for most other municipal employees was half pay after twenty-five years of service at a minimum age of fifty-five.

In addition, more devious pension improvements were also implemented during Lindsay's term in office. The unfunded $500 supplemental pension initially won by the TWU in 1966 would later be demanded, and won, by almost all city workers. And, in 1969, after he was denied renomination by the Republican party in his reelection campaign for mayor, Lindsay entered into a quid pro quo arrangement with the police, fire, sanitation, and corrections unions. In return for the political support of these unions, Lindsay granted an additional pension, a $1 per day annuity payment, which would be in addition to workers' regular pension, social security, and the $500 supplemental pension.

The way in which pension plans were "administered" also had a profound impact on both the level of benefits paid to pensioners and the cost to the city. In the early 1960s, retirement benefits for municipal employees were typically computed as a percentage (usually 50 percent) of the workers' average salaries for their last five years of service. Beginning in 1963, the state legislature passed a bill over the objections of Mayor

Wagner, which based police and fire pensions on their final year's pay, and other unions would soon emulate this precedent.[22] Finally, by the early 1970s, most municipal pensions were based on a percentage of the workers' total earnings their final year, including overtime. This practice became so abused that by 1978 the TA proposed that the base for workers' pensions be limited to 120 percent of their final year's salary.[23]

Throughout this period (1966-1976) the true cost of pensions was hidden from the public. By the mid-1970s it was estimated that municipal pensions were underfunded by at least $1 billion per year.[24] One way this ws accomplished was by using totally outdated mortality tables, in some instances dating back to 1918. By using estimates of life expectancy that said retirees would die much sooner than they would in reality, much less money would have to be set aside to fund these pensions.[25] A Securities and Exchange Commission (SEC) study of the city's pension system provides another example. Because they estimated the rate of return on pension investments during this period to be higher than it really was, the city under funded its pension contribution by $361.6 million.[26]

By 1977, the city's unfunded pension liability, money owed to future retirees but not set aside, was in excess of $8 billion. As a New York State Pension Commission study concluded: "The results of such gimmickry are almost tragic. They deceive the public employees and the taxpayers into believing that pension costs . . . have been met. In fact, such costs have not been met—they simply have not been paid. Therefore, next year's taxpayer not only must shoulder his proper share of government costs, but also the costs which have not been paid in prior years and which unfairly have been shifted to him."[27]

Public Policy Concern

From a public policy standpoint, a politician's reliance on image politics certainly raises cause for concern. At the least, an image-conscious politician will be less concerned with negotiating a "good" settlement than with enhancing his or her image. At the worst, the potential exists for an image-conscious politician to enter into a symbiotic relationship with a union, in which the union receives economic gains and the politician, image enhancement.

Notes

Prologue

1. Much of the following discussion initially appeared in Michael Marmo, "Multilateral Bargaining in the Public Sector: A New Perspective," *The Proceedings of the Industrial Relations Research Association, Annual Winter Meetings, 1982.*

2. Kenneth McLennan and Michael Moscow, "Multilateral Bargaining in the Public Sector," *Proceedings of the Twenty-First Annual Winter Meeting*, Industrial Relations Research Association, December 1968, p. 31.

3. Anthony Downs, *An Economic Theory of Democracy*, New York: Harper and Brothers, 1957, p. 2.

4. Walter Fogel and David Lewin, "Wage Determination in the Public Sector," *Industrial and Labor Relations Review*, April 1974, p. 414.

5. Murray Edelman, *Politics as Symbolic Action*, Chicago: Markham Publishing Company, 1971, p. 7.

6. Murray Edelman, *The Symbolic Uses of Politics*, Urbana: University of Illinois Press, 1964, p. 172.

7. James E. Combs, *Dimensions of Political Drama*, Santa Monica, Calif.: Goodyear Publishing Company, 1980, p. 123.

8. Cited in Edward Jay Epstein, *News From Nowhere: Television and the News*, New York: Random House, 1973, p. 164.

9. Ibid., p. 4.

10. Ibid, p. 262.

11. Daniel J. Boorstin, *The Image: A Guide to Pseudo-Events in America*, New York: Harper and Row, 1964.

12. David L. Altheide and John M. Johnson, *Bureaucratic Propaganda*, Boston: Allyn and Bacon, 1980, p. 72.

13. Doris Graber, *Mass Media and American Politics*, Washington, D.C.: Congressional Quarterly Press, 1970, p. 15.

14. Altheide and Johnson, op. cit., p. 23.

15. Peter Hall, "A Symbolic Interactionist Analysis of Politics," *Sociological Inquiry*, 42 (1972), p. 51.

16. Harry Wellington and Ralph E. Winter, Jr., "The Limits of Collective Bargaining in Public Employment," *Yale Law Journal*, 78 (June 1962), p. 63.

17. Dan Nimmo, *Political Communication and Public Opinion in America*, Santa Monica, Calif., Goodyear Publishing Company, 1978, p. 87.

18. Edelman, *Politics as Symbolic Action*, op. cit., p. 37.

19. Combs, op. cit., p. 60.

20. Edelman, *Politics as Symbolic Action*, *op. cit., p. 38.*

Chapter 1

1. Oliver R. Pilat, *Lindsay's Campaign—A Behind the Scenes Diary*, Boston: Beacon Press, 1968, p. 1.

2. Thomas P. Ronan, "Lindsay Says He Will Run," *New York Times*, May 14, 1965, p. 1.

3. Ibid.

4. "Candidate Lindsay," *New York Times*, May 16, 1965, Section 4, p. 1.

5. Robert J. Donovan, *The Future of the Republican Party*, New York: New American Library, 1964.

6. Pilat, op. cit., p. 9.

7. Warren Weaver, Jr., "Big Gamble of John Vliet Lindsay," *New York Times*, May 23, 1965, Section 6, p. 30.

8. Pilat, op. cit., p. 14.

9. Nat Hentoff, *A Political Life—The Education of John V. Lindsay*, New York: Alfred A. Knopf, 1969, p. 77.

10. Barbara Carter, *The Road to City Hall*, Englewood Cliffs, N.J.: Prentice-Hall, 1967, p. 20.

11. T.R. Dye and L.H. Zeigler, *American Politics in the Media Age*, Monterey, Calif.: Brooks/Cole Publishing Company, 1983, p. 148.

12. Warren Weaver, Jr., "This Tuesday's Winner—and Loser," *New York Times*, October 31, 1965, Section 6, p. 46.

13. William F. Buckley, Jr., *The Unmaking of a Mayor*, New York: The Viking Press, 1966, p. 282.

14. Gene Wyckoff, *The Image Candidates*, New York: Macmillan, 1968, p. 6.

15. Dan Nimmo, *The Political Persuaders*, Englewood Cliffs, N.J.: Prentice-Hall, 1970, p. 141.

16. Warren Weaver, Jr., "This Tuesday's Winner—and Loser," op. cit., p. 46.

17. Ibid.

18. Wyckoff, op. cit., p. 222.

19. Wyckoff, op. cit., p. 223.

20. Buckley, op. cit., p. 284.

21. Ibid.

22. William S. White, cited in Buckley, op. cit., p. 285.

23. Daniel R. Shanor, "The Columnists Look at Lindsay," *Journalism Quarterly*, Summer 1966, p. 287.

24. Ibid.

25. Hentoff, op. cit., p. 78.

26. The following discussion is drawn from James Q. Wilson, "The Mayors vs. the Cities," *The Public Interest*, Summer 1969, pp. 25-37.

27. Ibid.

28. Roger Starr, "Power and Powerlessness in a Regional City," *The Public Interest*, Summer 1969, p. 12.

29. Ibid., p. 31.

30. Ibid., p. 32.

31. Irving Kristol and Paul Weaver, "Who Knows New York? And Other Notes on a Mixed Up City," *The Public Interest*, Summer 1969, p. 42.

32. Murray Edelman, *The Symbolic Uses of Politics*, Urbana: University of Illinois Press, 1964, p. 78.

33. Dan Cordtz, "Lindsay Runs Scared," *Wall Street Journal*, October 20, 1965, p. 1.

34. Carter, op. cit., p. 101.

284 Notes

35. Hentoff, op. cit., p. 102.

36. Ibid.

37. Wyckoff, op. cit., p. 224.

38. Martin Tolchin, "Liberal Mantle Hotly Contested," *New York Times*, October 31, 1965, p. 82.

39. Wyckoff, op. cit., p. 224.

40. Dye and Zeigler, op. cit., p. 123.

41. Wyckoff, op. cit., p. 223.

42. Carter, op. cit., p. 101.

43. *Journal American*, October 29, 1965, p. 31.

44. Cited in Buckley, op. cit., p. 290.

45. Hentoff, op. cit., p. 42.

46. "Text of Rose's Address Reporting Endorsement of Lindsay," *New York Times*, June 29, 1965, p. 20.

47. Pilat, op. cit., p. 41.

48. Ibid., p. 101.

49. Buckley, op. cit., p. 282.

50. Hentoff, op. cit., p. 153.

51. Sidney Zion, "Dubinsky and Rose," *New York Times*, June 28, 1965, p. 24.

52. Ibid.

53. Nimmo, op. cit., p. 146.

54. Dye and Zeigler, op. cit., p. 153.

55. Carter, op. cit., p. 119.

56. Wyckoff, op. cit., p. 222.

57. Alan Otten, "Lindsay Faces Formidable Challenge," *Wall Street Journal*, December 30, 1965, p. 1.

58. Ibid.

59. Ibid.

60. Woody Klein, *Lindsay's Promise—The Dream That Failed*, New York: Macmillan, 1970, p. 28.

61. Ibid., p. 36.

62. Ibid., p. 29.

63. Hentoff, op. cit., p. 123.

64. Ibid.

65. Klein, op. cit., p. 44.

Chapter 2

1. Telegram sent by TWU to Mayor-Elect John Lindsay on November 3, 1965. Signed by Michael Quill, Matthew Guinan, Daniel Gilmartin, and Ellis Van Riper. Seen in the files of the TWU.

2. John G. Rogers and Sam Rubenstein, "Mike Quill's Congratulations—And Now The Contract Demands," *Herald Tribune*, November 5, 1965, p. 1.

3. Damon Stetson, "Quill Asks Pact Put At $250 Million By Transit Body," *New York Times*, November 5, 1965, p. 1.

4. Ibid.

5. Ibid.

6. Rogers and Rubenstein, op. cit., p. 1.

7. Damon Stetson, "Peril to 15-Cent Fare Rising Once Again," *New York Times*, November 7, 1965, p. 57.

8. Ibid.

9. Ibid.

10. Bernard Stengren, "Transit Problems Rooted in Politics," *New York Times*, December 24, 1965, p. 18.

11. New York City Transit Authority, *Exhibits for Contract Negotiations*, 1965, p. 35.

12. Albert L. Lincoln, "The New York City Subway Strike: An Explanatory Approach," *Public Policy 16*, Cambridge, Mass.: Harvard University Press, 1967, p. 273.

13. Emanuel Perlmutter, "Transit Problems Have....," *New York Times*, July 5, 1966, p. 43.

14. Ibid.

15. Edward Sussna, "Collective Bargaining on the New York City Transit System, 1940-1957," *Industrial and Labor Relations Review*, Vol. 11, No. 4, July 1958, p. 519.

16. Bernard Stengren, op. cit., p. 18.

17. Ibid.

18. Ibid.

19. *New York Times*, July 5, 1966, p. 9.

20. *New York Times*, July 26, 1955, p. 6.

21. "Biography of Joseph O'Grady," *New York Times*, January 5, 1966, p. 28.

22. "O'Grady Will Retire," *New York Times*, December 27, 1965, p. 1.

23. "Scholarly Foe of Crime—John Joseph Gilhooley," *New York Times*, April 7, 1965, p. 33.

24. Damon Stetson, "Peril to 15-cent Fare Rising Once Again," *New York Times*, November 7, 1965, p. 57.

25. "Editorial," *New York Times*, November 6, 1965, p. 28.

26. David Lewin, Raymond Horton, and James Kuhn, *Collective Bargaining and Manpower Utilization in Big City Governments*, Montclair, N.J.: Landmark Studies, Allanheld Osmun and Co., 1979, p. 48.

27. Robert F. Wagner, "Interim Order on the Conduct of Relations Between the City of New York and Its Employees," New York: Office of the Mayor, July 21, 1954.

28. Ibid.

29. Lewin, op. cit., p. 48.

30. Alice Cook, "Public Employees Bargaining in New York City," *Industrial Relations*, May 1970, p. 255.

31. Sterling D. Spero and John M. Capozzola, *The Urban Community and its Unionized Bureaucracies*, New York: Dunnellon Publishing, 1973, p. 65.

32. Emanuel Perlmutter, "Kheel Urges Rise in Bridge Tolls to Keep 15-cent Fare," *New York Times*, November 8, 1965, p. 1.

33. John Pascal, "Quill's Subway Strike Dirge—2d Verse, We're Flexible," *Herald Tribune*, November 8, 1965, p. 19.

34. Perlmutter, op. cit., p. 1.

35. Ibid.

36. Ibid.

37. Perlmutter, op. cit.

38. James Lynn, "Two Top Dems and Lindsay Talk it Over," *Herald Tribune*, November 9, 1965, p. 1.

39. Ibid.

40. Emanuel Perlmutter, "His Honor Talks of This and That," *New York Times*, November 9, 1965, p. 39.

41. Lynn, op. cit.

42. "Editorial—The Transit Balancing Act," *New York Times*, December 9, 1965, p. 42.

43. Damon Stetson, "Gilhooley Urges Transit Merger," *New York Times*, November 14, 1965, p. 53.

44. "Wagner's Board Shuns TWU Talks," *New York Times*, November 15, 1965, p. 39.

45. Ibid.

46. Ibid.

47. Thomas P. Ronan, "Lindsay Says City Needs Arbitration in Labor Disputes," *New York Times*, November 17, 1965, p. 1.

48. Paul Weissman, "Lindsay on Quill: It's All Up to Wagner," *Herald Tribune*, November 17, 1965, p. 1.

49. Don Flynn, "Lindsay Asks Cooling Off," *Herald Tribune*, November 19, 1965, p. 1.

50. Damon Stetson, "Lindsay to Meet Mayor On Transit," *New York Times*, November 19, 1965, p. 28.

51. Ibid.

52. News release issued by Mayor Robert F. Wagner on November 18, 1965. Seen in the files of the TWU.

53. Damon Stetson, op. cit.

54. "10 Listed By Lindsay For Transit Panel," *New York Times*, November 20, 1965, p. 18.

55. "Quill Says Demands Are For Bargaining," *New York Times*, November 22, 1965, p. 29.

56. Emanuel Perlmutter, "Transit Officials Put TWU Demand at $680 Million," *New York Times*, November 24, 1965, p. 1.

57. Ibid.

58. Ibid.

59. Daniel Gilmartin. Personal interview held in Gilmartin's office at 1980 Broadway, New York, N.Y., February 27, 1970.

60. "Local 100's Collective Bargaining Program," Seen in the files of the TWU.

61. Richard Madden, "Puerto Rico Hails Lindsay on Visit," *New York Times*, November 25, 1965, p. 55.

62. Emanuel Perlmutter, "Wagner Says 15-cent Fare Issue is Lindsay's Alone to Resolve," *New York Times*, November 28, 1965, p. 1.

63. Ibid.

64. Ibid.

65. Thomas Grubisich, "The TA Runs on Wheels and a Deficit," *Herald Tribune*, January 9, 1966, p. 12.

66. Daniel Scannell, Personal interview held in Scannell's office at 370 Jay Street, Brooklyn, N.Y., December 14, 1966.

67. Don Flynn, "TWU-Money Talks," *Herald Tribune*, December 19, 1965, p. 31.

68. Daniel Scannell, Interview, op. cit.

69. Martin Arnold, "State Gives City $100 Million Aid," *New York Times*, January 19, 1966, p. 30.

70. Bernard Stengren, op. cit.

71. Emanuel Perlmutter, "Strike Talks Show Gain," *New York Times*, January 9, 1966, p. 1.

72. Daniel Scannell, Interview, op. cit.

73. Thomas Grubisich, op. cit.

74. Thomas Grubisich, "All 10 Mediators Spurned by Quill," *Herald Tribune*, November 29, 1965, p. 1.

75. Emanuel Perlmutter, "Lindsay's Panel on Transit is Turned Down By Quill," *New York Times*, November 29, 1965, p. 1.

76. Ibid.

77. Emanuel Perlmutter, "Authority Lauds Transit Nominees," *New York Times*, November 30, 1965, p. 35.

78. Ibid.

79. Sue Reinart, "Lindsay Challenges Quill on Transit Strike Threat," *Herald Tribune*, November 30, 1965, p. 1.

80. Emanuel Perlmutter, "Authority Lauds Transit Nominees," op. cit.

81. Martin Gansberg, "New TWU Plea Made To Lindsay," *New York Times*, December 1, 1965, p. 93.

82. Telegram sent by TWU to Mayor-Elect John V. Lindsay on November 30, 1965. Telegram was signed by Michael Quill, Matthew Guinan, Daniel Gilmartin, and Ellis Van Riper. Seen in the files of the TWU.

83. Emanuel Perlmutter, "Quill Calls a Halt to Transit Talks," *New York Times*, December 2, 1965, p. 1.

84. Ibid.

85. Newton H. Fulbright, "Quill Ends TA Talks in Furor Over Lindsay," *Herald Tribune*, December 2, 1965, p. 1.

86. Emanuel Perlmutter, "Quill Calls Halt to Transit Talks," op. cit.

87. Ibid.

88. Homer Bigart, "Quill Threatens December 15 Walkout On Transit Lines," *New York Times*, December 3, 1965, p. 1.

89. Telegram from TWU to TA members, dated December 2, 1965. Seen in TWU files.

90. Homer Bigart, "Quill Threatens December 15 Walkout on Transit Lines," op. cit.

91. Ibid.

92. Ibid.

93. Shirley Quill, *Mike Quill Himself A Memoir*, Greenwich, Conn.: Devin-Adair Publishers, 1985, p. 264.

94. Ibid., p. 252.

95. Ibid.

96. Ibid., p. 253.

97. Ibid., p. 287.

98. Homer Bigart, "Quill Threatens Dec. 15 Walkout on Transit Lines," op. cit.

99. Ibid.

100. "Editorial," *New York Times*, December 3, 1965, p. 38.

101. Ibid.

102. Homer Bigart, "Kheel Angered, Bars Any Role In Transit Talks," *New York Times*, December 4, 1965, p. 1.

103. Ibid.

104. Ibid.

105. Emanuel Perlmutter, "Gilhooley Urges Wirtz To Mediate In Transit Talks," *New York Times*, December 5, 1965, p. 1.

106. Emanuel Perlmutter, "Quill Turns Down Wirtz As Transit Pact Mediator," *New York Times*, December 6, 1965, p. 1.

107. Ibid.

108. "Editorial," *New York Times*, December 6, 1965, p. 36.

109. Emanuel Perlmutter, "City Hall Talks On Transit Pact Called by Mayor," *New York Times*, December 7, 1965, p. 1.

110. Emanuel Perlmutter, "Lindsay Wants To Review Books of Transit Board," *New York Times*, December 8, 1965, p. 1.

111. Don Flynn and Robert Parella, "Quill Back, No Less Peppery," *Herald Tribune*, December 8, 1965, p. 3.

112. Ibid.

113. Emanuel Perlmutter, "Wagner Strives To Block Strike on Subways December 15," *New York Times*, December 9, 1965, p. 53.

114. Douglas Robinson, "Posters Proclaim a Citizens 'War' Against Quill," *New York Times*, December 9, 1965, p. 53.

115. Ibid.

116. L.H. Whittemore, *The Man Who Ran The Subways: The Story of Mike Quill*, New York: Holt, Rinehart and Winston, 1968, p. 274.

117. Homer Bigart, "Quill Calls Off Dec. 15 Walkout; 3 Will Mediate," op. cit.

118. A.H. Raskin, "What Makes Teddy Kheel Run?", *New York Times*, December 5, 1965, Section 6, p. 52.

119. "Mediator," *New Yorker*, January 22, 1966, p. 22.

120. Leonard Lyons, "The Lyons Den," *New York Post*, December 27, 1965, p. 29.

121. "Mediator," op. cit., p. 22.

122. Douglas MacMahon, Personal interview held in MacMahon's office at 1980 Broadway, New York, N.Y., December 22, 1966.

123. Daniel Scannell, Personal interview, op. cit.

124. John O'Donnell, Personal interview held in O'Donnell's office at 501 Fifth Avenue, New York, N.Y., December 19, 1966.

125. Timothy Costello, Personal interview held in Costello's office at 250 Broadway, New York, N.Y., December 14, 1966.

126. Theodore Kheel, Personal interview held in Kheel's office at 250 Park Avenue, New York, N.Y., December 21, 1966.

127. Richard Witkin, "The Power Brokers," *New York Times*, January 12, 1966, p. 17.

128. George Morris, "Lindsay's Advisors Are Responsible For Strike," *The Worker*, January 11, 1966, p. 1.

129. A.H. Raskin, "Still The Old Scenario," *New York Times*, December 27, 1965, p. 24.

130. Thomas P. Ronan, "Political Effect On Mayor Studied," *New York Times*, January 2, 1966, p. 58.

131. A.H. Raskin, "What Makes Teddy Kheel Run?", op. cit.

132. Ibid.

133. Timothy Costello, Personal interview, op. cit.

134. Homer Bigart, "Quill Calls Off Dec. 15 Walkout; 3 Will Mediate," op. cit.

135. "One Threat Down, One To Go," *New York Times*, December 10, 1965, p. 46.

Chapter 3

1. Woody Klein, *Lindsay's Promise—The Dream That Failed*, New York: MacMillan, 1970, p. 36.

2. Emanuel Perlmutter, "Lindsay Confers On Transit Pact, Promises Help," *New York Times*, December 13, 1965, p. 1.

3. Klein, op. cit.

4. "Lindsay To Name A Panel To Unify City's Transport," *New York Times*, December 14, 1965, p. 1.

5. Emanuel Perlmutter, "State Aid Sought By Mayor To Save 15-Cent Fare," *New York Times*, December 15, 1965, p. 1.

6. Ibid.

7. Damon Stetson, "Talks With Quill On Right Track, 3 Mediators Say," *New York Times*, December 23, 1965, p. 1.

8. John Cashman, "Quill's Rank-and-File: What They Really Want," *New York Post*, December 14, 1965.

9. Ibid.

10. Don Flynn, "Transit Talks Going Well," *Herald Tribune*, December 16, 1965.

11. Ibid.

12. Paul Weissman, "Lindsay Bill—Transport in 1 Agency," *Herald Tribune*, December 18, 1965, p. 1.

13. Emanuel Perlmutter, "Outside Meddling in Transit Talks Charged By Quill," *New York Times*, December 20, 1965, p. 1.

14. Ibid.

15. Thomas R. Brooks, "Lindsay, Quill and the Transit Strike," *Commentary*, March 1966, p. 52.

16. John O'Donnell, Personal interview held in O'Donnell's office at 501 Fifth Avenue, New York, N.Y., December 19, 1966.

17. "Mackell To Seek Transit Merger," *New York Times*, December 20, 1965, p. 42.

18. Ibid.

19. Leon Keyserling, *Higher Pay For N.Y.C. Transport Workers: The Workers Deserve It, The City Can Afford It*, December 1965. Seen in TWU files.

20. Ibid.

21. "Mediator," *The New Yorker*, January 22, 1966, p. 22.

22. Ibid.

23. Emanuel Perlmutter, "Wagner Enters Transit Dispute," *New York Times*, December 22, 1965, p. 1.

24. Damon Stetson, "Talks With Quill On Right Track....," op. cit.

25. Ibid.

26. Ibid.

27. Ibid.

28. Ibid.

29. Ibid.

30. Matthew Guinan, Speech made on WOR-TV in NYC on December 30, 1965. Transcript seen in TWU files.

31. Richard Witkin, "Turning Point: Late Sunday Night," *New York Times*, January 14, 1966, p. 29.

32. Richard Alden, "Hard Position is Adopted by Union's 'Second' Line— City May Raise Offer," *New York Times*, January 5, 1966, p. 1.

33. Douglas MacMahon, Personal interview held in MacMahon's office at 1980 Broadway, New York, N.Y., December 22, 1966.

34. Charles Grutzner, "Authority's Wages: Are They Fair or Too Low?", *New York Times*, January 6, 1966, p. 12.

35. Ibid.

36. *Exhibits For Contract Negotiations—1965*, NYC Transit Authority, p. 77. Seen in TWU files.

37. Ibid.

38. A.H. Raskin, "Politics Up-Ends the Bargaining Table," in *Public Workers and Public Unions*, ed. by Sam Zagoria, Englewood Cliffs, N.Y.: Prentice-Hall, 1972, p. 127.

39. Ibid.

40. Bernard Stengren, "Transit Problems Rooted in Politics," *New York Times*, December 24, 1963, p. 18.

41. Ralph Katz, "TWU Strike Off As Quill Defers Testing of Train," *New York Times*, December 14, 1961, p. 1.

42. Thomas R. Brooks, op. cit., p. 53.

43. Peter Kihss, "Cost of Strike Settlement," *New York Times*, January 14, 1966, p. 29.

44. Ibid.

45. Damon Stetson, "Feinsinger Irked by Transit Talks," *New York Times*, December 24, 1965, p. 20.

46. Ibid.

47. Ibid.

48. Ibid.

49. A.H. Raskin, "Politics Up-Ends Bargaining Table," op. cit.

50. Ibid.

51. J.K. Turncott, "Transit Labor in New York 1945-1959," in Theodore

Kheel and J.W. Turncott, *Transit and Arbitration*, Englewood Cliffs, N.J.: Prentice-Hall, 1960, p. 30.

52. Ibid.

53. Ibid.

54. Joshua Freeman, *The Transport Workers Union in New York City 1933-1948*, Ph.D. dissertation, Rutgers University, New Brunswick, N.J., 1983, p. 696.

55. Shirley Quill, *Mike Quill Himself A Memoir*, Greenwich, Conn.: Devin-Adair Publishers, 1985, p. 186.

56. Charles R. Morris, *The Cost of Good Intentions*, New York: W.W. Norton and Co., 1980, p. 87.

57. Ibid.

58. A.H. Raskin, "Politics Up-Ends the Bargaining Table," op. cit.

59. A.H. Raskin, Quoted in Charles R. Morris, op. cit., p. 89.

60. "Mediators Seek City Transit Pact," *New York Times*, December 4, 1961, p. 30.

61. Stanley Levey, "New Year's Transit Crisis Seen Despite City's New Peace Board," *New York Times*, December 7, 1961, p. 1.

62. "Quill Threatens Transit Walkout," *New York Times*, December 9, 1961, p. 1.

63. Ralph Katz, "TWU Strike Off As Kheel Defers Testing of Train," *New York Times*, December 14, 1961, p. 1.

64. Ellis Van Riper, Personal interview held in Van Riper's office at 1980 Broadway, New York, N.Y., March 2, 1970.

65. A.H. Raskin, Personal interview held in Raskin's office at 229 West 43rd Street, New York, N.Y., March 13 and 16, 1970.

66. Stanley Levey, "Strike Averted On City Transit, 15-cent Fare Is Kept," *New York Times*, December 29, 1961, p. 1.

67. Ibid.

68. "Issues in Transit Dispute," *New York Times*, December 27, 1963, p. 12.

69. Margaret Weil, "65-Million Is Added To TWU Demands," *New York Times*, October 3, 1963, p. 1.

70. Margaret Weil, "Subway Fare Rise Is Linked To Pay," *New York Times*, September 25, 1963, p. 25.

71. "Quill Optimistic On Transit Pact," *New York Times*, October 23, 1963, p. 33.

72. Emanuel Perlmutter, "Mayor Asks Speed On Transit Terms," *New York Times*, December 24, 1963, p. 18.

73. Damon Stetson, "Quill Walks Out Of Transit Talks; Gives Ultimatum," *New York Times*, December 29, 1963, p. 1.

74. "New Transit Talks Fail After 6,000 Vote A Walkout," *New York Times*, December 30, 1963, p. 1.

75. Emanuel Perlmutter, "Transit Strike Averted—Hard Bargaining Started 12 Hours Before Deadline," *New York Times*, January 2, 1964, p. 1.

76. Ibid.

77. Ibid.

78. McCandlish Phillips, "Transit Workers Happy It's Over," *New York Times*, January 2, 1964, p. 22.

79. Damon Stetson, "Transit Strike Averted ... 15-cent Fare Is Kept," *New York Times*, January 2, 1964, p. 1.

80. Emanuel Perlmutter, "Picketing Leads To Hasty Talks On Benefits," *New York Times*, January 8, 1964, p. 28.

81. Ibid.

82. Ibid.

83. Damon Stetson, "Quill Asks Union To Back Walkout," *New York Times*, December 25, 1965, p. 11.

84. Alfred Robbins, et al., "The Strike—The Shocking Blunders," *Journal American*, January 16, 1966, p. 18.

85. Timothy Costello, Personal interview held in Costello's office at 250 Broadway, New York, N.Y., December 14, 1966.

86. Emanuel Perlmutter, "Transit Walkout Voted For January 1 If Parleys Fail," *New York Times*, December 27, 1965, p. 1.

87. Ibid.

88. Ibid.

89. Douglas MacMahon, op. cit.

90. Emanuel Perlmutter, "Transit Walkout Voted For January 1 . . . .", op. cit.

91. Ibid.

92. Ibid.

93. Damon Stetson, "Peril To 15-cent Fare Rising Once Again," *New York Times,* November 7, 1965, p. 57.

94. Damon Stetson, "Gilhooley Urges Transit Merger," *New York Times,* November 14, 1965, p. 53.

95. Daniel Scannell, Personal interview held in Scannell's office at 370 Jay Street, Brooklyn, N.Y., December 14, 1966.

96. John O'Donnell, op. cit.

97. Theodore Kheel, Personal interview held in Kheel's office at 250 Park Avenue, New York, N.Y., December 21, 1966.

98. Woody Klein, op. cit.

99. Ibid.

100. Ibid.

101. Ibid.

102. Samuel Kaplan, "Lindsay To Seek Unified Transit," *New York Times,* November 9, 1965, p. 1.

103. "Words On Transit For Mr. Lindsay," *New York Times,* March 13, 1966, Section 4, p. 2.

104. The following discussion is drawn from Robert A. Caro, *The Power Broker: Robert Moses and the Fall of New York,* New York: Alfred A. Knopf, 1974.

105. Damon Stetson, "Transit Officials Plan Court Move to Bar a Strike," *New York Times,* December 29, 1965, p. 1.

106. George Syvertsen, "Lindsay Transit Imperative: No Strike," *Herald Tribune,* December 28, 1965, p. 1.

107. Ibid.

108. Woody Klein, op. cit.

109. Damon Stetson, "Transit Officials Plan Court Move To Bar a Strike," *New York Times,* December 29, 1965, p. 1.

110. Woody Klein, op. cit., p. 42.

111. Damon Stetson, "Financing Issue Delays Progress In Transit Talks," *New York Times,* November 30, 1965, p. 1.

112. Ibid.

113. Ibid.

114. Woody Klein, op. cit., p. 42.

115. Robert E. Dallos, "Businesses Plan For Transit Halt," *New York Times*, December 30, 1965, p. 1.

116. Ibid.

117. Ibid.

118. "Cliffs Edge In Transit," *New York Times*, December 30, 1965, p. 22.

119. Don Flynn, "Lindsay's Last-Day Transit Move," *Herald Tribune*, December 31, 1965, p. 1.

120. Damon Stetson, "Quill on TV Tears Up Court Order in Act of Defiance," *New York Times*, December 31, 1965, p. 1.

121. Ibid.

122. Statement issued by Transit Mediation Panel on December 30, 1965. Seen in TWU Files.

123. Selwyn Raab, "Mediator Tells the Inside Story," *World Telegram*, January 17, 1966, p. 1.

124. Damon Stetson, "Quill on TV Tears Up Court Order....", op. cit.

125. Peter Kihss, "Quill Faces Jail If Strike Occurs," *New York Times*, December 31, 1965, p. 8.

126. Damon Stetson, "Financing Issue Delays Progress of Transit Talks," *New York Times*, December 30, 1965, p. 1.

127. Damon Stetson, "Quill on TV Tears Up Court Order....", op. cit.

128. Robert E. Dallos, "Mayor-Elect Asks Curb on Autos in Case of Strike," *New York Times*, December 31, 1965, p. 8.

129. Ibid.

130. Woody Klein, op. cit.

131. Damon Stetson, "Transit Strike Apparently On....", *New York Times*, January 1, 1966, p. 1.

132. Woody Klein, op. cit.

133. L.H. Whittemore, *The Man Who Ran The Subways: The Story of Mike Quill*, New York: Holt, Rinehart and Winston, 1968, p. 279.

134. Damon Stetson, "Transit Strike Apparently On....", op. cit.

135. Thomas R. Brooks, op. cit., p. 52.

136. Damon Stetson, "Transit Strike Apparently On....", op. cit.

137. L.H. Whittemore, op. cit., p. 280.

138. Murray Schumach, "The Oath Is Taken," *New York Times*, January 1, 1966, p. 1.

139. Roger Starr, "Lindsay: A Political Portrait," *Commentary*, February 1970, p. 21.

140. Warren Weaver, "Big Gamble of John Vliet Lindsay," *New York Times*, May 23, 1965, p. 86.

141. Roger Starr, op. cit.

142. Ibid.

143. Ibid.

144. Nat Hentoff, *A Political Life: The Education of John V. Lindsay*, New York: Alfred A. Knopf, 1969, p. 166.

145. Ibid.

146. Ibid.

147. Larry L. King, "Lindsay of New York," *Harper's Magazine*, August 1968, p. 43.

148. Nat Hentoff, op. cit.

149. Richard Whalen, "This Lindsay Takes on 'That' City," *Fortune*, June 1966, pp. 127-28.

150. Larry L. King, op cit.

151. Ibid.

152. Ibid.

153. Roger Starr, op. cit., p. 29.

154. Ibid.

155. "Lindsay's Candidacy Gives New York GOP New Hope," *Congressional Quarterly Weekly Report*, June 18, 1965, p. 1187.

156. Ibid.

157. Ibid.

158. Ibid.

159. Daniel Button, *Lindsay: A Man For Tomorrow*, New York: Random House, 1965, p. 26.

160. Roger Starr, op. cit., p. 32.

161. Ibid.

Chapter 4

1. Damon Stetson, "Transit Strike Apparently On....", *New York Times*, January 1, 1966, p. 1.

2. Ibid.

3. Ibid.

4. Ibid.

5. Thomas R. Brooks, "Lindsay, Quill and the Transit Strike," *Commentary*, March 1966.

6. Woody Klein, *Lindsay's Promise—The Dream That Failed*, New York: Macmillan, 1970, p. 49.

7. Ibid.

8. Ibid.

9. Ibid.

10. Ibid.

11. Damon Stetson, op. cit.

12. Ibid.

13. Ibid.

14. Daniel Scannell, Personal interview held in Scannell's office at 370 Jay Street, Brooklyn, N.Y., on December 14, 1966.

15. Ellis Van Riper, Personal interview held in Van Riper's office at 1980 Broadway, New York, N.Y., on February 27, 1970.

16. Edward Herlihy, Personal interview held in Herlihy's office at 250 Broadway, New York, N.Y., March 11, 1970.

17. A.H. Raskin, "Lindsay and Labor," *New York Times*, September 29, 1968, Section 4, p. 3.

18. John O'Connell, Personal interview held in O'Connell's office at 1980 Broadway, New York, N.Y., March 3, 1970.

19. Daniel Scannell, op. cit.

20. Matthew Guinan, Personal interview held in Guinan's office at 1980 Broadway, New York, N.Y., March 4, 1970.

21. Damon Stetson, op. cit.

22. Woody Klein, op. cit.

23. "Strict Rules Set On Travel Into The City During Strike," *New York Times*, January 1, 1966, p. 1.

24. Terrence Smith, "City Prepares To Help Stranded Transit Riders," *New York Times*, January 1, 1966, p. 1.

25. Bernard Weinbraub, "Wagner's Slip Off On a Mexican Trip," *New York Times*, January 1, 1966.

26. "Editorial," *New York Times*, January 1, 1966, p. 16.

27. Damon Stetson, op. cit.

28. "Storage of Trains Begins Smoothly," *New York Times*, January 2, 1966, p. 59.

29. Woody Klein, op. cit., p. 53.

30. "Mediators Trying For Joint Talks," *New York Times*, January 2, 1966, p. 1.

31. Ibid.

32. Don Flynn and Rasa Gustaitis, "Strike-Crisis Talks Resume Today....," *Herald Tribune*, January 2, 1966, p. 1.

33. Edward N. Costikyan, "Who Runs New York," *New York*, December 23, 1968, p. 25.

34. "Mediators Trying For Joint Talks," op. cit.

35. Ibid.

36. L.H. Whittemore, *The Man Who Ran The Subways; The Story of Mike Quill*, New York: Holt, Rinehart and Winston, 1968.

37. "Transcript of Mayor Lindsay's Statement On The Transit Strike," *New York Times*, January 2, 1966, p. 59.

38. Ibid.

39. Woody Klein, op. cit., p. 54.

40. Ibid.

41. Ibid.

42. Ibid.

43. "Text of Lindsay's Inaugural Address at City Hall," *New York Times*, January 2, 1966, p. 56.

44. William Borders, "4,000 Dance Gaily at Mayor's Ball," *New York Times*, January 2, 1966, p. 56.

45. Bernard Weinraub, "Many Dismayed By Transit Tie-Up," *New York Times*, January 2, 1966, p. 59.

46. Ibid.

47. "Bicycle Rentals Soar As Result of Strike," *New York Times*, January 2, 1966, p. 59.

48. Weinraub, op. cit.

49. Ralph Blumenthal, "Even the Pickets Get There On Foot," *New York Times*, January 2, 1966, p. 59.

50. Note from the Americana Hotel of New York to people staying in their hotel; dated January 1, 1966. Seen in TWU files.

51. Emanuel Perlmutter, "Transit Board Questions Good Faith of Union's Offer," *New York Times*, January 3, 1966, p. 1.

52. Ibid.

53. Homer Bigart, "Lindsay Bids Workers Stay at Home," op. cit.

54. L.H. Whittemore, op. cit., p. 285.

55. Homer Bigart, "Lindsay Bids Workers Stay at Home," op. cit.

56. Ibid.

57. L.H. Whittemore, op. cit., p. 286.

58. John Noble Wilford, "Thousands Vent Grievances on Transit Dispute," *New York Times*, January 3, 1966, p. 18.

59. Raymond H. Anderson, "Lindsay Sets A Brisk Example By Walking 3 Miles To City Hall," *New York Times*, January 3, 1966, p. 17.

60. Ibid.

61. Ralph Blumenthal, "Mayor Tours City Control Post and Urges Caller to Stay Home," *New York Times*, January 3, 1966, p. 17.

62. Woody Klein, op. cit., p. 57.

63. Ralph Blumenthal, op. cit.

64. Woody Klein, op. cit., p. 59.

65. Homer Bigart, "Lindsay Bids Workers Stay at Home," op. cit.

66. Woody Klein, op. cit., p. 60.

67. "Transcript of Mayor Lindsay's Statement and News Conference," *New York Times*, January 3, 1966, p. 16.

68. Homer Bigart, "Lindsay Bids Workers Stay at Home," op. cit.

69. Philip H. Dougherty, "Walkout Snarles Holiday Return," *New York Times*, January 3, 1966, p. 18.

70. Irving Spiegel, "Pickets On The March Despite The Rain," *New York Times*, January 3, 1966, p. 17.

71. Bernard Weinraub, "City's Police Put In A 12-Hour Day," *New York Times*, January 3, 1966, p. 1.

72. Ibid.

73. Ibid.

74. Robert E. Dallos, "Hotels Filling Up For Duration; Elsewhere Crowds Are Thin," *New York Times*, January 3, 1966, p. 18.

75. John H. Allan, "Business Awaits Strike's Impact," *New York Times*, January 3, 1966, p. 18.

76. Ibid.

77. Robert E. Dallos, op. cit.

78. Joseph E. Ingraham, "50 Inspectors Set To Check Cabbies on Overcharging," *New York Times*, January 3, 1966, p. 18.

79. John Noble Wilford, op. cit.

80. Damon Stetson, "Quill Held In Contempt, Faces Jail Today," *New York Times*, January 4, 1966, p. 1.

81. Ibid.

82. Ibid.

83. Ibid.

84. Ibid.

85. Ibid.

86. "Excerpts From Quill's Radio Interview," *New York Times*, January 4, 1966, p. 17.

87. Murray Schumach, "13 Union Chiefs Supporting Quill," *New York Times*, January 4, 1966, p. 14.

88. "After 3-Mile Hike, Lindsay Uses Car and Gives 7 A Lift," *New York Times*, January 4, 1966, p. 14.

89. Woody Klein, op. cit., p. 60.

90. "Editorial," *New York Times*, January 3, 1966, p. 26.

91. Woody Klein, op. cit., p. 61.

92. Ibid., p. 62.

93. "Mayor Crosses Bridge Before He Comes To It," *New York Times*, January 4, 1966, p. 14.

94. Woody Klein, op. cit., p. 64.

95. Jack Newfield and Paul DuBrul, *The Permanent Government—Who Really Runs New York?*, New York: The Pilgrim Press, 1981, p. 137.

96. "Excerpts From the Mayor's 11 A.M. News Conference," *New York Times*, January 4, 1966, p. 17.

97. Jack Gould, "TV: 2 Disparate Personalities In The Transit Crisis," *New York Times*, January 4, 1966, p. 55.

98. Douglas Kneeland, "People With A Will Find A Way To Work," *New York Times*, January 4, 1966, p. 1.

99. Ibid.

100. Peter Kihss, "Doors at 2 Rail Stations Locked For Time In Crush," *New York Times*, January 4, 1966, p. 1.

101. Ibid.

102. Philip H. Dougherty, "Strike No Bonanza For Cabbies....," *New York Times*, January 4, 1966, p. 14.

103. Douglas Kneeland, op. cit.

104. Paul Hoffman, "Cots in Armories Aid The Stranded," *New York Times*, January 4, 1966, p. 17.

105. Bernard Weinraub, "Bronx Commuters Slow Down As Subway Stalls," *New York Times*, January 4, 1966, p. 15.

106. "Retailers' Losses Put at 35-Million," *New York Times*, January 4, 1966, p. 1.

107. Dan Dorfman, "A Disastrous Day For The City's Department Stores," *Herald Tribune*, January 4, 1966, p. 7.

108. Homer Bigart, "Retailers' Losses Put At 35-Million," op. cit.

109. Dan Dorfman, op. cit.

110. Homer Bigart, "Retailers' Losses Put At 35-Million," op. cit.

111. Ibid.

112. "New York's Transit Strike Leaders Ordered Jailed," *Wall Street Journal*, January 4, 1966, p. 2.

113. "Shows Go On, But Business Suffers," *New York Times*, January 4, 1966, p. 17.

114. Ronald Sullivan, "New Yorkers Win Wagner's Praise," *New York Times*, January 4, 1966, p. 17.

Chapter 5

1. Fred Ferretti, "Quill's Jail Collapse Embitters Strikers," *Herald Tribune*, January 5, 1966, p. 1.

2. Murray Schumach, "Union Chief Irate," *New York Times*, January 5, 1966, p. 1.

3. Fred Ferretti, op. cit.

4. "TWU's Quill Is Jailed," *Wall Street Journal*, January 5, 1966, p. 2.

5. L.H. Whittemore, *The Man Who Ran The Subways; The Story of Mike Quill*, New York: Holt, Rinehart and Winston, 1968, p. 290.

6. Murray Schumach, "Quill Jailed, Falls Ill, Taken To Hospital," *New York Times*, January 5, 1966, p. 1.

7. Ibid.

8. Fred Ferretti, op. cit.

9. Ibid.

10. Ibid.

11. Murray Schumach, "Quill Jailed, Falls Ill....," op. cit.

12. L.H. Whittemore, op. cit., p. 291.

13. Fred Ferretti, op. cit.

14. Murray Schumach, "Union Chief Irate," op. cit.

15. Fred Ferretti, op. cit.

16. L.H. Whittemore, op. cit., p. 293.

17. Ibid., p. 6.

18. Ibid., p. 9.

19. Joshua Freeman, "Catholics, Communists, and Republicans: Irish Workers and the Organization of the Transport Workers Union," in *Working Class America*, ed. by Michael H. Frische and Daniel J. Walkowitz, Urbana: University of Illinois Press, 1983, p. 257.

20. Ibid., p. 257.

21. Ibid., p. 262.

22. L.H. Whittemore, op. cit., p. 25.

23. Ibid., pp. 38-40.

24. Shirley Quill, *Mike Quill Himself A Memoir*, Greenwich, Conn.: Devin-Adair Publishers, 1985, p. 63.

25. Joshua Freeman, op. cit., p. 265.

26. Joshua Freeman, *The Transport Workers Union in New York City 1933-1948*, Ph.D. dissertation, Rutgers University, New Brunswick, N.J., 1983, p. 120.

27. Shirley Quill, op. cit., p. 63.

28. Joshua Freeman, "Catholics, Communists....," op. cit., p. 266.

29. L.H. Whittemore, op. cit., p. 42.

30. Joshua Freeman, Ph.D. dissertation, op. cit., p. 256.

31. Mark K. Maier, *City Unions, Managing Discontent in New York City*, New Brunswick, N.J.: Rutgers University Press, 1987, p. 17.

32. Joshua Freeman, "Catholics, Communists....," op. cit., p. 259.

33. Ibid., p. 260.

34. L.H. Whittemore, op. cit., p. 82.

35. Ibid., p. 93.

36. Ibid., p. 95.

37. Ibid., pp. 102-03.

38. Ibid., p. 104.

39. Ibid., p. 126.

40. Ibid., p. 126.

41. Ibid., p. 224.

42. Ibid., p. 39.

43. Joshua Freeman, "Catholics, Communists....," op. cit., p. 271.

44. L.H. Whittemore, op. cit., p. 39.

45. Joshua Freeman, "Catholics, Communists....," op. cit., p. 258.

46. Ibid., p. 272.

47. L.H. Whittemore, op. cit., p. 170.

48. Murray Schumach, "2 Faces of Quill: Public and Private," *New York Times*, January 2, 1966, p. 1.

49. Shirley Quill, op. cit., p. 119.

50. Murray Schumach, "2 Faces of Quill....," op. cit., p. 1.

51. From Quill's "Political Platform," when running for City Council in 1943. Included in TWU collection, Papers of Michael Quill, Councilmanic Pre-Sort, 1937-1944, Box No. 17, Tammiment Library, New York University.

52. Ibid.

53. L.H. Whittemore, op. cit., p. 78.

54. Ibid., p. 225.

55. Shirley Quill, op. cit., p. 296.

56. Ibid., pp. 296-297.

57. L.H. Whittemore, op. cit., p. 247.

58. Ibid., p. 251.

59. Ibid., p. 232.

60. Ibid., pp. 253-61.

61. Shirley Quill, op. cit., p. 277.

62. L.H. Whittemore, op. cit., p. 260.

63. "Transcript of Mayor's Statement," *New York Times*, January 11, 1966, p. 23.

64. John O'Donnell, Personal interview held in O'Donnell's office at 501 Fifth Avenue, New York, N.Y., December 19, 1968.

65. Steven V. Roberts, "Transit Agency Wary of Making Martyr of Quill," *New York Times*, January 4, 1966, p. 14.

66. Jimmy Breslin, "The Talkers, the Brave Ones, The Smart Ones... The Victims," *Herald Tribune*, January 9, 1966, p. 10.

67. Fern Marja Eckman, "Douglas MacMahon: Quill's Second Line," *New York Post*, January 9, 1966, p. 24.

68. Joshua Freeman, Ph.D. dissertation, op. cit., p. 140.

69. Shirley Quill, op. cit., pp. 200-201.

70. Edith Evans Asbury, "Man Who Takes Up Quill Baton Was Once His Foe," *New York Times*, January 5, 1966, p. 14.

71. Fern Marja Eckman, op. cit.

Chapter 6

1. "Hard Position Is Adopted By Union's 'Second Line'—No Progress In Talks," *New York Times*, January 5, 1966, p. 1.

2. Ibid.

3. Damon Stetson, "No Progress In Talks," *New York Times*, January 5, 1966, p. 1.

4. "Hard Position Is Adopted....," op. cit.

5. Woody Klein, *Lindsay's Promise—The Dream That Failed*, New York: MacMillan, 1970, pp. 66-67.

6. Fred Ferretti, "Quill's Jail Collapse Embitters Strikers," *Herald Tribune*, January 5, 1966, p. 1.

7. "Mediator," *The New Yorker*, January 22, 1966, p. 23.

8. Robert E. Dallos, "Defiant Pickets Supporting Quill," *New York Times*, January 5. 1966, p. 14.

9. Woody Klein, op. cit., p. 66.

10. Douglas E. Kneeland, "People Return To City, But Holiday Moon Is Over," *New York Times*, January 5, 1966, p. 16.

11. Peter Kihss, "Auto-Train Crisis Is More Serious," *New York Times*, January 5, 1966, p. 1.

12. Ibid.

13. Homer Bigart, "$100-Million Loss Each Day Is Seen," *New York Times*, January 5, 1966, p. 1.

14. Ibid.

15. Ibid.

16. Douglas E. Kneeland, op. cit.

17. Homer Bigart, op. cit.

18. Ibid.

19. Ibid.

20. "Most Schools Reopen, But Absenteeism Is High," *New York Times*, January 5, 1966, p. 15.

21. Eric Pace, "City's Blood Bank Dwindling...," *New York Times*, January 5, 1966, p. 1.

22. "Strike Halts Malcolm X Case," *New York Times*, January 5, 1966, p. 16.

23. Douglas Robinson, "Rock 'n Roll Producers Suing Transport Union....," *New York Times*, January 5, 1966, p. 14.

24. David R. Jones, "Strike....," *New York Times*, January 5, 1966, p. 17.

25. "Hard Position Is Adopted....," op. cit.

26. Ralph Blumenthal, "Absentees Can Get Jobless Benefits," *New York Times*, January 5, 1966, p. 1.

27. Richard Witkin, "Wagner's Early Departure Irks Some Liberals," *New York Times*, January 5, 1966, p. 17.

28. Damon Stetson, "Lindsay Sees 'Movement' In Transit Talks—Mayor Pressing," *New York Times*, January 6, 1966, p. 1.

29. Don Flynn, "Lindsay Reports New Transit Offers," *Herald Tribune*, January 6, 1966, p. 1.

30. Douglas MacMahon, Personal interview held in MacMahon's office at 1980 Broadway, New York, N.Y., December 22, 1966.

31. Damon Stetson, "Lindsay Sees 'Movement' In Transit Talks....," op. cit.

32. Murray Schumach, "Quill Is Reported 'Markedly' Better," *New York Times*, January 6, 1966, p. 1.

33. Ibid.

34. Ibid.

35. Sydney Schanberg, "Governor Scored In Transit Strike," *New York Times*, January 6, 1966, p. 13.

36. Ibid.

37. "Now Quill Has Rocky Doing It," *Herald Tribune*, January 6, 1966, p. 8.

38. Peter Kihss, "Four Areas South of 59th Street....," *New York Times*, January 6, 1966, p. 1.

39. "President Asked To Enter Strike," *New York Times*, January 6, 1966, p. 1.

40. John Pomfret, "President Voices Concern On Strike, Guidance Needed," *New York Times*, January 6, 1966, p. 1.

41. Homer Bigart, "President Asked To Enter Strike," op. cit.

42. Ibid.

43. Douglas MacMahon, op. cit.

44. Don Flynn and Jerome Zukosky, "Mayor Talks To TA About Quill Release....," *Herald Tribune*, January 7, 1966, p. 1.

45. Douglas Kiker, "Johnson Strategy In Helping Linsday," *Herald Tribune*, January 7, 1966, p. 1.

46. Damon Stetson, "Johnson Sends Wirtz To Transit Parley....," *New York Times*, January 7, 1966, p. 1.

47. Ibid.

48. Don Flynn and Jerome Zukosky, op. cit.

49. Damon Stetson, "Johnson Sends Wirtz To Transit Parley....," op. cit.

50. Murray Schumach, "Doctor Says Quill Had Minor Setback," *New York Times*, January 7, 1966, p. 1.

51. Damon Stetson, "Johnson Sends Wirtz To Transit Parley....," op. cit.

52. Peter Kihss, "Roads Jammed 6-1/2 Hours....," *New York Times*, January 7, 1966, p. 1.

53. Michael Stern, "Drizzle and Breakdowns Add To Problems," *New York Times*, January 7, 1966, p. 17.

54. Ibid.

55. Douglas Kneeland, "Staggered-Hours Plan Fails To Ease Traffic Jam," *New York Times*, January 7, 1966, p. 17.

56. Ibid.

57. Homer Bigart, "Daily Cost To City Put At $6-Million," *New York Times*, January 7, 1966, p. 1.

58. Ibid.

59. "Transit Unit Docks 2,500....," *New York Times*, January 7, 1966, p. 16.

60. Homer Bigart, "Daily Cost To City Put At $6-Million," op. cit.

61. Robert Alden, "Stores In Midtown Reel Under Losses They Lay To Strike," *New York Times*, January 7, 1966, p. 16.

62. "Many Draftees Decline To Fight The Strike," *New York Times*, January 7, 1966, p. 17.

63. Fred Hechinger, "Nearest Schools Open To Students," *New York Times*, January 7, 1966.

64. Steven V. Roberts, "How Do I Get To?....," *New York Times*, January 7, 1966, p. 17.

65. Terrence Smith, "Big Lindsay Week Ruined By Strike," *New York Times*, January 7, 1966, p. 34.

66. Ibid.

67. Homer Bigart, "Quill Threatens December 15 Walkout....," *New York Times*, December 3, 1965, p. 1.

68. Damon Stetson, "Transit Board Seeks $322,000-a-Day Fine....," *New York Times*, January 8, 1966, p. 1.

69. Selwyn Raab, "Mediator Tells Inside Story," *World Telegram*, January 17, 1966, p. 1.

70. Damon Stetson, "Transit Board Seeks $322,000-a-Day Fine....," op. cit.

71. "TA Won't Free Quill, Asks Union Fines," *Herald Tribune*, January 8, 1966, p. 1.

72. Damon Stetson, "Transit Board Seeks $322,000-a-Day Fine....," op. cit.

73. Emanuel Perlmutter, "MacMahon Blocked Move To Free Nine," *New York Times*, January 13, 1966, p. 20.

74. Douglas MacMahon, op. cit.

75. Thomas R. Brooks, "Lindsay, Quill and The Transit Strike," *Commentary*, March 1966, p. 54.

76. Murray Schumach, "Unions Maintain Silence On Strike," *New York Times*, January 3, 1966, p. 1.

77. Ibid.

78. Murray Schumach, "13 Union Chiefs Supporting Quill," *New York Times*, January 4, 1966, p. 14.

79. *TWU Express*, February 1966, p. 14.

80. Ibid.

81. Ibid.

82. Emanuel Perlmutter, "Labor Increases Backing Of Strike," *New York Times*, January 5, 1966, p. 14.

83. Ibid.

84. *TWU Express*, February 1966, p. 13.

85. Emanuel Perlmutter, "Labor Increases Backing of Strike," op. cit.

86. *TWU Express*, February 1966, p. 14.

87. Emanuel Perlmutter, "Labor Increases Backing of Strike," op. cit.

88. David R. Jones, "Wirtz Finding; Keep Bargaining," *New York Times*, January 8, 1966, p. 10.

89. Damon Stetson, "Transit Board Seeks $322,000-a-Day Fine....," op. cit.

90. Ibid.

91. "TA Won't Free Quill," *Herald Tribune*, January 8, 1966, p. 1.

92. Murray Schumach, "Hospital Refuses To Discuss Quill," *New York Times*, January 8, 1966, p. 10.

93. Martin Arnold, "2 Bridges and Tube Are Made One-Way In The Evening Rush," *New York Times*, January 8, 1966, p. 1.

94. Ibid.

95. Ibid.

96. Homer Bigart, "Rockefeller Requests Aid and Johnson Acts Quickly," *New York Times*, January 8, 1966, p. 1.

97. George Syvertsen and Paul Weissman, "City Assesses Workers' Loss In Strike," *Herald Tribune*, January 6, 1966, p. 8.

98. Homer Bigart, "Rockefeller Requests Aid and Johnson Acts Quickly," op. cit.

99. Leonard Katz and Helen Dudar, "Harlem Is Hit Hard By Strike, Faces Chaos," *New York Post*, January 6, 1966, p. 4.

100. Ibid.

101. Thomas Buckley, "Harlem's Pay Day No Gay Time As Strike Shrinks Pocket Books," *New York Times*, January 8, 1966, p. 11.

102. Ibid.

103. Ibid.

104. Seymour Krim, "Melancholia In Garment Center," *Herald Tribune*, January 12, 1966, p. 1.

105. Thomas Buckley, op. cit.

106. Robert Shelton, "One Comedian Meets Race Issue Squarely In Act," *New York Times*, December 31, 1965, p. 11.

107. Leonard Katz and Helen Dudar, op. cit.

108. Thomas Buckley, op. cit.

109. Ibid.

110. Ibid.

111. Paul Hoffman, "Student Shifting Works Smoothly," *New York Times*, January 8, 1966, p. 1.

112. Ibid.

113. Homer Bigart, "Rockefeller Requests Aid And Johnson Acts....," op. cit.

Chapter 7

1. Francis Sugrue, "Bus Drivers' Consensus—100 Percent Behind Quill," *Herald Tribune*, January 9, 1966, p. 11.

2. Victor Gotbaum, "Collective Bargaining and the Union Leader," in Sam Zagoria, ed., *Public Workers and Public Unions*, Englewood Cliffs, N.J.: Prentice-Hall, 1972, p. 78.

3. In an open shop, all workers are represented by the union, but union membership is optional.

4. Victor Gotbaum, op. cit.

5. Edward Sussna, "Collective Bargaining On The New York City Transit System, 1940-1957," *Industrial and Labor Relations Review*, 11 (July 1958), p. 522.

6. L.H. Whittemore, *The Man Who Ran The Subways, The Story of Mike Quill*, New York: Holt, Rinehart and Winston, 1968, pp. 211-12.

7. Ibid.

8. Theodore Kheel, "Introduction: Background and History," in Lawrence Chickering, ed., *Public Employee Unions*, Lexington, Mass.: Lexington Books, 1976, p. 7.

9. Edward Sussna, op. cit., p. 530.

10. Ibid., p. 532.

11. L.H. Whittemore, op. cit., p. 188.

12. Ibid., p. 187.

13. Ibid.

14. Leonard Ingalls, "TWU Gets Wide Support In Transit Workers' Voting," *New York Times*, June 26, 1954, p. 1.

15. Ibid.

16. L.H. Whittemore, op. cit., p. 213.

17. Ibid., p. 213.

18. Ibid., p. 214.

19. Ibid.

20. Ibid.

21. "Walkout in 1956 Delayed 750,000," *New York Times*, December 9, 1957, p. 28.

22. L.H. Whittemore, op. cit., p. 215.

23. Ibid.

24. Ibid., p. 217.

25. Ibid., p. 218.

26. Ibid., p. 217.

27. Emanuel Perlmutter, "7 Craft Unions Unite In Strike," *New York Times*, December 10, 1957, p. 1.

28. Emanuel Perlmutter, "Motormen Retort, Walkout Goes On," *New York Times*, December 11, 1957, p. 26.

29. Emanuel Perlmutter, "7 Craft Unions Unite In Strike," op. cit.

30. "Quill Sees 'Bluff' In Strike Threat," *New York Times*, December 9, 1957, p. 28.

31. Emanuel Perlmutter, "7 Craft Unions Unite In Strike," op. cit.

32. Emanuel Perlmutter, "Strikers Assert 'Low' Pay Is Issue," *New York Times*, December 12, 1957, p. 25.

33. A.H. Raskin, "Motormen Ask To See Wagner," *New York Times*, December 13, 1957, p. 1.

34. Stanley Levey, "Wagner Widens His Plan To End Subway Walkout," *New York Times*, December 15, 1957, p. 1.

35. Ibid.

36. "Transit Vote Today Tests Quill Strength," *New York Times*, December 16, 1957, p. 1.

37. "Text of Zelano's Appeal," *New York Times*, December 14, 1957, p. 15.

38. Peter Kihss, "TWU Re-Elected," *New York Times*, December 17, 1957, p. 1.

39. Leo Egan, "Republican Labor Coup," *New York Times*, December 17, 1957, p. 38.

40. Emanuel Perlmutter, "Motormen View Terms As Victory," *New York Times*, December 17, 1957, p. 38.

41. Edward Sussna, op. cit., p. 525.

42. Albert Lincoln, "The New York City Transit Strike: An Explanatory Approach," *Public Policy 16*, Cambridge, Mass.: Harvard University Press, 1967.

43. Stanley Levey, "2 Transit Unions Will Merge Here," *New York Times*, August 29, 1958, p. 1.

44. Stanley Levey, "TWU Wins Again In Transit Balloting," *New York Times*, May 28, 1959, p. 1.

45. "1,000 TWU Men Denounce Contract," *New York Times*, January 7, 1964, p. 39.

46. Harold W. Davey, Mario F. Bognanno, and David L. Estenson, *Contemporary Collective Bargaining*, Englewood Cliffs, N.J.: Prentice-Hall, 1986, p. 233.

47. Arthur M. Ross, *Trade Union Wage Policy*, Berkeley: University of California Press, 1948, p. 38.

48. See, for example, Seymour Martin Lipset and Martin Trow, "Reference Group Theory and Trade Union Policy," in Mirray Komarovsky, ed., *Common Frontiers of the Social Sciences*, Glencoe, Illinois: The Free Press, 1957.

49. Charles R. Perry, *Collective Bargaining and the Decline of the United Mine Workers*, Philadelphia: Industrial Research Unit, The Wharton School, University of Pennsylvania, 1984, p. 108.

50. Harry Katz, *Shifting Gears: Changing Labor Relations in the U.S. Automobile Industry*, Cambridge, Mass.: The MIT Press, 1985, p. 36.

51. Jacob Kaufman, *Collective Bargaining in the Railroad Industry*, New York: Russell and Russell, 1952, pp. 46-48.

52. Emanuel Perlmutter, "City Rights Aide Scored On Hiring," *New York Times*, June 12, 1963, p. 26.

53. Emanuel Perlmutter, "Negroes Seeking Top Transit Jobs," *New York Times*, February 17, 1968, p. 14.

54. Alfred Robbins, et al., "The Strike—The Shocking Blunders," *Journal American*, January 16, 1966, p. 18.

55. Joseph Carnegie, Chairman of the Rank-and-File Committee for a Democratic Union Within the NYCTA, "Letter to the Editor," *New York Times*, December 3, 1969, p. 54.

56. "Transit Workers Form Rights Unit," *New York Times*, June 9, 1963, p. 63.

57. Ibid.

Chapter 8

1. "Strike Talks Show Gains," *New York Times*, January 9, 1966, p. 1.

2. Ibid.

3. Don Flynn and Rasa Gustaitis, "It's Critical and Essential To End Transit Strike By Tonight," *Herald Tribune*, January 9, 1966, p. 1.

4. Ibid.

5. Terrence Smith, "Mayor Chats With Victims of Strike," *New York Times*, January 9, 1966, p. 1.

6. Don Flynn and Rasa Gustaitis, op. cit.

7. Ibid.

8. Ibid.

9. Terrence Smith, op. cit.

10. Don Flynn and Rasa Gustaitis, op. cit.

11. "Quill Called Better, Police Are Alerted By A Bomb Scare," *New York Times*, January 9, 1966, p. 42.

12. Thomas Buckley, "New Yorkers Relax And Traffic Eases After Hectic Week," *New York Times*, January 9, 1966, p.1.

13. Ibid.

14. "Boats Will Give Free Ride To Job For Staffs of 7 Hospitals Here," *New York Times*, January 9, 1966, p. 42.

15. George Dugan, "2 Rabbis Assail Union's Position," *New York Times*, January 9, 1966, p. 43.

16. Emanuel Perlmutter, "Joint Talks Held," *New York Times*, January 10, 1966, p. 1.

17. Daniel Scannell, Personal interview held in Scannell's office at 370 Jay Street, Brooklyn, N.Y., December 14, 1966.

18. Douglas MacMahon, Personal interview held in MacMahon's office at 1980 Broadway, New York, N.Y., December 22, 1966.

19. Selwyn Raab, "Mediator Tells The Inside Story," *World Telegram*, January 17, 1966.

20. Douglas MacMahon, op. cit.

21. Timothy Costello, Personal interview held in Costello's office at 250 Broadway, New York, N.Y., December 14, 1966.

22. Richard Madden, "Gilhooley Scores City-Transit Plan As Power Grab," *New York Times*, March 12, 1966, p. 1.

23. Ibid.

24. Thomas R. Brooks, "Lindsay, Quill and the Transit Strike," *Commentary*, March 1966, p. 55.

25. Theodore Kheel, Personal interview held in Kheel's office at 250 Park Avenue, New York, N.Y., December 21, 1966.

26. Thomas R. Brooks, op. cit., p. 55.

27. Ibid.

28. Daniel Scannell, op. cit.

29. Richard Witkin, "Turning Point: Late Sunday Night," New York Times, January 14, 1966, p. 29.

30. A Edward Schneyer, Personal interview held in Schneyer's office at 370 Jay Street, Brooklyn, N.Y., December 7, 1966.

31. Daniel Scannell, op. cit.

32. Matthew Guinan, Personal interview held in Guinan's office at 1980 Broadway, New York, N.Y., March 4, 1970.

33. Edward Herlihy, Personal interview held in Herlihy's office at 250 Broadway, New York, N.Y., March 11, 1970.

34. This statement was corroborated in interviews by two "active" participants in the negotiations. Neither wished to be cited as the source of the quote.

35. Thomas R. Brooks, op. cit.

36. Ibid.

37. Damon Stetson, "Talks at Impasse," New York Times, January 11, 1966, p. 1.

38. Michael T. Kaufman, "3 Pickets At Jail For Union Chiefs," New York Times, January 10, 1966, p. 12.

39. Ibid.

40. Peter Kihss, "Traffic Rules Altered," New York Times, January 10, 1966, p. 1.

41. Raymond H. Anderson, "Small-Business Owners Rush To U.S. Loan Office," New York Times, January 10, 1966, p. 1.

42. "Its Impact Staggers....," Wall Street Journal, January 10, 1966, p. 1.

43. Ibid.

44. Robert Alden, "Impact of Strike Felt Across the U.S.," New York Times, January 11, 1966, p. 1.

45. Samuel Lubell, "Any Settlement of the Strike Will Leave Bitterness," World Telegram, January 10, 1966, p. 3.

46. Fred Ferretti, "Strikers Rally, 12,00 Strong," *Herald Tribune*, January 11, 1966, p. 1.

47. Ibid.

48. Fred Ferretti, "Strikers Rally, 12,000 Strong," op. cit.

49. Ibid.

50. Woody Klein, *Lindsay's Promise—The Dream That Failed*, New York: MacMillan, 1970, p. 71.

51. "Transcript of Lindsay's Opening Statement at His News Conference Yesterday," *New York Times*, January 11, 1966, p. 16.

52. Ibid.

53. Ibid.

54. Theodore Kheel, op. cit.

55. Timothy Costello, op. cit.

56. Ibid.

57. Ibid.

58. Douglas MacMahon, op. cit.

59. A. Edward Schneyer, op. cit.

60. Theodore Kheel, op. cit.

61. Emanuel Perlmutter, "Price Visited Imprisoned Quill....," *New York Times*, January 18, 1966, p. 1.

62. Ibid.

63. Ibid.

64. John O'Donnell, Personal interview held in O'Donnell's office at 501 Fifth Avenue, New York, N.Y., December 19, 1966.

65. A.H. Raskin, "Why New York Is 'Strike City,' " *New York Times Magazine*, December 22, 1968, p. 7.

66. Ibid.

67. Nicholas Peleggi, "Rules of the Power Game," *New York*, December 23, 1968, p. 33.

68. A.H. Raskin, "Why New York Is 'Strike City,' " op. cit., p. 7.

69. Ibid.

70. Ibid.

71. "Mayor Demands," *New York Times*, January 11, 1966, p. 1.

72. Ibid.

73. Ibid.

74. "Record Traffic Jam," *New York Times*, January 11, 1966, p. 1.

75. Ibid.

76. Richard Witkin, "Further Strike Action Weighed....," *New York Times*, January 11, 1966, p. 17.

77. Leonard Buder, " 'Outside' Students Jam High Schools," *New York Times*, January 11, 1966, p. 17.

78. Bernard Weintraub, "Jobless Claims Show Sharp Rise," *New York Times*, January 11, 1966, p. 16.

79. Michael Kaufman, "Transit Strikers Tighten Budgets in Lieu of Any Aid," *New York Times*, January 11, 1966, p. 16.

80. Judy Michaelson, "One Striker's Solution: Raise The Fare," *New York Post*, January 11, 1966, p. 15.

81. Michael Kaufman, op. cit.

82. "Strike Deadlock," *New York Times*, January 12, 1966, p. 1.

83. "Meany Predicts Quick Strike End," *New York Times*, January 12, 1966, p. 17.

84. Ibid.

85. Dom Bonafede, "Meany Offers Assistance To Union....," *Herald Tribune*, January 12, 1966, p. 1.

86. "Meany Predicts Quick Strike End," op. cit.

87. Dom Bonafede, op. cit.

88. Robert Alden, "Business Groups Demand Drastic Strike Action," *New York Times*, January 12, 1966, p. 1.

89. Ibid.

90. Ibid.

91. Peter Kihss, "5th and Madison Avenues Become One Way Friday," *New York Times*, January 12, 1966, p. 1.

92. Ibid.

93. "New Yorkers Clamber Onto Anything Afloat," *Wall Street Journal*, January 12, 1966, p. 12.

94. "Advertisers Appeal To Walk Weary New Yorkers....," *Advertising Age*, January 10, 1966, p. 78.

95. Thomas Buckley, "Traffic Directed By Policewomen," *New York Times*, January 12, 1966, p. 1.

96. "Editorial—This Beleaguered City," *New York Times*, January 12, 1966, p. 20.

97. Eric Pace, "Police Overtime—$2-Million A Week," *New York Times*, January 12, 1966, p. 17.

98. Leonard Buder, "City Fears A Prolonged Strike Could Hurt College Aspirants," *New York Times*, January 12, 1966, p. 16.

99. Ibid.

100. Marshall Peck, "Jobless Aid Due For Each Day Missed," *Herald Tribune*, January 12, 1966, p. 6.

101. John Sibley, "Governor Speeds Jobless Aid Here," *New York Times*, January 12, 1966, p. 1.

102. "City Employees Told Absence Will Count On Sick Leave Time," *New York Times*, January 12, 1966, p. 17.

103. "Strike Rivals Unite To Fight Condon-Wadlin Suit," *New York Times*, January 12, 1966, p. 16.

104. Ibid.

105. John C. Devlin, "2 Transit Unions Report On Assets," *New York Times*, January 12, 1966, p. 16.

Chapter 9

1. Damon Stetson, "Package Is Put AT $52-Million," *New York Times*, January 13, 1966, p. 1.

2. Peter Kihss, "Panel Proposes Pay Rises To 15%," *New York Times*, January 13, 1966, p. 1.

3. Martin Steadman and Don Flynn, "We Roll For $60-Million," *Herald Tribune*, January 13, 1966, p. 1.

4. Woody Klein, *Lindsay's Promise—The Dream That Failed*, New York: MacMillan, 1970, p. 73.

5. Terrence Smith, "Kennedy Is Critical of Lindsay's Timing On Strike," *New York Times*, January 13, 1966, p. 20.

6. Woody Klein, op. cit.

7. Terence Smith, op. cit.

8. "Transit Strike Accord Is Reached," *New York Times*, January 13, 1966, p. 1.

9. "We Roll," *Herald Tribune*, January 13, 1966, p. 1.

10. John O'Donnell, Mimeographed copy of speech, "1966 Transit Strike," given at Labor-Management Luncheon at the New School for Social Research, May 14, 1966. Seen in TWU files.

11. "Text of Report Submitted By Mediators," *New York Times*, January 13, 1966, p. 12.

12. Ibid.

13. Ibid.

14. Ibid.

15. Ibid.

16. Ibid.

17. Peter Kihss, "Panel Proposes Pay Raises To 15%," op. cit.

18. Woody Klein, op. cit.

19. "Mayor Lindsay's Remarks," *New York Times*, January 14, 1966, p. 28.

20. "Transit Strike Accord Is Reached," op. cit.

21. Timothy Costello, Personal interview held in Costello's office at 250 Broadway, New York, N.Y., December 14, 1966.

22. Ibid.

23. David R. Jones, "Johnson Asks Law To Deal With Strikes Hurting U.S.," *New York Times*, January 13, 1966, p. 1.

24. Homer Bigart, "Meany's Thrust at Quill Stirs the Anger of a Loyal Woman," *New York Times*, January 13, 1966, p. 20.

25. Ibid.

26. Murray Schumach, "Subways and Buses Roar Back To Life," *New York Times*, January 14, 1966, p. 1.

27. Ibid.

28. Ibid.

29. Robert E. Tomasson, "Authority Drops Its Damage Suit," *New York Times*, January 14, 1966, p. 30.

30. "Quill Discharged From Bellevue After 8 Associates Leave Jail," *New York Times*, January 14, 1966, p. 30.

31. Ibid.

32. Ibid.

33. "Hospital Expecting Quill To Leave Soon," *New York Times*, January 16, 1966, p. 78.

34. Robert E. Tomasson, op. cit.

35. John D. Pomfret, "President Warns Issue Is Inflation," *New York Times*, January 14, 1966, p. 1.

36. Damon Stetson, "President Stuns Weary City Hall," *New York Times*, January 14, 1966, p. 1.

37. "Mediator," *The New Yorker*, January 22, 1966, p. 27.

38. Damon Stetson, "President Stuns Weary City Hall," op. cit.

39. Ibid.

40. James Lynn, "Rockefeller: $100 Million To Save 15-Cent Fare," *Herald Tribune*, January 14, 1966, p. 1.

41. Thomas P. Ronan, "Governor To Act," *New York Times*, January 14, 1966, p. 1.

42. Ibid.

43. Ibid.

44. James Lynn, op. cit.

45. Ralph Blumenthal, "Normal Day Again: City Traffic Flows With Hardly a Snag," *New York Times*, January 14, 1966, p. 1.

46. Ibid.

47. Ibid.

48. Robert Alden, "Picking Up Pieces Is Chief Aim Now," *New York Times*, January 14, 1966, p. 29.

49. Ibid.

50. Ibid.

51. Ibid.

52. James W. Sullivan, "Lindsay's Image—It's As Shiny As A New 15-Cent Token," *Herald Tribune*, January 14, 1966, p. 1.

53. Damon Stetson, "President Stuns Weary City Hall," op. cit.

54. James W. Sullivan, op. cit.

55. "Poll Shows Voters Still Back Lindsay," *New York Times*, March 1, 1966, p. 44.

56. "Editorial," *New York Times*, January 3, 1966, p. 26.

57. "Editorial," *New York Times*, January 7, 1966, p. 28.

58. "Editorial," *New York Post*, January 11, 1966, p. 24.

59. "Editorial," *New York Post*, January 13, 1966, p. 24.

60. "Editorial," *Journal American*, January 2, 1966, p. 32L.

61. "Editorial," *Journal American*, January 13, 1966, p. 20.

62. "Editorial," *Herald Tribune*, January 2, 1966, p. 18.

63. "Editorial," *Daily News*, January 4, 1966, p. 23.

64. "Editorial," *Daily News*, January 5, 1966, p. 33.

65. "Editorial," *World Telegram and Sun*, January 2, 1966, p. 9.

66. "Editorial," *World Telegram and Sun*, January 10, 1966, p. 14.

67. "Editorial," *Amsterdam News*, January 8, 1966, p. 10.

68. "Writers Ruffle Quill's Feathers," *Editor and Publisher*, January 8, 1966, p. 12.

69. "Editorial," WINS Radio, Aired on January 3, 1966, and January 4, 1966, by Joel Chaseman, General Manager of WINS. Seen in TWU files.

70. "Editorial," WABC Radio, Aired on January 7, 1966 by John O. Gilbert, General Manager of WABC-TV. Seen in TWU files.

71. "Editorial," WCBS-TV, Aired on January 3, 1966, and January 4, 1966, by Michael F. Keating, General Manager of WCBS-TV. Seen in TWU files.

72. *World Telegram and Sun*, January 6, 1966, p. 14.

73. Ibid.

74. *Journal American*, January 6, 1966, p. 18.

75. *Daily News*, January 6, 1966, p. 27.

76. Ibid.

77. *New York Times*, January 6, 1966, p. 18.

78. Ibid.

79. *Journal American*, January 6, 1966, p. 18.

80. Robert E. Tomasson, "Strike Penalties Barred By Court," *New York Times*, January 15, 1966, p. 1.

81. "Wirtz Declares Lindsay Ignored TWU Pay Advice," *New York Times*, January 15, 1966, p. 1.

82. Damon Stetson, "Mayor Maps Plan For Labor Peace," *New York Times*, January 15, 1966, p. 1.

83. Ibid.

84. Emanuel Perlmutter, "Rockefeller Seeks New Way To Curb Municipal Strikes," *New York Times*, January 16, 1966, p. 79.

85. Theodore Kheel, Personal interview held in Kheel's office at 250 Park Avenue, New York, N.Y., December 21, 1966.

86. Robert E. Lane and David O. Sears, *Public Opinion*, Englewood Cliffs, N.J.: Prentice-Hall, 1964, p. 62.

87. Ibid.

88. Angus Campbell, et al., *The American Voter*, New York: John Wiley and Sons, 1964, p. 28.

89. Murray Edelman, *The Symbolic Uses of Politics*, Urbana: University of Illinois Press, 1964, pp. 76-78.

90. Douglas MacMahon, Personal interview held in MacMahon's office at 1980 Broadway, New York, N.Y., December 22, 1966.

91. Jack Gould, "TV: 2 Disparate Personalities in Transit Crisis," *New York Times*, January 4, 1966, p. 55.

92. Douglas MacMahon, op. cit.

93. Richard Phalon, "Gilhooley Sees $51-Million Need In 1966 Alone To Save 15-Cent Fare," *New York Times*, January 16, 1966, p. 79.

94. Richard L. Madden, "Rockefeller Says He Can't Give City $600-Million More," *New York Times*, January 18, 1966, p. 1.

95. Ibid.

96. Martin Arnold, "State Gives City $100-Million Aid," *New York Times*, January 19, 1966, p. 30.

97. Martin Arnold, "Court Opens Way To Suits Seeking To Punish TWU," *New York Times*, January 22, 1966, p. 1.

98. Damon Stetson, "Quill Demands Strike Inquiry," *New York Times*, January 26, 1966, p. 1.

99. Ibid.

100. Murray Schumach, "Quill Dies of Heart Attack....," *New York Times*, January 29, 1966, p. 1.

101. Ibid.

102. Brian J. Cudahy, *Under The Sidewalks of New York*, Brattleboro, Vt.: The Stephen Greene Press, 1979, p. 132.

103. "TWU Votes Pacts With City and Five Bus Lines," *New York Times*, February 8, 1966, p. 32.

104. Robert E. Tomasson, "State Court Finds Transit Pay Rises Given Illegaly," *New York Times*, February 10, 1966, p. 1.

105. Ibid.

106. Damon Stetson, "2d Transit Crisis Is Looming in City," *New York Times*, February 11, 1966, p. 29.

107. Emanuel Perlmutter, "Governor To Ask About Transit Pay Vote In Albany Today," *New York Times*, February 14, 1966, p. 1.

108. Ibid.

109. Sydney Schanberg, "Legislature Cool To Bill Allowing Transit Pay Raise," *New York Times*, February 15, 1966, p. 1.

110. Sydney Schanberg, "Transit Pay Rise Stalled A 2d Day," *New York Times*, February 16, 1966, p. 1.

111. Ibid.

112. Ibid.

113. Ibid.

114. Ibid.

115. Sydney Schanberg, "Transit Pay Bill Passed In Albany To Avert Strike," *New York Times*, February 17, 1966, p. 1.

116. Ibid.

117. Ibid.

118. Ibid.

119. Murray Schumach, "Labor in 2 Moods Greets Governor," *New York Times*, February 18, 1966, p. 18.

120. Sydney Schanberg, "Legislature Cool To Bill Allowing Transit Pay Raise," op. cit.

121. Murray Schumach, "Labor in 2 Moods Greets Governor," op. cit.

122. "Governor Spurs Legislature To Validate TWU Contract," *TWU Express*, March 1966, p. 3.

123. Daniel Gilmartin, "Political Action in Albany," *TWU Express*, March 1966, p. 15.

124. Daniel Gilmartin, "Support Those Who Helped Us," *TWU Express*, April 1966, p. 14.

125. Michael Stern, "Suit Challenges Transit Pay Bill," *New York Times*, February 26, 1966, p. 23.

126. "Mayor Backs Strike Exemption For Social Workers," *New York Times*, March 1, 1966, p. 44.

127. Robert Tomasson, "Court Hears Suits Against Law Giving Raises To Transit Unions," *New York Times*, March 9, 1966, p. 83.

128. "Transit Wage Rise Begins Tomorrow," *New York Times*, March 16, 1966, p. 88.

129. Robert Tomasson, "Court Hears Suits....," op. cit.

130. Homer Bigart, "Court Backs Special Law Clearing Transit Strikers," *New York Times*, March 25, 1966, p. 1.

Epilogue

1. Kurt L. Hanslowe, *The Emerging Law of Labor Relations in Public Employment*, ILR Paperback No. 4, Ithaca: New York State School of Industrial and Labor Relations, 1967, pp. 94-95.

2. *Government Employees Relations Review* (BNA), No. 134, April 4, 1966.

3. "5 More Hit Labor Bill," *Chief*, October 7, 1966, p. 2.

4. Felix Nigro, *Management-Employee Relations in the Public Service*, Chicago: Public Personnel Association, 1969.

5. Steven R. Weisman, "Why Lindsay Failed as Mayor," *The Washington Monthly*, April, 1972, p. 50.

6. Ibid.

7. Ibid.

8. Jack Newfield and Paul DuBrul, *The Permanent Government—Who Really Runs New York?*, New York: The Pilgrim Press, 1981, p. 137.

9. Larry L. King, "Lindsay of New York," *Harper's Magazine*, August 1968, p. 42.

10. Newfield and DuBrul, op. cit., p. 136.

11. Steven R. Weisman, op. cit., p. 43.

12. Douglas Yates, "The Urban Jigsaw Puzzle: New York Under Lindsay," *New York Affairs*, Vol. 2, Winter 1974, p. 3.

13. Jerome Zukosky, "Book Review," *Commentary*, September 1970.

14. Newfield and DuBrul, op. cit., p. 141.

15. Ibid., p. 137.

16. Charles R. Morris, *The Cost of Good Intentions*, New York: W.W. Norton, 1980, p. 97.

17. Ibid., p. 98.

18. Ibid., p. 101.

19. Weisman, op. cit., p. 47.

20. Charles R. Morris, op. cit., p. 101.

21. Ibid., p. 102.

22. Ken Auletta, *The Streets Were Paved With Gold*, New York: Random House, 1979, p. 61.

23. Ibid., p. 49.

24. Newfield and DuBrul, op. cit., p. 203.

25. Ibid.

26. Auletta, op. cit., p. 51.

27. Ibid.

Index

Abraham and Strauss, 152
Abyssinian Baptist Church, 173
Ackley, Gardner, 238
Actors' Equity, 151
Akers, Anthony B., 99
Amalgamated Association of Street, Electric Railway and Motor Coach Employees, 182, 189
Amalgamated Clothing Workers Union, 135; New York Joint Board, 168
Amalgamated Lithographers of America, 167
Amalgamated Transit Union, 28, 187; officials arrested, 131, 168
American Federation of State, County, and Municipal Employees: Local 371, 263; District Council 37, 271
American Federation of Teachers, 168
American Labor Party, 23, 135, 139
The American Voter, 253
Amsterdam News, 245
Ancient Order of Hibernians, 134
Association of Catholic Trade Unionists, 136
Audience, 18-19
Aurelio, Richard, 273

Bakke, E. Wight: Taylor Law, 251, 270
Bailer, Lloyd, 45
Barnes, Henry, 88, 114, 157, 160, 171, 214, 219
Beame, Abraham: background, 14; Lindsay campaign for mayor, 14-26; old-style politics, 16-17; political ideology, 15
Becker, Daniel, 264
Bergerman, Milton, 214

Black, Algernon, 25
Blaikie, Robert B., 267
Bloomingdale's, 152
Board of Transportation, 31, 136
Boorstin, Daniel, 5
Brandes, Sidney, 89, 101, 165, 236
Broderick, Vincent, 109, 116, 122, 157, 197
Brooklyn Museum, 128
Brotherhood of Interborough Employees, 132
Brotherhood of Locomotive Engineers, 172, 181, 182
Brotherhood of Railroad Trainmen, 90, 172
Brownell, Herbert, 98
Brownstein, Irwin, 222, 257
Brydges, Earl W., 156, 222, 257, 262, 263, 264
Buckley, Charles, 21
Buckley, William F.: Lindsay campaign for mayor, 17; use of National Guard, 215; image politics, 274

Cambridge, Godfrey, 174
Carnegie, Joseph, 194
Caudert, Frederic R., 99
Change in administration, 80-81, 128
Citizens Union, 214
Clague, Ewan, 45
Cochrane, W.R., 173
Cogen, Charles, 168
Cole, David L.: Motormen's Benevolent Association, 186; role in 1963 negotiations, 78; Taylor law, 251, 270; Transit Labor Board, 36, 38-39, 73, 77
Columbia University, 93

Commerce and Industry Association of New
York, 151, 172, 218, 242
Committee on Transit, 89
Communications Workers of America, 169
Conant, Frank E., 157
Condensation symbols, 7
Condon-Wadlin Act, 46, 47, 77, 89, 92,
101, 155, 262; Weinstein suit, 223, 237,
248-249, 258, 260, 264, 265, 267
Constituents, 18-19
Coolidge, Calvin, 46
Corbett, Raymond R., 168
Costello, Timothy: change in administration,
81; impact of strike on city, 121, 127, 158,
164-165, 173; Lindsay's image, 53;
mediation panel, 53, 55; power brokers,
208; preparing for strike, 88, 121; Transit
Authority/city relationship, 200
Costikyan, Edward, 108
Cost of TWU proposals, 40
Cox, Archibald, 45
Curran, Joseph, 170

Davey, Harold, 192
Davis, Meyer, 110
Davis, Sammy Jr., 110
Death-gamble, 65, 229
DeLury, John, 169, 272
Dewey, Thomas E.: creation of Transit
Authority, 31-32, 182
Donegan, James J., 189
Donovan, Bernard, 153, 163, 175, 197, 215,
233
Downs, Anthony, 1
Dubinsky, David, 23; Lindsay advisor, 54,
154, 170; American Labor Party, 135
DuBrul, Paul, 123, 273, 274
Dunlop, John T.: Taylor law, 251, 270
Dworkis, Martin, 99
Dye, T.R., 15

Edelman, Murray, 3, 20, 254
Editor and Publisher, 246
Erie-Lackawanna Railroad, 125, 219
Ethical Culture Society, 25
Executive Order 49, 34-35, 72

Feinsinger, Nathan: jailing Quill, 148;
Lindsay formula for ending strike, 217;

named mediator, 45, 52, 55, 57; role in
negotiations, 60, 62, 63, 68, 83, 89, 94,
195, 210; settlement announced, 232;
strike reaction, 103; wage-price
guideposts, 231, 238, 239
Ferrer, Irene, 237
Fifth Avenue Association, 157, 218, 242
Fifth Avenue Coach Lines, 29
$500-dollar supplementary pension,
200-201, 229, 238
Flas, Florence, 175
Flynn, Edward J., 71
Fogel, Walter, 1
Frank, Reuven, 5
Freedom National Bank, 173, 175
Freeman, Joshua, 71, 138
Friendly Sons of Saint Patrick, 133-134

Garrett, Sylvester: Lindsay formula for
ending strike, 213; named mediator, 52,
55, 57; role in negotiations, 170
Garth, David, 207
Geller, Abraham N., 118-120, 130, 144,
155, 159, 165, 213, 236
Gellhorn, Walter, 45
Gilhooley, John J.: named to Transit
Authority, 32; naming mediation panel,
43, 47-48; retention of fifteen-cent fare,
37, 41; role in negotiations, 40, 84, 91;
Transit Labor Board, 38; wage-price
guideposts, 239
Gilmartin, Daniel, 131, 228, 236, 263, 265,
266
Gimbels, 127, 152
Goldberg, Arthur J., 155
Goldwater, Barry, 12
Goodman, Roy M., 162
Goodwin, Elliot, 99
Gotbaum, Victor, 177-178, 271
Gottehrer, Barry, 207
Gould, Jack, 123, 255
Greater New York Hospital Association, 153
Greenberg, Max, 169
Greenberg, Samuel L., 257
Gross, Ralph, 151, 172, 218, 242
Grosso, Michael B., 242
Guinan, Matthew: Lindsay's role in
negotiations, 104, 201; role in
negotiations, 48, 64, 228; jailed, 131, 159;
succeeds Quill, 260